THE EAGLE
Handbook of
BIBLE
Promises

THE EAGLE
Handbook of
BIBLE
Promises

compiled by

MARTIN MANSER
and
MIKE BEAUMONT

eagle
Eagle Publishing
Guildford, Surrey

Photographic credits

The Image Bank, London, has supplied the majority of the images and photographs used throughout this book. The publisher wishes to thank them for their help and permission. Credits for the other photographs are as follows:

Jon Arnold: 116, 129, 172, 188, 241, 284, 345, 354-3

The Daily Telegraph Photographic Library: 194,197, 254-5, 307, 325, 327, 335, 344, 348

Tony Stone Images: 97, 120, 205, 214, 262, 290, 319, 334, 370-1

The Tate Gallery: 332-3

Mike Webb (Tear Fund): 96

Archive material: 21, 29, 62, 87, 94, 130, 147, 148, 150-1, 164, 228-9, 230, 232, 233, 234, 287

British Library Cataloguing in Publication Data. A catalogue record for this book is available from the British Library.

Published by Eagle Publishing, PO Box 530, Guildford, Surrey GU2 4FH

Typeset by Eagle Publishing
Page layout and design by Roger Judd

Printed in

ISBN 0 86347 374 1

Contents

Introduction

One of Mike's earliest memories is of his grandmother's Promise Box. Covered in heavy gold paper and measuring some 20 by 10 centimetres, this priceless treasure would come out on Sunday afternoons during visits to her home. For her, it was the climax of the visit! The lid would carefully be lifted, as though something might escape, and a miniature pair of tongs be removed. Inside the box were rolled up lots of little scrolls of paper, all neatly standing to attention like a brigade of guards, waiting to be picked out. Your hand would waver with indecision (rather like trying to decide which chocolate to pick from a chocolate box), until finally you thrust the tongs into the chosen scroll, removed it with great care (so as not to pull all the others out!), unrolled it, and with a great sense of ceremony read out the promise for that day.

While that was one of Mike's first introductions to the promises of God (and no doubt brought much pleasure and blessing at the time), it is our conviction that this is not really how God intended his promises to be used – to be pulled out at random for a quick blessing, or to be taken as a 'spiritual aspirin' so that all our problems disappear. The promises of God are given so that we can come to know the God of the promises. They are there to show us more of who he is and what he is like; to take hold of our hearts and minds and draw them to himself and into his way of thinking and acting; to get us so familiar with him that it becomes second nature to us to call on his promises in the ordinary everyday events of life, just as Jesus did, and to see our lives transformed as we do so.

The Eagle Handbook of Bible Promises has been designed, not as a Promise Box therefore, but as a handbook of practical Christian living. We have looked at the promises of the Bible and have tried to see how they work out in practice, so that they can become a part of your own life as you are challenged and encouraged by them.

The material is arranged in six major themes. We begin with the persons of the Trinity: God the Father, the Lord Jesus Christ, and the Holy Spirit. Then we move on to how our life with God finds expression – in belonging to God's church and living for him in the world: these are the next two major themes. In the final theme we look forward to the future and draw together some of the chief strands of the Bible's teaching about the hope we have for then, and also how it affects us now.

Each of these major themes, Knowing God, Trusting Jesus, Growing in the Spirit, Belonging to the church, Living in the world, Getting ready for the future, is divided into seven chapters. Within each chapter, we explore a particular topic, beginning with a key thought and a key Bible verse to set the scene. After the main study material, comes a hymn (which can be used as a response), a conclusion and a final Bible quotation, all designed to help you retain the main emphases of the teaching. In each section we try to look for the relevance of the promise for us today.

The book has been designed particularly for personal use, but those leading small groups will also find it a helpful resource book – as may a hard-pressed preacher wanting a quick sermon outline!

In writing the book, we have tried to be honest and realistic . . . about our failures as well as our successes; for God's promises only really begin to work out when we are realistic about ourselves as well as about him. The ultimate aim of the book is to help us all become more like the people God intends us to be, as we make our own 'his very great and precious promises' (2 Peter 1:4).

Martin Manser
Mike Beaumont

PART ONE

Knowing God

CHAPTER ONE

This is your God!

> If we can grasp God's promises about who he is and what
> he is like, it will completely change our outlook on life.
> We will be able to trust him and see him at work!
>
> *'Here is your God!' See, the Sovereign LORD comes with power ...*
> (Isaiah 40:9–10)

'Just how big is God?' This child's question has no doubt stumped many a parent! But actually, it is a question many of us ask, consciously or unconsciously, when problems come our way. 'Is God big enough to deal with this?' We may not speak the words; but when we do not trust, we are certainly thinking the thought. This is exactly what God's people were thinking in Isaiah's day, some seven hundred years before the birth of Jesus; but Isaiah knew that if we could just see how big God is, we would not have to ask the question!

The greatness of God: Isaiah 40

Having spoken of the coming judgment of God on the disobedient Jewish nation, Isaiah looks forward to the time when God is about to restore them to their own land.

Four facts about God

In verses 1–11 we hear tender voices speaking to Jerusalem that her time in exile is soon to come to an end: the Lord is coming to her rescue! But this comfort given is nothing 'airy-fairy'; it is based on four facts about God:

God has dealt with his people's sin

Comfort, comfort my people, says your God. Speak tenderly to Jerusalem, and proclaim to her that her hard service has been completed, that her sin has been paid for, that she has received from the LORD's hand double for all her sins.

(Isaiah 40:1–2)

Dealing with sin is always God's first step in bringing change to people's lives. As we trust in Jesus, we too can know our sins forgiven:

In him [Jesus] we have redemption through his blood, the forgiveness of sins, in accordance with the riches of God's grace . . .

(Ephesians 1:7)

God himself is coming

What makes a difference to every situation is God coming in. This is what would change their situation too, said Isaiah. When God comes, things change!

A voice of one calling: 'In the desert prepare the way for the LORD; make straight in the wilderness a highway for our God. Every valley shall be raised up, every mountain and hill made low; the rough ground shall become level, the rugged places a plain. And the glory of the LORD will be revealed, and all mankind together will see it. For the mouth of the LORD has spoken.'

(Isaiah 40:3–5)

You who bring good tidings to Zion, go up on a high mountain. You who bring good tidings to Jerusalem, lift up your voice with a shout, lift it up, do not be afraid; say to the towns of Judah, 'Here is your God!' See, the Sovereign Lord comes with power, and his arm rules for him. See, his reward is with him, and his recompense accompanies him.

(Isaiah 40:9–10)

The presence of God always changes things! See also 2 Chronicles 32:7–8; Luke 7:16

God's word and promise are unchanging and eternal

The grass withers and the flowers fall, but the word of our God stands for ever.

(Isaiah 40:8)

See also Psalm 119:89; Isaiah 55:10–11; Matthew 5:18

God comes with power, but also with tenderness

Here is the amazing thing about God! He has limitless power; yet he exercises that power with amazing tenderness, looking after his people as a shepherd looks after his sheep.

He tends his flock like a shepherd: He gathers the lambs in his arms and carries them close to his heart; he gently leads those that have young.

(Isaiah 40:11)

See also Genesis 48:15; Psalm 23:1–4; 28:9; Micah 5:4; John 10:11

There is no one like God!

Verses 12–26 show God as the creator and controller of everything. There is no one like him; nothing compares with his greatness.

• Just look at his majestic acts in creation; mighty oceans and great mountains are as nothing to him (v 12)! From whom did he take advice in how to do all this (vv 13–14)? He has no need to consult anyone!
See also Job 38:1–40:5

• Now look at the great countries and empires of the world, which seem so powerful. But what are they to God? Merely a drop in a bucket! (vv 15–17) Could any idol or other 'god' have done all this (vv 18–20)?
See also Jeremiah 10:1–16

• Next, think about the world – its vast size, its teeming millions. But what is this in comparison to God (v 22)? And what about the world's great leaders: leaders of nations and superpowers? See them in relation to God (vv 23–24).
See also 2 Kings 19:15–19

• Finally, think about the stars – innumerable and light years upon light years away. What are they to this God (v 26)? No, he really is unique (v 25).

> O LORD, Our Lord,
> how majestic is your name in all the
> earth!
> You have set your glory
> above the heavens.
> From the lips of children and infants
> you have ordained praise
> because of your enemies,
> to silence the foe and the avenger.
> When I consider your heavens,
> the work of your fingers,
> the moon and the stars,
> which you have set in place,
> what is man that you are mindful of him,
> the son of man that you care for him?
> You made him a little lower than the
> heavenly beings,
> and crowned him with glory and
> honour.'
>
> **(Psalm 8:1–5)**

God cannot forget!

Of course, there are always the cynics around in life, aren't there? Or the grumblers who have lost their perspective or think that God has somehow forgotten them (see, e.g. Lamentations 5:19–22). But what about you? Have you ever thought, 'My way is hidden from the LORD; my cause is disregarded by my God' (v 27)? Are you perhaps thinking it today?

But can it really be that this unique God (v 25) is just too great to care about his people? No! He is simply too great to fail us! He cannot fail us, he cannot forget us. He never grows old or tired; his understanding is beyond the depths of human reason.

Do you not know? Have you not heard? The LORD is the everlasting God, the Creator of the ends of the earth. He will not grow tired or weary, and his understanding no-one can fathom.

(Isaiah 40:28)

Can a mother forget the baby at her breast and have no compassion on the child she has borne? Though she may forget, I will not forget you! See, I have engraved you on the palms of my hands.

(Isaiah 49:15–16)

See also Psalm 27:10; Isaiah 44:21; Jeremiah 31:20

God's power for weary people

Verses 29–31 show us how God's power can be experienced in our everyday lives. We may get weary – even the youngest and most energetic of us (v 30); but as we put our trust in God each day (v 31, 'hope in the LORD') we can know *our* weak power being exchanged for *his* great power and can soar above the pressures or the problems like an eagle soaring far above!

He gives strength to the weary and increases the power of the weak. Even youths grow tired and weary, and young men stumble and fall; but those who hope in the LORD will renew their strength. They will soar on wings like eagles; they will run and not grow weary, they will walk and not be faint.

(Isaiah 40:29–31)

See also Psalm 68:35; Isaiah 26:8; 41:10; Matthew 11:28

What about us?

So, what about us? How great is God in our thinking? If he is not great in our thinking, he will never be great in our living!

J. I. Packer, in his excellent book *Knowing God*, says that the question of verse 25 'rebukes wrong thoughts about God'. "Your thoughts of God are too human," said Luther to Erasmus. This is where most of us go astray. Our thoughts of God are not great enough; we fail to reckon with the reality of His limitless wisdom and power. Because we ourselves are limited and weak, we imagine that at some points God is too, and find it hard to believe that He is not. We think of God as too much like what we are. Put this mistake right, says God; learn to acknowledge the full majesty of your incomparable God and Saviour.'

Little wonder we find it difficult to grasp God's promises or God's presence if all he is in our thinking is a slightly bigger version of us – perhaps even with all the same weaknesses and faults – but rather nicer! (But that is how we often think if we are honest!) If we can start to see the greatness of God, however, and understand that he never gets tired, never runs out of resources, then we will increasingly be happy to 'wait upon the LORD' (v 31, KJV) until his strength becomes ours.

Remember: God is a God who loves to act on behalf of those who wait on him!

Since ancient times no-one has heard, no ear has perceived, no eye has seen any God besides you, who acts on behalf of those who wait for him.

(Isaiah 64:4)

Blessed is the man who listens to me, watching daily at my doors, waiting at my doorway.

(Proverbs 8:34)

'Our God is too small' was the title of a book by J. B. Phillips. And it's true! How often we underestimate God; how much we need to have our whole being filled with far bigger thoughts of him. When that happens, life looks different. The wonder of Isaiah's teaching here is that God – in his greatness – cares about me, even me! What a thought when we are tired or depressed – the God of the whole universe knows about me and my life! What a transformation that brings to life with all its cares, and all its opportunities! But it is only as we stop and wait on him that the 'penny begins to drop' about this. When it does, what a joyful response to his greatness it brings!

Who among the gods is like you, O LORD? Who is like you – majestic in holiness, awesome in glory, working wonders?

(Exodus 15:11)

See also Psalm 93:1–2; 96:6–9

It is because God is so great that he is able to do what he promises:

Yet he [Abraham] did not waver through unbelief regarding the promise of God, but was strengthened in his faith and gave glory to God, being fully persuaded that God had power to do what he had promised.

(Romans 4:20–21)

Little wonder, then, that the Bible says that such a great God should be listened to reverently and closely!

For the LORD is the great God,
the great King above all gods.
In his hand are the depths of the earth,
and the mountain peaks belong to him.
The sea is his, for he made it,
and his hands formed the dry land.
Come, let us bow down in worship,
let us kneel before the Lord our Maker;
for he is our God
and we are the people of his pasture,
the flock under his care.
Today, if you hear his voice,
do not harden your hearts . . .

(Psalm 95:3–8)

Relevance for today

If God is so great, as Isaiah had grasped him to be, then we need to remember:

No need is beyond God's reach

Then he [Jesus] went up and touched the coffin, and those carrying it stood still. He said, 'Young man, I say to you, get up!' The dead man sat up and began to talk, and Jesus gave him back to his mother. They were all filled with awe and praised God. 'A great prophet has appeared among us,' they said. 'God has come to help his people.'

(Luke 7:14–16)

See also 1 Kings 17:12–16; Matthew 6:25–33; John 11:21–44

No problem is bigger than God

'Be strong and courageous. Do not be afraid or discouraged because of the king of Assyria and the vast army with him, for there is a greater power with us than with him. With him is only the arm of flesh, but with us is the LORD our God to help us and to fight our battles.'

(2 Chronicles 32:7–8)

See also Numbers 14:9; 2 Kings 6:16–17; Daniel 3:16–18; Romans 8:38–3

No detail is too insignificant to God

'Are not five sparrows sold for two pennies? Yet not one of them is forgotten by God. Indeed, the very hairs of your head are all numbered. Don't be afraid; you are worth more than many sparrows.'

(Luke 12:6–7)

See also Deuteronomy 10:17–18; Matthew 6:26,28–29; John 21:5–6

No opportunity is bigger than God

'The land we passed through and explored is exceedingly good. If the LORD is pleased with us, he will lead us into that land, a land flowing with milk and honey, and will give it to us. Only do not rebel against the LORD. And do not be afraid of the people of the land, because we will swallow them up. Their protection is gone, but the LORD is with us.

(Numbers 14:7–9)

See also Nehemiah 2:1–8; 1 Corinthians 16:

No circumstance can ever make God forget me

'Remember these things, O Jacob, for you are my servant, O Israel. I have made you, you are my servant; O Israel, I will not forget you. I have swept away your offences like a cloud, your sins like the morning mist. Return to me, for I have redeemed you.'

(Isaiah 44:21–22)

See also Deuteronomy 4:31; Isaiah 49:15–21; Hebrews 6:10

No event will ever take God by surprise

For you created my inmost being; you knit me together in my mother's womb. I praise you because I am fearfully and wonderfully made; your works are wonderful, I know that full well. My frame was not hidden from you when I was made in the secret place. When I was woven together in the depths of the earth, your eyes saw my unformed body. All the days ordained for me were written in your book before one of them came to be.

(Psalm 139:13–16)

See also Isaiah 48:3–7; Jeremiah 1:5; Daniel 2:19–22

No sin is bigger than God's power to deal with it

'Come now, let us reason together,' says the LORD. 'Though your sins are like scarlet, they shall be as white as snow; though they are red as crimson, they shall be like wool.'

(Isaiah 1:18)

See also 2 Samuel 12:13; Psalm 51:7; 103:8–12; Isaiah 44:22

Little wonder, in the light of all of this, that Paul could write:

'What, then, shall we say in response to this? If God is for us, who can be against us?'

(Romans 8:31)

15

This hymn writer certainly grasped a sense of the greatness of God, yet also the intimacy of God's love and care for him:

My God, how wonderful Thou art,
*　Thy majesty how bright!*
How beautiful Thy mercy-seat,
*　In depths of burning light!*

How dread are Thine eternal years.
*　O everlasting Lord,*
By prostrate spirits day and night
*　Incessantly adored!*

O how I fear Thee, Living God,
*　With deepest, tenderest fears,*
And worship Thee with trembling hope,
*　And penitential tears!*

Yet I may love Thee, too, O Lord,
*　Almighty as Thou art,*
For Thou hast stooped to ask of me
*　The love of my poor heart.*

How wonderful, how beautiful,
*　The sight of Thee must be,*
Thine endless wisdom, boundless power,
*　And aweful purity!*

Frederick William Faber, 1814–63

Conclusion

In a busy world, we (like Martha long ago) find it hard to 'stop'. But Isaiah 40 is a 'stop signal' – an invitation to stop and think about the greatness of our God; but also a promise, that those who do stop, who do 'wait', will renew their strength.

You are awesome, O God, in your sanctuary; the God of Israel gives power and strength to his people.

(Psalm 68:35)

God is Special

As we capture again a sense of God in his holiness and glory, so our own lives become renewed and ready to serve God.

'My eyes have seen the King, the LORD Almighty.' (Isaiah 6:5)

'Holiness'. For many of us, the word conjures up all sorts of images – mostly of the kind we don't like! Perhaps we think of someone carrying a big Bible, dressed in a drab outfit, frowning at us because we look like we are enjoying ourselves. The 'frowners' were around in Jesus' day too (the Pharisees); but Jesus showed that holiness is an exciting thing that touches every part of life, for it touches the very heart of what God is like.

The holiness of God: Isaiah 6

The world must have seemed like it had fallen apart; for, after a reign of 52 years, during which Judah's national pride had flourished and its borders grown, the godly king Uzziah had died (v 1). What would happen now? Who would take over? How would things go? God's answer for Isaiah's anxious foreboding was a revelation of himself. The earthly king might have died; but the king of glory was still on his throne!

The things Isaiah saw

In his vision, Isaiah saw things in a way he had never seen before.

Isaiah saw things about God

First he saw that God is great, holy, almighty and full of glory.

In the year that King Uzziah died, I saw the Lord seated on a throne, high and exalted, and the train of his robe filled the temple. Above him were seraphs, each with six wings: With two wings they covered their faces, with two they covered their feet, and with two they were flying. And they were calling to one another: 'Holy, holy, holy is the LORD Almighty; the whole earth is full of his glory.' At the sound of their voices the doorposts and thresholds shook and the temple was filled with smoke.

(Isaiah 6:1–4)

See also Exodus 15:11; 19:18–24; 40:34–35; 2 Chronicles 7:1–3; Psalm 89:6-8

Isaiah saw things about himself

As he saw this wonderful vision, he also saw that, in comparison to this holy God, he was so unclean:

'Woe to me!' I cried. 'I am ruined! For I am a man of unclean lips, and I live among a people of unclean lips, and my eyes have seen the King, the LORD Almighty.'

(Isaiah 6:5)

See also Job 42:5–6; Luke 5:8

When we see God's holiness, we see just how sinful we really are. The clearer we see him, the clearer we see ourselves, and the more that prepares us for serving him. 'It is integral to Isaiah's message that his words will be those of a forgiven man, himself as guilty as those to whom he will offer life or death' (Derek Kidner).

There is no-one righteous, not even one.

(Romans 3:10)

. . . all have sinned and fall short of the glory of God.

(Romans 3:23)

If we claim to be without sin, we deceive ourselves and the truth is not in us.

(1 John 1:8)

What shall we conclude then? Are we any better? Not at all! We have already made the charge that Jews and Gentiles alike are all under sin.

(Romans 3:9)

Isaiah saw how God makes people holy

The amazing thing about God is that he shows us our sin – then takes action himself to deal with it!

Then one of the seraphs flew to me with a live coal in his hand, which he had taken with tongs from the altar. With it he touched my mouth and said, 'See, this has touched your lips; your guilt is taken away and your sin atoned for.'

(Isaiah 6:6–7)

This understanding that it is God himself who deals with people's sins – and not their own efforts – runs through the Bible.

For the life of a creature is in the blood, and I have given it to you to make atonement for yourselves on the altar; it is the blood that makes atonement for one's life.

(Leviticus 17:11)

You see, at just the right time, when we were still powerless, Christ died for the ungodly. Very rarely will anyone die for a righteous man, though for a good man someone might possibly dare to die. But God demonstrates his own love for us in this: While we were still sinners, Christ died for us.

(Romans 5:6–8)

For Christ died for sins once for all, the righteous for the unrighteous, to bring you to God.

(1 Peter 3:18)

Isaiah saw that 'being cleaned up' comes before 'being sent out'

It was only as Isaiah had this encounter with the Holy God, which in turn led to his being made holy, that he was in a place to offer himself to be used by God.

Then I heard the voice of the LORD saying, 'Whom shall I send? And who will go for us?' And I said, 'Here am I. Send me!'

(Isaiah 6:8)

This is something that David had discovered too. When confronted about his adulterous relationship with Bathsheba (2 Samuel 12:1–13), he did not try to cover it up, but confessed his sin quickly, knowing that only then would he be in a place to serve God again.

Create in me a pure heart, O God, and renew a steadfast spirit within me. Do not cast me from your presence or take your Holy Spirit from me. Restore to me the joy of your salvation and grant me a willing spirit to sustain me. Then I will teach transgressors your ways . . .

(Psalm 51:10–13)

See also Acts 9:1–22

Good-heartedness can never come before God-heartedness. Trying to serve God without first knowing his forgiveness and renewing power in our lives will only ever lead to frustration (e.g. Job 19:7–8).

Isaiah saw that God's message would not always be welcomed by everyone

It is one thing to be ready to 'go' with God's word; it is another to be prepared to be rejected when people reject it. Isaiah is warned that that people will block their ears and harden their hearts to his message, and that God himself will underline their decision (vv 9–10).

See also Isaiah 53:1; John 1:11–12; 12:37–38

Whether people hear or not, respond or not, God's servant is still to 'stick at it' (vv 11–13).

What is holiness?

So, what do we mean by holiness? To many people the whole idea of holiness is something negative, associated with lots of 'don'ts' – don't go to the disco, don't smoke, don't drink, etc. In short, don't enjoy yourself! This was what characterized the Pharisees of Jesus' day. Their whole idea of holiness was to do with how you looked on the outside (see Mark 7:1–8). But when we think like this, we have lost a sense of holiness as being an aspect of God's very nature.

Holiness and God

The original Hebrew word for holy has the idea of 'being separate', 'set apart', perhaps even 'special', which is a positive word. God is special! He is special because he is different, separate from everything else. This is why his holiness is related to his glory (Isaiah 6:3).

All three Persons of the Godhead are described as holy:

God the Father is holy

His names in the Old Testament include 'the Holy One' (Psalm 22:3; Proverbs 9:10; Hosea 11:9; Habakkuk 1:12) and 'the Holy One of Israel' (Isaiah 10:20; 30:11–12; 30:15).

God the Son, the Lord Jesus Christ, is holy

The angel Gabriel declared him holy (Luke 1:35), demons recognized him as holy (Mark 1:24), and the church gladly honoured him as holy (Acts 4:27).

God the Spirit is holy

While the Spirit is referred to only three times in the Old Testament as 'Holy Spirit' (e.g. Isaiah 63:10), this becomes his usual designation by the New Testament (e.g. Luke 11:13; Acts 2:4; Ephesians 4:30). In fact, it has almost become his name!

Holiness and God and the people of God

God's holiness does not stand in isolation, as something 'out there'. He is 'the Holy One of Israel' (see, e.g. 2 Kings 19:22; Psalm 71:22; Isaiah 1:4; 12:6; 31:1; Jeremiah 51:5; Ezekiel 39:7). In other words, he is involved with people 'down here'. That is why his people are challenged to be like him.

'I am the LORD who brought you up out of Egypt to be your God; therefore be holy, because I am holy.'

(Leviticus 11:45)

'Now if you obey me fully and keep my covenant, then out of all nations you will be my treasured possession. Although the whole earth is mine, you will be for me a kingdom of priests and a holy nation.'

(Exodus 19:5–6)

Therefore, I urge you, brothers, in view of God's mercy, to offer your bodies as living sacrifices, holy and pleasing to God – this is your spiritual act of worship.

(Romans 12:1)

See also Colossians 3:1–14; 1 Thessalonians 4:3–7; 1 Peter 1:13–16

(See also the chapter 'Growing like Jesus')

God is determined that his holiness will be seen:

'I will show the holiness of my great name, which has been profaned among the nations, the name you have profaned among them. Then the nations will know that I am the LORD, declares the Sovereign LORD, when I show myself holy through you before their eyes.'

(Ezekiel 36:23)

God's holiness and us

God's holiness – his utter purity and his just and perfect rule – stands in glaring contrast with our sinfulness. God cannot look on evil (Habakkuk 1:13), and his perfect justice demands his wrath against sin. This wrath is not a crude fitful human 'temper tantrum', but 'the holy revulsion of God's being against that which is the contradiction of his holiness' (John Murray). But thankfully, his wrath is not the last word!

If God were simply to stand at a distance and call to us to be holy, who of us would ever make it? Who of us could avoid his wrath? But that is not what God is like: he tells us to be holy – and then provides a means of it happening!

By giving his own Son to die on the cross to bear the punishment for our sin, God himself makes us clean so that we can now come into his holy presence. With his prophetic insight, Isaiah looked ahead some seven hundred years and caught a wonderful glimpse of what Jesus would one day do for us:

Surely he took up our infirmities and carried our sorrows, yet we considered him stricken by God, smitten by him, and afflicted. But he was pierced for our transgressions, he was crushed for our iniquities; the punishment that brought us peace was upon him, and by his wounds we are healed. We all, like sheep, have gone astray, each of us has turned to his own way; and the Lord has laid on him the iniquity of us all.

(Isaiah 53:4–6)

See also Romans 3:25–26; Hebrews 10:19–23

Relevance for today

If we are going to live with this holy God, then we need to remember:

I cannot hide my sin from a holy God

Nothing in all creation is hidden from God's sight. Everything is uncovered and laid bare before the eyes of him to whom we must give account.

(Hebrews 4:13)

'Can anyone hide in secret places so that I cannot see him?' declares the LORD. 'Do not I fill heaven and earth?' declares the LORD.

(Jeremiah 23:24)

See also Psalm 33:13–15; 119:168; Proverbs 5:21; Jeremiah 16:17; 29:23; Acts 5:1–11

The wonderful thing that Isaiah discovered, however, was that we do not need to hide our sin! God is graciously waiting to forgive it!

God does not deal with us as our sins deserve

The LORD is compassionate and gracious, slow to anger, abounding in love. He will not always accuse, nor will he harbour his anger for ever; he does not treat us as our sins deserve or repay us according to our iniquities. For as high as the heavens are above the earth, so great is his love for those who fear him; as far as the east is from the west, so far has he removed our transgressions from us. As a father has compassion on his children, so the LORD has compassion on those who fear him; for he knows how we are formed, he remembers that we are dust.

(Psalm 103:8–14)

See also Ezra 9:13; Romans 6:23

Despite God being so holy, he says that no sin is too bad to be forgiven

'Come now, let us reason together,' says the LORD. 'Though your sins are like scarlet, they shall be as white as snow; though they are red as crimson, they shall be like wool.'

(Isaiah 1:18)

See also 1 Corinthians 15:9–10; 1 Timothy 1:15

Holiness is not so much about what I do on the outside, as what I am like on the inside

This is not to say that what we are like on the outside is unimportant! But God wants the outside to be a genuine reflection of what is on the inside, and not a 'cover-up' for what is going on there.

'What comes out of a man is what makes him "unclean". For from within, out of men's hearts, come evil thoughts, sexual immorality, theft, murder, adultery, greed, malice, deceit, lewdness, envy, slander, arrogance and folly. All these evils come from inside and make a man "unclean".'

(Mark 7:20–23)

Encounters with the holiness of God are for our good and not our harm

While Isaiah felt like running from God's holiness (Isaiah 6:5–7), God encountered him in holiness only to reveal himself to him and to change him. We do not need to run from God's holiness!

'When they see among them their children, the work of my hands, they will keep my name holy; they will acknowledge the holiness of the Holy One of Jacob, and will stand in awe of the God of Israel.'

(Isaiah 29:23)

And a highway will be there; it will be called the Way of Holiness. The unclean will not journey on it; it will be for those who walk in that Way; wicked fools will not go about on it. No lion will be there, nor will any ferocious beast get up on it; they will not be found there. But only the redeemed will walk there, and the ransomed of the LORD will return. They will enter Zion with singing; everlasting joy will crown their heads. Gladness and joy will overtake them, and sorrow and sighing will flee away.

(Isaiah 35:8–10)

But now that you have been set free from sin and have become slaves to God, the benefit you reap leads to holiness, and the result is eternal life.

(Romans 6:22)

Holiness cannot begin to grow in me until this is the sort of God and the sort of life that I choose to follow

'Now fear the LORD and serve him with all faithfulness. Throw away the gods your forefathers worshipped beyond the River and in Egypt, and serve the LORD. But if serving the LORD seems undesirable to you, then choose for yourselves this day whom you will serve . . .'

Joshua said to the people, 'You are not able to serve the LORD. He is a holy God; he is a jealous God. He will not forgive your rebellion and your sins. If you forsake the LORD and serve foreign gods, he will turn and bring disaster on you and make an end of you, after he has been good to you.' But the people said to Joshua, 'No! We will serve the LORD.' Then Joshua said, 'You are witnesses against yourselves that you have chosen to serve the LORD.' 'Yes, we are witnesses,' they replied. 'Now then,' said Joshua, 'throw away the foreign gods that are among you and yield your hearts to the LORD, the God of Israel.' And the people said to Joshua, 'We will serve the LORD our God and obey him.'

(Joshua 24:14–15, 19–24)

Holy, holy, holy, Lord God Almighty!
Early in the morning our song shall rise to
  Thee;
Holy, holy, holy! merciful and mighty
God in Three Persons, blessed Trinity!

Holy, holy, holy! all the saints adore Thee,
Casting down their golden crowns around
  the glassy sea;
Cherubim and seraphim falling down before
  Thee,
Who wert, and art, and evermore shalt be.

Holy, holy, holy! though the darkness hide
  Thee
Though the eye of sinful man Thy glory may
  not see
Only Thou art holy, there is none beside
  Thee
Perfect in power, in love, and purity.

Holy, holy, holy, Lord God Almighty!
All Thy works shall praise Thy Name, in
  earth and sky and sea;
Holy, holy, holy! merciful and mighty,
God in Three Persons, blessed Trinity!

Reginald Heber, 1783–1826

Conclusion

God alone is completely pure and free from all evil. So it is not possible for those who do wrong to come into his presence until they have been made clean. The great news is – that is exactly what God wants to do for us!

'Holy, holy, holy is the LORD Almighty; the whole earth is full of his glory.'

(Isaiah 6:3)

CHAPTER THREE

The Friendship of God

> God loves people. God commits himself to people. In fact, he calls us to be his friends, to follow him in the world and to share that friendship with others.
>
> *'I will walk among you and be your God, and you will be my people.'* (Leviticus 26:12)

All of us know what it is like to have friendships, perhaps even a 'special friend' – one with whom we can really be ourselves; one with whom we can laugh and cry; one we trust implicitly through thick and thin; one who loves us enough even to tell us the truth!

The Bible says that this is the sort of relationship which God wants with people – ordinary people like you and me. In fact, this was one of the things that marked Jesus out. He was a real 'people person'. He loved making friendships – not with the 'religious specialists', but with ordinary people. He was a *friend* to them. Little wonder that 'the common people heard him gladly' (Mark 12:37, KJV). For Jesus, helping people to discover the friendship of God was one of the most important things in life.

This friendship was no ordinary friendship, however. It was the friendship of *covenant*.

A special relationship

'I will be your God and you will be my people.' This amazing sentence, with slight variations, occurs again and again throughout the Bible. Look, for example, at one of the first promises of such a friendship, the one made to Abraham:

'I will establish my covenant as an everlasting covenant between me and you and your descendants after you for the generations to come, to be your God and the God of your descendants after you.'

(Genesis 17:7)

Or consider the promise God made to Moses, as he underlined once again that promise to Abraham:

'I will take you as my own people, and I will be your God. Then you will know that I am the Lord your God.'

(Exodus 6:7)

Or consider the promise repeated yet again, as Jeremiah encouraged God's people in a time of bleak prospects:

'So you will be my people, and I will be your God.'

(Jeremiah 30:22)

From the first book of the Bible to the last, this message rings through.

See also e.g. Leviticus 26:12; Deuteronomy 7:6; Jeremiah 11:3–5; 31:33; 32:38; Ezekiel 11:20; 37:27; 2 Corinthians 6:16; Revelation 21:3

These words sum up the special relationship or covenant that God has with his people. In Bible times a 'covenant' was a binding agreement or unbreakable contract. That is a hard concept for us to grasp these days, because we are so used to slick lawyers being able to break anything!

God says: this is the sort of agreement I want to make with people – one that can't be broken, no matter what happens.

But this covenant is not some mere legal contract – technical, hard, and cold; it is a contract of intimacy, loyalty, and friendship.

A relationship initiated by God

This special relationship or covenant is initiated completely by God. Again and again, it is God who takes the first step, often while people are attending to everyday affairs. Abraham was settling down to life in Haran, having just migrated there from Ur, when God revealed himself (Genesis 11:31–12:5); Moses was tending his father-in-law's flock in the desert when God appeared to

him in a burning bush that wouldn't burn and gave his life new directions (Exodus 3:1–6); and Jesus' encounter with his first disciples was when they were hard at work fishing (Mark 1:16–18).

The making of the relationship is shown again and again to be God's from start to finish! It is an act of complete condescension on his part: he acts in grace towards us. It isn't that we are better than others; we're not! The initiative lies fully with God and his love, as Moses

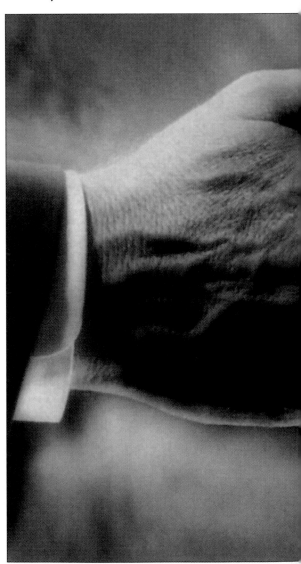

reminded God's people as they stood on the edge of the promised land:

'The LORD did not set his affection on you and choose you because you were more numerous than other peoples, for you were the fewest of all peoples. But it was because the LORD loved you and kept the oath he swore to your forefathers that he brought you out with a mighty hand and redeemed you from the land of slavery, from the power of Pharaoh king of Egypt. Know therefore that the LORD your God is God; he is the faithful God, keeping his covenant of love to a thousand generations of those who love him and keep his commands.'

(Deuteronomy 7:7–9)

See also Deuteronomy 9:4–6; Ezekiel 36:22–23; Ephesians 1:4–6

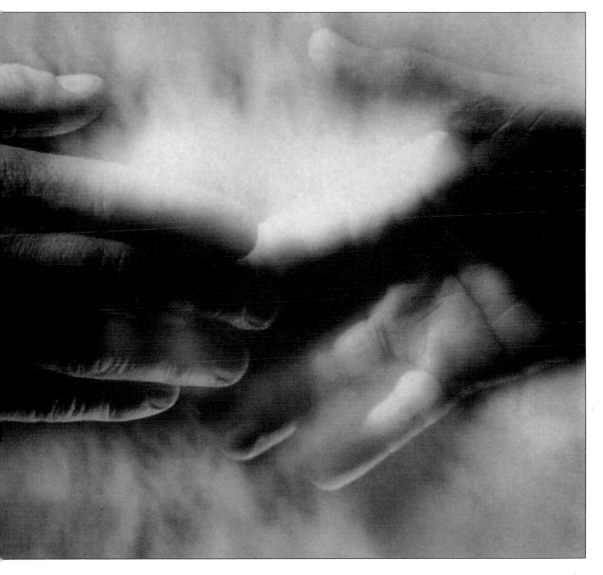

A relationship established by God

In some contracts, there is provision for negotiation between the two parties – but not in this one! It isn't an agreement between equal parties; God alone establishes it and decides the terms of the agreement. We see this, for example, in the covenant established with Abraham, where God even puts him into a deep sleep so that he can contribute absolutely nothing to it, other than experience it in a vision (see Genesis 15:12–21).

Jesus will underline the same principle when he reminds his disciples how it was that they were called into relationship with him:

'You did not choose me, but I chose you and appointed you to go and bear fruit – fruit that will last.'

(John 15:16)

Does this mean we have reason to be afraid? Not at all! For the terms of this contract have been determined by the most loving, the most understanding, the most just being in the whole cosmos!

Key covenants in the Bible

The covenant with Noah –
to protect humanity (Genesis 9:8–17)

The covenant with Abraham –
to build a special family (Genesis 12:1–3; 15:1–6; 17:1–8)

The covenant with Moses –
to make a great nation (Exodus 3:7–17; 19:3–6)

The covenant with David –
to establish an eternal kingdom (2 Samuel 7:8–16; Psalm 89:19–29)

The new covenant –
to change the human heart (Jeremiah 31:31–34; Matthew 26:26–29; Hebrews 8:7–13)

A relationship of the heart

God knows that laying down rules for us will not get us to walk in his covenant; only a miraculous change of our heart can do that. So that is just what God does! He changes the hearts of those who belong to him so we find that in our inmost being we now want to walk with him and keep his law.

'This is the covenant that I will make with the house of Israel after that time,' declares the LORD. 'I will put my law in their minds and write it on their hearts. I will be their God, and they will be my people.'

(Jeremiah 31:33)

See also Ezekiel 36:26–27; 2 Corinthians 3:3

A relationship open to all

There was a time when the covenant was open only to the Jewish nation – but not any longer! In fact, from the earliest days, God showed that he always had a much, much bigger plan in mind (Genesis 12:2–3; 15:5–6).

The covenant is open to *everyone*. All we need to do to become part of it is to repent and believe:

'Repent and be baptised, every one of you, in the name of Jesus Christ for the forgiveness of your sins. And you will receive the gift of the Holy Spirit. The promise is for you and your children and for all who are far off – for all whom the Lord our God will call.'

(Acts 2:38–39)

If you confess with your mouth, 'Jesus is Lord,' and believe in your heart that God raised him from the dead, you will be saved. ... As the Scripture says, 'Anyone who trusts in him will never be put to shame.' For there is no difference between Jew and Gentile – the same Lord is Lord of all and richly blesses all who call on him, for, 'Everyone who calls on the name of the Lord will be saved.'

(Romans 10:9, 11–13)

'Here I am! I stand at the door and knock. If anyone hears my voice and opens the door, I will come in and eat with him, and he with me.'

(Revelation 3:20)

A relationship involving the whole Trinity
The covenant that we as believers stand in with God involves the three Persons of the Trinity:
• The Father, who gave a people to his Son and sent him into the world to save them (John 6:37–40);
• The Son, who is the guarantee of the covenant (Hebrews 7:22) and the perfect go-between (Hebrews 7:26–27), fulfilling the demands that the Law makes on us (Matthew 5:17–18) by living a perfect life for us and dying in our place (John 10:14–18). The covenant is in fact ratified by Jesus' blood (Matthew 26:28) and he himself is the mediator of the covenant (Hebrews 9:11–15).
• The Holy Spirit, through whose power Christ offered himself on the cross (Hebrews 9:14) and who applies the effects of that death to us (1 Corinthians 2:9-12; 1 Thessalonians 1:5).

Old words, eternal message

Charles Spurgeon, a great Baptist preacher of the nineteenth century, wrote the following, which sums up so much about this friendship of God. While the language may seem dated, the message most definitely is not!

'Those who fear God need not fear want. Through all these long years the Lord has always found meat for his own children, whether they have been in the wilderness, or by the brook Cherith, or in captivity, or in the midst of famine. Hitherto the Lord has given us day by day our daily bread, and we doubt not that He will continue to feed us till we want no more.

'As to the higher and greater blessings of the covenant of grace, He will never cease to supply them as our case demands. He is mindful that He made the covenant, and never acts as if He regretted it. He is mindful of it when we provoke Him to destroy us. He is mindful to love us, keep us, and comfort us, even as He engaged to do. He is mindful of every jot and tittle of His engagements, never suffering one of His words to fall to the ground.

'We are sadly unmindful of our God, but He is graciously mindful of us. He cannot forget His Son who is the Surety of the Covenant, nor His Holy Spirit who actively carries out the covenant, nor His own honour, which is bound up with the covenant. Hence the foundation of God standeth sure, and no believer shall lose his divine inheritance . . .'

Relevance for today

To be practical, what does all this mean?

It is possible to be friends with God!

The scripture was fulfilled that says, 'Abraham believed God, and it was credited to him as righteousness,' and he was called God's friend.

(James 2:23)

See also Exodus 33:11; Isaiah 41:8

'You are my friends if you do what I command. I no longer call you servants, because a servant does not know his master's business. Instead, I have called you friends, for everything that I learned from my Father I have made known to you.'

(John 15:14–15)

Have I found that friendship for myself?

God will never let us go!

Our friendship with God is based on the covenant. We are no longer foreigners to the covenants of the promise, without hope and without God in the world' (Ephesians 2:12). We are in a stable, unchanging, committed relationship with God and he will never let us go.

'As I was with Moses, so I will be with you; I will never leave you nor forsake you.'

(Joshua 1:5)

Be strong and courageous. Do not be afraid or terrified because of them, for the LORD your God goes with you; he will never leave you nor forsake you.

(Deuteronomy 31:6)

God has said, 'Never will I leave you; never will I forsake you.' So we say with confidence, 'The Lord is my helper; I will not be afraid. What can man do to me?'

(Hebrews 13:5)

God's covenant with us is eternal!

Because this covenant is eternal, it gives us a solid promise to lay hold of when we feel far from God. As the hymn puts it: 'His oath, His cov'nant, and blood, Support me in the 'whelming flood'.

The Lord has sworn and will not change his mind: 'You are a priest for ever.' Because of this oath, Jesus has become the guarantee of a better covenant.

(Hebrews 7:21–22)

But you have come to Mount Zion, to the heavenly Jerusalem, the city of the living God. You have come to thousands upon thousands of angels in joyful assembly, to the church of the firstborn, whose names are written in heaven. You have come to God, the judge of all men, to the spirits of righteous men made perfect, to Jesus the mediator of a new covenant, and to the sprinkled blood that speaks a better word than the blood of Abel.

(Hebrews 12:22–24)

May the God of peace, who through the blood of the eternal covenant brought back from the dead our Lord Jesus, that great Shepherd of the sheep, equip you with everything good for doing his will, and may he work in us what is pleasing to him, through Jesus Christ, to whom be glory for ever and ever. Amen.

(Hebrews 13:20–21)

The covenant brings responsibilities

This wonderful covenant of friendship with God gives us a responsibility to live a life of holiness and righteousness, being faithful to our God.

Make every effort to live in peace with all men and to be holy; without holiness no-one will see the Lord.

(Hebrews 12:14)

See also Luke 1:72–75; Romans 12:1–2; Ephesians 4:1

Covenant faithfulness should characterize all our relationships

God's relationship of absolute faithfulness with us should be reflected in every relationship that we have with others – especially marriage (Ephesians 5:21–33; Hebrews 13:4) and our commitment to one another in the body of Christ, the church (e.g. Romans 13:8–10; Galatians 5:13–14).

Finally, all of you, live in harmony with one another; be sympathetic, love as brothers, be compassionate and humble. Do not repay evil with evil or insult with insult, but with blessing, because to this you were called so that you may inherit a blessing. For, 'Whoever would love life and see good days must keep his tongue from evil and his lips from deceitful speech. He must turn from evil and do good; he must seek peace and pursue it. For the eyes of the Lord are on the righteous and his ears are attentive to their prayer, but the face of the Lord is against those who do evil.'

(1 Peter 3:8–12)

Dear friends, let us love one another, for love comes from God . . . Since God so loved us, we also ought to love one another. No-one has ever seen God; but if we love one another, God lives in us and his love is made complete in us.

(1 John 4:7, 11–12)

Covenant friendship is important to God

Loyal friendship is the very hallmark of God's covenant with us; he therefore expects us to demonstrate that in all our relationships.

• God wants us to be loyal and dependable friends to others:

'Where you go I will go, and where you stay I will stay. Your people will be my people and your God my God.'

(Ruth 1:16)

A friend loves at all times, and a brother is born for adversity.

(Proverbs 17:17)

Two are better than one, because they have a good return for their work: If one falls down, his friend can help him up.

(Ecclesiastes 4:9–10)

See also 1 Samuel 18:1–4; 20:42; 2 Samuel 15:21; Proverbs 17:9; 18:24

• God wants us to know that gossip destroys friendship and breaks covenant:

A perverse man stirs up dissension, and a gossip separates close friends.

(Proverbs 16:28)

He who covers over an offence promotes love, but whoever repeats the matter separates close friends.

(Proverbs 17:9)

See also Proverbs 26:18–20; James 1:26; 3:3–12

My hope is built on nothing less
Than Jesus' blood and righteousness;
I dare not trust the sweetest frame,
But wholly lean on Jesus' Name.

On Christ, the solid Rock, I stand;
All other ground is sinking sand.

When darkness veils His lovely face,
I rest on His unchanging grace;
In every high and stormy gale,
My anchor holds within the veil.

His oath, His cov'nant, and blood,
Support me in the 'whelming flood;
When all around my soul gives way,
He then is all my hope and stay.

When He shall come with trumpet sound,
O may I then in Him be found!
Clothed in His righteousness alone,
Faultless to stand before the throne.

Edward Mote, 1797-1874

Conclusion

God is the best friend in the world, and he seals
that friendship in covenant. Knowing that we
are in a covenant relationship with him is meant
to make us confident, but not proud. It should
produce a deep sense of gratitude to God which
is reflected in the way we live and act towards
others.

*Jesus has become the guarantee of a better
covenant.*

(Hebrews 7:22)

CHAPTER FOUR

God is Faithful

True friends stay faithful – no matter what happens.
God's friendship is like that, staying faithful to us even when
we get things wrong, even when we let him down.

'Great is your faithfulness.' (Lamentations 3:23)

'I won't be your friend any more if you don't!' How often we must have heard children saying that. Come to think of it, how often we must have heard adults saying that too – but in a far more sophisticated way, of course! God's friendship is not like that, however. Through Jesus, he has made a covenant with us (as we saw in the previous chapter) to stay our friend, come what may and to work his purposes out, come what may. It is this 'come what may' that characterizes God's faithfulness.

God's faithfulness

Moses made a rather dangerous request one day: he asked to see God's glory (Exodus 33:18). If he had stopped to think about it, he might have thought twice! But God, in his kindness, called him up Mount Sinai to experience just what he had requested. But instead of the thunder and lightning and trembling mountains he might have expected (see Exodus 19:16–19), what he actually encountered was a revelation of the essence of God's heart.

And he passed in front of Moses, proclaiming, 'The LORD, the LORD, the compassionate and gracious God, slow to anger, abounding in love and faithfulness, maintaining love to thousands, and forgiving wickedness, rebellion and sin.'

(Exodus 34:6–7)

This is probably one of the most important passages in the Old Testament, revealing as it does God's own declaration of what he is like and how he promises to deal with people. Right at the heart of this stands God's assertion of his faithfulness. In fact, God is not just faithful – he abounds in faithfulness!

The promise of God's faithfulness

Again and again, the Bible assures us of God's faithfulness:

He is the Rock, his works are perfect, and all his ways are just. A faithful God who does no wrong, upright and just is he.

(Deuteronomy 32:4)

Your love, O LORD, reaches to the heavens, your faithfulness to the skies.

(Psalm 36:5)

No temptation has seized you except what is common to man. And God is faithful; he will not let you be tempted beyond what you can bear. But when you are tempted, he will also provide a way out so that you can stand up under it.

(1 Corinthians 10:13)

The one who calls you is faithful and he will do it.

(1 Thessalonians 5:24)

See also Genesis 24:27; Psalm 89:1–8; Isaiah 25:1; Lamentations 3:22–23; 1 Corinthians 1:9; 10:13; 2 Thessalonians 3:3; Hebrews 10:23

God's faithfulness is rooted in his inability to lie or do wrong.

God is not a man, that he should lie, nor a son of man, that he should change his mind. Does he speak and then not act? Does he promise and not fulfil?

(Numbers 23:19)

See also Deuteronomy 32:4; 1 Samuel 15:29; Titus 1:2; Hebrews 7:21

God promises to keep his covenant with those who love and obey him

Know therefore that the LORD your God is God; he is the faithful God, keeping his covenant of love to a thousand generations of those who love him and keep his commands.

(Deuteronomy 7:9)

See also Deuteronomy 5:10; Nehemiah 1:5; Psalm 18:25; Daniel 9:4

God promises to stay faithful, even when we are faithless

If we are faithless, He remains faithful, for He cannot deny Himself.

(2 Timothy 2:13, NASB)

See also Deuteronomy 4:25–31; Romans 3:3–4

The extent of God's faithfulness

But just how far does God's faithfulness go? Are there limits to it? Might I go beyond its reach or exhaust its resources? To think that the answer to such questions might be 'yes' shows that we have not yet grasped how big the God of the Bible really is!

God's faithfulness is great

Yet this I call to mind and therefore I have hope: Because of the LORD's great love we are not consumed, for his compassions never fail. They are new every morning; great is your faithfulness.

(Lamentations 3:21–23)

God's faithfulness is immeasurable

Your love, O LORD, reaches to the heavens, your faithfulness to the skies.

(Psalm 36:5)

God's faithfulness is unshakeable

'Though the mountains be shaken and the hills be removed, yet my unfailing love for you will not be shaken nor my covenant of peace be removed,' says the LORD, who has compassion on you.

(Isaiah 54:10)

God's faithfulness is enduring

Your word, O LORD, is eternal; it stands firm in the heavens. Your faithfulness continues through all generations.

(Psalm 119:89–90)

Expressions of God's faithfulness

Just as a diamond has many facets to it, each beautiful in its own right, but increasing the whole beauty when considered together, so is God's faithfulness. Each expression of his faithfulness is amazing; but seen together, it is awe-inspiring!

God's faithfulness is seen in:

The natural order of creation

As long as the earth endures, seedtime and harvest, cold and heat, summer and winter, day and night will never cease.

(Genesis 8:22)

See also Jeremiah 33:20–21; Matthew 5:45; 6:26

The keeping of his promises

The LORD is faithful to all his promises and loving towards all he has made.

(Psalm 145:13)

See also Joshua 23:14; Hebrews 10:23

His fulfilling of his word

As the rain and the snow come down from heaven, and do not return to it without

35

watering the earth and making it bud and flourish, so that it yields seed for the sower and bread for the eater, so is my word that goes out from my mouth: It will not return to me empty, but will accomplish what I desire and achieve the purpose for which I sent it.

(Isaiah 55:10–11)

See also 2 Chronicles 36:21–22; Luke 24:25–27, 44–47

His calling of us and his commitment to complete the work already begun in us

He will keep you strong to the end, so that you will be blameless on the day of our Lord Jesus Christ. God, who has called you into fellowship with his Son Jesus Christ our Lord, is faithful.

(1 Corinthians 1:8–9)

See also Philippians 1:6; 1 Thessalonians 5:23–24

His forgiveness of our sins

If we claim to be without sin, we deceive ourselves and the truth is not in us. If we confess our sins, he is faithful and just and will forgive us our sins and purify us from all unrighteousness.

(1 John 1:8–9)

See also Micah 7:18–19; Hebrews 2:17

His helping us when we are tempted

For we do not have a high priest who is unable to sympathise with our weaknesses, but we have one who has been tempted in every way, just as we are – yet was without sin. Let us then approach the throne of grace with confidence, so that we may receive mercy and find grace to help us in our time of need.

(Hebrews 4:15–16)

See also Matthew 4:11; Luke 22:43; 1 Corinthians 10:13

His helping us when we need protection

You are my hiding-place; you will protect me from trouble and surround me with songs of deliverance.

(Psalm 32:7)

See also Psalm 61:7; 91:4–7; John 17:11–15; 2 Thessalonians 3:3

The proof of God's faithfulness

But what proof do we have of God's faithfulness? Thankfully, it is not left to our feelings or to our emotions or even to other people's experience of it. The New Testament says that God has given one great, unshakeable piece of proof that God is faithful; a piece of proof that no one can take away – the resurrection of the Lord Jesus Christ!

We tell you the good news: What God promised our fathers he has fulfilled for us, their children, by raising up Jesus.

(Acts 13:32–33)

See also John 2:18–22; Acts 2:22–28; 17:29–31

Our response

Listening or learning?

Listening to stories about God's faithfulness is wonderful. But we do not learn about God's faithfulness in the classroom or from books. Rather, it is in the 'nitty-gritty' of life, with all its troubles, its rough and tumble, that we prove it for ourselves. It is only when it is 'put to the test' that we truly grasp it. That is what Abraham discovered long ago when God put him to the test by asking him to sacrifice his long-awaited, promised son, and then miraculously intervening (Genesis 22:1–18). It was not Abraham's son that God wanted, but Abraham's heart!

Limited or liberated?

Of course, our picture of God's faithfulness may need sharpening. Our understanding of it may be limited, coming from our experiences and views of human faithfulness: perhaps the faithfulness of the 'party faithful', who staunchly support their leader at a political conference on one occasion only to turn their backs on him or her in later years; perhaps the faithfulness of a husband, who makes vows to his wife at their wedding, only to abandon her shortly afterwards for the 'latest model'; perhaps the faithfulness of a friend who said they would always stand by us, but who then drops us when we go through a hard time.

If our view of God's faithfulness is limited by such experiences of life, we need to be liberated! This is simply not what God is like. God is a friend who is absolutely dependable, reliable, trustworthy: one you can always count on to be there and help; one who will never let you down, never let you go.

'Never will I leave you; never will I forsake you.'

(Hebrews 13:5)

If we recognize that our view of faithfulness has been limited and spoilt by such experiences, then we need to ask God to release us by a revelation of his truth (John 8:32) and a renewing of our minds and thinking (Romans 12:2).

Faith and faithfulness

So, how are we to respond to such a God? By trusting the One who is trustworthy; by putting our faith in the One who is faithful – not only once when we become Christians, but also in the here and now: in the life of today, in your life and ours this week, this day, this moment.

Trust in the LORD with all your heart and lean not on your own understanding; in all your ways acknowledge him, and he will make your paths straight.

(Proverbs 3:5–6)

When faced with something that seems impossible, Martin sometimes prays something like this: 'Lord, this is where I need your grace and your help, right here and now.' What happens? An answer is always provided! Something happens. The situation is seen in a different light; an alternative solution is discovered; an attitude or outlook is changed; circumstances get transformed. Why? Because God always responds to the one who calls out in faith.

We need to respond to God's faithfulness in the reality of personal faith. It has always been like this. Notice that all this isn't something static; it's something growing – because it is all about a relationship with God through Christ – and relationships, by their very nature, grow and get stretched.

God's blessing

Is exercising faith in God's faithfulness worthwhile? Absolutely! The Bible is full of promises and examples of how God always blesses those who have faith in him. Sometimes it is risky! But God never lets his people down.

So all who believe as Abraham believed are blessed just as Abraham was.

(Galatians 3:9, NCV)

See also Joshua 14:6–14; Daniel 6:19–23;
Matthew 24:45–47; Luke 1:45; John 20:29;
Hebrews 11:1–2

Relevance for today

God's heart and promise is for us to know him and his faithfulness

'I will betroth you to me for ever; I will betroth you in righteousness and justice, in love and compassion. I will betroth you in faithfulness, and you will acknowledge the LORD.'

(Hosea 2:19–20).

See also Deuteronomy 7:7–9

Our experiences of limited and imperfect human faithfulness do not have to colour how we relate to God

Christ has come to set us free from everything that hinders a true understanding of what God is really like – including our past experiences of un-faithfulness.

Then you will know the truth, and the truth will set you free . . . So if the Son sets you free, you will be free indeed.

(John 8:32, 36)

See also 2 Corinthians 3:17

God's faithfulness means he is always with us and will never forget us

There can never be an occasion when he is not with us, no matter what the circumstances, pressures, threats or outlook.

'Can a mother forget the baby at her breast and have no compassion on the child she has borne?

Though she may forget, I will not forget you! See, I have engraved you on the palms of my hands.'

(Isaiah 49:15–16)

See also Isaiah 44:21; 1 Corinthians 10:13

God's faithfulness should be a recurring theme of our praise

As we look back and remember what he has done in the past, and praise him for it, it encourages us to trust him for what he will do in the future.

I will proclaim the name of the LORD. Oh, praise the greatness of our God! He is the Rock, his works are perfect, and all his ways are just. A faithful God who does no wrong, upright and just is he.'

(Deuteronomy 32:3–4)

See also Psalm 89:1–8; 92:1–2; Isaiah 25:1

Faithfulness is for living out in the world, not merely reading about in the study

'Be strong and courageous, and do the work. Do not be afraid or discouraged, for the LORD God, my God, is with you. He will not fail you or forsake you until all the work for the service of the temple of the LORD is finished.'

(1 Chronicles 28:20)

See also 2 Timothy 4:16–18

God wants us to live as faithful people

• towards him (1 Kings 3:6; 2 Chronicles 30:20–21; Psalm 18:25; Revelation 2:10),
• towards the tasks that he gives us (Matthew 25:14–21; 1 Corinthians 4:1–2),
• towards one another (Proverbs 31:26; 1 Corinthians 4:15–17; Ephesians 1:1; Colossians 4:7-9; 1 Timothy 5:9–10).
If we do not live as faithful people, we have probably not understood God's faithfulness towards us.

Let love and faithfulness never leave you; bind them around your neck, write them on the tablet of your heart. Then you will win favour and a good name in the sight of God and man.

(Proverbs 3:3–4)

*'Great is Thy faithfulness', O God my
    Father,
There is no shadow of turning with Thee;
Thou changest not, Thy compassions they fail
    not;
As Thou hast been Thou for ever wilt be.*

   *'Great is Thy faithfulness! Great is Thy
        faithfulness!'
    Morning by morning new mercies I see!
    All I have needed Thy hand hath provided –
    'Great is Thy faithfulness', Lord, unto me!*

*Summer and winter, and springtime and
    harvest,
Sun, moon and stars in their courses above,
Join with all Nature in manifold witness
To Thy great faithfulness, mercy and love.*

*Pardon for sin and a peace that endureth
Thy own dear presence to cheer and to guide,
Strength for today and bright hope for
    tomorrow,
Blessings all mine, with ten thousand beside!*

Thomas O. Chisholm, 1866–1960

Conclusion

God's faithfulness is not merely an 'attribute' of his character to be thought about. It is right at the heart of who he is and how he shows himself. He is faithful and this fact can be – and is to be – experienced in our daily lives as we depend on him.

God, who has called you into fellowship with his Son Jesus Christ our Lord, is faithful.

(1 Corinthians 1:9)

CHAPTER FIVE

Amazing Grace!

> God does not give us what we deserve; he gives us *more* than we could ever deserve.
>
> *The God of all grace.* (1 Peter 5:10)

'It's just not fair!' How many times have you heard (or said!) those words? Perhaps someone got promotion when you felt they didn't deserve it; perhaps you felt someone received a better gift or a better deal than you did; perhaps life seemed to serve you a hard blow. Whenever we get less than we feel we should have done, we immediately cry, 'Unfair!' and think that, if only the world were just, then surely everything would be 'fair'.

But here is a shocking piece of news! The Bible tells us that God is not 'fair'! What! How can we say that? Well, it's true! For if God were fair, none of us would last a moment; his 'fairness' would judge our sin and wipe us from the face of the earth without a moment's hesitation. But here is the wonderful news: God is not fair; he is *more than fair!* That is what the Bible means by the grace of God.

Grace discovered: Exodus 34:1–7

We cannot explore this amazing theme of God's more-than-fairness without returning to the passage we looked at in the previous chapter when Moses went up the mountain to discover God as he really was.

And he passed in front of Moses, proclaiming, 'The LORD, the LORD, the compassionate and gracious God, slow to anger, abounding in love and faithfulness, maintaining love to thousands, and forgiving wickedness, rebellion and sin.'

(Exodus 34:6–7)

Moses discovered that not only was God a faithful God, he was also a gracious God. In fact 'compassionate' and 'gracious' were the first words from God's lips as he described himself. How sad it is, therefore, when people today do not see these qualities as the first thing that God wants us to know about him.

From start to finish, the Bible is full of promises and assurances of God's grace. Here are just some of them:

*'The L*ORD *bless you and keep you; the L*ORD *make his face shine upon you and be gracious to you; the L*ORD *turn his face towards you and give you peace.'*

(Numbers 6:24–26)

*The L*ORD *is gracious and compassionate, slow to anger and rich in love. The L*ORD *is good to all; he has compassion on all he has made.*

(Psalm 145:8-9)

*Yet the L*ORD *longs to be gracious to you; he rises to show you compassion. For the L*ORD *is a God of justice. Blessed are all who wait for him!*

(Isaiah 30:18–19)

The Word became flesh and made his dwelling among us. We have seen his glory, the glory of the One and Only, who came from the Father, full of grace and truth. John

testifies concerning him. He cries out, saying, 'This was he of whom I said, "He who comes after me has surpassed me because he was before me." ' From the fulness of his grace we have all received one blessing after another. For the law was given through Moses; grace and truth came through Jesus Christ.

(John 1:14–17)

Therefore, since we have been justified through faith, we have peace with God through our Lord Jesus Christ, through whom we have gained access by faith into this grace in which we now stand.

(Romans 5:1–2)

But he said to me, 'My grace is sufficient for you, for my power is made perfect in weakness.'

(2 Corinthians 12:9)

See also Genesis 21:1; 2 Kings 13:23; 2 Chronicles 30:9; Psalm 86:15; 103:8–18; Joel 2:13; Acts 14:3; 1 Corinthians 15:10; 2 Corinthians 8:9; 2 Thessalonians 1:2; 2 Timothy 2:1; Titus 2:11; Hebrews 4:16; 1 Peter 5:10; Revelation 22:21.

But because of his great love for us, God, who is rich in mercy, made us alive with Christ even when we were dead in transgressions – it is by grace you have been saved. And God raised us up with Christ and seated us with him in the heavenly realms in Christ Jesus, in order that in the coming ages he might show the incomparable riches of his grace, expressed in his kindness to us in Christ Jesus. For it is by grace you have been saved, through faith – and this not from yourselves, it is the gift of God – not by works, so that no-one can boast.

(Ephesians 2:4–9)

Grace discovered: Matthew 20:1–16

Two important truths stand out in this parable about the grace of God:

God's grace is free

Note that the landowner (who clearly stands for God) was a caring person. He gave work to those who needed it and agreed to pay them a fair wage: a day's pay for a day's work (vv 1–2).

But he gets more and more generous as the day goes on. Each worker, regardless of how long he has worked, gets paid a day's wages (vv 3–7, 9). Each received what he needed in order to keep his family, not what he deserved on a strict hourly rate. The landowner chose to pay them according to their need, according to his grace.

Jesus pays particular attention to the group hired at the eleventh hour (5 pm by our reckoning). How generously they were treated! They, as well as the others, needed money to support their families; the landowner saw their need and so offered them work, paying them way beyond what they might have expected. When the other workers complained that it was not 'fair' (vv 11–12), the landowner simply said he was not being unfair, but more-than-fair (vv 13–15).

God sees our need, too: how we are sinners who need saving from judgment and hell. The miracle of grace is that God does not deal with us according to what we deserve or what we have 'earned'. In spite of our sin, he loves us. In love, he gave his Son to die on the cross. That's grace: **G-R-A-C-E** – God's Riches At Christ's Expense

This righteousness from God comes through faith in Jesus Christ to all who believe. There is no difference, for all have sinned and fall short of the glory of God, and are justified freely by his grace through the redemption that came by Christ Jesus

(Romans 3:22–24)

In him we have redemption through his blood, the forgiveness of sins, in accordance with the riches of God's grace that he lavished on us with all wisdom and understanding.

(Ephesians 1:7–8)

See also Romans 4:4–5; Ephesians 2:8–9; 2 Timothy 1:9

This freely available grace is not just about our sin being dealt with and our being saved from judgment and hell at 'the End', however. God's grace is available for our lives every day, right here and now! Little wonder, then, that the writer of Hebrews says:

Let us then approach the throne of grace with confidence, so that we may receive mercy and find grace to help us in our time of need.

(Hebrews 4:16)

God's grace is sovereign

God's grace is not only free; it is also sovereign. By that we mean that God has the right to choose what he wants to do (just as in the parable, v 15, 'Don't I have the right to do what I want with my own money?'). How do we find ourselves reacting to this? How do we react when we see other Christians 'being blessed' by God more than we seem to be blessed? Are we envious because God is generous to others (v 15)?

There is a shop in Martin's town where they know his name, say hello cheerily as he enters, and seem to treat him nicely. They make him feel important! But one day he noticed that the assistants acted in the same way with other people as well. His reaction: he felt cheated! Why? Because he wanted to be the only one who came in for special treatment! He had not understood grace at that moment.

God's grace requires that we do not grumble (v 11) at how others are treated. God can treat us however he wants: he is God, after all; so who are we to question him?

But who are you, O man, to talk back to God? 'Shall what is formed say to him who formed it, "Why did you make me like this?" ' Does not the potter have the right to make out of the same lump of clay some pottery for noble purposes and some for common use?

(Romans 9:20–21)

See also Isaiah 29:16; 45:9–11

God is not unfair to any of us (v 13 of the parable). If he treated any of us justly, we would be condemned to hell. The wonder of his *mercy* is that he does not give us what we deserve (judgment!); the wonder of his *grace* is that he gives us more than we could ever deserve, loving us despite our sin (Ephesians 2:1–10). Grace is the free gift of God, given, as God freely chooses, to those who deserve the opposite. It is completely undeserved by us; it depends only upon God's own will.

Grace maintained

As we saw earlier, God chose a people to be his own, pledging himself in covenant to them, and remaining faithful to them even when they were unfaithful to him. (See, e.g., 2 Samuel 7:12–16; Hosea 11:1–9.)

Such grace does not mean 'softness' however! God is not some weak father who 'lets his children get away with anything' – he loves us far too much for that! That is why, in his grace, he promises to bring tender, fatherly discipline into our lives when it is needed. Such discipline proves we are truly loved!

My son, do not despise the LORD's discipline and do not resent his rebuke, because the LORD disciplines those he loves, as a father the son he delights in.

(Proverbs 3:11–12)

See also Deuteronomy 8:5; Job 5:17–18; Psalm 94:12–14; Proverbs 1:7; 6:23; Jeremiah 30:11; 1 Corinthians 11:32; Hebrews 12:5–13; Revelation 3:19

Grace experienced

The Bible is very clear that we cannot do anything to put ourselves right with God (Romans 3:20). Praying, going to church, trying to 'be spiritual', doing charitable work – none of this can change our standing before God one iota! This is exactly why we need the grace of God!

In his grace God wants to save us

Getting in a right relationship with God is all about his gracious work from start to finish!

We are called by God's grace

[God] who has saved us and called us to a holy life – not because of anything we have done but because of his own purpose and grace. This grace was given us in Christ Jesus before the beginning of time, but it has now been revealed through the appearing of our Saviour, Christ Jesus, who has destroyed death and has brought life and immortality to light through the gospel.

(2 Timothy 1:9–10)

See also Galatians 1:15; 1 Peter 5:10

We are put right with God by grace

For it is by grace you have been saved, through faith – and this not from yourselves, it is the gift of God – not by works, so that no-one can boast.

(Ephesians 2:8)

See also Romans 3:24; 4:16; 5:21

All of this is centred on the cross (Romans 3:24–25; 5:8–9; Titus 3:4–7) and it can be taken hold of, even by us today, simply through faith (Romans 3:25; 4:16; Ephesians 2:8).

In his grace God wants to forgive us

God's grace means that he forgives our sins – absolutely and completely, no matter what they may have been – and then replaces that sin with life!

Where sin increased, grace increased all the more.

(Romans 5:20)

'Come now, let us reason together,' says the LORD. 'Though your sins are like scarlet, they shall be as white as snow; though they are red as crimson, they shall be like wool.'

(Isaiah 1:18)

Praise the LORD, O my soul, and forget not all his benefits – who forgives all your sins and heals all your diseases . . . he does not treat us as our sins deserve or repay us according to our iniquities. For as high as the heavens are above the earth, so great is his love for those who fear him; as far as the east is from the west, so far has he removed our transgressions from us.

(Psalm 103:2–3, 10–12)

See also Isaiah 43:25; 55:6–7; Jeremiah 31: 33–34; Micah 7:18–20; Hebrews 10:17; 1 John 1:9

Remember: no matter how bad our sin may have been, the power of the blood to cleanse me is greater than the power of sin to stain me.

In his grace God wants to keep us

God never starts something he cannot finish! That is why, when his grace gets to work on our life, we can be sure it will 'stick with us' right to the end. God's grace will always keep us and see us through.

There has never been the slightest doubt in my mind that the God who started this great work in you would keep at it and bring it to a flourishing finish on the very day Christ Jesus appears.

(Philippians 1:6 The Message)

See also Isaiah 49:16; John 10:27–29; 1 Corinthians 1:8–9

Relevance for today

God wants us to know him as the gracious God

Yet the LORD longs to be gracious to you; he rises to show you compassion. For the LORD is a God of justice. Blessed are all who wait for him!

(Isaiah 30:18)

See also Exodus 34:5–6

We should take care not to miss the grace of God in our lives

As God's fellow-workers we urge you not to receive God's grace in vain. For he says, 'In the time of my favour I heard you, and in the day of salvation I helped you.' I tell you, now is the time of God's favour, now is the day of salvation.

(2 Corinthians 6:1–2)

See also Jonah 2:8; Hebrews 12:15

The grace of God is there for everyday life

To keep me from becoming conceited because of these surpassingly great revelations, there was given me a thorn in my flesh, a messenger of Satan, to torment me. Three times I pleaded with the Lord to take it away from me. But he said to me, 'My grace is sufficient for you, for my power is made perfect in weakness.' Therefore I will boast all the more gladly about my weaknesses, so that Christ's power may rest on me. That is why, for Christ's sake, I delight in weaknesses, in insults, in hardships, in persecutions, in difficulties. For when I am weak, then I am strong.

(2 Corinthians 12:7–9)

See also Luke 2:40; Acts 4:32–33; 2 Corinthians 8:7; Titus 2:11–12

We should never think that we have been too bad to experience the grace of God

For I am the least of the apostles and do not even deserve to be called an apostle, because I persecuted the church of God. But by the grace of God I am what I am, and his grace to me was not without effect.

(1 Corinthians 15:9–10)

See also Acts 22:3–16; 26:9–18

Humility is the key to receiving the grace of God

All of you, clothe yourselves with humility towards one another, because, 'God opposes the proud but gives grace to the humble.' Humble yourselves, therefore, under God's mighty hand, that he may lift you up in due time.

(1 Peter 5:5–6)

See also Proverbs 3:34; James 4:6

We should pass on the grace of God to others and live as gracious people

Each one should use whatever gift he has received to serve others, faithfully administering God's grace in its various forms.

(1 Peter 4:10)

See also Luke 4:22; Colossians 4:6

Amazing grace! (how sweet the sound)
That saved a wretch like me!
I once was lost, but now am found;
Was blind, but now I see.

'Twas grace that taught my heart to fear,
And grace my fears relieved;
How precious did that grace appear
The hour I first believed!

Through many dangers, toils and snares
I have already come;
'Tis grace has brought me safe thus far,
And grace will lead me home.

The Lord has promised good to me,
His Word my hope secures;
He will my shield and portion be
As long as life endures.

Yes, when this flesh and heart shall fail
And mortal life shall cease,
I shall possess within the veil
A life of joy and peace.

When I've been there a thousand years,
Bright shining as the sun,
I've no less days to sing God's praise
Than when I first begun.

John Newton, 1725–1807

Conclusion

Our God is 'the God of all grace' (1 Peter 5:10) and therefore everything he does is full of grace. This is what the God of the promises is like.

May the grace of the Lord Jesus Christ, and the love of God, and the fellowship of the Holy Spirit be with you all.

(2 Corinthians 13:14)

CHAPTER SIX

The Names of God

> Through his different names in the Bible, God reveals something of the greatness of his character and shows that he is wholly trustworthy and able to meet all our needs.
>
> *Moses said to God, 'Suppose I go to the Israelites and say to them, "The God of your fathers has sent me to you," and they ask me, "What is his name?" Then what shall I tell them?' (Exodus 3:13)*

'Hide and seek' has always been a popular children's game. One child covers his face while the others hide in as difficult places as they can find, in the hope they will not be discovered. Thankfully, God never plays 'Hide and seek' with us. If he were to, we would never find him. God's great delight is not in hiding himself, but in revealing himself. He loves to be found! (See Deuteronomy 4:29; Proverbs 8:17; Jeremiah 29:13; Acts 17:27)

One of the ways God has revealed himself is through his names. In Bible times a name was far more than something to distinguish you from someone else; it summed up who you really were.

There are almost 150 different Hebrew and Greek words used for 'God' in the Bible. That in itself tells us how wonderful he is and how difficult it is to describe him!

General names of God

El

This Hebrew word means 'God' or 'god' in the widest sense. While sometimes found alone (e.g. Genesis 31:13) it is frequently found combined with other words to show God's distinctive nature and to distinguish him from false pagan gods.

For example, God reveals himself as:

El Shaddai – God Almighty (Genesis 17:1; 28:3; 35:11; Exodus 6:3; Ezekiel 10:5)

El Elyon – God the Most High (Genesis 14:18–20)

El Olam – Eternal God (Genesis 21:33)
El Roi – God who sees (Genesis 16:13)

Other words linked with his name include: holy (Isaiah 5:16), righteous (Isaiah 45:21), jealous (Exodus 20:5), faithful (Deuteronomy 7:9), merciful (Deuteronomy 4:31).

A common 'combination name', especially in the Old Testament, is 'the living God'.

As the deer pants for streams of water, so my soul pants for you, O God. My soul thirsts for God, for the living God.

(Psalm 42:1–2)

David asked the men standing near him, 'What will be done for the man who kills this Philistine and removes this disgrace from Israel? Who is this uncircumcised Philistine that he should defy the armies of the living God?'

(1 Samuel 17:26)

For he is the living God and he endures for ever; his kingdom will not be destroyed, his dominion will never end.

(Daniel 6:26)

See also Joshua 3:10; 2 Kings 19:16; Psalm 84:2; Jeremiah 10:10; Hosea 1:10; Matthew 16:16; 26:63

Mike travels to India quite often and there the name the Living God is often used by Christians. Just as in Bible times, where there was also a multiplicity of 'gods' to choose from, this term marks out the true God as quite distinct from all other so-called 'gods' and from 'dead' and 'worthless' idols. (See 2 Corinthians 6:16; 1 Thessalonians 1:9.) This is why we are commanded not to make any idols for ourselves (Exodus 20:3–4; 1 Kings 16:26; Jeremiah 14:22; Ezekiel 20:7). God is not dead (as an idol is) but living!

Elohim

This word and its compounds occurs over 2,000 times in the Bible. It is a plural word, referring to God's majesty (rather like the royal 'we') or to the persons of the Trinity (e.g. Genesis 1:1–2, 26). This word reveals God as the God of creation and providence, the supreme God, in contrast to other created beings.

Sometimes the names of people or places included the word El to serve as a reminder of their God. Look out for them when you are reading the Bible. Here are some examples:

Israel – He struggles with God
Genesis 32:28

Ishmael – God hears
Genesis 16:15

Elijah – The Lord is my God
1 Kings 17:1

Elisha – God is salvation
1 Kings 19:19

Eliab – God is Father
1 Samuel 16:6

Eleazar – God has helped
Deuteronomy 10:6

Elizabeth – God is my oath
Luke 1:5

Bethel – House of God
Genesis 28:19

The covenant or 'personal' name of God

On Mount Sinai, as Moses stood before the burning bush that was not consumed, God revealed to him the name by which he wished to be known – Yahweh (or Jehovah), represented in most English versions as LORD (in capital letters).

The background to the name

As the original Hebrew word YHWH did not contain any vowels, we are not one hundred per cent sure how it was pronounced! After the exile, Jews increasingly felt this name of God was too sacred to be spoken and so substituted another word, Adonai (Lord, in lower-case letters), when reading it in the Scriptures. Some texts combined the vowels of Adonai with the consonants of YHWH to remind readers to pronounce God's 'personal name' as Adonai. It was a misunderstanding of this that led some people later to think that God's personal name was therefore Jehovah, rather than the more likely 'Yahweh'.

The meaning of the name

God said to Moses, 'I AM WHO I AM. This is what you are to say to the Israelites: "I AM has sent me to you."' God also said to Moses, 'Say to the Israelites, "The LORD [YAHWEH], the God of your fathers – the God of Abraham, the God of Isaac and the God of Jacob – has sent me to you." This is my name for ever, the name by which I am to be remembered from generation to generation.'

(Exodus 3:14–15)

God is saying far more here than 'I exist'; he is saying, 'I am always, actively present.' In fact, the phrase translated, 'I am who I am' could also be translated: 'I will be who I will be' (as in v 12). God is promising that he is always there – he always has been, and always will be. He is the God of the past, the present, and the future.

Grace and peace to you from him who is, and who was, and who is to come.

(Revelation 1:4)

'I am the Alpha and the Omega,' says the Lord God, 'who is, and who was, and who is to come, the Almighty.'

(Revelation 1:8)

See also Revelation 11:17; 16:5

This is why he can forgive what is past, know what is ahead, and use both for his purposes in the present. Nothing is outside of the reach or power of such a God! Nothing can separate us from us his love

(Romans 8:35–39 The Message)

Combination names

As with El, the general name for God, God's personal name (here retained as the more traditional Jehovah) was also combined with other words. For example,

Jehovah-Jireh (the LORD will provide, Genesis 22:8, 14), when the Lord provided a ram as a substitute for Isaac.

Our God is a God who promises to provide for his people:

And my God will meet all your needs according to his glorious riches in Christ Jesus.

(Philippians 4:19)

See also Psalm 65:9; 1 Timothy 6:17

Jehovah-Nissi (the LORD is my banner, Exodus 17:15), when Israel defeated the Amalekites.

Our God is a God who promises to defend his people:

The LORD is my rock, my fortress and my deliverer; my God is my rock, in whom I take refuge. He is my shield and the horn of my salvation, my stronghold. I call to the LORD, who is worthy of praise, and I am saved from my enemies.

(Psalm 18:2–3)

See also Psalm 28:8; 46:5–7; 68:5; Song of Songs 2:4

Jehovah-Shalom (the LORD is peace, Judges 6:24), when Gideon first encountered God and feared he would die.

Our God is a God who promises to bring us his peace:

You will keep in perfect peace him whose mind is steadfast, because he trusts in you. Trust in the LORD for ever, for the LORD, the LORD, is the Rock eternal.

(Isaiah 26:3–4)

See also John 14:27; Philippians 4:6–7

Jehovah-Tsidkenu (the LORD our righteousness, Jeremiah 23:6; 33:16), when Jeremiah looked forward to God's coming Messiah.

Our God is a God who himself provides righteousness for people:

Abram believed the LORD, and he credited it to him as righteousness.

(Genesis 15:6)

See also Isaiah 42:6–7; 61:1–3, 10–11; Romans 3:21–22; 4:22–24; 5:17–18

Jehovah-Tsebaoth (Sabaoth) (the LORD Almighty, or, in older English versions, 'the LORD of hosts', 1 Samuel 1:3; 17:45).

Our God is a God who is sovereign over all the powers of heaven and earth:

Sovereign LORD, you have made the heavens and the earth by your great power and outstretched arm. Nothing is too hard for you . . . O great and powerful God, whose name is the LORD Almighty, great are your purposes and mighty are your deeds. Your eyes are open to all the ways of men; you reward everyone according to his conduct and as his deeds deserve. You performed miraculous signs and wonders in Egypt and have continued them to this day, both in Israel and among all mankind, and have gained the renown that is still yours. You brought your people Israel out of Egypt with signs and wonders, by a mighty hand and an outstretched arm and with great terror.

(Jeremiah 32:17–22)

That power is like the working of his mighty strength, which he exerted in Christ when he raised him from the dead and seated him at his right hand in the heavenly realms, far above all rule and authority, power and dominion, and every title that can be given, not only in the present age but also in the one to come.

(Ephesians 1:19–21)

See also Daniel 7:13–14; Philippians 2:9–11

Jehovah-Ra-ah (the LORD my shepherd, Psalm 23:1).

Our God is a God who tenderly shepherds and cares for his people:

See, the Sovereign LORD comes with power, and his arm rules for him. See, his reward is with him, and his recompense accompanies him. He tends his flock like a shepherd: He gathers the lambs in his arms and carries them close to his heart; he gently leads those that have young.

(Isaiah 40:10–11)

See also Psalm 80:1–3; John 10:11–16

Jehovah-Rophi (the LORD my healer, Exodus 15:26).

Our God is a God who promises healing to his people:

'If you listen carefully to the voice of the LORD your God and do what is right in his eyes, if you pay attention to his commands and keep all his decrees, I will not bring on you any of the diseases I brought on the Egyptians, for I am the LORD, who heals you.'

(Exodus 15:26)

See also Numbers 21:6–9; Psalm 103:1–5; 147:3; Isaiah 53:5; Malachi 4:2; Matthew 8:16–17; Acts 10:38; Revelation 22:1–2

Others include: *Jehovah-Mekaddishkem* (the LORD who makes holy, Exodus 31:13); *Jehovah-Shammah* (the LORD who is there, Ezekiel 48:35); *Jehovah-Elohe-Yisrael* (the LORD God of Israel, Judges 5:3; Isaiah 17:6; Zephaniah 2:9).

Two testaments, one God

Sometimes people have driven a 'wedge' between the Old and New Testaments, as if God were somehow different in each – all wrath and judgment in the Old, all kindness and grace in the New. Nothing could be further from the truth! It is the same God who speaks and reveals himself in both and all his characteristics can be found in both. This can be seen in the following two examples:

God as Father

God is the Father of the human race in general, because of creation:

Have we not all one Father? Did not one God create us?

(Malachi 2:10)

'For in him we live and move and have our being.' As some of your own poets have said, 'We are his offspring.' Therefore since we are God's offspring, we should not think that the divine being is like gold or silver or stone – an image made by man's design and skill.

(Acts 17:28–29)

But God is the Father of his people in particular, because of salvation:

I will lead them beside streams of water on a level path where they will not stumble, because I am Israel's father, and Ephraim is my firstborn son.

(Jeremiah 31:9)

I will be a Father to you, and you will be my sons and daughters, says the Lord Almighty.

(2 Corinthians 6:18)

See also Psalm 2:7; 68:5; 89:26; Isaiah 9:6; Jeremiah 3:19; John 1:12; 1 John 3:1–2

With the coming of Jesus, however, this fatherhood becomes so intimate that we can now even call God Abba – the Aramaic for 'daddy'!

For you did not receive a spirit that makes you a slave again to fear, but you received the Spirit of sonship. And by him we cry, 'Abba, Father.'

(Romans 8:15)

See also Mark 14:36; Galatians 4:6

God as Lord

When the Old Testament was translated into Greek, the word *kyrios* was used to translate Yahweh (LORD). But here is the amazing thing! In the New Testament, they chose exactly the same word – *kyrios* – for Jesus. The word used for Yahweh is used for Jesus Christ! Why? Because they understood that this Jesus was no less than the eternal Yahweh come among them!

On many occasions in the New Testament, Old Testament passages that referred to Yahweh are unashamedly applied to Christ (e.g. Acts 2:34–35 applies Psalm 110:1; Romans 10:13 applies Joel 2:32; Philippians 2:9–11 applies Isaiah 45:23). Furthermore, Jesus took the very name of God, Yahweh (I am, Exodus 3:14) and often, and unhesitatingly, applied it to himself:

'I tell you the truth,' Jesus answered, 'before Abraham was born, I am!'

(John 8:58)

See also e.g. John 6:35; 10:14; 11:25; 15:1

Relevance for today

We can call on the name of the Lord and be saved

And everyone who calls on the name of the Lord will be saved.

(Acts 2:21)

The many names of God remind us of how great he is

God is so great that there is simply no one like him:

There is no-one like the God of Jeshurun, who rides on the heavens to help you and on the clouds in his majesty. The eternal God is your refuge, and underneath are the everlasting arms.

(Deuteronomy 33:26–27)

Yahweh – I AM – is always there, always with us, no matter what situation we are in

'The LORD himself goes before you and will be with you; he will never leave you nor forsake you. Do not be afraid; do not be discouraged.'

(Deuteronomy 31:8)

See also Deuteronomy 31:6; Joshua 1:5; Isaiah 54:10; Hebrews 13:5

God is big enough to embrace my past, present and future, and therefore I need not doubt or fear

But now, this is what the LORD says – he who created you, O Jacob, he who formed you, O Israel: 'Fear not, for I have redeemed you; I have summoned you by name; you are mine. When you pass through the waters, I will be with you; and when you pass through the rivers, they will not sweep over you. When you walk through the fire, you will not be burned; the flames will not set you ablaze. For I am the LORD, your God, the Holy One of Israel, your Saviour.'

(Isaiah 43:1–4)

We should not take any of the names of the Lord our God in vain

Whether through blasphemy, or through using them in a manipulative way, we should not take any of the names of the Lord in vain. God's name is always to be hallowed' (Matthew 6:9)

*'Our Father in heaven,
hallowed be your name . . .'*

(Matthew 6:9)

You shall not misuse the name of the LORD your God, for the LORD will not hold anyone guiltless who misuses his name.

(Exodus 20:7)

Reflecting on the names of God can fuel our spiritual walk and growth

It can help us in our worship (Psalm 8:1), our praying (1 Kings 8:28–30), and in spiritual warfare (Psalm 20:7).

Some trust in chariots and some in horses, but we trust in the name of the LORD our God.

(Psalm 20:7)

55

The God of Abraham praise,
Who reigns enthroned above,
Ancient of everlasting days,
And God of love.
Jehovah! Great I AM!
By earth and heaven confessed;
I bow and bless the sacred Name
For ever blessed.

The God of Abraham praise,
At whose supreme command
From earth I rise, and seek the joys
At His right hand.
I all on earth forsake
Its wisdom, fame, and power –
And Him my only portion make,
My shield and tower.

The God of Abraham praise,
Whose all-sufficient grace
Shall guide me all my happy days
In all my ways.
He is my faithful Friend,
He is my gracious God;
And He shall save me to the end
Through Jesus' blood.

He by Himself hath sworn,
I on His oath depend:
I shall, on eagles' wings upborne,
To heaven ascend;
I shall behold His face,
I shall His power adore,
And sing the wonders of His grace
For evermore.

The whole triumphant host
Give thanks to God on high;
Hail, Father, Son, and Holy Ghost!
They ever cry.
Hail, Abraham's God, and mine!
I join the heavenly lays;
All might and majesty are Thine,
And endless praise.

Thomas Olivers, 1725–99

Conclusion

Left alone, none of us can find God or fully understand him. But he has chosen to reveal himself; and in his names we begin to sense something of the greatness of the One who has declared himself to be our Father.

'I tell you the truth,' Jesus answered, 'before Abraham was born, I am!'

(John 8:58)

CHAPTER SEVEN

Can We Really Trust God?

> The example of Abraham shows us how to make the promises of God our own by trusting him, even when everything seems impossible.
>
> *He [Abraham] did not waver through unbelief regarding the promise of God, but was strengthened in his faith and gave glory to God, being fully persuaded that God had power to do what he had promised.* (Romans 4:20–21)

'Trust' is a rare commodity as we enter the third millennium. Can we trust politicians, newspapers, our insurance company, our employer, our friend? Often, their 'track record' will be a fairly good indicator, for if they haven't been trustworthy in the past, it is unlikely they will be in the future.

God is not afraid of our looking at his 'track record'. If we can begin to grasp what the Bible says about him and his ways, then we will begin to see that it is the most natural thing in the world to trust him.

But the founder of the 'family of faith' – Abraham – had absolutely nothing to go on at first. For Abraham, God had no track record! But he steadily learned from experience that you really can trust God. Let's look at some key incidents from his life.

The example of Abraham
Genesis 12:1–9

Like so many of us, Abram (his name wasn't changed to Abraham until later, see Genesis 17:5) started out by not believing in God. Coming from the city of Ur (Genesis 11:31) a centre of worship of the Moon god, Abram was almost certainly a 'pagan'. But our background makes no difference when it comes to getting to know God! (See e.g. Galatians 3:28–29)

God does not always tell us everything 'up front'

He told Abram to 'go to the land I will show you' (v 1) – but he didn't tell him which one! Only when he got to Shechem did God say, 'This is it!' (vv 6–7).

See also Acts 7:3; 8:26–29; 20:22–24; Hebrews 11:8

Faith is about 'risking it'

Abram had to leave first Ur, then Haran, his family, his friends, his old way of life and step out into an unknown world. If he hadn't stepped out in faith and trusted God's promise (vv 2–3), he would never have known whether it was true or not. Faith doesn't drop out of the sky; it grows as we risk stepping out with God.

Faith requires practical steps at times

The Promised Land didn't drop at his feet – he had to set out and find it, following God's leading as he went. Notice his step-by-step practical and spiritual response in verses 4–9.

However, taking practical steps is not the same as 'helping God out'. Whenever Abraham tried to do that, things always went disastrously wrong (Genesis 12:10–20; 16:1–16; 20:1–18).

What do we mean by 'faith'? Here is the definition of Hebrews 11:1 in several different English translations:
• Now faith is being sure of what we hope for and certain of what we do not see. (NIV)
• Now faith is the assurance of things hoped for, the conviction of things not seen. (NASB & NRSV)
• Only faith can guarantee the blessings that we hope for, or prove the existence of the realities that are unseen. (NJB)
• Faith makes us sure of what we hope for and gives us proof of what we cannot see. (CEV)
• Faith means being sure of the things we hope for and knowing that something is real even if we do not see it. (NCV)
One contemporary paraphrase (The Message) sees faith in this passage as 'our handle on what we can't see'. That is exactly what faith is: it 'gives us a handle' on God's promises until they come into being.

Genesis 15:1–7

Four striking phrases

In these verses, for the first time in the Bible, come four striking phrases that recur throughout the Scriptures and that are keys to trusting God:

'The word of the LORD came' (v 1)

We cannot trust God until we have heard him. Without this, faith is little more than 'hoping for the best'; but once we know God has spoken, it is so much easier to trust. Consider the example of Elijah:

Then the word of the LORD came to Elijah: 'Leave here, turn eastward and hide in the Kerith Ravine, east of the Jordan. You will drink from the brook, and I have ordered the ravens to feed you there.' So he did what the LORD had told him. He went to the Kerith Ravine, east of the Jordan, and stayed there. The ravens brought him bread and meat in the morning and bread and meat in the evening, and he drank from the brook.

(1 Kings 17:2–6)

See also 1 Samuel 15:10; 2 Samuel 7:4; Isaiah 38:4; Jeremiah 1:4

'Do not be afraid' (v 1)

When God tells us what he wants us to do, it can sometimes seem scary at first! That is why God often encourages his people not to be afraid:

Moses answered the people, 'Do not be afraid. Stand firm and you will see the deliverance the LORD will bring you today. The Egyptians you see today you will never see again. The LORD will fight for you; you need only to be still.'

(Exodus 14:13–14)

'Peace I leave with you; my peace I give you. I do not give to you as the world gives. Do not let your hearts be troubled and do not be afraid.'

(John 14:27)

See also Deuteronomy 1:21; Isaiah 40:9; Luke 1:30; John 14:27; Acts 27:24

'I am your shield' (v 1)

A shield is for protection. If we are stepping out in obedience to God, he will protect us – even if we do encounter opposition or get it wrong.

Many are saying of me, 'God will not deliver him' But you are a shield around me, O LORD; you bestow glory on me and lift up my head.

(Psalm 3:2–3)

Surely he will save you from the fowler's snare and from the deadly pestilence. He will cover you with his feathers, and under his wings you will find refuge; his

faithfulness will be your shield and rampart.
(Psalm 91:3–4)
See also 2 Samuel 22:3; Psalm 7:10; 84:11;
Proverbs 2:7

'Abram believed' (v 6)

'Believing' is simply taking God at his word. Abraham was not asked to comprehend some profound theological truth, simply to believe God's specific promise about having many descendants. The Roman centurion took Jesus at his word:

'But just say the word, and my servant will be healed.'
(Matthew 8:8)
See also Exodus 4:29-31; Jonah 3:5; John 20:8;
Acts 4:4; Ephesians 1:13

For Abraham, the excitement of just having defeated King Kedorlaomer (Genesis 14:17) was past. He was now back to everyday life, and nothing of what God had promised seemed to be on the horizon. Little wonder he was beginning to have questions (vv 2–3). But it is at such times that God speaks exactly to our needs (vv 1 and 4–5). 'God does not content Himself with vague assurances. He gives us solid ground for comfort in some fresh revelation of Himself' (F. B. Meyer).

Specific faith

Note what it was that God asked Abraham to believe. It wasn't anything 'mystical', but rather something very tangible and specific. He took him outside to look at the stars in the clear night sky (v 5). All of us know what that is like: the more you look, what happens? Yes! The more you see! And as he saw more and more, God whispered to him, 'That's how many descendants you're going to have Abram!' And Abram simply said, 'I believe it Lord!' – despite circumstances that seemed completely hopeless from a human point of view (Genesis 15:2; 18:11–12; Romans 4:19). Faith keeps its focus on God, not on the circumstances.

By faith Abraham, even though he was past age – and Sarah herself was barren – was enabled to become a father because he considered him faithful who had made the promise. And so from this one man, and he as good as dead, came descendants as numerous as the stars in the sky and as countless as the sand on the seashore.
(Hebrews 11:11–12)

Against all hope, Abraham in hope believed and so became the father of many nations, just as it had been said to him, 'So shall your offspring be.' Without weakening in his faith, he faced the fact that his body was as good as dead – since he was about a hundred years old – and that Sarah's womb was also dead. Yet he did not waver through unbelief regarding the promise of God, but was strengthened in his faith and gave glory to God, being fully persuaded that God had power to do what he had promised.
(Romans 4:18–21)

Signs of encouragement

God gave Abram sure grounds for his faith as he made a covenant (see Chapter 3 of this part) with him (vvs 9–21 and 17:1–27). God loves to encourage us with tangible 'signs' that he is with us on the journey of faith and as a pledge that his promise will come to pass – though such signs should not become a substitute for our faith!
See also Exodus 3:11–12; Judges 6:17–22, 31–40; Isaiah 7:10–14; John 2:11; Acts 14:3

For Christians, the greatest 'sign' of all that he is with us is the presence of the Holy Spirit within us:

[God] put his mark on us to show that we are his, and he put his Spirit in our hearts to be a guarantee for all he has promised.
(2 Corinthians 1:22, NCV)
See also 2 Corinthians 5:5; Ephesians 1:13–14

Genesis 22:1–19

It's very easy to say we believe in God; but sometimes God puts that faith to the test! Yes, God (v 1)! This wasn't the only test of Abraham's faith, but it was certainly the most stretching. Yet because Abraham had known and trusted God for many years, he was now ready for such a test. God's tests are always appropriate to the point where we are at in our faith; he never stretches us beyond what he knows we can carry.

Abraham knew that sacrificing Isaac would mean giving up all hope of seeing God's promises fulfilled: there would be no great nation, no promised land, and no coming Saviour. Yet because God had made these promises to Abraham – and had stressed that they would come to pass through Isaac, and no one else (Genesis 17:17–22) – Abraham just knew that God would do it somehow, whatever it took – even if it meant raising him from the dead (see Hebrews 11:17–19)!

Abraham's faith was seen, not in mere words, but in action. Faith is not faith until we step out!

Do you want evidence that faith without deeds is useless? Was not our ancestor Abraham considered righteous for what he did when he offered his son Isaac on the altar? You see that his faith and his actions were working together, and his faith was made complete by what he did. And the scripture was fulfilled that says, 'Abraham believed God, and it was credited to him as righteousness,' and he was called God's friend.

(James 2:20–23)

His faith was met by God's wonderful provision (vv 9–14) – a provision that foreshadows the sacrifice of the Son of God himself (see John 3:16; 1 John 4:9–10).

Romans 4:18–24

Abraham – referred to 68 times in the New Testament – was clearly seen as a man from whom we can learn. Romans 4, which is full of references to him, notes the following things about his trusting of God:

'against all hope' (v 18). Faith does not let itself be shaped by the circumstances; it looks circumstances squarely in the face and says, 'You can change!'

'without weakening in his faith' (v 19). Faith recognizes that things don't always happen overnight. Sometimes we have to keep hold of the promise and just keep going. Simply 'keeping going' is at times faith!

'he faced the fact' (v 19). Faith is not about 'burying our heads in the sand'. We face up to the reality of the situation, but simply see God as bigger than that.

'he did not waver through unbelief' (v 20). Faith doesn't keep doubting what God has said; it keeps hold of it and keeps coming back to it.

'was strengthened in his faith' (v 20). Faith needs strengthening along the way – through things like prayer, the Word of God, and the encouragement of God's people.

'gave glory to God' (v 20). Faith doesn't take credit for the person exercising it; it points constantly to God, to his promise and to what he is doing.

'being fully persuaded that God had power to do what he had promised' (v 21). Faith works best where it knows God best! The more we know him, the more confident we can be.

61

The testing of our faith

Abraham stood up to the test of faith. But how do we react when God tests our faith, and when trusting him seems to be the last thing on earth that we want to do?

When testing comes to us, it is important to remember certain things:

God tests us, not because he doesn't love us, but because he does love us.

He wants us to grow – and to grow up. A young sapling grows into a sturdy mature tree by putting down roots, by growing in the face of the wind, rain and the weather. God wants his people to grow in this way too.

'I am the true vine, and my Father is the gardener. He cuts off every branch in me that bears no fruit, while every branch that does bear fruit he prunes so that it will be even more fruitful.'

(John 15:1-2)

See also Job 1:4–12; 42:5; John 15:1–8; 1 Peter 1:6–7

Friendship with God is a key

Abraham, amazingly, was called God's friend!

And the scripture was fulfilled that says, 'Abraham believed God, and it was credited to him as righteousness,' and he was called God's friend.

(James 2:23)

See also 2 Chronicles 20:7; Isaiah 41:8

As a friend, he had got to know God; there was a closeness between them. And as God's promises had become part of his life over the years, and as God himself had become precious to him, so Abraham had learnt to trust the God of the promise. That's why he didn't give up even when everything seemed impossible. Developing friendship with God is a key to experiencing his promises and to keeping going when things don't seem to be working out.

Faith, on its own, is meaningless

Abraham didn't just say he trusted God; he did something about it. He obeyed; he acted on his professed faith.

By faith Abraham, when called to go to a place he would later receive as his inheritance, obeyed and went, even though he did not know where he was going.

(Hebrews 11:8)

See also Genesis 12:4;17:23; 22:1–18; Hebrews 11:17–19

It's all too easy to say, 'Yes, I believe; yes, I have faith,' but then not to act on that faith in everyday life – in the lifestyle we live, the decisions we make, and the promises of God we claim. The way we handle these things are all evidence of our faith and trust in God – or not, as the case may be!

Faith by itself, if it is not accompanied by action, is dead.

(James 2:17)

See also Galatians 5:6; 1 Thessalonians 1:3; James 2:18–26; 2 Peter 1:5–7

Relevance for today

The more we get to know God, the more we can trust his promises

Remember: God really does want us to know him!

'No longer will a man teach his neighbour, or a man his brother, saying, "Know the LORD," because they will all know me, from the least of them to the greatest,' declares the LORD.

(Jeremiah 31:34)

'You are my witnesses,' declares the LORD, 'and my servant whom I have chosen, so that you may know and believe me and understand that I am he. Before me no god was formed, nor will there be one after me. I, even I, am the LORD, and apart from me there is no saviour.'

(Isaiah 43:10–11)

The more we get to know this God of the promises, the more we then grow in our ability to trust the promises of God and to claim them for ourselves.

I have sought your face with all my heart; be gracious to me according to your promise.

(Psalm 119:58)

Those who know your name will trust in you, for you, LORD, have never forsaken those who seek you.

(Psalm 9:10)

See also Genesis 22:7–8; 2 Samuel 7:18–29; Psalm 71:5–6

As we look at God's track record, we can be strengthened in our faith

God wants us to be strengthened in our faith as we take encouragement from the Scriptures and the testimony of others. Hearing of what God has done encourages us to trust him for ourselves.

For everything that was written in the past was written to teach us, so that through endurance and the encouragement of the Scriptures we might have hope.

(Romans 15:4)

Therefore, since we are surrounded by such a great cloud of witnesses, let us throw off everything that hinders and the sin that so easily entangles, and let us run with perseverance the race marked out for us. Let us fix our eyes on Jesus, the author and perfecter of our faith, who for the joy set before him endured the cross, scorning its shame, and sat down at the right hand of the throne of God. Consider him who endured such opposition from sinful men, so that you will not grow weary and lose heart.

(Hebrews 12:1–3)

See also Romans 1:11–12; Colossians 2:1–3; 1 Thessalonians 3:6–8

God invites us to 'go for it' and to see for ourselves whether he and his promises are good

Taste and see that the LORD is good; blessed is the man who takes refuge in him.

(Psalm 34:8)

Your promises have been thoroughly tested, and your servant loves them.

(Psalm 119:140)

'Bring the whole tithe into the storehouse, that there may be food in my house. Test me in this,' says the LORD Almighty, 'and see if I will not throw open the floodgates of heaven and pour out so much blessing that you will not have room enough for it.'

(Malachi 3:10)

In times of testing, we need to surround ourselves with encouragement to help 'keep us going'

God's Word and God's people are two key provisions to help us in this, which is why the devil tries to keep us away from both.

Let us hold unswervingly to the hope we profess, for he who promised is faithful. And let us consider how we may spur one another on towards love and good deeds. Let us not give up meeting together, as some are in the habit of doing, but let us encourage one another – and all the more as you see the Day approaching.

(Hebrews 10:23–25)

'I will strengthen them in the LORD and in his name they will walk,' declares the LORD.

(Zechariah 10:12)

See also Isaiah 35:3–4; Psalm 119:28; Luke 22:32; 1 Thessalonians 3:1–3

God's promises all find their 'Yes!' in Jesus

For no matter how many promises God has made, they are 'Yes' in Christ.

(2 Corinthians 1:20)

Conclusion

Trusting God is hard at times. Yet, because it is all part of knowing God, we come to see that it is the only way to grow in our faith and relationship with him.

They cried to you and were saved; in you they trusted and were not disappointed.

(Psalm 22:5)

It is as we come to know God personally through faith in Jesus Christ that we can really begin to claim the promises of God in earnest. And so it is to Jesus that we turn in the next part of this book.

Put thou thy trust in God,
In duty's path go on;
Walk in His strength with faith and hope,
So shall thy work be done.

Give to the winds thy fears;
Hope, and be undismayed:
God hears thy sighs and counts thy tears;
God shall lift up thy head.

Commit thy ways to Him,
Thy works into His hands,
And rest on His unchanging word,
Who heaven and earth commands.

Though countless years go by,
His covenant shall endure;
Though clouds and darkness hide His path,
The promised grace is sure.

Through waves and clouds and storms
His power will clear thy way:
Wait thou His time; the darkest night
Shall end in brightest day.

Leave to His sovereign sway
To choose and to command;
So shalt thou, wondering, own His way,
How wise, how strong, His hand.

Let us in life, in death,
His steadfast truth declare,
And publish with our latest breath
His love and guardian care.

Paul Gerhardt, 1607–76
translated by John Wesley, 1703–91

PART TWO

Trusting Jesus

CHAPTER ONE

The Promised Saviour

After God's first promise of Christ (Genesis 3:15), he is never lost sight of in the Old Testament as the promised one. Someone is coming!

For no matter how many promises God has made, they are 'Yes' in Christ. (2 Corinthians 1:20)

'I promise I'll come!' We wonder if you have ever said those words, but then found later that you couldn't keep the promise. Something happened – an unforeseen visitor, a crisis at work or in the family, the car broke down, time just flew by – and you felt dreadful as you realized you just wouldn't be able to make it after all. God is never like that. What he means, he says; what he says, he does. Nothing can ever 'crop up' that takes him by surprise or 'upsets his plans'.

Right at the beginning, after the fall of Adam and Eve, God promised that someone would come; someone who could deal with humanity's most basic problem – sin. That someone would be no less a person than his Son. It took many years of preparation before the time was right; but throughout the Old Testament period, God kept reinforcing his promise again and again: 'He's coming! He's coming!' In fact, there are so many promises in the Old Testament about the coming of Jesus that it is hard to see how anyone could not possibly believe in him! It's those promises that we summarize in this chapter.

Promise and fulfilment

There are over 300 prophecies in the Old Testament that we see fulfilled in the New Testament in the Lord Jesus Christ, covering many different aspects of who he is and what he came to do. At first, Jesus' disciples did not understand this (nor would we have done!); but gradually, 'the penny began to drop'. It started soon after the resurrection, the event that put everything in a new perspective for them. For example, look at what happened as he met with two of his followers as they walked along the road to Emmaus:

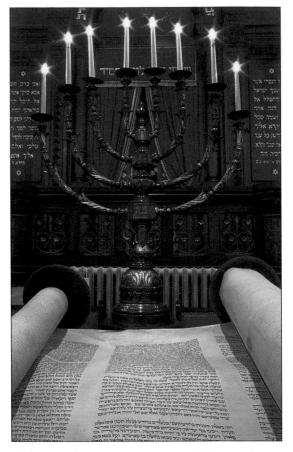

He [Jesus] said to them, 'How foolish you are, and how slow of heart to believe all that the prophets have spoken! Did not the Christ have to suffer these things and then enter his glory?' And beginning with Moses and all the Prophets, he explained to them what was said in all the Scriptures concerning himself . . . When he was at the table with them, he took bread, gave thanks, broke it and began to give it to them. Then their eyes were opened and they recognised him, and he disappeared from their sight. They asked each other, 'Were not our hearts burning within us while he talked with us on the road and opened the Scriptures to us?'

(Luke 24:25–27, 30–31)

See also Luke 24:36–47; Acts 1:1-3

Our hearts can still 'burn within us' as we read the Old Testament, asking Jesus to interpret it to us through his Holy Spirit and to show us how it all relates to him.

In this chapter we are going to take a rather different approach to the one adopted so far in this book. For the most part, we simply list here some of the key Old Testament prophecies, backed up each time by verses from the New Testament. This is so that you can use this chapter as a resource for your own further reading and investigations.

Christ's person and birth

The New Testament makes very clear that Jesus was not just another man like other men; or a specially enlightened prophet or guru; rather, he was the very Son of God, who had been with the Father from the beginning.

In the beginning was the Word, and the Word was with God, and the Word was God. He was with God in the beginning . . . The Word became flesh and made his dwelling among us. We have seen his glory, the glory of the One and Only, who came from the Father, full of grace and truth.

(John 1:1–2, 14)

See also 1 John 1:1–2

While this was not easy for Jesus' disciples to grasp, they saw many prophecies of it as they searched the Scriptures.

Jesus as God

For in Christ all the fulness of the Deity lives in bodily form.

(Colossians 2:9)

The Son is the radiance of God's glory and the exact representation of his being, sustaining all things by his powerful word.

(Hebrews 1:3)

. . . Christ, who is God over all.

(Romans 9:5)

The conviction of the early church was that when you were looking at Jesus you were looking at no one less than God himself! As they searched the Scriptures, they found many promises that backed this up.

- He is the eternal Son of God (Psalm 2:7; Proverbs 8:22–31; Matthew 16:16; 26:63–64; Colossians 1:13–19; Hebrews 5:6)
- He is the Lord (Psalm 110:1; Matthew 22:41–45; Luke 2:11)
- He is Immanuel (which means, 'God with us') (Isaiah 7:14; Matthew 1:22–23)
- He is an eternal priest, like (yet far superior to) the priest-king Melchizedek (Psalm 110:4; Hebrews 5:6; 7:1–22)
- He is God himself (Isaiah 9:6-7; John 1:1; Romans 9:5; 1 John 5:20)

Jesus as a man

This Jesus had not come among them as some sort of 'ghost' or 'spirit', pretending to be a man; he truly had become a human being in every sense of the word.

*That which was from the beginning, which we have **heard**, which we have **seen** with our eyes, which we have **looked at** and our hands have **touched** – this we proclaim concerning the Word of life. The life appeared; we have seen it and testify to it, and we proclaim to you the eternal life, which was with the Father and has appeared to us.*

(1 John 1:1–2, our emphasis)

The New Testament shows Jesus doing all the things that characterize human beings: getting tired (John 4:6), being thirsty (John 4:7), getting hungry (Matthew 4:2), sleeping (Luke 8:23), experiencing emotions (John 2:13–17), enjoying children (Mark 10:13–16), relaxing with people over a meal (Matthew 9:10), grieving (John 11:35), suffering, both emotionally (Luke 22:44) and physically (Luke 22:63), dying (John 19:30, 33–34).

Once again, as they searched their Scriptures they found many prophecies and promises that this, strange though it seemed, was exactly what God had been planning.

- He is the Son of Man (Daniel 7:13–14; Matthew 8:20; Mark 14:62; John 5:27; Revelation 1:13)
- He would be a descendant of Abraham (Genesis 22:18; Matthew 1:1; Luke 3:33; Galatians 3:16)
- He would be a descendant of David (2 Samuel 7:12–13; Matthew 1:1; Luke 1:32; 2:4; 3:31; Romans 1:3)
- He would be born of a woman (Genesis 3:15; Matthew 1:18; Galatians 4:4)
- He would be born in Bethlehem (Micah 5:2; Matthew 2:1–6; Luke 2:4–6; John 7:42)
- Children would be killed at the time of his birth (Jeremiah 31:15; Matthew 2:16–18)
- He would be called out of Egypt (Hosea 11:1; Matthew 2:13–15)

How could these two aspects come together?

Clearly it is no ordinary event of life for God to become a man! So how could this happen? Again, as they searched the Scriptures, two key

facts began to explain it:
- He would be born of a *virgin* (Isaiah 7:14; Matthew 1:18–22; Luke 1:34–35)
- He would be anointed with *the Holy Spirit* (Isaiah 11:2; 42:1; Matthew 3:16; Luke 4:14–19; Acts 10:38)

His being born of a virgin stressed that this was no mere normal conception; Jesus had laid aside his divine glory (Philippians 2:6–7) and taken upon himself a brand new, unspoilt human nature created by the Holy Spirit for him within Mary's womb. This 'incarnation' is indeed nothing less than a miracle. But then, who wants a God who cannot do miracles?

Christ's character, life and work

As God, Christ could properly have claimed many rights and dignities; but he did not! The whole 'atmosphere' of his life and work was that of servanthood.

I am among you as one who serves.
(Luke 22:27)

Who, being in very nature God, did not consider equality with God something to be grasped, but made himself nothing, taking the nature of a servant
(Philippians 2:6–7)
See also Matthew 20:25–28; John 13:1–17; Acts 4:27–30

A servant God! This could have seemed beyond belief were it not for the fact that, once again, it was prophesied in the Scriptures.

His character
- His servanthood (Isaiah 42:1–4; 49:5–6; Matthew 12:15–21)
- His sinlessness (Isaiah 53:9; John 8:46; 2 Corinthians 5:21; 1 Peter 2:22)
- His meekness (Isaiah 42:1–4; Matthew 12:15–21; 2 Corinthians 10:1)
- His unflagging zeal (Psalm 69:9; John 2:17)
- His commitment to do the will of God (Psalm 40:6–8; Hebrews 10:5–7)
- His suffering of insults (Psalm 69:7, 9; Romans 15:3)

His life and work

- His forerunner who would prepare the way for him (Isaiah 40:3; Malachi 3:1; Matthew 3:1–3)
- His ministry in Galilee (Isaiah 9:1–2; Matthew 4:12–17, 23)
- His ministry amongst the poor and needy (Isaiah 61:1–2; Luke 4:16–21)
- His teaching in parables (Psalm 78:2; Matthew 13:34–35)
- His prophetic ministry (Deuteronomy 18:15; Matthew 21:11; Acts 3:22–23)
- His great miracles (Isaiah 35:5–6; Matthew 11:2–6)
- His rejection by his brothers (Psalm 69:8; John 1:11; 7:3–5)
- His offence to Israel (Isaiah 8:14; Luke 2:34; Romans 9:32–33; 1 Peter 2:6–8)
- His entrance into Jerusalem (Zechariah 9:9; Matthew 21:1–11)
- His rejection by the Jewish rulers (Psalm 118:22–23; Matthew 21:42)

His suffering and death

Jesus made many promises to his disciples during the three years they spent together; the promises that they found hardest to grasp were those concerning his death and resurrection.

From that time on Jesus began to explain to his disciples that he must go to Jerusalem and suffer many things at the hands of the elders, chief priests and teachers of the law, and that he must be killed and on the third day be raised to life. Peter took him aside and began to rebuke him. 'Never, Lord!' he said. 'This shall never happen to you!' Jesus turned and said to Peter, 'Get behind me, Satan! You are a stumbling-block to me; you do not have in mind the things of God, but the things of men .'

(Matthew 16:21-23)

See also Matthew 17:22–23; Luke 18:31–32

Once again, an amazing amount of detail about his suffering and death is to be found in the Old Testament:

- His betrayal by a friend (Psalm 41:9; Matthew 26:20–25, 47–50; John 13:18)
- The falling away of his disciples (Zechariah 13:7; Matthew 26:31, 56)
- His being sold for thirty pieces of silver (Zechariah 11:12; Matthew 26:14–15)
- The purchase of a potter's field (Zechariah 11:13; Matthew 27:3–10)
- His suffering (Genesis 3:15; Psalm 22:1–24; Matthew 16:21; Luke 24:25–27; Acts 3:18; 17:2–3)
- His suffering in the place of others (Isaiah 53:4–5; Mark 10:45; 1 Peter 2:24)
- His silence before his accusers (Isaiah 53:7: Matthew 26:62–63; 27:12–14)
- His disfigured face (Isaiah 52:14; Mark 15:17)
- The beating of him and spitting upon him (Isaiah 50:6; Matthew 26:67–68)
- The nailing of him to the cross (Psalm 22:16; John 19:18; 20:25)
- The mocking of him by those around (Psalm 22:6–8; Matthew 27:39–44)
- The abandoning of him by God (Psalm 22:1; Matthew 27:46)
- The offering of wine vinegar to him (Psalm 69:21; Matthew 27:48; John 19:28–29)
- The dividing of his clothes (Psalm 22:18; Matthew 27:35; John 19:24)
- His prayer for those who crucified him (end of Isaiah 53:12; Luke 23:34)
- His death (Isaiah 53:12; Matthew 27:50; John 19:30)
- His bones were not broken (Numbers 9:12; Psalm 34:20; John 19:32–36)
- The piercing of his side (Zechariah 12:10; John 19:34–37)
- His burial (Isaiah 53:9; Matthew 27:57–60)

Either all of this minute detail is the most amazing coincidence (on a level with the proverbial chimpanzee banging on the keys of a computer and happening to type out the Oxford English Dictionary); or Jesus was indeed the promised Saviour.

Christ's resurrection, ascension, and reign

On the third day he will rise again.

(Luke 18:33)

Not only did Jesus prophesy his death, with increasing detail and clarity as the cross drew closer (see e.g. Matthew 12:39–40; 16:21; 17:22–23), he also prophesied his resurrection and what would follow it. This too, the early church would later see, could all be found in the Old Testament.

As his custom was, Paul went into the synagogue, and on three Sabbath days he reasoned with them from the Scriptures, explaining and proving that the Christ had to suffer and rise from the dead. 'This Jesus I am proclaiming to you is the Christ,' he said.

(Acts 17:2–3)

Just look at some of the things they found about Jesus in the Scriptures:
- His resurrection (Psalm 16:8–11; Matthew 28:1–7; Luke 24:6–8; Acts 2:24–28; 1 Corinthians 15:3–5)
- His ascension (Psalm 68:18; Luke 24:51; Acts 1:9; Ephesians 4:8–10)
- His reign in heaven (Psalm 110:1; Acts 2:33–36; Romans 8:34; 1 Peter 3:22)
- His bringing of salvation to all nations (Isaiah 11:10; 42:6; Luke 2:30-32; Acts 10:45; Romans 15:8–12; Revelation 5:9; 7:10)
- His just rule (Psalm 45:6–7; Hebrews 1:8–9; Revelation 19:11–15)
- His everlasting kingdom (Isaiah 9:7; Daniel 7:14; Luke 1:32–33; Revelation 11:15)
- His disciples' appointment of a successor to Judas (Psalm 109:8; Acts 1:15–26)
- His coming again on the clouds (Daniel 7:13; Acts 1:11; Matthew 24:29–31; 1 Thessalonians 4:16–17) (See also Part 6, Chapter 2.)

He [Jesus] said to them, 'This is what I told you while I was still with you: Everything must be fulfilled that is written about me in the Law of Moses, the Prophets and the Psalms.' Then he opened their minds so they could understand the Scriptures.

(Luke 24:44–45)

Relevance for today

God keeps his promises

God always keeps his promises, even though at times there may be a long wait between the promise (Genesis 3:15) and its fulfilment (Luke 1:30–33).

But when the time had fully come, God sent his Son, born of a woman, born under law, to redeem those under law, that we might receive the full rights of sons.

(Galatians 4:4)

The Lord is not slow in keeping his promise, as some understand slowness. He is patient with you

(2 Peter 3:9)

The focus of prophecies

The focus and fulfilment of all Old Testament prophecies is Jesus. The Old Testament comes alive when we put our 'Jesus spectacles' on, looking at everything there through him.

For I tell you that Christ has become a servant of the Jews on behalf of God's truth, to confirm the promises made to the patriarchs so that the Gentiles may glorify God for his mercy.

(Romans 15:89)

For no matter how many promises God has made, they are 'Yes' in Christ.

(2 Corinthians 1:20)

A witness to Jesus

The Old Testament believers who looked ahead to Jesus stand as witnesses to us to urge us to keep moving on with the Jesus they were looking for and longing for.

Therefore, since we are surrounded by such a great cloud of witnesses, let us throw off everything that hinders and the sin that so easily entangles, and let us run with perseverance the race marked out for us. Let us fix our eyes on Jesus, the author and perfecter of our faith .

(Hebrews 12:1–2)

With so many prophecies about Christ in the Old Testament – often in such amazing detail – it is hard to see how people can fail to believe in him! Perhaps it is because all of this requires not only intellectual assent, but also a change of heart for us to grasp and make these promises our own. It is this change of heart, and how it can come about that we look at in the following chapters.

Father of mercies, in Thy Word
What endless glory shines!
For ever be Thy Name adored
For these celestial lines.

Here may the blind and hungry come,
And light and food receive;
Here shall the lowliest guest have room,
And taste and see and live.

Here springs of consolation rise
To cheer the fainting mind,
And thirsting souls receive supplies,
And sweet refreshment find.

Here the Redeemer's welcome voice
Spreads heavenly peace around;
And life and everlasting joys
Attend the blissful sound.

O may these heavenly pages be
My ever dear delight;
And still new beauties may I see,
And still increasing light!

Divine Instructor, gracious Lord,
Be Thou for ever near;
Teach me to love Thy sacred Word,
And view my Saviour there.

Anne Steele, 1717–78

Conclusion

You cannot think about these prophecies for long without realizing how the Lord Jesus Christ permeates the whole Bible. Everything points to him. Truly, he has kept his promise!

Philip found Nathanael and told him, 'We have found the one Moses wrote about in the Law, and about whom the prophets also wrote – Jesus of Nazareth, the son of Joseph.'

(John 1:45)

Making the Promise Our Own

> If we want to know God personally, then the only way we will find him is through Jesus Christ, his Son.
>
> *Only Jesus has the power to save! His name is the only one in all the world that can save anyone.* (Acts 4:12, CEV)

Mike's teaching ministry often takes him to the Third World. Wherever he goes, he can be sure of being pestered by traders to buy bargains he does not need or by guides to visit sights he does not want to see. The thing about guides, especially in India, is that they often have no idea of where they are taking you, or of how to direct you somewhere. But since it is deemed rude not to know or not to tell, they will guide you anyway! The philosophy seems to be: going somewhere is better than going nowhere!

Going somewhere is better than going nowhere. That sums up much religion today. And since, we are told, 'all roads lead to God in the end', why worry anyway? 'None is wrong, and none is right; they are just different.'

But the Christian faith disagrees, for Jesus disagreed. In fact, he said the *only* way to God was through him. But how do we know he was right? Well, Christianity is unique among world religions, for it alone has God coming to look for people, rather than the other way round. Jesus was no mere teacher, prophet, guru, or guide; as we saw in the previous chapter, he actually *is* God himself, God come to us *in person*. And that is why he, and he alone, is the only guide worth trusting, the only One who knows the true way to God and who can help us make the promise our own.

'I am the way and the truth and the life. No-one comes to the Father except through me.'

(John 14:6)

Seeing our need

The first step to finding our way to somewhere is to find out where we are now; or, to put it a different way, the first step to solving a problem is to see the need. The same is true with our lives. The Bible pictures our need, or 'where we are now', in many different ways. Here are some of those ways it describes us, and some of God's promises to those who acknowledge that this is what they are like.

Empty

Being hungry and thirsty for reality is often our experience.

Come, all you who are thirsty, come to the waters; and you who have no money, come, buy and eat! Come buy wine and milk without money and without cost. Why spend money on what is not bread, and your labour on what does not satisfy? Listen, listen to me, and eat what is good, and your soul will delight in the richest of fare.

(Isaiah 55:1–2)

See also John 4:13–14; 6:35; 7:37–38

Weary

Life with its pressures and problems often tires us.

'Come to me, all you who are weary and burdened, and I will give you rest. Take my yoke upon you and learn from me, for I am gentle and humble in heart, and you will find rest for your souls. For my yoke is easy and my burden is light.'

(Matthew 11:28–29)

See also Psalm 31:9–10; Isaiah 40:29–31

Blind

We often cannot see where we are going in life.

The god of this age has blinded the minds of unbelievers, so that they cannot see the light of the gospel of the glory of Christ, who is the image of God. For we do not preach ourselves, but Jesus Christ as Lord . . . For God, who said, 'Let light shine out of darkness,' made his light shine in our hearts to give us the light of the knowledge of the glory of God in the face of Christ.

(2 Corinthians 4:4–6)

See also Matthew 4:16: John 8:12; 9:39–40

Lost

We are often helpless to know which way to go.

My sheep wandered over all the mountains and on every high hill. They were scattered over the whole earth, and no-one searched or looked for them . . . I [the Sovereign Lord] will search for the lost and bring back the strays.

(Ezekiel 34:6, 16)

See also Numbers 17:12; Psalm 119:176; Jeremiah 50:6; Matthew 10:6; Luke 19:10

Poor

We are spiritually bankrupt, without resources for life.

The poor and needy search for water, but there is none; their tongues are parched with thirst. But I the Lord will answer them; I, the God of Israel, will not forsake them.

(Isaiah 41:17)

See also Psalm 109:22; Luke 4:18; 2 Corinthians 8:9; Revelation 3:17

Purposeless

Life is without meaning without God.

Show me, O Lord, my life's end and the number of my days; let me know how fleeting is my life. You have made my days a mere handbreadth; the span of my years is as nothing before you. Each man's life is but a breath. Man is a mere phantom as he goes to and fro: He bustles about, but only in vain; he heaps up wealth, not knowing who will get it. But now, Lord, what do I look for? My hope is in you.

(Psalm 39:4–7)

See also Ecclesiastes 1:2; 3:19; 12:8

Ignorant

We cannot understand God and his ways without his help.

He [God] has made everything beautiful in its time. He has also set eternity in the hearts of men; yet they cannot fathom what God has done from beginning to end . . . I know that everything God does will endure for ever; nothing can be added to it and nothing taken from it. God does it so that men will revere him.

(Ecclesiastes 3:11, 14)

See also Job 38:2; Ecclesiastes 8:7–8; Matthew 16:2–3

Oppressed

We can easily be downtrodden by circumstances, other people, or even our own sin.

'I have indeed seen the misery of my people in Egypt. I have heard them crying out because of their slave drivers, and I am concerned about their suffering. So I have come down to rescue them . . .'

(Exodus 3:7)

See also Deuteronomy 28:47–48; Psalm 119:134; Zechariah 10:2; Luke 4:18–19

Not a pretty picture of the human race, is it? But all of these needs are not the key issue. They are but symptoms of an underlying disease. They are signs of an illness, not the illness itself. The Bible calls this illness sin. And, like any diagnosis of a serious illness, the identifying of this most basic human condition is not popular; for being called 'sinners' hits right at our pride. Yet it is only when we recognize and acknowledge that our fundamental problem is sin that we can begin to see a way out.

So, what does the Bible mean by 'sin'?

What 'sin' is

In today's world 'sin' is a rather quaint idea. These days 'anything goes', as long as it 'doesn't harm anyone else'. So we may talk about mistakes, or momentary lapses, or errors of judgment, or little character weaknesses – but never 'sin'. The trouble is, all these words 'let us off the hook'. So, the husband doesn't need to say 'sorry', the politician doesn't need to resign, the wrongdoer doesn't need to own up. At best, it was always someone else's fault; at worst, it was just one of our little weaknesses.

All of this, however, underplays what the Bible means by sin. Sin isn't a lapse in my morals, behaviour or deeds; sin is an offence against God (Psalm 51:3–4). This comes out in the very words the Bible uses for 'sin', all of which concern God.

We do not always see the fuller meaning of the word 'sin' in our English translations; but here are some of the meanings behind the Hebrew and Greek words that are used. In each case, the word translated 'sin' carries the meaning given:

* ***missing the mark or target*** (e.g. Lamentations 5:7; John 8:46; 1 John 1:8) The

target that we are meant to aim at (as, in a natural way, in Judges 20:16) is God's glory, and every one of us has fallen short of this (Romans 3:23).

• *stepping over a boundary* (e.g. 1 Samuel 15:24; Ezekiel 14:11; 18:26) God's standard is laid down and, rebelling against authority as we do, we think we know better and so 'cross the line'.

• *twisting of a standard* (e.g. Daniel 9:5) We are 'un-right' creatures, distorted and misshapen by sin. Consequently, everything we do has a 'twist' to it.

• *rebellion* (e.g. Isaiah 1:28) This is the defiance of God's rule over our lives; our saying 'No!' (rather like a child in a wilful mood) to God.

In all of these pictures it is God who is at the centre: it is God's target that is not hit, God's law that is transgressed, God's purpose that is twisted, God's will that is defied. Sin is going against God, turning our back on him, rebelling against him. It is living for ourselves, not for the One who made us. It is living independently from him, doing what we want, not what he wants – and then wondering why life doesn't turn out right! And it is in this state of sin that we all naturally find ourselves.

What 'sin' does

The truth is: not all of God's promises are exciting and wonderful! For example, he makes some promises about what sin actually does to our lives – and they do not make for pleasant reading, if we are honest! But we are foolish not to listen to what God says about it. Here are some of the results of sin, considered from the all-seeing viewpoint of God.

Sin puts us out of relationship with God
The minute this happens, God seems distant and unreal in our lives.

But your iniquities have separated you from your God; your sins have hidden his face from you, so that he will not hear.

(Isaiah 59:2)

Sin makes us hardened or 'calloused'

'For this people's heart has become calloused; they hardly hear with their ears, and they have closed their eyes.'

(Matthew 13:15, quoting Isaiah 6:10)

Just as skin can become calloused – hard and insensitive – so our hearts can become calloused too. We no longer have a conscience about the thoughts we have or the things we do, and what used to trouble us does so no more. Sin has deceived us into a hardness of heart. The writer of Hebrews warns Christians that this can happen to them too if they are not careful! (See Hebrews 3:12–13.)

Sin makes us slaves to our actions and habits
We find there are things that we just cannot stop doing, even if we want to.

I do not understand what I do. For what I want to do I do not do, but what I hate I do . . . For I have the desire to do what is good, but I cannot carry it out. For what I do is not the good I want to do; no, the evil I do not want to do – this I keep on doing.

(Romans 7:15, 18–19)

See also John 8:34

Sin renders us helpless
We are unable to do anything about it! Deep inside, we might want to change; but we just can't.

When we were unable to help ourselves, at the moment of our need, Christ died for us, although we were living against God.

(Romans 5:6, NCV)

Sin brings upon us God's condemnation

We deserve God's wrath (his righteous anger) because of our sin, for it offends his holiness.

The wrath of God is being revealed from heaven against all the godlessness and wickedness of men who suppress the truth by their wickedness.

(Romans 1:18)

See also Jeremiah 42:18; Ezekiel 18:20

Sin leads to death

As human beings, we all face death. George Bernard Shaw once wrote: 'Death is the ultimate statistic; one out of one die.' But the Bible sees death, not as an inevitable end to life, but as the direct consequence of sin.

For the wages of sin is death, but the gift of God is eternal life in Christ Jesus our Lord.

(Romans 6:23)

See also Genesis 2:16–17; 3:19; Psalm 90:10

But the Bible also speaks of another death, not just one at the end of life. It says that, without Jesus, we are spiritually 'dead' right now (Ephesians 2:1–3)! Little wonder it is hard for us to find 'life'!

Sin leads to God's judgment

Just as man is destined to die once, and after that to face judgment, so Christ was sacrificed once to take away the sins of many people.

(Hebrews 9:27)

See also Psalm 1:4–5; Romans 14:10; Hebrews 10:26–27

What can be done?

We have just seen that, of ourselves, we are utterly incapable of doing anything about our hopeless state. So, what can be done? Is there a cure for sin? Yes! God himself has provided the answer in Christ! It is by means of Christ's death on the cross that our whole condition is changed:

But God demonstrates his own love for us in this: While we were still sinners, Christ died for us.

(Romans 5:8)

For Christ died for sins once for all, the righteous for the unrighteous, to bring you to God.

(1 Peter 3:18)

He himself bore our sins in his body on the tree, so that we might die to sins and live for righteousness; by his wounds you have been healed.

(1 Peter 2:24)

See also Hebrews 9:12-15, 24-28; 10:19-23

But all this happened two thousand years ago. How can it be relevant for today?

Relevance for today

No change in 2,000 years

People are still the same; we have the same inner needs as people two thousand years ago. But Jesus too is the same!

Jesus Christ is the same yesterday and today and for ever.

(Hebrews 13:8)

Because he is still the same, he can therefore still meet those needs. As the eternal Son of God, what he did two thousand years ago is eternally relevant and redeeming (Hebrews 9:12).

Without Jesus, we are all lost

In Luke 15:3–31 Jesus tells three parables, all about 'lost things' – a lost sheep (vv 3–7), a lost coin (vv 8–10) and a lost son (vv 11–31); all are pictures of our lives without him. This is serious, for our eternal destiny is certainly not a light matter. Yet the emphasis of the parables is that, with Jesus, lost things can be found!

For the Son of Man came to seek and to save what was lost.

(Luke 19:10)

God still provides the gift of repentance as a way of escape

To repent means 'to do a U-turn'; to stop going our own way and turn round and start living God's way. It means being truly sorry for our former way of life and turning from our sin to God. In the words of J.A. Motyer, 'Repentance is the door into safety.'

Seek the LORD while he may be found; call on him while he is near. Let the wicked forsake his way and the evil man his thoughts. Let him turn to the LORD, and he will have mercy on him, and to our God, for he will freely pardon.

(Isaiah 55:6–7)

When the people heard this, they were cut to the heart and said to Peter and the other apostles, 'Brothers, what shall we do?' Peter replied, 'Repent and be baptised, every one of you, in the name of Jesus Christ for the forgiveness of your sins.'

(Acts 2:37–38)

Don't you know that the reason God is good to you is because he wants you to turn to him?

(Romans 2:4, CEV)

See also Matthew 4:17; Acts 3:19; 14:15; 17:30–31; 26:20

Make these promises your own

One way to make these promises your own is as simple as A-B-C.

- *Accept* what God says about you – that you are a sinner (Romans 3:9–20, 23). Stop explaining things away or blaming others and 'come clean' before the holy God. Accept you can't do a thing to save yourself (Philippians 3:7–9; Titus 3:4–5). The Holy Spirit will help you to do this (John 16:7–9)!
- *Believe* that Jesus died on the cross for you and that, three days later, God raised him to life to prove his sacrifice for sins had been accepted (John 3:16-18; Romans 10:9–10; 1 Corinthians 15:3–4; Acts 2:22–39; 16:30–31).
- *Commit* your life to him (John 1:12). Let him take complete control of every aspect; make him 'Lord' of everything! (Ephesians 5:8–10; Colossians 1:10–12; 2:6)

And here is the promise of God's Word for those who do this:

If you confess with your mouth, 'Jesus is Lord,' and believe in your heart that God raised him from the dead, you will be saved. For it is with your heart that you believe and are justified, and it is with your mouth that you confess and are saved. As the Scripture says, 'Anyone who trusts in him will nerver be put to shame.'

(Romans 10:9–10)

Just as I am, without one plea,
But that Thy blood was shed for me,
And that Thou bidd'st me come to Thee,
O Lamb of God, I come.

Just as I am, and waiting not
To rid my soul of one dark blot,
To Thee, whose blood can cleanse each spot,
O Lamb of God, I come.

Just as I am, though tossed about
With many a conflict, many a doubt,
Fightings and fears within, without,
O Lamb of God, I come.

Just as I am, poor, wretched, blind;
Sight, riches, healing of the mind,
Yea, all I need, in Thee to find,
O Lamb of God, I come.

Just as I am, Thou wilt receive,
Wilt welcome, pardon, cleanse, relieve;
Because Thy promise I believe,
O Lamb of God, I come.

Just as I am – Thy love unknown
Has broken every barrier down;
-Now to be Thine, yea, Thine alone,
O Lamb of God, I come.

Just as I am, of that free love
The breadth, length, depth, and height to
prove,
Here for a season, then above,
O Lamb of God, I come.

Charlotte Elliott, 1789–1871

Conclusion

God wants us to make the promise our own. If we come to him, truly wanting to turn from our sins, and believing in the Lord Jesus Christ and his death on the cross for us, then he will save us.

Come to me, all you who are weary and burdened, and I will give you rest.

(Matthew 11:28)

CHAPTER THREE

The Promise of a New Beginning

> Putting our faith in Jesus is the start, not the end, of the matter!
> A whole new life has now opened up for us.
>
> *If anyone is in Christ, he is a new creation; old things have passed away; behold, all things have become new.*
> (2 Corinthians 5:17, NKJV)

There are few of us who do not find the birth of a baby a moving event. Grown adults suddenly become cooing and gurgling idiots before the presence of new life! Perhaps it is the baby's freshness, or helplessness; everything just seems so perfect.

Little wonder, then, that there are times when we say, 'If only I could start again.' 'If only my mistakes could be wiped out; if only the messes could be undone; if only I could have another chance.'

Jesus says, 'You can!' When we put our trust in him, a whole new life begins for us; the past is over and done with, and we have a fresh, new start. We truly become 'a new creation' (2 Corinthians 5:17).

The importance of 'conversion'

Being a Christian is not just a matter of believing in Jesus; it is about something actually happening to you; it is about being 'converted'.

Being changed

And he [Jesus] said, 'I tell you the truth, unless you change and become like little children, you will never enter the kingdom of heaven.'

(Matthew 18:3)

Conversion is not a change brought about by self-effort or by 'pulling ourselves up by our bootstraps', however. It is a change that happens in the heart. The Old Testament had many promises about God one day bringing such a change in people's hearts.

'I will give you a new heart and put a new spirit in you; I will remove from you your heart of stone and give you a heart of flesh. And I will put my Spirit in you and move you to follow my decrees and be careful to keep my laws.'

(Ezekiel 36:26–27)

See also Jeremiah 31:33–34; Ezekiel 11:19–20; 18:31–32

Through Jesus this change now becomes possible.

Being born again

This 'change of heart' in conversion is such a profound experience that the New Testament writers could only describe it as being 'born all over again'.

'I tell you the truth, no-one can see the kingdom of God unless he is born again.'

(John 3:3)

For you have been born again, not of perishable seed, but of imperishable, through the living and enduring word of God.

(1 Peter 1:23)

See also John 3:1–8; James 1:18; Titus 3:4–7; 1 John 4:7

Both these things – being changed and being born again – are things done to us, not by us

Neither can be achieved by ourselves, whether by self-effort or self-improvement techniques. Nicodemus (John 3:1) and Paul (Philippians 3:5) had both spent their lives trying to do this. As Pharisees, they had been committed to the punctilious and legalistic fulfilment of the Jewish law, in all its minute details and all its various interpretations by the rabbis; but they discovered that it simply didn't work; it didn't change a thing. (See Paul's own testimony about this in Philippians 3:4–9.)

Rather, this new beginning is God's work from start to finish:

'No-one can come to me [Jesus] unless the Father who sent me draws him . . . '

(John 6:44)

See also Lamentations 5:21; Ephesians 2:12–13

It is God alone who can transform us from being sinners to sons.

No longer a slave, but a son.

(Galatians 4:7)

This theme of our becoming 'sons of God' or 'children of God' is a strong one in the New Testament. It brings home the fact that when we are 'born again', we really do become part of God's family.

But when the fullness of the time had come, God sent forth His Son, born of a woman, born under the law, to redeem those who were under the law, that we might receive the adoption as sons. And because you are sons, God has sent forth the Spirit of His Son into your hearts, crying out, 'Abba, Father!' Therefore you are no longer a slave but a son, and if a son, then an heir of God through Christ.

(Galatians 4:4–7, NKJV)

See what love the Father has given us, that we should be called children of God; and that is what we are.

(1 John 3:1, NRSV)

See also John 1:12–13; Romans 8:14–17; 2 Corinthians 6:18; Galatians 3:26; Ephesians 1:5 (Note: The New Testament's stress on 'sons' does not exclude 'daughters'! In those days it was the son who received the inheritance, and the Bible is stressing that all God's children have an inheritance in Christ.)

How do we get 'converted' or 'born again'?

If it is God's doing, what is our involvement in all this? As we saw in the previous chapter, it is to repent – to be finished with our old sinful life – and to have faith – to trust in Christ and what he did on the cross. Repentance and faith always go together (Mark 1:15; Acts 3:19 and 4:4; 10:43–44 and 11:18; 17:30 and 17:34; 20:21).

The promises are for all

Who are these promises of new life in Christ for? For everyone who comes in faith! Everyone can have a new beginning.

And everyone who calls on the name of the Lord will be saved.

(Joel 2:32, quoted by Peter in Acts 2:21)

To all who received him [Jesus], to those who believed in his name, he gave the right to become children of God.

(John 1:12)

What tremendous assurance these verses give us! If we have truly come to Christ and trusted in him for salvation, then the Bible says we are saved. A promise that helped Martin greatly when he first became a Christian was this one:

'All that the Father gives me will come to me, and whoever comes to me I will never drive away.'

(John 6:37)

What a promise! Jesus will never reject anyone who comes to him!

The activity of God

If we have truly come to Christ, then certain things have been going on in our lives – some of them even before we knew it!

God chose us

Some people find this teaching of 'being chosen' ('election') difficult, but it is in the Bible and so we need to understand God's heart in it.

God's choosing of us was planned in eternity and made in time

It was certainly before we knew anything about it and underlines how very much our salvation has nothing to do with us!

But we ought always to thank God for you, brothers loved by the Lord, because from the beginning God chose you to be saved through the sanctifying work of the Spirit and through belief in the truth.

(2 Thessalonians 2:13)

. . . [God], who has saved us and called us to a holy life – not because of anything we have done but because of his own purpose and grace. This grace was given us in Christ Jesus before the beginning of time, but it has now been revealed through the appearing of our Saviour, Christ Jesus . . .

(2 Timothy 1:9–10)

See also John 15:16; Romans 8:28–30; Ephesians 1:4–5

God's choosing of us is not because we are special or good

It is a choice made entirely by his mercy, grace and love, and is not based on anything within us or on anything we have done.

The LORD did not set his affection on you and choose you because you were more numerous than other peoples, for you were the fewest of all peoples. But it was because the LORD loved you . . .

(Deuteronomy 7:7–8)

Is God unjust? Not at all! For he says to Moses, 'I will have mercy on whom I have mercy, and I will have compassion on whom I have compassion.' It does not, therefore, depend on man's desire or effort, but on God's mercy.

(Romans 9:14)

Brothers, think of what you were when you were called. Not many of you were wise by human standards; not many were influential; not many were of noble birth. But God chose the foolish things of the world to shame the wise; God chose the weak things of the world to shame the strong. He chose the lowly things of this world and the despised things – and the things that are not – to nullify the things that are, so that no-one may boast before him.

(1 Corinthians 1:26–29)

See also Deuteronomy 4:32–38; 10:14–15; Ephesians 2:8–9

God's choosing of us does undermine our own responsibility

We are not lost or saved against our will! No one is 'forced into heaven'; and no one is picked out 'not to have a chance'. Those who are not called are simply those who do not want to have anything to do with the gospel; those who are called, do.

For the message of the cross is foolishness to those who are perishing, but to us who are being saved it is the power of God.

(1 Corinthians 1:18)

God never forces anyone to believe!

See also Deuteronomy 7:7–11; Joshua 24:2–15; Matthew 22:1–14

God's choosing of us is for purpose not for pride

Sadly, God's people in the Old Testament forgot this. They became complacent in simply 'being' the people of God, rather than doing anything as a result of it, and so were often chided by God for this.

'But I am the LORD your God, who brought you out of Egypt. You shall acknowledge no God but me, no Saviour except me. I cared for you in the desert, in the land of burning heat. When I fed them, they were satisfied; when they were satisfied, they became proud; then they forgot me.'

(Hosea 13:4–6)

See also Deuteronomy 8:10–18; Isaiah 2:12–18; Ezekiel 33:28

God's purposes for us, as followers of Jesus, include his promises of our –

Becoming like Jesus

For those God foreknew he also predestined to be conformed to the likeness of his Son, that he might be the firstborn among many brothers. And those he predestined, he also called; those he called, he also justified; those he justified, he also glorified.

(Romans 8:29)

See also 1 Corinthians 15:49; 2 Corinthians 3:18; Philippians 3:20–21

Declaring God's praises

But you are a chosen people, a royal priesthood, a holy nation, a people belonging to God, that you may declare the praises of him who called you out of darkness into his wonderful light.

(1 Peter 2:9)

See also Psalm 35:28; Isaiah 43:20–21; Acts 2:11; Romans 15:9–11

87

Bearing good fruit

'You did not choose me, but I chose you and appointed you to go and bear fruit – fruit that will last. Then the Father will give you whatever you ask in my name.'

(John 15:16)

See also Psalm 1:1–3; 92:12–15; Matthew 3:8; John 15:5–8

Doing good works prepared for us

For we are God's workmanship, created in Christ Jesus to do good works, which God prepared in advance for us to do.

(Ephesians 2:10)

See also Titus 2:14; 1 Peter 2:12

God's choosing of us should give us security

God has not chosen us to then let us go! We are too precious to him for that! Listen to this promise of Jesus:

'My sheep listen to my voice; I know them, and they follow me. I give them eternal life, and they shall never perish; no-one can snatch them out of my hand. My Father, who has given them to me, is greater than all; no-one can snatch them out of my Father's hand.'

(John 10:27–29)

See also John 6:39–40; Romans 8:31–39

God's choosing us does not mean waiting for some 'mystical experience' of 'being chosen'

We are not just to sit here and 'wait for something to happen' or wait to somehow see if we are 'chosen'; we are commanded to repent and believe. If we don't, we are lost; if we do, we will be saved. This will then be the evidence that we have been called!

'Whoever believes and is baptised will be saved, but whoever does not believe will be condemned.'

(Mark 16:16)

'For God did not send his Son into the world to condemn the world, but to save the world through him. Whoever believes in him is not condemned, but whoever does not believe stands condemned already because he has not believed in the name of God's one and only Son.'

(John 3:17–18)

God 'births' us

God's calling of us is something creative. He gives us a new nature and a new will. Now we can start all over again! And with his Spirit, we find that we now want to do (and can do!) what we did not want to do before.

We are given new life

We who were once spiritually dead are brought to life (Ephesians 2:15; Colossians 2:13–15; 1 Peter 1:3, 23).

We are given a new nature

The new birth means the implanting of a new nature in us (Romans 6:4; 2 Corinthians 5:17; Titus 3:5–6).

We are given a new heart

This new heart is one that is responsive to God (Ezekiel 11:19–20; 36:26–27; 2 Timothy 2:22; Hebrews 10:19–22).

All of this – a complete 'regeneration' – is brought about by the sovereign, mysterious work of God (John 3:5–8).

Promises for the new-born

Once we have made this 'new beginning' with God, a whole number of promises follow:

Jesus is always with us

'And surely I am with you always, to the very end of the age.'

(Matthew 28:20)

See also Deuteronomy 31:6–8; Joshua 1:5; Acts 18:10; Hebrews 13:5–6

The Holy Spirit is within us

'And I [Jesus] will ask the Father, and he will give you another Counsellor to be with you for ever – the Spirit of truth. The world cannot accept him, because it neither sees him nor knows him. But you know him, for he lives with you and will be in you.'

(John 14:16–17)

See also Acts 2:38; Romans 8:15–16; 1 Corinthians 12:13

Our sins are completely forgiven

Everyone who believes in him [Jesus] receives forgiveness of sins through his name.

(Acts 10:43)

See also Romans 8:1; Ephesians 1:7–8; 1 John 1:8–9

We are put right with God ('justified')

'Therefore, my brothers, I want you to know that through Jesus the forgiveness of sins is proclaimed to you. Through him everyone who believes is justified from everything you could not be justified from by the law of Moses.'

(Acts 13:38–39)

See also Luke 18:9-14; Romans 3:22–24; 5:1, 9; 8:30; 1 Corinthians 6:9–11; Galatians 2:15–16; Titus 3:4–7

We are made friends ('reconciled') with God

Once you were alienated from God and were enemies in your minds because of your evil behaviour. But now he has reconciled you by Christ's physical body through death to present you holy in his sight, without blemish and free from accusation.

(Colossians 1:21-22)

See also Romans 5:10; 2 Corinthians 5:18–20; Ephesians 2:11-18

We have the gift of eternal life

'For God so loved the world that he gave his one and only Son, that whoever believes in him shall not perish but have eternal life.'

(John 3:16)

See also John 6:47; 17:3; Romans 6:23

We have access into the presence of God

For through him [Jesus] we both have access to the Father by one Spirit.

(Ephesians 2:18)

See also Romans 5:1–2; Ephesians 2:18; 3:12; Hebrews 10:19–22

We are now 'in Christ'

This phrase was one of Paul's favourite expressions for describing how, once we put our faith in Christ, we are completely identified with him.

Therefore, if anyone is in Christ, he is a new creation; the old has gone, the new has come!

(2 Corinthians 5:17)

See also John 15:5; 1 Corinthians 1:2, 30; Ephesians 1:3–10

We are no longer under the dominating control of sin

No-one who is born of God will continue to sin, because God's seed remains in him; he cannot go on sinning, because he has been born of God.

(1 John 3:9)

See also Romans 6:1–14; 1 John 5:18

We are secure for ever

He who began a good work in you will carry it on to completion until the day of Christ Jesus.

(Philippians 1:6)

See also John 6:37–40; 10:27–28; Romans 8:31–39

Practical steps

These great spiritual realities require practical steps from us in response to them. Let us look at the steps the apostles laid out for their first new converts (Acts 2:37–47). Here we see the new believers -

- *being baptized* (v 41) (see also Acts 8:12, 36–38; 9:18; 10:47–48; 16:15, 33; 18:8; 19:3–5).
- *joining the church* (v 41) (see also Acts 2:47; 5:14).
- *enjoying Christian fellowship* (vv 42–47), expressed in teaching, meeting together, breaking bread ('communion'), praying and practical sharing in their needs (see also Acts 2:1; 5:12; 6:1–7; 1 Corinthians 14:26).
- *experiencing the reality of God's presence* (v 43) (see also Acts 4:31; 5:1–11, 12–14; 8:4–7; 10:44–48; 11:21; 12:1–24; 14:3; 19:11–12; 20:7–12; 27:22–25; 28:1–6).
- *seeing continual growth in their numbers* (v 47) (see also Acts 2:41; 4:4; 5:14; 6:1, 7; 9:31; 11:21, 24; 14:1, 21; 16:5; 17:4, 12).

Relevance for today

New beginnings do not happen by self-effort or self-improvement (Philippians 3:4-9), but by new birth (John 3:3).

No matter what a mess we may have made of our lives so far, God can give us a new beginning (1 Corinthians 15:9–10).

We do not have to settle for just believing about Jesus or even believing in Jesus; we too can be 'born again' and come to truly know Jesus (John 1:12–13).

If I have trusted in Christ, I have been 'chosen' and can therefore be sure about my relationship with God and my eternal destiny. I need have no fears! (Romans 8:31).

If I have put my trust in Christ, I really am 'a new creation' (2 Corinthians 5:17) and do not need to listen to the accusations of my heart (1 John 3:19–20) or of the devil (Revelation 12:10–11).

*To God be the glory! great things He hath
  done!*
*So loved He the world that He gave us His
  Son;*
Who yielded His life an atonement for sin,
And opened the life-gate that all may go in.

  *Praise the Lord! praise the Lord! Let the
    earth hear His voice!*
  *Praise the Lord! praise the Lord! Let the
    people rejoice!*
  *O come to the Father through Jesus the
    Son:*
  *And give Him the glory! great things He
    hath done!*

O perfect redemption, the purchase of blood!
To every believer the promise of God;
The vilest offender who truly believes,
That moment from Jesus a pardon receives.

*Great things He hath taught us, great things
He hath done,*
*And great our rejoicing through Jesus the
  Son;*
*But purer and higher and greater will be
Our wonder, our transport, when Jesus we
  see!*

Frances Jane Van Alstyne, 1820–1915

Conclusion

How wonderful it is to know we can make a new beginning! And coming to Jesus is only the start; he is the doorway to all the promises and blessings of God.

And He who sits on the throne said, 'Behold, I am making all things new.'

(Revelation 21:5, NASB)

CHAPTER FOUR

The Promise of Peace

Peace is a quality of life that we all want, yet often find so hard to have. The Bible shows us the way to experience this peace.

Therefore, since we have been justified through faith, we have peace with God through our Lord Jesus Christ. (Romans 5:1)

'All I want is a little bit of peace!' How often have you said those words? Even in our hi-tech world, with all its 'mod cons' and labour-saving devices, 'a little bit of peace' can often seem hard to find, can't it? For the parent with a toddler, for the business executive with a schedule, for the student with a deadline, for the worker with a quota – finding a few minutes of peace would be wonderful. And as for those in war-torn areas, peace would be worth anything.

Even when we find peace, it seems as if everything that can spoil it will try to. In the week that Mike was writing this chapter, for example, his peace was severely challenged (at a time he could well have done without it) when, not only did his computer keep crashing, but he also got himself trapped on a train heading for a place he didn't want to go to!

God wants us to experience peace, and to experience it in every circumstance of life. The Bible says that true peace does not depend on where we are or what is going on around us. True peace can be found anywhere; for true peace is found in the heart.

Peace is such a wonderful thing that the Bible shows many different aspects of it.

Peace with God

Therefore, since we have been justified through faith, we have peace with God through our Lord Jesus Christ, through whom we have gained access by faith into this grace in which we now stand.

(Romans 5:1–2)

It is this aspect of peace that is the foundation of our lives as believers. It is not a feeling, but a permanent state into which we are brought as we make Christ's work on the cross our own through faith. The hostilities are over – for

good! We now know that God is with us and for us; and his peace is our constant inner assurance that our sins are forgiven – for ever!

See also Job 22:21; Luke 2:14; Acts 10:36

We cannot achieve our own peace with God

Some peace can be negotiated; but not this one! There is no bargaining or negotiating in the world that could let us arrange terms with God. The only way that peace could be made was when Christ died on the cross and rose again, having paid the price of our sin. God himself was the one who made the peace for us, even though the hostilities began on our side!

Surely he took up our infirmities and carried our sorrows, yet we considered him stricken by God, smitten by him, and afflicted. But he was pierced for our transgressions, he was crushed for our iniquities; the punishment that brought us peace was upon him, and by his wounds we are healed.

(Isaiah 53:4–5)

And through Christ, God has brought all things back to himself again – things on earth and things in heaven. God made peace through the blood of Christ's death on the cross.

(Colossians 1:20, NCV)

See also Luke 2:10–14; Acts 10:36; 1 Peter 1:1–2

Peace with God came though a person

People generally negotiate a peace; but this peace is different. Jesus didn't simply negotiate the peace; he was the peace! 'He himself is our peace,' wrote the apostle Paul (Ephesians 2:14). Peace is a person – the person of the Lord Jesus Christ. It was Jesus himself who removed the barrier, both between people and God, and between people and people, so that both Jews and Gentiles alike might come near to God together.

He will stand and shepherd his flock in the strength of the LORD, in the majesty of the name of the LORD his God. And they will live securely, for then his greatness will reach to the ends of the earth. And he will be their peace.

(Micah 5:4–5)

See also Isaiah 9:6; Romans 5:1; Ephesians 2:14–22

In Ephesians 2:14-22 Paul uses three images to bring out the depth and reality of this new-found peace with God through Jesus. He writes of Jesus making one people, or 'man' (v 15), one family (vv 18–19), one temple (vv 20–22) – all images that show that this peace is to be experienced, not alone, but together.

The peace of God

Not only does God make peace, he gives peace

The peace of God, which transcends all understanding, will guard your hearts and your minds in Christ Jesus.

(Philippians 4:7)

The context of this passage shows that such a peace comes as a result of:
- knowing the joy of the Lord in our lives (v 4)
- showing a gentle, considerate spirit to everyone we meet (v 5)
- praying constantly, particularly about the things that trouble us (v 6)

See also Numbers 6:24–26; Psalm 4:8; 29:11; 85:8; Isaiah 26:12

Peace is the gift of Jesus

'Peace I leave with you; my peace I give you. I do not give to you as the world gives. Do not let your hearts be troubled and do not be afraid.'

(John 14:27)

See also Luke 24:36; John 20:21; Colossians 3:15

This peace is the gift of Jesus, not something we have to work for. It's this calm, unruffled, unflappable spirit, which was so obvious throughout Christ's life. Just think, for example, of how he simply walked through a mob anxious to kill him (Luke 4:28–30) or waited in Gethsemane for his betrayer to arrive (Matthew 26:45–56). It is this sort of peace, for the pressured times of life, that Jesus wants to give us.

The more we let him rule or bring his 'government' into our life, the more of his peace we will know:

And he will be called Wonderful Counsellor, Mighty God, Everlasting Father, Prince of Peace. Of the increase of his government and peace there will be no end.

(Isaiah 9:6–7)

Peace is a fruit of the Holy Spirit

This peace is a fruit of the Holy Spirit (Galatians 5:22–23). As a fruit, peace is something that grows from deep within. The more we draw on Jesus and his Spirit, the more this fruit of peace will grow. Here are some of the ways that it grows:

Growth through trust

The more we trust God, the more we will we know peace. A key to this is learning how to keep our hearts and minds fixed on him, rather than letting them get blown around with every circumstance or problem that arises.

You will keep in perfect peace him whose mind is steadfast, because he trusts in you. Trust in the LORD for ever, for the LORD, the LORD, is the Rock eternal.

(Isaiah 26:3–4)

May the God of hope fill you with all joy and peace as you trust in him, so that you may overflow with hope by the power of the Holy Spirit.

(Romans 15:13)

See also Psalm 112:6–8; Proverbs 3:5–8; Romans 8:6; Colossians 3:15

Growth through love

The more we love God and obey his word, the more we will know peace.

Great peace have they who love your law, and nothing can make them stumble.

(Psalm 119:165)

If only you had paid attention to my commands, your peace would have been like a river, your righteousness like the waves of the sea.

(Isaiah 48:18)

See also Leviticus 26:3–6; Isaiah 54:13

Growth through righteous living

The fruit of righteousness will be peace; the effect of righteousness will be quietness and confidence for ever.

(Isaiah 32:17)

The more we live righteously before God, the more we will know peace. While the devil may try to convince us otherwise, as he did with Eve for example (see Genesis 3:1–5), we cannot expect to do what God says is wrong and still experience his peace. If we 'do bad' we will 'feel bad'; but if we do what God says is right, his peace and blessing will follow.

See also Psalm 85:10; Romans 14:17; 2 Timothy 2:22; Hebrews 12:11

Growth through the Holy Spirit

The more we are filled with the Holy Spirit, the more we will know peace.

For the kingdom of God is not a matter of eating and drinking, but of righteousness, peace and joy in the Holy Spirit.

(Romans 14:17)

But the fruit of the Spirit is love, joy, peace, patience, kindness, goodness, faithfulness, gentleness and self-control.

(Galatians 5:22–23)

See also Romans 8:6; 15:13

Growth through contentment

The more content we are in life, the more we will know peace. There is nothing like always wanting 'more' to rob us of our peace. Jesus addressed this issue in the Sermon on the Mount (Matthew 5–7). He taught that learning to be content with what we have is a great recipe for peace (Matthew 6:25–34).

'So do not worry, saying, "What shall we eat?" or "What shall we drink?" or "What shall we wear?" For the pagans run after all these things, and your heavenly Father knows that you need them. But seek first his kingdom and his righteousness, and all these things will be given to you as well.'

(Matthew 6:31–33)

The apostle Paul had also grasped this lesson:

Do not be anxious about anything, but in everything, by prayer and petition, with thanksgiving, present your requests to God. And the peace of God, which transcends all understanding, will guard your hearts and your minds in Christ Jesus.

(Philippians 4:6–7)

Always wanting 'more' and worrying about things will rob us of our peace.

See also Ecclesiastes 2:22–25; Luke 12:15–21

This peace of God, then, is far more than just not feeling troubled or fearful, though it certainly includes that (John 14:27); it is the quiet assurance within that we are God's children, and that our heavenly Father is therefore always with us, whatever our circumstances (Psalm 46:1–11).

> *God is our refuge and strength,*
> *an ever-present help in trouble.*
> *Therefore we will not fear, though the earth*
> *give way*
> *and the mountains fall into the heart of*
> *the sea,*
> *though its waters roar and foam*
> *and the mountains quake with their surging.*
>
> *There is a river whose streams make glad the*
> *city of God,*
> *the holy place where the Most High dwells.*
> *God is within her, she will not fall;*
> *God will help her at break of day.*
> *Nations are in uproar, kingdoms fall;*
> *he lifts his voice, the earth melts.*
>
> *The LORD Almighty is with us;*
> *the God of Jacob is our fortress.*
>
> *Come and see the works of the LORD,*
> *the desolations he has brought on the earth.*
> *He makes wars cease to the ends of the earth;*
> *he breaks the bow and shatters the spear,*
> *he burns the shields with fire.*
> *'Be still, and know that I am God;*
> *I will be exalted among the nations,*
> *I will be exalted in the earth.'*
>
> *The LORD Almighty is with us;*
> *the God of Jacob is our fortress.*
>
> **(Psalm 46:1–11)**

Peace from God

Grace and peace to you from God our Father and from the Lord Jesus Christ.

(Romans 1:7)

This opening of Paul's letter to the Romans is the form of greeting found, with minor variations, in all his letters (1 Corinthians 1:3; 2 Corinthians 1:2; Galatians 1:3; Ephesians 1:2; Philippians 1:2; Colossians 1:2; 1 Thessalonians 1:1; 2 Thessalonians 1:2; 1 Timothy 1:2; 2 Timothy 1:2; Titus 1:4; Philemon 3). Clearly it was an important concept to him!

Bible commentator William Hendriksen writes of this peace, 'It is not the reflection of an unclouded sky in the tranquil waters of a picturesque lake, but rather the cleft of the rock in which the Lord hides his children when the storm is raging.' Paul's life certainly knew many pressures and turmoils (2 Corinthians 1:8–9; 6:4–10; 11:23–28; 12:7–10); but through it all he could take hold of, and share with others, the peace of God, flowing like a constant stream in many practical ways.

I have learned to be content whatever the circumstances. I know what it is to be in need, and I know what it is to have plenty. I have learned the secret of being content in any and every situation, whether well fed or hungry, whether living in plenty or in want. I can do everything through him who gives me strength.

(Philippians 4:11–13)

The God of peace

God himself is described as 'the God of peace' (Hebrews 13:20), and the Lord Jesus Christ is prophesied as being the 'Prince of Peace' (Isaiah 9:6). Jesus brought peace to the natural elements (Mark 4:39), peace to troubled minds, bodies and spirits (Mark 1:23–26; 5:34; Luke 7:48–50), peace to fearful and confused followers (John 20:19, 21, 26). The gospel is about peace from start to finish; it is 'the gospel of peace' (Ephesians 6:15). And yet, Jesus said, its challenge may well bring conflict, even within families (Matthew 10:21–22, 34–36).

Peacemakers with God

Peace is not just an inner experience, however. The Christian is called to make peace (Matthew 5:9; James 3:18) and to seek peace with all people (Romans 12:18; Hebrews 12:14). It is only those who know God's peace who can resist the pressures and conflicts of the world and radiate this peace to others.

Peace is to be portrayed in our churches

The church should be a place where peace abounds. Christ has given peace to us; our task is to now live it out and maintain it (Ephesians 4:3; Colossians 3:15). All barriers, like that between Jews and Gentiles in the early church, have been broken down (Ephesians 2:14–17). Everything we do in our church life should now reflect that (1 Corinthians 11:11–33; 12:14–27; 14:12) and love for one another should be the hallmark of everything we do (1 Corinthians 13:1–13).

Peace is to be pursued in our world

One day peace and righteousness will be established throughout the world, as many of the prophets foresaw:

In the last days the mountain of the LORD's temple will be established as chief among the mountains; it will be raised above the hills, and peoples will stream to it. Many nations will come and say, 'Come, let us go up to the mountain of the LORD, to the house of the God of Jacob. He will teach us his ways, so that we may walk in his paths.' The law will go out from Zion, the word of the LORD from Jerusalem. He will judge between many peoples and will settle disputes for strong nations far and wide. They will beat their swords into ploughshares and their spears into pruning hooks. Nation will not take up sword against nation, nor will they train for war any more. Every man will sit under his own vine and under his own fig-tree, and no-one will make them afraid, for the Lord Almighty has spoken.

(Micah 4:1–4)

See also Isaiah 2:1–4; 11:6–9; 32:17–18; Revelation 21:1–5

What a wonderful day that will be! But we do not have to sit back and just wait for it; we can start playing our small part now. We can bless people with peace (Luke 10:5–6), pray for peace in the world (Psalm 122:6–7), pray for our nation and government (Jeremiah 29:7; 1 Timothy 2:1–4), encourage some of God's people to take significant positions that can help bring about change (Daniel 1:17–20; 2:48–49). No organization or individual can ultimately change the sin of people's hearts – only God can do that; but that does not mean we should sit by and see God's world fall apart!

Relevance for today

True peace
True peace and rest can only to be found in the presence of God himself.

The LORD replied, 'My Presence will go with you, and I will give you rest.'

(Exodus 33:14)

See also Matthew 11:28–30; 1 John 3:19–20

Peace for all who trust
Peace with God is available to all who trust in Christ.

Therefore, since we have been justified through faith, we have peace with God through our Lord Jesus Christ.

(Romans 5:1)

See also Luke 7:50; Romans 15:13

Barriers to peace
Activity and busyness (Luke 10:38–40) can sometimes get in the way of our knowing God's peace (Luke 10:41–42). True peace and strength are found in quietly trusting in God.

This is what the Sovereign LORD, the Holy One of Israel, says: 'In repentance and rest is your salvation, in quietness and trust is your strength."

(Isaiah 30:15)

See also Exodus 14:13–14; Isaiah 40:30–31

God sustains us
We can find peace by casting our cares daily on the Lord.

Cast your cares on the LORD and he will sustain you.

(Psalm 55:22)

See also 1 Peter 5:6–7

Peace comes with listening
Peace comes as we learn to stop talking and doing, and listen to God instead.

Be still, and know that I am God.

(Psalm 46:10)

This well-known verse hides a rather striking message in the original Hebrew. Its true meaning comes out in various paraphrases, which include 'Relax!', 'Quiet!', and even 'Shut up!' There are times when we just need to stop talking and start listening!

Possessions do not bring peace
In a consumer society, we need to remember that 'a man's life does not consist in the abundance of his possessions' (Luke 12:15). Constantly worrying about 'getting more' will rob us of our peace (Matthew 6:25–34). We could gain the whole world, yet lose our soul (Matthew 16:26).

Peace with one another
Our peace with God must be reflected in peace with one another. This means we must be ruthless in removing any attitudes within ourselves that work against this (e.g. James 2:13). Our churches should be a living example of the peace of God.

Let us therefore make every effort to do what leads to peace and to mutual edification.

(Romans 14:19)

See also Romans 12:17–18; 1 Corinthians 7:15; 14:33; Ephesians 4:3; Colossians 3:15; 1 Thessalonians 5:13; Hebrews 12:14

Aim for perfection, listen to my appeal, be of one mind, live in peace. And the God of love and peace will be with you.

(2 Corinthians 13:11)

*Peace, perfect peace, in this dark world of
    sin?
The blood of Jesus whispers peace within.*

*Peace, perfect peace, by thronging duties
    pressed?
To do the will of Jesus, this is rest.*

*Peace, perfect peace, with sorrows surging
    round?
On Jesus' bosom nought but calm is found.*

*Peace, perfect peace, with loved ones far
    away?
In Jesus' keeping we are safe, and they.*

*Peace, perfect peace, our future all
    unknown?
Jesus we know, and He is on the throne.*

*Peace, perfect peace, death shadowing us and
    ours?
Jesus has vanquished death and all its
    powers.*

*It is enough: earth's struggles soon shall
    cease,
And Jesus call us to heaven's perfect peace.*

Edward Henry Bickersteth, 1825–1906

Conclusion

The one who is our peace gives peace for those
who are at peace with God.

*Now may the Lord of peace himself give you
peace at all times and in every way. The
Lord be with all of you.*

(2 Thessalonians 3:16)

CHAPTER FIVE

The Promise of Forgiveness

Knowing God's forgiveness in our own lives every day is a releasing and transforming power.

If we confess our sins, he is faithful and just and will forgive us our sins and purify us from all unrighteousness.
(1 John 1:9)

'I can never forgive them.' Perhaps all of us have heard (even said?) those words. Of course, they are often understandable – especially in the heat of the moment, or under extreme pressure, or in a dreadful crisis. But how sad if we can never let go of those words. For not to forgive, Jesus said, is to lock ourselves in a prison that is impossible to get out of (Matthew 18:21–35).

Mike well remembers the mother of a child who was murdered in the town where he led his first church. Of course, it was absolutely horrific, and we cannot imagine the agony that family went through. But throughout that lady's life, the one thing that 'kept her going' was bitterness and a desire for revenge. In fact, she died a bitter, twisted and lonely lady. Sadly, she had put herself in prison and thrown away the key.

God's heart is that we should experience something far better than that, no matter what circumstances we might go through.

Sinless Christians?

'Now I am a Christian, I never sin any more.' We might think that anyone who spoke like that lived on a different planet! But, strange as it may seem, there were people in New Testament times who thought just like that; and that was one reason why John wrote his first letter.

John's heart for God's people was that they should not sin – 'My dear children, I write this to you so that you will not sin' (1 John 2:1); but he was real enough to know that they were not perfect yet and that they still did sin. Anyone claiming to be without sin was simply deceiving themselves, he said (1:8); but anyone who owned up to their sin could be sure Jesus would forgive it.

If we claim to be without sin, we deceive ourselves and the truth is not in us. If we confess our sins, he is faithful and just and will forgive us our sins and purify us from all unrighteousness. If we claim we have not sinned, we make him out to be a liar and his word has no place in our lives. My dear children, I write this to you so that you will not sin. But if anybody does sin, we have one who speaks to the Father in our defence – Jesus Christ, the Righteous One. He is the atoning sacrifice for our sins, and not only for ours but also for the sins of the whole world.

(1 John 1:8–2:2)

Only by a strange re-definition of sin, or by deceitfulness of heart, can we claim to be sinless – at least, on this side of heaven anyway! Only when we are finally with Jesus will we be free of sin and at last like him (Philippians 3:20–21). In fact, John says, if we claim to be sinless in this life, we are making God out to be a liar (1:10).

Here is both challenge and encouragement then: the challenge is – don't sin! The encouragement is: but when you do, Jesus will be there to forgive.

The forgiveness of our sins

So, what about us? We are truly born-again, living our daily lives when . . . suddenly, we fall flat on our face, or we do or say something that pulls us up with a start. Have we been play-acting, not really living out the Christian life, all along? No, not at all! We are simply discovering the reality of living as forgiven people while still remaining in a fallen world – and we are not on our own!

We all fall at times

Even Paul knew an inner struggle against sin at times (see Romans 7:15–25). He didn't always do what he wanted to and sometimes did what he didn't want to, just like you and me; but he also knew the answer to this struggle:

What a wretched man I am! Who will rescue me from this body of death? Thanks be to God - through Jesus Christ our Lord!

(Romans 7:24–25)

Some of the greatest saints in the Bible failed God terribly at times; but, like Paul, each of them knew that their sin was not the last word; the last word always lies with God, who promises always to forgive those who repent.

Then David said to Nathan, 'I have sinned against the LORD.' Nathan replied, 'The LORD has taken away your sin. You are not going to die.

(2 Samuel 12:13)

God will forgive us

Going back to God, like David did, is always the answer. No matter how many times we fail, God is willing to forgive. The effectiveness of Jesus' sacrifice on the cross is so great that there is no limit to how far, or how often, it can reach out to cleanse. The power of the blood to cleanse me is always greater than the power of sin to stain me!

If my people, who are called by my name, will humble themselves and pray and seek my face and turn from their wicked ways, then will I hear from heaven and will forgive their sin and will heal their land.

(2 Chronicles 7:14)

Cleanse me with hyssop, and I shall be clean; wash me, and I shall be whiter than snow.

(Psalm 51:7)

If you, O LORD, kept a record of sins, O LORD, who could stand? But with you there is forgiveness; therefore you are feared.

(Psalm 130:3–4)

See also Numbers 14:19–20; Psalm 103:1–5; Micah 7:18–19; Matthew 9:2–7; Colossians 1:13–14; Hebrews 10:19–22; James 5:13–16; 1 John 2:12

The devil will always try to convince us that our particular sin is unforgivable or that we have done it just once too often (which is why he is called 'the accuser', Revelation 12:10); or our conscience may accuse us and tell us that God will never forgive us now; but it is at such times that we need to stand on the truth of God's word. Believe the truth, not the lie!

'Coming clean'

When we as Christians do something wrong (or neglect to do something right), or think or speak in this way, it is sin. The problem, as we saw earlier, is that this isn't a very popular word today. Even we, as Christians, don't like it! But it is when we are aware of it that we need to do something about it. We need to 'come clean' in order to 'get clean'.

Confess the sin

John says, 'If we confess our sin,' (1 John 1:9). To confess means to be real with God about it, to admit it, to 'call a spade a spade', to face up to it – not to explain it away or blame others, as King Saul tried to do (1 Samuel 13:11–14; 15:13–23). Confession is often the thing we want to run away from; yet it is the thing that opens up the door for God to come in.

When I kept silent, my bones wasted away through my groaning all day long. For day and night your hand was heavy upon me; my strength was sapped as in the heat of summer. Then I acknowledged my sin to you and did not cover up my iniquity. I said, 'I will confess my transgressions to the LORD' – and you forgave the guilt of my sin.

(Psalm 32:3–5)

He who conceals his sins does not prosper, but whoever confesses and renounces them finds mercy.

(Proverbs 28:13)

See also Leviticus 5:5–6; 26:40–42; 2 Chronicles 6:24–25; Nehemiah 9:1–3

Receive God's forgiveness

As we confess our sin, God promises to cleanse us.

If we confess our sins, he is faithful and just and will forgive us our sins and purify us from all unrighteousness.

(1 John 1:9)

See also 2 Chronicles 7:14; Psalm 51:1–7; 103:1–12; Acts 3:19; Ephesians 1:7–8; 1 John 1:7

Remember: it is in God's very nature to forgive!

The LORD, the LORD, the compassionate and gracious God, slow to anger, abounding in love and faithfulness, maintaining love to thousands, and forgiving wickedness, rebellion and sin.

(Exodus 34:6–7)

Remember the price!

God's forgiveness is not brought about by his simply 'waving a magic wand'. No, it cost him the life of his Son. 'It is shallow nonsense to say God forgives us because he is love. The only ground upon which God can forgive us is the

cross' (Oswald Chambers). God, in his justice (1 John 1:9), has paid the price of satisfying his righteous anger (wrath) against our sin, by sending his Son to die in our place as an 'atoning sacrifice' (NIV, NRSV) or 'propitiation' (KJV, NASB) (1 John 2:2; see also Romans 3:25).

For you know that it was not with perishable things such as silver or gold that you were redeemed from the empty way of life handed down to you from your forefathers, but with the precious blood of Christ, a lamb without blemish or defect.

(1 Peter 1:18–19)

'But I've sinned too badly!'

Ever felt like that? That you have sinned too badly for God to forgive you? Then take a look at some of the sinners in the Bible who discovered the gracious and forgiving heart of God. If God can forgive them, God can forgive anyone! No one is ever beyond the reach of God's grace.

Here are some people from the Bible who must have felt their sin excluded them from God's forgiveness – but it never did! God forgave them and still used them.

- Abraham – deceitfulness (Genesis 12:10–20; 20:1–18)
- Moses – murder (Exodus 2:10–15)
- David – adultery and conspiracy to murder (2 Samuel 11:1–12:13; Psalm 51)
- Peter – denial of Jesus (Matthew 26:69–75)
- Paul – persecution of Christians (Acts 7:58–8:1; 9:1–19; 1 Corinthians 15:9–10; Galatians 1:13–15)
- Zacchaeus – fraudulent business practice (Luke 19:1–10)
- An unnamed woman – prostitution (Luke 7:36–50)

Remember: Jesus never avoided mixing with 'sinners' (Luke 5:29–32). He was always ready to extend his forgiveness to them; but equally, to extend the challenge, 'Go now and leave your life of sin' (John 8:11). None of us should let past sin keep us from enjoying God's friendship. We simply need to come to him and 'come clean'. We too can then be forgiven and sent out to 'sin no more'.

Jesus said to them, 'It is not the healthy who need a doctor, but the sick. I have not come to call the righteous, but sinners.'

(Mark 2:17)

Steps to forgiveness

What then are the steps for us, as Christians, to know God's gift of forgiveness?

Be serious
The first step to 'getting clean' is to be serious with God about our sin, just as David was (Psalm 51:1–3). Don't treat sin lightly, for it breaks both God's law and God's heart. It is an offence against the holy God who hates sin.

Your eyes are too pure to look on evil; you cannot tolerate wrong.

(Habakkuk 1:13)

Be specific
Tell God exactly what you did wrong. Of course, he knows already! But like any parent with their child, he wants to hear it from our own lips. Don't be vague; be specific (e.g. Isaiah 6:5; Luke 15:17–19); confess it before him and call it what it is – sin!

Be sorry
This means being genuinely repentant for what you have been done. It is not about being sorry that you were caught out, or that things 'went wrong'; but about seeing that you have grieved your heavenly Father (Psalm 51:4). Agree with God's perspective on the matter, just as David did (Psalm 51:4–5).

Be strong
Turn resolutely and decisively away from the sin to God. Take whatever action is needed to remove the source of the sin. Resolve that, with God's help, you will not do it again (John 8:10–11).

'Be strong in the Lord and in his mighty power'.

(Ephesians 6:10)

Be settled
Be settled in what you fix your eyes on and what you put your hope in. If you keep looking at yourself and your failure, you will stay defeated and discouraged. It does not depend on you, but on Jesus who is 'the author and perfecter of our faith' (Hebrews 12:2). Look again at the cross where the penalty for your sin was laid upon him (Isaiah 53:4–6).

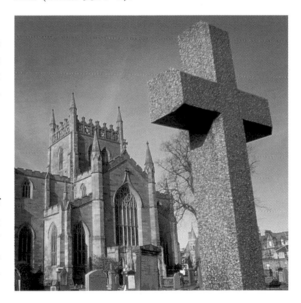

Be sure
God really does want us to receive afresh the certainty of his forgiveness and to realize that he no longer holds our sin against us (Psalm 32:1–5; 103:12; Hebrews 10:22; Romans 5:1). Ask the Holy Spirit to minister this deep into your heart and mind.

Be sensible

The Bible tells us to 'be very careful, then, how you live – not as unwise but as wise' (Ephesians 5:15). Wisdom means that we may need to avoid certain places, things, or people that we find difficult to handle or that tempt us into sin. There is little point your putting your head in the lion's mouth and then praying that it will not get bitten off! Be sensible; take whatever decisive and practical steps you need to in order to avoid that particular sin again. Consider being accountable to a more mature Christian.

Ready to forgive?

O ne measure of how genuinely we appreciate God's forgiveness, Jesus said, is how forgiving we ourselves are towards others. A phrase in the Lord's Prayer, and a comment after it, underlines this:

'Forgive us for our sins, just as we have forgiven those who sinned against us.'

(Matthew 6:12, NCV)

'For if you forgive men when they sin against you, your heavenly Father will also forgive you. But if you do not forgive men their sins, your Father will not forgive your sins.'

(Matthew 6:14–15)

See also Matthew 18:21–35; Mark 11:25; Luke 6:37; James 2:13

If we have experienced God's forgiveness, we will be amazed at his kindness towards us. Our natural response will be love towards him (Luke 7:37-38, 44-47) and kindness towards others (Ephesians 4:32; 1 Peter 4:8). There is simply no place for anger or judgmental attitudes towards others who are simply as flawed as us (Matthew 7:1-5); no place for feelings of hurt, injury or resentment towards others who have wronged us. Anger will be replaced by favour and kindness if we have truly understood and received forgiveness. This is something we can't do by ourselves; we truly need God's grace.

Relevance for today

God is still the God of forgiveness

The God who does not change (Malachi 3:6) is as ready to forgive sin today as the day he promised to do it, for forgiveness is part of his very nature (Exodus 34:6).

You are forgiving and good, O Lord, abounding in love to all who call to you.

(Psalm 86:5)

The LORD is compassionate and gracious, slow to anger, abounding in love. He will not always accuse, nor will he harbour his anger for ever; he does not treat us as our sins deserve or repay us according to our iniquities. For as high as the heavens are above the earth, so great is his love for those who fear him; as far as the east is from the west, so far has he removed our transgressions from us. As a father has compassion on his children, so the LORD has compassion on those who fear him.

(Psalm 103:8–13)

If you, O LORD, kept a record of sins, O LORD, who could stand? But with you there is forgiveness; therefore you are feared.

(Psalm 130:3–4)

I, even I, am he who blots out your transgressions, for my own sake, and remembers your sins no more.

(Isaiah 43:25)

God alone is able to forgive sin

There is no counselling or psychotherapy in the world that can deal with sin; only God can. No matter how much time or money we might spend on such things, it will never deal with the root of our problem.

There is no God apart from me, a righteous God and a Saviour; there is none but me. Turn to me and be saved, all you ends of the earth; for I am God, and there is no other.

(Isaiah 45:21–22)

Who can forgive sins but God alone?

(Mark 2:7)

God forgives sin only through Christ's death on the cross

While earthly debts may have various means of payment, this debt has just one means – Christ's death on the cross. Nothing can be added to it and nothing taken away from it.

Surely he took up our infirmities and carried our sorrows, yet we considered him stricken by God, smitten by him, and afflicted. But he was pierced for our transgressions, he was crushed for our iniquities; the punishment that brought us peace was upon him, and by his wounds we are healed. We all, like sheep, have gone astray, each of us has turned to his own way; and the LORD has laid on him the iniquity of us all.

(Isaiah 53:5–6)

For there is one God and one mediator between God and men, the man Christ Jesus, who gave himself as a ransom for all men.

(1 Timothy 2:5–6)

See also Ephesians 1:7; Colossians 1:20; 1 Peter 2:24

There is not a thing we can add to this; all we can do is to respond in repentance and faith (Acts 2:37–39; Romans 3:21–25).

No matter what sins I may have committed, God is prepared to forgive them

'Come now, let us reason together,' says the LORD. 'Though your sins are like scarlet, they shall be as white as snow; though they are red as crimson, they shall be like wool.'

(Isaiah 1:18)

There is no sin too bad for God to forgive. The issue is not whether he will forgive, but whether I will repent.

Conscience is God's gift to me

It is important to respond to our conscience when it 'pricks' us, for this is God's inner voice, telling us when something is wrong.

'So I [Paul] strive always to keep my conscience clear before God and man.'

(Acts 24:16)

See also 1 Samuel 24:5–6; 2 Samuel 24:10; Job 27:6; Romans 13:5; 2 Corinthians 1:12; 1 Timothy 1:18–19; 4:1–2; Titus 1:15; Hebrews 10:22; 1 Peter 3:16

If I cannot forgive, I have not understood forgiveness

There is good ground for wondering whether I myself have truly been forgiven if I cannot forgive someone else who offends against me. God commands, not invites, the forgiven to forgive.

'For if you forgive men when they sin against you, your heavenly Father will also forgive you. But if you do not forgive men their sins, your Father will not forgive your sins.'

(Matthew 6:14–15)

See also Matthew 18:21–35; Ephesians 4:32

Great God of wonders! all Thy ways
Are matchless, godlike, and divine;
But the fair glories of Thy grace
More godlike and unrivalled shine;

Who is a pardoning God like Thee?
Or who has grace so rich and free?

Such dire offences to forgive,
Such guilty, daring worms to spare;
This is Thy grand prerogative,
And in the honour none shall share:

In wonder lost, with trembling joy,
We take the pardon of our God,
Pardon for sins of deepest dye,
A pardon sealed with Jesus' blood:

O may this strange, this wondrous grace,
This matchless miracle of love,
Fill the wide earth with grateful praise,
And all the angelic choirs above:

Samuel Davies, 1723–61

Conclusion

Experiencing the forgiveness of God will release us into a deeper worship of God, a greater sorrow for our sin and a stronger love for other people.

Who is a God like you, who pardons sin and forgives the transgression . . . ? You do not stay angry for ever but delight to show mercy.

(Micah 7:18)

The Promise of Jesus' Presence

As Christians, we can know Jesus as our constant companion and friend. He is always with us!

'I have called you friends, for everything that I learned from my Father I have made known to you.' (John 15:15)

Knowing that someone is *there* with you can make such a difference. Think of the mother giving birth, or the aged person dying, or the child trying to learn to ride a bicycle; just having someone nearby is so reassuring at such times. *Being there* makes such a difference.

We have already seen that God is 'the God who is there' (Part 1, Chapter 6) and that he reaches out to people in friendship (Part 1, Chapter 3). It should not surprise us, therefore, that when God came into this world in the person of his Son, he came to *be there* with us.

'The virgin will be with child and will give birth to a son, and they will call him Immanuel' – which means, *'God with us.'*

(Matthew 1:23)

But he is more than simply 'there'; he is there *as a friend*. Not only was the word 'friend' often found on his lips (e.g. Luke 5:20; John 11:11; 15:13–15; 21:5), he acted as a true friend to everyone he encountered, especially to those who felt they did not deserve it (Luke 7:34), and even to the one who betrayed him (Matthew 26:50). Such is the depth of his friendship!

Jesus, our companion

The promises of God are precious. But his presence is even better than his promises! Whatever happens to us, there is one who is our constant companion.

'Surely I am with you always, to the very end of the age.'

(Matthew 28:20)

One night the Lord spoke to Paul in a vision: 'Do not be afraid; keep on speaking, do not be silent. For I am with you, and no-one is going to attack and harm you, because I have many people in this city.'

(Acts 18:9–10)

Jesus our companion is always with us

Although he was returning to the Father, Jesus promised that, through his Holy Spirit, his presence would always be with his followers. He promised that:

- He and the Father would dwell with us

Jesus replied, 'If anyone loves me, he will obey my teaching. My Father will love him, and we will come to him and make our home with him.'

(John 14:23)

- He would fellowship with us

'Here I am! I stand at the door and knock. If anyone hears my voice and opens the door, I will come in and eat with him, and he with me.'

(Revelation 3:20)

- We would not be left as orphans

'I will not leave you as orphans; I will come to you.'

(John 14:18)

- Jesus our companion draws close in life

Jesus demonstrated by his actions that we can have his risen presence with us along life's journey.

And they talked together of all these things which had happened. So it was, while they conversed and reasoned, that Jesus Himself drew near and went with them.

(Luke 24:14–15, NKJV)

Still today, Jesus wants to draw near and go with us in everyday life. His presence always transformed both people (e.g. Luke 19:1–10) and situations (e.g. John 2:1–11). Through his Spirit, the same still happens today.

Jesus our companion is always there in every situation

- He encourages us in times of difficulty

The following night the Lord stood near Paul and said, 'Take courage! As you have testified about me in Jerusalem, so you must also testify in Rome.'

(Acts 23:11)

See also Matthew 14:26–27; Acts 27:21–25

- He comforts us in times of sorrow

'Blessed are those who mourn, for they will be comforted.'

(Matthew 5:4)

See also Luke 24:17–32; John 11:17–44; 2 Corinthians 1:3–6; Philippians 2:1

- He strengthens us in times of weakness

To keep me from becoming conceited because of these surpassingly great revelations, there was given me a thorn in my flesh, a messenger of Satan, to torment me. Three times I pleaded with the Lord to take it away from me. But he said to me, 'My grace is sufficient for you, for my power is made perfect in weakness.' Therefore I will boast all the more gladly about my weaknesses, so that Christ's power may rest on me. That is why, for Christ's sake, I delight in weaknesses, in insults, in hardships, in persecutions, in difficulties. For when I am weak, then I am strong.

(2 Corinthians 12:7–10)

I can do everything through him who gives me strength.

(Philippians 4:13)

See also Ephesians 3:16; Colossians 1:11; 1 Timothy 1:12

Jesus, our friend

Being a companion, could, of course, be a rather clinical arrangement. A stranger could become, for a little while, a travelling companion; but enduring friendship is unlikely to arise from it. Thankfully, that is not how it is with Jesus! Jesus is not just a companion – someone there with us on the journey; he is a friend. Listen to what he said to his disciples:

'I no longer call you servants, because a servant does not know his master's business. Instead, I have called you friends, for everything that I learned from my Father I have made known to you.'

(John 15:15)

When Mike was young, he had a friend whose parents owned an ice-cream factory. How exciting to be drawn into such a business for a day, because of his friend! But what Jesus offers is far better than that. Through friendship with him, we are drawn into our heavenly Father's business and purpose for eternity.

Marks of his friendship

The friend who stays close

He is the one of whom it is written:

. . . there is a friend who sticks closer than a brother.

(Proverbs 18:24)

A friend loves at all times, and a brother is born for adversity.

(Proverbs 17:17)

The friend who stands by us

Jesus knows what it is like to be deserted by friends (Mark 14:50); but he will never do that to us. Listen to Paul's testimony:

At my first defence, no-one came to my support, but everyone deserted me. May it not be held against them. But the Lord stood at my side and gave me strength, so that through me the message might be fully proclaimed and all the Gentiles might hear it. And I was delivered from the lion's mouth. The Lord will rescue me from every evil attack and will bring me safely to his heavenly kingdom. To him be glory for ever and ever.

(2 Timothy 4:16–18)

The friend who stays faithful

Such is his friendship, that he comes to us even when we have failed him. He is the friend who helps us up when we fall (Ecclesiastes 4:10). Peter had denied him three times (Mark 14:66–72), but Jesus forgave him and gave him a threefold commission to care for his sheep (John 21:15–19). He always stays faithful, even when we do not.

Here is a trustworthy saying: If we died with him, we will also live with him; if we endure, we will also reign with him. If we disown him, he will also disown us; if we are faithless, he will remain faithful, for he cannot disown himself.

(2 Timothy 2:11–13)

The friend who loves us

'Greater love has no-one than this, that he lay down his life for his friends. You are my friends if you do what I command.'

(John 15:13–14)

Not only does he love us; he loves us enough to be truthful with us. At times he asks searching questions to reveal what is in our heart (John 21:15–22). Sometimes the love of a true friend will hurt!

Better is open rebuke than hidden love. Wounds from a friend can be trusted . . .

(Proverbs 27:5–6)

The friend who has 'been there'

Whatever circumstance, pressure or temptation we might face, it is good to remember that Jesus, our friend, has already 'been there'.

For we do not have a high priest who is unable to sympathise with our weaknesses, but we have one who has been tempted in every way, just as we are – yet was without sin. Let us then approach the throne of grace with confidence, so that we may receive mercy and find grace to help us in our time of need.

(Hebrews 4:15–16)

Not only has he 'been there' and faced all these things, he has come through them victoriously! He faced temptation (Matthew 4:1–11), tiredness (John 4:4–8), the risk of being misunderstood (John 4:9), false accusations (Matthew 27:12–14; Mark 3:1–6; John 8:3–11). What an encouragement to know that our friend Jesus walked this earth, facing the things that we do, and that he conquered them all, and that through his Spirit he can help us face the same sort of things today.

The friend who is inclusive

Some human friendships are so exclusive that they are unhealthy. They become cliques that no one else can break into. But Jesus' heart and kingdom are so big that there is room for all (e.g. John 14:2). He made room for men and women (Matthew 14:21); Jew and non-Jew (Matthew 15:21-28); young and old (Matthew 21:14-16); the religious and the 'sinner' (Luke 7:36-50). None was excluded! Never believe that you will be.

In good company!

If we are friends of our God, then we are in good company! People like Abraham (2 Chronicles 20:7; Isaiah 41:8; James 2:23) and Moses (Exodus 33:11) are among that number who were called "God's friend". And, in Christ, so are you and I! We too are now friends (John 15:15), children (1 John 3:1), part of his flock (Luke 12:32). We are not left alone, but are part of a huge family (Ephesians 2:19), stretching across heaven and earth (Ephesians 3:14-15) and across every nation (Revelation 7:9).

Keys to true friendship with Jesus

There are certain things that can help a friendship grow – or hinder it! So, what helps friendship with Jesus to grow?

Honesty and openness of heart

No true friendship can develop where secrets are kept or hearts are not opened. It is the same between us and Jesus. And because he already knows the worst about us (e.g. Mark 2:8; 12:14-15; Hebrews 4:13), there is nothing we can tell him that will shock him or make him change his mind about us.

Obedience

Because our friend is Lord of the universe, it is important to listen to what he says. Indeed, a measure of how much we are his friends will be reflected in how much we obey him.

'You are my friends if you obey me.'

(John 15:14, CEV)

And this is love: that we walk in obedience to his commands.

(2 John 6)

See also John 14:23; Romans 1:5; 2 Corinthians 9:13; 1 Peter 1:2

This is not Jesus putting a condition on our friendship – 'I won't be your friend unless you obey me.' Rather this is him saying, 'How can you claim to be my friend, to love me and trust me, if you don't put into practice what I say?' Obedience shows we are true friends; and that is why the New Testament urges us to pursue it. It is only as we have a reverence ('fear') of God, demonstrated in obedient lives, that he can he take us into his confidence:

The Lord confides in those who fear him.

(Psalm 25:14)

'You are my friends if you obey me. I no longer call you servants, because a master doesn't confide in his servants. Now you are my friends, since I have told you everything the Father told me.'

(John 15:14–15, NLT)

See also Job 29:4; Proverbs 3:32

As we obey God, we will experience a deeper friendship with Jesus and he will confide his secrets in us.

Godly lifestyle

If there are things in our life that are not given over to Jesus, things we are holding back from doing, or wrong things we are doing, then this will hinder the friendship. The devil may try to convince us that it doesn't matter, but it does!

What do righteousness and wickedness have in common? Or what fellowship can light have with darkness? . . . 'Therefore come out from them and be separate, says the Lord. Touch no unclean thing, and I will receive you.' 'I will be a Father to you, and you will be my sons and daughters, says the Lord Almighty.'

(2 Corinthians 6:14, 17–18)

See also Galatians 5:19–21; 6:7–8; Ephesians 5:3–11; 1 John 1:5–6

The depth of Christ's friendship

How do you show how much you love someone? TV advertisements say by giving your beloved their favourite chocolate, or by buying your family that new car. For the Son of God, it was nothing so trivial!

Life for friends

'Greater love has no one than this, than to lay down one's life for his friends.'

(John 15:13, NKJV)

Jesus voluntarily gave up his own life for his friends, such was the depth of his love.

See also John 10:11; 13:1

We can understand how a true friend might be prepared to sacrifice his life for someone for whom he had true affection. But the Bible says there is more. For the great wonder is that our heavenly friend died on the cross, not for his friends, but for his enemies!

Life for enemies!

While we were God's enemies, he made friends with us through the death of his Son.

(Romans 5:10, NCV)

See also Romans 5:7–8; Colossians 1:21–22

This is amazing – that we were rescued while we were still his enemies! What a friend!

Don't abuse friendship!

But as we close this chapter, let's just stop and remember who it is who is our friend. It is 'Immanuel' – God with us (Matthew 1:23). It is God who is our friend! It is God who is with us in all of daily life.

And this is why we should take care not to become over-familiar with him. He is not a 'mate' – he is Almighty God! The line between enjoyment of his friendship and abuse of it can be fine; let us ensure we do not cross it, and so enjoy to the full the presence and the promises of the One who loved us so much that he came in person.

Relevance for today

Jesus still comes to save us from our sin

Here is a trustworthy saying that deserves full acceptance: Christ Jesus came into the world to save sinners – of whom I am the worst. But for that very reason I was shown mercy so that in me, the worst of sinners, Christ Jesus might display his unlimited patience as an example for those who would believe on him and receive eternal life.

(1 Timothy 1:15–16)

See also Matthew 1:21; John 3:17; Acts 4:12; 5:30–31; Romans 5:9

Jesus still comes to guide us and direct our way

'My sheep listen to my voice; I know them, and they follow me . . . no-one can snatch them out of my hand.'

(John 10:27–28)

See also John 10:2–5; 16:13; 2 Corinthians 2:14

Jesus still comes to care for us

'I am the good shepherd; I know my sheep and my sheep know me – and I lay down my life for the sheep.'

(John 10:14–15)

See also Matthew 9:36; 11:28–30; 14:14; Mark 8:2–3; 1 Peter 5:7

Jesus still comes to strengthen us

I can do all things through Christ, because he gives me strength.

(Philippians 4:13, NCV)

See also 2 Corinthians 12:9; Ephesians 3:16–17; 6:10–13; 1 Timothy 1:12; 2 Timothy 4:17

Jesus still comes to aid us in times in times of temptation

Because he himself suffered when he was tempted, he is able to help those who are being tempted.

(Hebrews 2:18)

See also Luke 22:31–32; Hebrews 4:15–16

Jesus still comes to draw us near to him in difficult times

This is what Paul discovered through his 'thorn in the flesh' (2 Corinthians 12:7–10). Days of difficulty, or days when God seems remote, perhaps through loneliness or loss, may test our faith; yet he is always with us in such periods and we will come through them all the stronger and will be able to say, like Job,

I know that you can do all things; no plan of yours can be thwarted . . . My ears had heard of you but now my eyes have seen you.

(Job 42:2, 5)

115

I've found a Friend, O such a Friend!
He loved me ere I knew Him;
He drew me with the cords of love,
And thus He bound me to Him;
And round my heart still closely twine
Those ties which nought can sever;
For I am His, and He is mine,
For ever and for ever.

I've found a Friend, O such a Friend!
He bled, He died to save me;
And not alone the gift of life,
But His own self He gave me.
Nought that I have mine own I'll call,
I'll hold it for the Giver;
My heart, my strength, my life, my all
Are His, and His for ever.

I've found a Friend, O such a Friend!
All power to Him is given,
To guard me on my onward course,
And bring me safe to heaven.
The eternal glories gleam afar,
To nerve my faint endeavour;
So now to watch! to work! to war!
And then – to rest for ever.

I've found a Friend, O such a Friend.
So kind, and true, and tender!
So wise a Counsellor and Guide,
So mighty a Defender!
From Him who loves me now so well
What power my soul can sever?
Shall life or death, or earth or hell?
No! I am His for ever.

James Grindlay Small, 1817

Conclusion

We will experience a growing friendship with Jesus the more we follow him and do what he wants.

'All authority in heaven and on earth has been given to me. Therefore go and make disciples of all nations . . . And surely I am with you always, to the very end of the age.'
(Matthew 28:18–20)

The Promise of Being Discipled

Having brought us into this new life with him, Jesus promises to now train (or 'disciple') us in how to live it. Jesus isn't looking simply for converts – he's looking for disciples!

'Come, follow me . . . and I will make you . . .' (Mark 1:17)

There are few worthwhile things in life that we do, or at least do well, at the first attempt. Even such basics as eating, speaking and writing took lots of attempts (and lots of failures!) before we mastered them.

Being a Christian is no different. We saw earlier in Part 2 that becoming a Christian is about being 'born again' (John 3:3). As such, we are new babies who need to learn lots of new skills for our new life. Discipleship (what we might call 'apprenticeship') is what Jesus promises to take us through to bring this about. Just as in our natural life, this process of learning, growing and maturing never stops. In fact, the day we stop, we die! Discipleship is for life.

The call to discipleship

The call to discipleship lay at the heart of Jesus' ministry (Mark 1:14–18). The calling of his first disciples sums it up:

'Come, follow me,' Jesus said, 'and I will make you fishers of men.'

(Mark 1:17)

See also Matthew 19:21; Luke 9:57–59; 19:5; John 1:39; 7:37

Jesus called all sorts of people to be his followers from all walks of life. No one was excluded! The list includes:

- fishermen (Matthew 4:18–20)
- tax collectors (Matthew 9:9)
- homemakers (Mark 15:41; Luke 8:3)
- religious experts (John 3:1; 19:38–39)
- freedom fighters (Luke 6:15; the Zealots were a revolutionary group committed to violent overthrow of Rome.)
- soldiers (Matthew 8:5–13)
- prostitutes (Matthew 21:31–32)

There really is room for everyone in Jesus' school of discipleship!

This call can be seen to be made up of three different elements.

A call to decision

When Jesus said, 'Come!' a decision had to be made; a decision that would change life from now on. While many responded gladly and spontaneously (e.g. Mark 1:18), others failed to do so because of the pull of other things (e.g. Matthew 8:21; 19:21–22).

A call to difference

We cannot 'follow' while staying where we are! When we follow Jesus, change is required, and many things will be different from now on.

Location
Some were called to follow Jesus literally, leaving behind their homes (Luke 5:11; 18:29–30) or their business (Luke 5:27–28). Others, however, were sent back home to be a witness to Jesus there (e.g. Mark 5:19).

Lifestyle
While not everyone had to leave their home, everyone certainly had to change their lifestyle and 'move on' with Jesus. Some responded to this challenge gladly (e.g. Luke 19:5–9), while others stumbled at it (e.g. Matthew 19:16–22).

Learning
Whether called to stay or move, discipleship meant learning for everyone. 'A student is not above his teacher, nor a servant above his master' (Matthew 10:24). But it is not 'learning for learning's sake'. As we learn, change will be required in our thinking and consequently in our living. Discipleship is not just about challenge, but change.

A call to destiny

When Jesus said 'And I will make you . . .' this was a call to be brought into God's eternal purposes for that individual's life. Jesus is in the business of making us into something beyond what we could have ever imagined! (See e.g. Matthew 16:18; Galatians 1:15–16.)

No matter how long or how short a time we have been a Christian, Jesus still brings these three challenges to us on a daily basis (Luke 9:23).

The characteristics of discipleship

So what does true discipleship involve?

Counting the cost

Wherever Jesus went, large crowds would gather. His healings or miracles or good teaching would ensure that (e.g. Matthew 4:25; 7:28; 13:2; 14:13–14; 15:30; 19:2). But although he happily preached to the crowd, he said there was a great cost in becoming a disciple (e.g. Luke 14:25–33). It involved:

Changing established loyalties

While we are to honour our parents (Exodus 20:12), they can no longer take first place in our lives. Love for them must almost seem like 'hate' in comparison to love for Jesus (Luke 14:26). Even loyalty to our possessions (Luke 14:33) and our very selves will be challenged (Luke 14:27).

Being ready to finish what we start

Like a man planning a building project, the would-be disciple must first sit down and think about whether he can finish what he starts (Luke 14:28–30).

Considering the cost first

Like a king going out to battle, the would-be disciple must consider the cost before beginning (Luke 14:31–32). Jesus is not looking for a blind and easy commitment that doesn't understand what it is letting itself in for.

Being ready to make sacrifices

Discipleship involves a readiness to make sacrifices, whether of our time and possessions (Luke 14:18–20) or even of life itself (Luke 14:27).

Then he [Jesus] said to them all: 'If anyone would come after me, he must deny himself and take up his cross daily and follow me. For whoever wants to save his life will lose it, but whoever loses his life for me will save.

(Luke 9:23–24)

See also Matthew 10:34–39; Luke 17:33; John 12:25

This all sounds so costly doesn't it? But for those who are ready to follow in this way, Jesus reassures them that it will by no means be to their loss!

Peter answered him, 'We have left everything to follow you! What then will there be for us?' Jesus said to them, 'I tell you the truth, at the renewal of all things, when the Son of Man sits on his glorious throne, you who have followed me will also sit on twelve thrones, judging the twelve tribes of Israel. And everyone who has left houses or brothers or sisters or father or mother or children or fields for my sake will receive a hundred times as much and will inherit eternal life.'

(Matthew 19:27–29)

Setting new priorities

All of us give priority to what is important to us. In fact, it is amazing what we can squeeze into life if we want to! But for us as Christians, we have a new and very simple priority:

119

'Seek first his kingdom and his righteousness, and all these things will be given to you as well.'

(Matthew 6:33)

Jesus said this in the context of teaching his disciples not to worry about such basics as food and clothing (Matthew 6:25-34) – the very things that are our priorities so often! But get this new priority in place, Jesus said, and all these will fall into place as well. This does not come naturally to us; and that is why we need discipling in this area.

This new priority of seeking first God's kingdom involves:

Seeking to become more like Jesus

'A student is not above his teacher, nor a servant above his master. It is enough for the student to be like his teacher, and the servant like his master.'

(Matthew 10:24–25)

I [Paul] want to know Christ and the power of his resurrection and the fellowship of sharing in his sufferings, becoming like him in his death, and so, somehow, to attain to the resurrection from the dead.

(Philippians 3:10–11)

Acknowledging Jesus as Lord

It is no good just saying we are disciples; we need to live like disciples.

'Not everyone who says to me, "Lord, Lord," will enter the kingdom of heaven, but only he who does the will of my Father who is in heaven.'

(Matthew 7:21)

To call him 'Lord', but not to obey what he says, is as foolish as building a house on sand, Jesus went on to say (Matthew 7:24–27). It isn't enough to read (or write!) books like this one and to listen to sermons. The word has to be put into practice; the Lord has to be obeyed.

See also Luke 8:21; James 1:22–25; 2:14–26

Keeping the 'greatest commandment'

' "Love the Lord your God with all your heart and with all your soul and with all your mind." This is the first and greatest commandment. And the second is like it: "Love your neighbour as yourself"'.'

(Matthew 22:37–39)

When asked which was the greatest commandment, Jesus replied with two: loving God and loving our neighbour as ourselves. They belong together for the disciple of Jesus and cannot be separated.

See also Matthew 5:43–47; James 2:8–9

Loving our fellow Christians

'A new command I give you: Love one another. As I have loved you, so you must love one another. By this all men will know that you are my disciples, if you love one another.'

(John 13:34–35)

See also John 13:14–15; Romans 13:8–10; Ephesians 4:2; 1 Peter 1:22; 3:8; 1 John 3:11–23; 4:7–12

Being a faithful witness to Jesus

'But you will receive power when the Holy Spirit comes on you; and you will be my witnesses in Jerusalem, and in all Judea and Samaria, and to the ends of the earth.'

(Acts 1:8)

The God of our fathers has chosen you to know his will and to see the Righteous One and to hear words from his mouth. You will be his witness to all men of what you have seen and heard.

(Acts 22:14–15)

See also Mark 5:19; Acts 3:15–16; 5:29–32; 10:39–43; 13:26–31; Revelation 2:12–13

Being fruitful

'I [Jesus] am the vine; you are the branches. If a man remains in me and I in him, he will bear much fruit; apart from me you can do nothing. If anyone does not remain in me, he is like a branch that is thrown away and withers; such branches are picked up, thrown into the fire and burned. If you remain in me and my words remain in you, ask whatever you wish, and it will be given you. This is to my Father's glory, that you bear much fruit, showing yourselves to be my disciples.'

(John 15:5–8)

See also Matthew 3:8; 7:15–20; 21:43; John 15:16; Romans 7:4–6; Galatians 5:22–23

Not looking back

'No-one who puts his hand to the plough and looks back is fit for service in the kingdom of God.

(Luke 9:62)

A farmer who keeps looking back over his shoulder while ploughing will end up with very ragged furrows. Likewise, we cannot follow Jesus if we are constantly looking back, pre-occupied all the time with our old ways and what we might have left behind or be missing out on.

See also Genesis 19:26; Luke 17:30–32

Giving up the right to our own way of life

'If anyone would come after me, he must deny himself and take up his cross daily and follow me.'

(Luke 9:23)

See also Matthew 10:38; Luke 14:27

'Denying' ourselves means there will be times when we just have to say 'no' to ourselves – to what we would like, or what we would like to do, or where we would, or would not, like to go.

Personal ambitions, comfort and agendas have to stop being 'number one' for us. Only when we have grasped the principle of 'dying to self' can we face persecution and get blessing out of it (Matthew 5:10–12) and find 'life' coming out of 'death'. Whenever we 'risk it' in this way, there will always be a return.

'I tell you the truth, unless a grain of wheat falls to the ground and dies, it remains only a single seed. But if it dies, it produces many seeds.'

(John 12:24)

What you sow does not come to life unless it dies.

(1 Corinthians 15:36)

Finishing with sin

Jesus straightened up and asked her, 'Woman, where are they? Has no-one condemned you?' 'No-one, sir,' she said. 'Then neither do I condemn you,' Jesus declared. 'Go now and leave your life of sin.'
(John 8:10–11)

Jesus forgives our sin; but he expects us then to walk away from it, rather than keep going back to it. With the help of the Spirit, we are called upon to put to death sin in our lives.

Therefore, brothers, we have an obligation – but it is not to the sinful nature, to live according to it. For if you live according to the sinful nature, you will die; but if by the Spirit you put to death the misdeeds of the body, you will live, because those who are led by the Spirit of God are sons of God.
(Romans 8:12–14)

Having a more mature Christian as a 'mentor' can help us keep accountable in dealing ruthlessly with sin.

Receiving discipline

'Discipleship' involves 'discipline' – correction! Let's face it, none of us likes that – especially in a society where not being judgmental about anything or anyone is the norm. Yet any serious athlete knows how important discipline is if they want to achieve the right end result. That is how it is with God and us.

Discipline from God

God is not afraid to discipline his children; but it is *always* out of love and for good purpose.

Blessed is the man whom God corrects; so do not despise the discipline of the Almighty. For he wounds, but he also binds up; he injures, but his hands also heal.
(Job 5:17–18)

And you have forgotten that word of encouragement that addresses you as sons: 'My son, do not make light of the Lord's discipline, and do not lose heart when he rebukes you, because the Lord disciplines those he loves, and he punishes everyone he accepts as a son.' Endure hardship as discipline; God is treating you as sons.
(Hebrews 12:5–7)
See also Deuteronomy 8:5; Proverbs 3:11–12; John 15:1–2; 1 Corinthians 11:32; Hebrews 12:8–11; Revelation 3:19

Discipline from others

God delegates his authority to others to discipline and train us too – whether to the state (Romans 13:1–5), our parents (Proverbs 15:5; Ephesians 6:1–4), or our spiritual leaders (Hebrews 13:17). It is even something we can receive from one another (e.g. Proverbs 15:31–32; 27:5–6; Ephesians 5:21; Colossians 3:16).

Finding our destiny

Discipleship is not without purpose – just 'there' for its own sake. Its aim is to bring us into the eternal purpose and destiny that God has for our lives.

For he chose us in him before the creation of the world to be holy and blameless in his sight. In love he predestined us to be adopted as his sons through Jesus Christ, in accordance with his pleasure and will.

(Ephesians 1:4–5)

While our ultimate destiny is to become 'his sons', that destiny has a particular 'shape' for each one of us. Finding our destiny is about finding what we were made for. Do you remember how in the film *Chariots of Fire* Eric

Liddell said he felt God's pleasure when he was running? In giving himself back to God, he knew that his true self was being realized. For Eric, it was running; for Peter, it was building the church (Matthew 16:18–19); for Paul, it was preaching the gospel to Jews and Gentiles (Acts 9:15); for Aquila and Priscilla, it was running a business from which they supported the church (Acts 18:1–3, 26; 1 Corinthians 16:19). But you too have a purpose and destiny in God! Ask him to show you just what it is! Discipleship is one of God's tools to help bring out that call and gifting in us.

The failures in discipleship

If you are anything like us, then you will often feel you fail in your discipleship – perhaps by not being as radical as we should be or by trying to 'serve two masters' (Matthew 6:24) after all! Sometimes we all fail to hit the target. But when we do, we are in good company. Just look at those first disciples:

• They didn't always understand what Jesus said (Mark 9:30–32; Luke 8:9; John 12:16; 20:9).
• They didn't always use the power that was theirs (Mark 9:14–19), and even when they wanted to, it was not always in the right way (Luke 9:52–56).
• They failed Jesus at the crucial moment (Matthew 26:40–45, 56, 69–75; Mark 14:50).
• The group leader was even told once he was doing Satan's work for him! (Matthew 16:23)

But remember: a disciple is a learner, an apprentice. Learning means failing at times, as well as succeeding. But every failure can be the seed-ground of the success of the next attempt. We take encouragement from the fact that God tells us to 'learn to do right' (Isaiah 1:17). He knows that doing right does not always come instinctively to us, and that we will sometimes get it wrong as we seek to do so; but he 'gives us space' to fail in order to train us to succeed.

Relevance for today

Making disciples should be a high priority for us

If one of the final commands of Jesus was to 'make disciples' (Matthew 28:19), then this should still be a high priority for us today. Am I personally making disciples? Am I being one?

Discipleship keeps us accountable

God gives each of us opportunities and gifts. All of us need the opportunity to be accountable for how we use them for the benefit of the whole church and the advancement of the kingdom (e.g. Luke 9:1–3, 10).

Discipleship releases me to try, even if I fail, rather than not to try

Just as when Peter stepped out of the boat to join Jesus as he walked on the lake (Matthew 14:25–33), Jesus would rather that we tried and failed, than that we never tried. His word to us, as 'learners', when we do try is still the same:

'Take courage! It is I. Don't be afraid . . . Come.'

(Matthew 14:27–29)

Discipleship leads to an effective, fruitful Christian life

Discipleship 'prunes' our life, just like a fruit tree, to stop it being unproductive and to make it more fruitful.

'I am the true vine, and my Father is the gardener. He cuts off every branch in me that bears no fruit, while every branch that does bear fruit he prunes so that it will be even more fruitful.'

(John 15:1–2)

Discipleship ensures the gospel is passed on faithfully

If we are unwilling to be accountable or submit ourselves to others, there is a very real danger that we will twist the message of the gospel into our own shape, as some did in New Testament times (e.g. 1 Timothy 1:3-4; Titus 1:10–14), or that we will become arrogant (e.g. 3 John 9–10). Maintaining the heart of a disciple is what ensures the true gospel is passed on faithfully from one generation to another (e.g. 2 Timothy 1:5; 2:2).

Discipleship brings great joy as we see our children in the faith becoming mature

I have no greater joy than to hear that my children are walking in the truth.

(3 John 4)

It is only as we are disciples that we can truly be called 'Christians'

The disciples were called Christians first at Antioch.

(Acts 11:26)

Conclusion

Following Jesus on his terms is costly – though not to follow him on his terms is even more costly!

'If anyone would come after me, he must deny himself and take up his cross and follow me. For whoever wants to save his life will lose it, but whoever loses his life for me and for the gospel will save it.'

(Mark 8:34–35

The choice is not whether we as Christians want to be disciples; but rather, whether we will so be disciples that we can be called Christians!

O the bitter shame and sorrow,
That a time could ever be,
When I let the Saviour's pity
Plead in vain, and proudly answered,
'All of self, and none of Thee!'

Yet He found me; I beheld Him
Bleeding on the accursed tree,
Heard Him pray, 'Forgive them, Father!'
And my wistful heart said faintly —
'Some of self, and some of Thee.'

Day by day His tender mercy,
Healing, helping, full, and free,
Sweet and strong, and, ah! so patient,
Brought me lower, while I whispered,
'Less of self, and more of Thee.'

Higher than the highest heavens,
Deeper than the deepest sea,
Lord, Thy love at last hath conquered;
Grant me now my supplication –
'None of self, and all of Thee.'

Theodore Monod, 1836–1921

PART THREE

Growing in the Spirit

CHAPTER ONE

The Promised Spirit

The Holy Spirit, once the preserve of only 'special' people, now comes, just as God promised, in a different way. He comes to all believers as our empowering Counsellor–Friend.

'I will ask the Father, and he will give you another Counsellor to be with you for ever.' (John 14:16)

'Always vote for the man who promises least; that way, you'll be disappointed the least.' So goes a rather cynical (but perhaps fairly accurate!) comment on politics. We are all accustomed to politicians making promises of what they will do if they get into power; and we also know that, generally speaking, we will end up disappointed. But you can never say this about God. What he promises, he does.

In the Old Testament, God made many promises about a new experience of his Spirit for his people; and, unlike our politicians, he did not disappoint us.

In the past

The Holy Spirit has always been active, right from the beginning:

In the beginning God created the heavens and the earth. The earth was barren, with no form of life; it was under a roaring ocean covered with darkness. But the Spirit of God was moving over the water.

(Genesis 1:1–2, CEV)

But the Spirit did not then suddenly disappear until New Testament times! He continued to be at work throughout the Old Testament period.

What did the Spirit do?

Among his many activities in the Old Testament, we see him:
- **Creating** – both at the beginning (Genesis 1:2; Psalm 33:6) and in an ongoing way (Job 33:4; Psalm 104:24–30)
- **Renewing people's hearts** (1 Samuel 10:6, 9; Psalm 51:10–12)
- **Revealing God's truth and will** (Numbers 24:2–4; 2 Samuel 23:2)
- **Anointing and empowering people for leadership** (1 Samuel 16:13)
- **Equipping people with creative skills** (Exodus 31:1–5)

Who did the Spirit empower?

In Old Testament times, the Spirit's empowering of people was generally restricted to leaders. For example:
- elders (e.g. Numbers 11:16–25)
- judges (e.g. Judges 3:7–11; 6:34)
- kings (e.g. 1 Samuel 10:9–10; 16:13)
- priests (e.g. 2 Chronicles 24:20)
- prophets (e.g. Ezekiel 2:2; Micah 3:8)
- other leaders (e.g. 1 Chronicles 12:18)

They were 'set apart' to these roles by having oil poured over them ('being anointed'), symbolic of the Spirit being 'poured out' over their lives (e.g. Exodus 30:30; 1 Samuel 10:1–2).

However, the Spirit generally 'came and went' as needed; and Saul lost his presence through disobedience (1 Samuel 16:14). David was perhaps one of the few to experience a more permanent presence of the Spirit (1 Samuel 16:13 says, 'from that day on the Spirit of the LORD came upon David in power'), and hence his cry to God not to take his Spirit from him (Psalm 51:11).

How was the Spirit seen?

Throughout the Old Testament period, the Spirit was rarely seen as a person, but more as the presence or power of God. This is reflected in the fact that he is hardly ever called the 'Holy Spirit' (emphasizing his relationship with the Holy God). In fact, the term is used just three times, whereas in the New Testament it occurs 91 times and has virtually become his 'name'.

The promise of the Spirit

But God had something far better in mind than a temporary anointing by what was seen as an impersonal power for a select few. He promised a time, linked with the age of the Messiah, when *all* his people, from the greatest to the least, would experience his Spirit in their lives.

The promise made

Anointing for the Messiah

The Old Testament promised that the Messiah would himself be anointed by the Spirit.

The Spirit of the LORD will rest on him – the Spirit of wisdom and of understanding, the Spirit of counsel and of power, the Spirit of knowledge and of the fear of the LORD.

(Isaiah 11:2)

See also Psalm 2:2; Isaiah 42:1; 61:1

It would be at Jesus' baptism that the Spirit would descend on him (Luke 3:22), anointing him for the work ahead (Acts 10:38). In fact, until this anointing, Jesus could do no work for his Father. Only after it could he claim the fulfilment of Isaiah's prophecy, with its implications for each of us:

'The Spirit of the Lord is on me, because he has anointed me to preach good news to the poor. He has sent me to proclaim freedom for the prisoners and recovery of sight for the blind, to release the oppressed, to proclaim the year of the Lord's favour.'

(Luke 4:18–19)

Anointing for God's people
The Old Testament also foresaw how, in the age of the Messiah, the Spirit would be given in a different *way* and in fuller measure.

First, the gift of the Spirit would be a matter of internals, not externals:

'I will give you a new heart and put a new spirit in you; I will remove from you your heart of stone and give you a heart of flesh. And I will put my Spirit in you and move you to follow my decrees and be careful to keep my laws.'

(Ezekiel 36:26–27)

See also Ezekiel 11:19–20; 18:31

Second, the gift of the Spirit would be irrespective of who we were:

'And afterwards, I will pour out my Spirit on all people. Your sons and daughters will prophesy, your old men will dream dreams, your young men will see visions. Even on my servants, both men and women, I will pour out my Spirit in those days.'

(Joel 2:28–29)

See also Acts 2:14–21; 10:44–48

The promise confirmed

Jesus not only experienced the Spirit's presence and power for himself; he confirmed all that the prophets had promised about us experiencing him too.

'Another Counsellor'
Jesus promised his disciples that when he left them, they would not be left alone; 'another Counsellor' would take his place.

'And I will ask the Father, and he will give you another Counsellor to be with you for ever.'

(John 14:16)

See also John 14:26; 15:26; 16:7

Other translations of 'Counsellor' include 'Comforter' (KJV), 'Helper' (NASB, NKJV, NCV), 'Advocate' (NRSV, JB), 'Friend' (*The Message*), 'Someone to stand by you' (J.B. Phillips). Clearly this is a word with many strands of meaning!

An illustration from the Bayeux Tapestry, portraying the Norman invasion of Britain in 1066, might help. In one scene King Harold prods his spear into the backside of a soldier, and underneath it says: 'Harold comforts his troops'. That may seem a strange way of 'comforting'! But what he was doing was saying, 'Go on; you can do it!' And that is exactly what the Holy Spirit does for us. He is there within us saying,

Go on – you can do it! I'm here! I'll help you!'

He is 'the one who comes alongside us to help us' (which is the literal translation of the Greek word for 'counsellor'). We are not left alone! The promised Spirit is here!

The gift of the Father

Jesus also confirmed the promise of the prophets that the Spirit would be given to us as the Father's gift.

'Which of you fathers, if your son asks for a fish, will give him a snake instead? Or if he asks for an egg, will give him a scorpion? If you then, though you are evil, know how to give good gifts to your children, how much more will your Father in heaven give the Holy Spirit to those who ask him!'

(Luke 11:11–13)

'I am going to send you what my Father has promised; but stay in the city until you have been clothed with power from on high.'

(Luke 24:49)

'. . . for God gives the Spirit without limit.'

(John 3:34)

See also John 14:26; 15:26; 16:7

The need for faith

This gift of the Spirit would not be automatic, however; Jesus promised him to all who believe:

'Whoever believes in me, as the Scripture has said, streams of living water will flow from within him.' By this he meant the Spirit, whom those who believed in him were later to receive.

(John 7:38–39)

See also Luke 11:11–13; Acts 2:38

The promise kept

After Jesus' death, resurrection and ascension (John 7:38–39), the way was opened for the promised baptism with the Holy Spirit.

'Wait here to receive the promise from the Father which I told you about. John baptized people with water, but in a few days you will be baptized with the Holy Spirit.'

(Acts 1:4–5, NCV)

See also Matthew 3:11; Luke 24:49; Acts 2:33

At Pentecost it happened! The promised Spirit came, with external signs so that there could be no doubting his arrival:

All of them were filled with the Holy Spirit and began to speak in other tongues as the Spirit enabled them.

(Acts 2:4)

But Pentecost was just the start! This experience was not a 'one-off' for the early church, something to 'get it going'; but rather something open to every individual who believed – Jew and Gentile, man and woman, young and old, near and far.

'The promise is for you and your children and for all who are far off – for all whom the Lord our God will call.'

(Acts 2:39)

See also Acts 8:14–17; 10:44–47; 19:1–6

Who is the Holy Spirit?

In the New Testament, the Holy Spirit is seen, not as an impersonal power, but as the third person of the Trinity.

The Holy Spirit is a person

Throughout the New Testament the Spirit is constantly referred to as 'he', not 'it' (e.g. John 14:17; 15:26; 16:7–8) – even though the Greek word for 'Spirit' is a 'neuter' gender, grammatically requiring the use of 'it'. (In other words, they were so convinced the Spirit was a person that they broke the rules of grammar to make their point!) As a person the Holy Spirit is shown to have thoughts, feelings and will.

What an amazing person the Holy Spirit is! Just look at some of the personal things we find him doing in the New Testament:

- thinking (1 Corinthians 2:11)
- searching things out (1 Corinthians 2:10)
- deciding (1 Corinthians 12:11)
- hearing (John 16:13)
- speaking (Acts 8:29)
- testifying to our sonship (Romans 8:16)
- interceding (Romans 8:26)
- experiencing love (Romans 15:30)
- bearing witness (John 15:26)
- revealing (John 16:14–15)
- teaching (John 14:26)
- restraining (Acts 16:6–7)
- convicting (John 16:7–11)
- guiding (John 16:13)
- leading (Romans 8:14)
- bringing glory to Christ (John 16:14)
- raising the dead (Romans 8:11)
- giving gifts (1 Corinthians 12:7–11)
- helping (Romans 8:26)
- being lied to (Acts 5:3–4)
- being grieved (Ephesians 4:30)
- being tested (Acts 5:9)
- being resisted (Acts 7:51)
- being insulted (Hebrews 10:29)
- being blasphemed against (Matthew 12:31).

Clearly the Holy Spirit is no mere impersonal force – an 'it'. He is a *he*, a person of the Trinity, God at work among us.

The Holy Spirit is God

Not only is the Holy Spirit a person; he is the person of God.

The Spirit is equated with God

Passages referring to the Father in the Old Testament are unashamedly applied to the

131

Spirit in the New. For example, in Acts 28:26–27 Paul ascribes to the Spirit words spoken by the Father (Isaiah 6:9–10).

See also Hebrews 3:7–11, quoting Psalm 95:7–11; Hebrews 10:15–16, quoting Jeremiah 31:33.

The Spirit has the characteristics of God

He is seen as eternal [without beginning or end] (Hebrews 9:14), omnipresent [everywhere all the time] (Psalm 139:7–10), omniscient [knowing everything] (Isaiah 40:13–14; 1 Corinthians 2:10–11), and omnipotent [able to do all he wants to] (1 Corinthians 12:11).

The Spirit does the works of God

He is Creator (Job 33:4); he works miracles (Matthew 12:28; Hebrews 2:4); he gives new birth (John 3:5–6); he gives life to the dead (Romans 8:11); he transforms believers to become more like Jesus (2 Corinthians 3:18); he is the author of Scripture (2 Timothy 3:16; 2 Peter 1:20–21). Only God can do these works of God!

The Spirit receives the honour due to God

Baptism is in his name along with Father and Son (Matthew 28:19); he can be blasphemed against, just as Father God can (Matthew 12:31–32); he is included in Paul's prayer of blessing of the three-in-one God (2 Corinthians 13:14).

He is called God!

If all this were not enough, the Holy Spirit is at times actually called God (Acts 5:3–4; 1 Corinthians 3:16; 2 Corinthians 3:17–18).

Relevance for today

- If the Holy Spirit is God, then I should respect him, respond to him, and receive from him.

Do you not know that your body is a temple of the Holy Spirit, who is in you, whom you have received from God? You are not your own; you were bought at a price. Therefore honour God with your body.

(1 Corinthians 6:19)

See also Romans 8:5–16; 1 Corinthians 3:16–17

- If I am still seeing the Holy Spirit more as a power than a person, I am living under the old covenant rather than the new!
- If the Holy Spirit is a person, then I should be careful not to treat him like a 'commodity' or a 'thing' to be used at my command.

When Simon saw that the Spirit was given at the laying on of the apostles' hands, he offered them money and said, 'Give me also this ability so that everyone on whom I lay my hands may receive the Holy Spirit.' Peter answered: 'May your money perish with you, because you thought you could buy the gift of God with money! You have no part or share in this ministry, because your heart is not right before God.'

(Acts 8:18–21)

- If God has promised his Spirit to us, then I need to ensure that I have received what he promised. The saints of the Old Testament longed for what we have, but did not receive it.

These were all commended for their faith, yet none of them received what had been promised. God had planned something better for us so that only together with us would they be made perfect.

(Hebrews 11:39–40)

How foolish of us, therefore, if we miss out on the new covenant experience of the Spirit that God had promised, or if we revert to trying to do God's will by our own effort (Galatians 3:1–5).

- If Jesus, the Messiah, needed the promised empowering of the Spirit, how much more do we.

'You know the message God sent to the people of Israel, telling the good news of peace through Jesus Christ, who is Lord of all. You know what has happened throughout Judea, beginning in Galilee after the baptism that John preached – how God anointed Jesus of Nazareth with the Holy Spirit and power, and how he went around doing good and healing all who were under the power of the devil, because God was with him.'

(Acts 10:36–38)

As for you, the anointing you received from him remains in you . . .

(1 John 2:27)

- If baptism in the Holy Spirit is the promise of Jesus for us, I should ensure I have received him in this way.

'Repent and be baptised, every one of you, in the name of Jesus Christ for the forgiveness of your sins. And you will receive the gift of the Holy Spirit. The promise is for you and your children and for all who are far off – for all whom the Lord our God will call.'

(Acts 2:38–39)

While Apollos was at Corinth, Paul took the road through the interior and arrived at Ephesus. There he found some disciples and asked them, 'Did you receive the Holy Spirit when you believed?' They answered, 'No, we have not even heard that there is a Holy Spirit.' So Paul asked, 'Then what baptism did you receive?' 'John's baptism,' they replied. Paul said, 'John's baptism was a baptism of repentance. He told the people to believe in the one coming after him, that is, in Jesus.' On hearing this, they were baptised into the name of the Lord Jesus. When Paul placed his hands on them, the Holy Spirit came on them, and they spoke in tongues and prophesied.

(Acts 19:1–6)

- The promised Holy Spirit is God's promise of yet more to come.

Now it is God who makes both us and you stand firm in Christ. He anointed us, set his seal of ownership on us, and put his Spirit in our hearts as a deposit, guaranteeing what is to come.

(2 Corinthians 1:21–22)

Come down, O Love divine,
Seek Thou this soul of mine,
And visit it with Thine own ardour glowing;
O Comforter, draw near,
Within my heart appear,
And kindle it, Thy holy flame bestowing.

O let it freely burn,
Till earthly passions turn
To dust and ashes, in its heat consuming;
And let Thy glorious light
Shine ever on my sight,
And clothe me round, the while my path
  illuming.

Let holy charity
Mine outward vesture be.
And lowliness become mine inner clothing;
True lowliness of heart,
Which takes the humbler part,
And o'er its own shortcomings weeps with
  loathing.

And so the yearning strong,
With which the soul will long,
Shall far outpass the power of human telling;
For none can guess its grace,
Till he become the place
Wherein the Holy Spirit makes His dwelling.

Bianco da Siena, c. 1350–1434
translated by Richard Frederick Littledale,
1833–90

Conclusion

The Holy Spirit is to us *now* what Jesus was to his disciples *then*. In having the Holy Spirit, we have Christ himself.

'And I will put my Spirit in you . . .'
(Ezekiel 36:27)

CHAPTER TWO

The Activity of the Spirit

The Spirit constantly points us to Jesus and helps us live more like he did.

. . . The Spirit of Jesus . . . (Acts 16:7)

In the early church, leaders spent centuries debating hotly the person of Christ and the Holy Spirit. Christ received all their attention initially, the Spirit having a mere 'And (I believe) in the Holy Spirit' in the creeds. (Not very much for the third Person of the Trinity!) As their attention gradually turned to him, arguments raged about whether he proceeded *from* the Father *with* the Son, or *from* the Father *and* the Son. To us, it rather seems an argument about nothing doesn't it?

While we might not argue over such theological details today, the Spirit can still be a source of disagreement (if not contention) amongst Christians. What is important is not only good theology but also good practice. For the Spirit was given, not to be a source of doctrine, but a source of life.

Remember who he is!

As writers, we come from different church backgrounds. Mike pastors a church where more 'overt' manifestations of the Spirit are not unusual and so feels at ease with them; Martin confesses to being more cautious at times about some aspects of the Spirit's work and can identify with a friend who when he became a Christian once described some of the Spirit's manifestations as 'weird'. The truth is, there are some of us who are rather afraid of the Spirit's work, while others 'take it in their stride'.

So, how can those fears be allayed? By remembering who the Spirit is!

The Spirit of Jesus

As we saw in the last chapter, the Spirit is personal. This means he is also relational. That is why he is called 'the Spirit of Jesus' (Acts 16:7) or 'the Spirit of Christ' (Romans 8:9). The relationship between Spirit and Saviour is so intimate that the Spirit's work can barely be separated from Christ's work. 'Remember that the Spirit is the Spirit of Jesus, who is gentle and loving and wants the very best for our lives' (Michael Green). If this is the case, then why should we be afraid?

If the Spirit is the Spirit of Jesus, then we have nothing to fear from him!

The Spirit of truth

Jesus described the Spirit as 'the Spirit of truth' (John 14:17; 15:26) and the apostle John underlined this (1 John 4:6; 5:6). He is truth in person, leading God's people into that truth.

'But when he, the Spirit of truth, comes, he will guide you into all truth.'

(John 16:13)

See also John 14:26; 1 Corinthians 2:12–13

This truth is not just about right doctrine, however, important as that is; it is also truth in terms of right living. There is little that rings 'true' if we 'stand up for truth' but are arrogant and ungracious in doing so, or preach holiness but live in secret sin.

Do I want to stand up for truth in the world? Then I will look to the Spirit to lead me, just as Paul did (Acts 13:8–12). Do I want to live out the truth? Then I will obey the Scriptures the Spirit inspired (2 Timothy 3:16–17) and respond to his promptings (e.g. Acts 8:26–29; 16:6). Do I want to worship in truth? Then I will follow the Spirit's leadings (John 4:23–24; 1

Corinthians 12:7–11; 14:26). Remember: truth is for living, not just learning!

If the Spirit is the Spirit of truth, then we have nothing to fear from him!

The Spirit of sonship

The Holy Spirit who lives in us (Romans 8:9) reminds us that we really are God's children.

For you did not receive a spirit that makes you a slave again to fear, but you received the Spirit of sonship. And by him we cry, 'Abba, Father.' The Spirit himself testifies with our spirit that we are God's children.

(Romans 8:15–16)

Since you are God's children, God sent the Spirit of his Son into your hearts, and the Spirit cries out, 'Father.' So now you are not a slave; you are God's child, and God will give you the blessing he promised, because you are his child.

(Galatians 4:6–7, NCV)

Think of how children sometimes say to one another, 'My dad is bigger than yours!' – meaning, 'I'm not scared of you!' That's what the Holy Spirit does when we are afraid or in difficulties. He says, 'Remember who your Dad is!' Paul reminded Timothy that the Holy Spirit is not 'a spirit of timidity, but a spirit of power, of love and of self-discipline' (2 Timothy 1:7). The Spirit urges us to 'be strong in the Lord and in his mighty power' (Ephesians 6:10) by reminding us who we are in Christ and what resources we can call upon.

If the Spirit is the Spirit of sonship, then we have nothing to fear from him!

As Bruce Milne writes in *Know the Truth*, 'Alarm at an authentic ministry of the Spirit needs the reassurance the disciples received hen they saw Jesus walking on the Sea of Galilee and cried out for fear it was a ghost, "Take courage! It is I. Don't be afraid".' (Matthew 14:27).

The work of the Spirit

The main focus of the Spirit's work is to 'point to Jesus'.

'He will bring glory to me [Jesus] by taking from what is mine and making it known to you.'
(John 16:14)

Jim Packer calls this 'a floodlight ministry'. Floodlights are positioned, not to draw attention to themselves, but to the building or football pitch they are directed to. So it is with the Spirit: he is, as it were, the hidden floodlight shining onto Jesus. His role is completely self-effacing. How, then, does he do this?

The Spirit convicts of sin

One of the first things he does is to bring home to people the reality of their sin and what it means to reject Jesus.

'When he comes, he will convict the world of guilt in regard to sin and righteousness and judgment: in regard to sin, because men do not believe in me; in regard to righteousness, because I am going to the Father, where you can see me no longer; and in regard to judgment, because the prince of this world now stands condemned.'

(John 16:8–11)

See also Acts 2:37; 24:25

The Spirit gives new birth

Having convicted us of our sin, the Spirit then helps us understand and believe what Jesus did for us in dying on the cross in our place. As we do so, he brings about a 'new birth' within us. (See Part 2, Chapter 3.)

Jesus answered, 'I tell you the truth, no-one can enter the kingdom of God unless he is born of water and the Spirit. Flesh gives birth to flesh, but the Spirit gives birth to spirit.'
(John 3:5–6)

But when the kindness and love of God our Saviour appeared, he saved us, not because of righteous things we had done, but because of his mercy. He saved us through the washing of rebirth and renewal by the Holy Spirit, whom he poured out on us generously through Jesus Christ our Saviour, so that, having been justified by his grace, we might become heirs having the hope of eternal life.

(Titus 3:4–7)

The Spirit lives within us

Having brought about the new birth in us, the Spirit then remains permanently within us, making the presence of Jesus real to us.

'You know Him, for He dwells with you and will be in you. I will not leave you as orphans; I will come to you.'

(John 14:17–18, NKJV)

See also Acts 2:38–39; Romans 8:9; 1 Corinthians 6:19

The Spirit 'seals' us

When we believe, we become 'marked people', spiritually speaking.

Having believed, you were marked in him with a seal, the promised Holy Spirit, who is a deposit guaranteeing our inheritance until the redemption of those who are God's possession – to the praise of his glory.

(Ephesians 1:13–14)

And do not grieve the Holy Spirit of God, with whom you were sealed for the day of redemption.

(Ephesians 4:30)

The Holy Spirit identifies us as God's own, genuine people, just as a wax seal marked an ancient document as genuine. His Spirit is the certain, secure deposit of our future inheritance (2 Corinthians 1:21–22).

The Spirit makes Christ's resurrection life real to us

He applies the effects of Christ's death, resurrection and present life to us. Why not take a few minutes to read through Romans 8 and see how exciting this is!

The Spirit inspires and interprets the Scriptures

The Holy Spirit is the one who inspired the Scriptures which help us see Jesus.

He inspired the writers

Above all, you must understand that no prophecy of Scripture came about by the prophet's own interpretation. For prophecy never had its origin in the will of man, but men spoke from God as they were carried along by the Holy Spirit.

(2 Peter 1:20–21)

The word used for 'carried along' was used of a ship carried along on the sea by the wind. That is how the Scriptures were written; the writers, as it were, 'hoisted their sails' to the Holy Spirit, and were 'carried along' by him, so that what they wrote was exactly what he wanted written.

He inspired the writings

All Scripture is God-breathed and is useful for teaching, rebuking, correcting and training in righteousness, so that the man of God may be thoroughly equipped for every good work.

(2 Timothy 3:16–17)

The words of Scripture are the very 'breath' of God, timeless truth caught in time by the inspiring work of the Holy Spirit. All the Scriptures, whether Old or New Testaments, point us towards Jesus (e.g. Luke 24:27; 1 Peter 1:10–12).

He inspires the readers

Without the Spirit's help, the Bible remains a 'closed book'; a fascinating but not very relevant piece of ancient literature. With the Spirit's help, however, the Bible comes alive to us, revealing God's heart, purposes and ways.

The Spirit searches all things, even the deep things of God. For who among men knows the thoughts of a man except the man's spirit within him? In the same way no-one knows the thoughts of God except the Spirit of God. We have not received the spirit of the world but the Spirit who is from God, that we may understand what God has freely given us.

(1 Corinthians 2:10–12)

The Holy Spirit's baptism

'For John baptised with water, but in a few days you will be baptised with the Holy Spirit.'

(Acts 1:5)

Jesus clearly expected believers to be baptized with (or 'in' or 'by') the Holy Spirit; but different Christians have different understandings of this. For some, Spirit baptism is an aspect of what it means to become a Christian; for others, it is a distinct experience after becoming a Christian.

Of the seven references in the New Testament to being 'baptized with the Holy Spirit', six (Matthew 3:11; Mark 1:8; Luke 3:16; John 1:33; Acts 1:5; 11:16) contrast John the Baptist's preparatory ministry (baptizing with water) with Jesus' ministry (baptizing with the Spirit). The seventh (1 Corinthians 12:13) describes the unity of the experience of the Spirit for all believers who are 'baptised by one Spirit into one body'. This suggests that

139

'baptism with the Spirit' is, at heart, an aspect of what it means to become a Christian.

But while this 'baptism' experience was expected to be the norm, whenever there was any lack in understanding or experience of it, the apostles took steps to rectify the situation immediately (e.g. Acts 8:14–17; 19:1–7), so that a 'baptism' was exactly what people experienced. Jesus does not want us to just believe in baptism with the Spirit; he wants us to experience it!

Peter's sermon on the Day of Pentecost holds a helpful key. When asked by his hearers what they must do to be saved, he replied:

'Repent and be baptised every one of you, in the name of Jesus Christ for the forgiveness of your sins. And you will receive the gift of the Holy Spirit.'

(Acts 2:38)

Peter outlines in his reply four things that make a Christian: repentance, baptism, assurance of forgiveness and receiving the Spirit. These four things are like four strands of a rope. While the strands can be separated, the rope is simply not a rope unless they are bound together. So it is for us in Christ. All four aspects of Christian initiation are needed. But if, for whatever reason, any is lacking, the most obvious thing is to get it in place quickly. We become aware that we have not repented? Let us do so right now! We have not been baptized in water? Let us get baptized! We are lacking assurance? Let us seek it! We are aware the Spirit's presence is not a reality? Let us receive him!

Be filled with the Spirit!

While there may be differing views about 'baptism in the Spirit', there can be no uncertainty concerning the Bible's instruction to us to be filled with the Spirit.

Do not get drunk on wine, which leads to debauchery. Instead, be filled with the Spirit.
(Ephesians 5:18)

Note that this is:

a personal command
This is not a command to 'the church' in a general way; it is a command to each one of us personally. And if it is a command, then we are not to sit around waiting for something to happen; there must be something we can do about it!

a plural command
In American English, Paul's wording would be: 'You *all* be filled with the Spirit.' It's up to all of us! Just think what could happen if we really had Spirit-filled churches!

a passive command
'Being filled' is something 'done to us' rather than our 'doing something'. We are commanded to seek it; but we cannot 'work it up' or 'make it happen'. Our part is to allow the Holy Spirit to fill us, by being clean, obedient and available (2 Timothy 2:20–22).

a progressive command
This is not something that just happens once; it is ongoing. It can, and should, happen again and again. The Greek literally means: 'be *continually* filled'; '*go on* being filled'. It is not a one-off event that we can look back on with contentment (or pride!). It certainly was not a one-off event in New Testament times (see Luke 1:15, 41, 67; 4:1; Acts 2:4; 4:8, 31; 6:3; 7:55; 9:17; 13:9, 52). We too need to go on and on being filled with God himself!

Being filled with the Spirit will affect the way we live, as he becomes the main influencer in our lives. Sometimes, there may be dramatic signs of his presence (e.g. Acts 2:2–4; 4:31; 10:45–46; 19:6); but always there will be a change of lifestyle (e.g. Acts 2:44–45; 13:52; Ephesians 4:30–32).

Relevance for today

Do not fear the Spirit's work

If the Spirit is 'the Spirit of Jesus' (Acts 16:7), then we have no cause to fear him or his work. Past experiences, or 'horror stories' from others, should not lead us to 'quench the Holy Spirit' (1 Thessalonians 5:19, NASB) or to 'grieve the Holy Spirit of God' (Ephesians 4:30) by our unresponsiveness.

The priority is 'filling' not 'fighting'

The urgent priority for us all is to be 'filled with the Spirit' (Ephesians 5:18), not to argue with one another about words (Titus 3:9).

Truth for the way we live

The Spirit is given, not just to lead us into truth about doctrine, but into truth in the way we live

'I have much more to say to you, more than you can now bear. But when he, the Spirit of truth, comes, he will guide you into all truth. He will not speak on his own; he will speak only what he hears, and he will tell you what is yet to come.'

(John 16:12-13)

The Spirit is the truth.

(1 John 5:6)

See also John 4:23; Ephesians 4:25; Philippians 4:8

Do not be afraid if the Spirit does 'strange things'

We do not need to be afraid if the Spirit sometimes does 'strange things'. By and large, we are traditionally very 'cerebral' in the West; everything has to be understood before we can accept it. This can make us very sceptical, if not cynical, about 'unusual happenings'. Yet the Spirit often did 'strange things' in the New Testament church: he came as wind and fire (Acts 2:2–3); he shook rooms (Acts 4:31); he did miracles (Acts 8:6–8); he suddenly moved individuals from where they were (Acts 8:39–40); he gave strange visions (Acts 10:9–16); he rescued people from prison (Acts 12:5–10; 16:25–34); he gave gifts of tongues and prophecy (Acts 19:6). If we exclude such things today, or if we are fearful when they do happen, we will be in danger of missing what the Spirit may want to do among us.

Spirit-filled churches

The command is to be Spirit-filled churches, not just Spirit-filled individuals. The challenge for each of us is: Is my own church responding to this?

141

Breathe on me, Breath of God;
Fill me with life anew,
That I may love what Thou dost love,
And do what Thou wouldst do.

Breathe on me, Breath of God,
Until my heart is pure,
Until with Thee I will one will,
To do and to endure.

Breathe on me, Breath of God,
Till I am wholly Thine,
Until this earthly part of me
Glows with Thy fire divine.

Breathe on me, Breath of God;
So shall I never die,
But live with Thee the perfect life
Of Thine eternity.

Edwin Hatch, 1835–89

Conclusion

No matter how we understand our first receiving of the Holy Spirit, what is vital is that we do not neglect his continuing work in our lives. The challenge to us is: do we really know the Spirit's activity in our lives today?

'He will bring glory to me.'

(John 16:14)

CHAPTER THREE

The Help of the Spirit

As Christians we are completely dependent on the Holy Spirit to help us live the Christian life.

For you did not receive a spirit that makes you a slave again to fear, but you received the Spirit of sonship. (Romans 8:15)

'Can I help you?' How many times has someone asked you that and you have answered, 'Oh no, that's fine! I can manage by myself, thank you!' or, 'I don't want to trouble you.' However we might dress this up, it all comes down to being independent!

The trouble is, we give those answers to God at times! The Holy Spirit comes to help us and we say (by action if not by word), 'I can manage, thanks!' But we cannot answer God like that, and be a real Christian! Christians are those who know they need God's help through the Spirit to live their life in Christ, who know they need his help not only to get in to the kingdom, but to get on in the kingdom.

The Spirit helps us to know

The Holy Spirit wants to help us know – with 100 per cent certainty! – that we are God's children who know they can 'draw near to God with a sincere heart in full assurance of faith' (Hebrews 10:22).

But isn't this rather presumptuous to say that we are God's children, that we know him and that we are confident of going to heaven? The Bible says 'No!' Being sure of our faith ('assurance') is the right of every child of God, and comes through a combination of the Spirit (Romans 8:16) and the Scriptures (John 20:30–31; 1 John 5:13).

The Spirit himself testifies with our spirit that we are God's children.

(Romans 8:16)

How does the Spirit do this? John gives us some answers in his first letter (1 John). He says: Here is how you can know. Ask yourself these questions:

Do you love God and his commandments?
If you do, you will be making an honest attempt to keep those commandments.

We know that we have come to know him if we obey his commands. The man who says, 'I know him,' but does not do what he commands is a liar, and the truth is not in him. But if anyone obeys his word, God's love is truly made complete in him.

(1 John 2:3–5)

This is love for God: to obey his commands. And his commands are not burdensome.

(1 John 5:3–4)

See also John 14:15; Titus 1:16

As we saw in Part 2, Chapter 5, it is not about being sinless (1 John 1:8–10), but about

recognizing that we cannot go on sinning (1 John 3:6) or go on sinning carelessly (1 John 3:9). Just having this desire to be free of sin is, in itself, a sign of the Spirit working in us. It means God really is with us, or we wouldn't be worried about it!

Do you love other Christians?

We know that we have passed from death to life, because we love our brothers.

(1 John 3:14)

And this is his command: to believe in the name of his Son, Jesus Christ, and to love one another as he commanded us.

(1 John 3:23)

Believing in Jesus and loving our spiritual brothers and sisters go together, John says. But why on earth would you love them unless God had done something in your life? The very fact you love them shows that you are indeed 'children of God' (1 John 3:1, 10, 14), part of the same big family (Ephesians 3:14–15; Hebrews 2:11).

Do you believe the truth about Jesus?

This is how you can recognise the Spirit of God: Every spirit that acknowledges that Jesus Christ has come in the flesh is from God, but every spirit that does not acknowledge Jesus is not from God. This is the spirit of the antichrist, which you have heard is coming and even now is already in the world. You, dear children, are from God and have overcome them, because the one who is in you is greater than the one who is in the world.

(1 John 4:2–4)

If anyone acknowledges that Jesus is the Son of God, God lives in him and he in God. And so we know and rely on the love God has for us.

(1 John 4:15–16)

Do you believe, John asks, that Jesus is indeed the Son of God, come among us as a man? Why on earth would you believe that unless the Spirit had done something in your heart?

See also 1 Corinthians 12:3; 1 John 2:23; 5:1, 13

Do you know the Spirit has been at work in you?

And this is how we know that he lives in us: We know it by the Spirit he gave us.

(1 John 3:24)

We know that we live in him and he in us, because he has given us of his Spirit.

(1 John 4:13)

Just look back over your life as a Christian and see how the Spirit has changed you, helped you, filled you. This is his work within (Romans 5:5; 8:16; Galatians 4:6). It is all a sign that you are truly his!

So, how do you respond to these questions of John's? If we can answer 'Yes!' to them, then we can 'know that we have come to know him' (1 John 2:3), we can be sure we have eternal life (1 John 3:14), and that we are indeed being led by the Spirit of God. Paul put it this way:

Those who are led by the Spirit of God are sons of God.

(Romans 8:14)

Whenever we have doubts about our faith (as most of us do at times), it is important to rely, not on our feelings at that moment, but on what we *know*. That is what John does in this letter, and is why he can exclaim:

How great is the love the Father has lavished on us, that we should be called children of God! And that is what we are!

(1 John 3:1)

God really wants us to be sure of our relationship with him, and the Holy Spirit is his gift to us to help us know with certainty that we belong to him. Let's not let the devil rob us of that promise!

The Spirit helps us to understand

Do you ever find there are things you don't understand – in the Bible or in life? Or about how God works or what he is doing? We confess we do! But that is when we can call on the Spirit whose role it is to help us understand.

'When he, the Spirit of truth, comes, he will guide you into all truth. He will not speak on his own; he will speak only what he hears, and he will tell you what is yet to come. He will bring glory to me by taking from what is mine and making it known to you.'

(John 16:13–14)

'What is mine'

What did Jesus mean by 'what is mine'? J. I. Packer explains it like this: 'He must have meant, at least, "everything that is real and true about me as God incarnate, as the Father's agent in creation, providence and grace, as this world's rightful lord, and as the one who actually is master of it whether men acknowledge me or not." But surely he also meant, "all that is real and true about me as your divine lover, your mediator, your surety in the new covenant, your prophet, priest and king, your Saviour from the guilt and power of sin and from the world's corruptions and the devil's clutches; and all that is true of me as your shepherd, husband, and friend, your life and your hope, the author and finisher of your faith, the lord of your own personal history, and the one who will some day bring you to be with me and share my glory, who am thus both your path and your prize." '

'Making it known to you'

To whom was Jesus referring when he said that the Spirit would 'make it known to you' (v 16)? Obviously, his disciples who were listening. But it was to us too. The same Spirit who inspired some of them to *write* the Scriptures (2 Timothy 3:16; 2 Peter 1:21) is the one who inspires us to *understand* them. We have probably all known times, when reading the Bible, when a truth suddenly leapt out and dawned on us in a fresh way. That is the work of the Spirit. And he wants us to keep asking him to help in this way.

'He will guide you into all truth'

But it is not just through Scripture that God reveals truth and brings guidance; nor is his revelation confined to doctrine. The Holy Spirit also gives special gifts to bring truth into specific situations. Some 'spiritual gifts' operate in this way. For example,

'words of wisdom' (1 Corinthians 12:8)
Through 'words of wisdom' the Spirit brings God's way of resolving a difficult problem or crisis that lies beyond our ordinary ability to 'work out a solution'.

See e.g. Matthew 22:18–21; Luke 21:15; Acts 15:19–21; Ephesians 1:17; James 1:5

'words of knowledge' (1 Corinthians 12:8)
A word of knowledge is the Spirit's revelation of something to someone that they could not possibly have known by any human means.

See e.g. Matthew 9:4; John 4:16–18; Acts 5:3–4

'prophecy' (1 Corinthians 12:10)
Prophecy is the Spirit's inspiring of people to bring a direct word from God, as he lays God's thoughts on their heart. While some New Testament prophecy concerned revealing the future (e.g. Acts 11:27–30; 21:10–14), it was more usually for 'strengthening, encouragement and comfort' (1 Corinthians 14:3). Prophecy is always to be weighed when it is given (1 Corinthians 14:29).

See Acts 2:18; 11:27–28; Romans 12:6; 1 Corinthians 14:1; 1 Thessalonians 5:19–21

Through gifts such as these the Spirit can bring us into more understanding of what is the Father's heart and purpose in any situation, or bring specific guidance in times of need. That is why Paul wrote:

Follow the way of love and eagerly desire spiritual gifts, especially the gift of prophecy.
(1 Corinthians 14:1)

The Spirit helps us to pray

Prayer is not instinctive to us, for we learn to get by in life without asking for help. Even when we do pray, we want instant answers and certainly do not want to hang around in God's presence too long – just in case he shows us a thing or two! Little wonder Paul recognized our human 'weakness' when it comes to prayer (Romans 8:26–27)! But the Holy Spirit is part of God's answer to this.

Praying 'in the Spirit'

Paul tells us to 'pray in the Spirit' (Ephesians 6:18). That is because we can't do it on our own; we need his help. Praying in the Spirit means letting the Spirit show us what to pray for, how to pray, when to pray; he is ready to do this, if only we ask him! For some, praying in tongues is one aspect of praying in the Spirit.

For if I pray in a tongue, my spirit prays, but my mind is unfruitful. So what shall I do? I will pray with my spirit, but I will also pray with my mind; I will sing with my spirit, but I will also sing with my mind.
(1 Corinthians 14:14–15)

And pray in the Spirit on all occasions with all kinds of prayers and requests.

(Ephesians 6:18)

In the same way, the Spirit helps us in our weakness. We do not know what we ought to pray for, but the Spirit himself intercedes for us with groans that words cannot express. And he who searches our hearts knows the mind of the Spirit, because the Spirit intercedes for the saints in accordance with God's will.

(Romans 8:26–27)

The Spirit answers all who listen

Often we do not hear anything from God because we do not stop and listen. But when we do, the Spirit will often put a word from God into our minds. Paul expected to hear from God in his praying (2 Corinthians 12:8–10); the church leaders at Antioch heard the Spirit speaking during a time of prayer (Acts 13:2); it was after a night of prayer that Jesus knew whom to choose as his disciples (Luke 6:12–13). We too need to learn to listen to the whispers of the Spirit.

See also 1 Kings 19:12–13; Acts 10:30–33; Hebrews 5:7

But you, dear friends, build yourselves up in your most holy faith and pray in the Holy Spirit.

(Jude 20)

The Spirit intercedes with us and for us

When we are praying it is good to remember that the Holy Spirit is right alongside, praying with us, prompting us, helping us to keep going when it is difficult or, as with the disciples in Gethsemane, when our 'spirit is willing, but the body is weak' (Mark 14:38). And not only does he help us to pray, he actually prays for us too, just as Jesus does (Romans 8:34; Hebrews 7:25). Since the Spirit knows the Father's heart so well, his praying is always right on target! Remember, and claim, this promise when next you are struggling.
.

The Spirit helps us to witness

'Do not worry about what to say or how to say it. At that time you will be given what to say, for it will not be you speaking, but the Spirit of your Father speaking through you.'

(Matthew 10:19–20)

'But you will receive power when the Holy Spirit comes on you; and you will be my witnesses in Jerusalem, and in all Judea and Samaria, and to the ends of the earth.'

(Acts 1:8)

See also Luke 24:48–49; Acts 2:11; 4:8–13; 5:27–32

cause anyone to stumble, whether Jews, Greeks or the church of God – even as I try to please everybody in every way. For I am not seeking my own good but the good of many, so that they may be saved.

(1 Corinthians 10:31–33)

See also Matthew 5:13–16; 1 Corinthians 6:1–20; Ephesians 4:17–24

Acts of kindness

Let us not become weary in doing good, for at the proper time we will reap a harvest if we do not give up.

(Galatians 6:9)

See also Matthew 5:16; Acts 4:9; 9:36; 10:38

Be ready to pray for people

'It is Jesus' name and the faith that comes through him that has given this complete healing to him, as you can all see.'

(Acts 3:16)

Another major feature of the Spirit's work is to help us in our witnessing to Jesus. If we are constantly being 'filled' but are never 'flowing', there is something wrong. The 'streams of living water' that Jesus promised (John 7:38) are meant to flow out of us, not stagnate within us!

Not all of us are 'evangelists'; but all of us can, and should, be 'witnesses'. We are asked to do a number of things.

Tell what we know

'For we cannot help speaking about what we have seen and heard.'

(Acts 4:20)

See also Luke 7:16–17; 8:38–39; John 9:25

Live differently from those around us

So whether you eat or drink or whatever you do, do it all for the glory of God. Do not

Many opportunities for sharing the gospel in the New Testament came as a direct result of praying for others to be healed or set free. They did not ask them to become Christians first; they simply prayed for them and left the Spirit to do the rest. Such miracles can break people's 'mind-set' on what they think about God, or whether they even believe in him!

See also e.g. Mark 16:20; Acts 3:1–16; 8:5–8; 14:8–20; 19:11–12; 28:1–10

Explain the gospel when asked

'We tell you the good news: What God promised our fathers he has fulfilled for us, their children, by raising up Jesus.'

(Acts 13:32–33)

See also Acts 8:26–35; 13:14–43; 17:1–4, 19–34; Colossians 4:6; 1 Peter 3:15–16

Relevance for today

The Spirit is still here to help us

Because the Spirit is 'the eternal Spirit' (Hebrews 9:14), he is still with us today. He did not stop working two thousand years ago! Paul encourages us to draw on 'the help of the Holy Spirit who lives in us' (2 Timothy 1:14) and 'the help given by the Spirit of Jesus Christ' (Philippians 1:19).

The Spirit still helps us to be sure

I write these things to you who believe in the name of the Son of God so that you may know that you have eternal life.

(1 John 5:13)

God wants us to be 100 per cent certain that we are his children (1 John 3:1–2; 5:2) and that we have eternal life. If we do not have this assurance, the Spirit wants to help us understand what Jesus has done to make this possible. The Spirit is God's '*deposit,* guaranteeing what is to come' (2 Corinthians 1:22).

The Spirit still ministers life through the word

The Bible may be an ancient book, but it is 'living and active' (Hebrews 4:12), revealing the Father's heart and truth, and is 'the sword of the Spirit' (Ephesians 6:17) that can be used in battle. Whenever we feel down, depressed or discouraged, we should not let our feelings have the last word, but rather focus on the Spirit's truth through God's word. As we read the word, the Spirit ministers its life to us.

The Spirit is a Counsellor not a creed

The Spirit is not a doctrine to be discussed, but a person to be known. He does not want us to restrict him to just an intellectual level of faith; his work is far more dynamic than that! Do I respond to him in this way?

We can still 'hoist our sails' to the Spirit

Just as the writers of Scripture 'hoisted their sails' to the Spirit (see page 136), so we can do the same whenever we need his help or inspiration. All we need to do is to ask!

Pause for thought:

Am I too proud to ask for help? For *his* help?

Father of everlasting grace,
Thy goodness and Thy truth we praise,
Thy goodness and Thy truth we prove;
Thou hast, in honour of Thy Son.
The gift unspeakable sent down,
The Spirit of life, and power, and love.

Send us the Spirit of Thy Son,
To make the depths of Godhead known,
To make us share the life divine;
Send Him the sprinkled blood to apply,
Send Him our souls to sanctify,
And show and seal us ever Thine.

So shall we pray, and never cease,
So shall we thankfully confess
Thy wisdom, truth, and power, and love;
With joy unspeakable adore,
And bless and praise Thee evermore,
And serve Thee as Thy hosts above:

Till, added to that heavenly choir,
We raise our songs of triumph higher,
And praise Thee in a bolder strain,
Out-soar the first-born seraph's flight,
And sing, with all our friends in light,
Thy everlasting love to man.

Charles Wesley, 1707–88

Conclusion

We should not resist the help of the Spirit. It is he who encourages us to be confident, yet humble, in our walk with God and who helps us in every circumstance of life.

The Spirit helps us in our weakness

(Romans 8:26)

CHAPTER FOUR

Becoming Like Jesus

The Holy Spirit wants to make us 'holy' – becoming more like Jesus and showing the love and grace of God to those around.

Christ loved the church and gave himself up for her to make her holy. (Ephesians 5:25)

All of us have heard children saying, 'When I grow up, I want to be a . . .'. Mike wanted to be a train driver and a teacher (achieving the latter but never the former!); Martin wanted to write dictionaries (and certainly achieved that). Whether we become what we imagined or not, such desires are part of the process of growing up.

In the heart of every Christian should be a desire to grow up (1 Peter 2:2), not into our own plans and ambitions, but into becoming like Jesus. The Holy Spirit is the One who helps us to do this.

Happiness and holiness

One of the greatest priorities of people in the West is *happiness;* but God's priority for us is *holiness.* Some 1,500 Bible verses concern holiness, and the words 'holy' or 'holiness' occur some 550 to 600 times (depending on the translation used). This in itself should tell us that holiness is important to God. At first sight, holiness and happiness might seem the very opposite of one another. Yet if we see holiness as 'becoming like Jesus', we will understand that it is when we are at our holiest that we are also at our happiest.

151

The priority of holiness

We have already seen (Part 1, Chapter Two), that God is holy. It should not surprise us, then, to find that he wants us to share that holiness too.

Christ loved the church and gave himself up for her to make her holy, cleansing her by the washing with water through the word, and to present her to himself as a radiant church, without stain or wrinkle or any other blemish, but holy and blameless.

(Ephesians 5:25–27)

From this passage we can note several things:

How he called us

'He gave himself up for her' (v 25). This was the only thing that could make the church clean – Jesus offering himself as a sacrifice for our sins on the cross. He has given everything to call us!

See also Colossians 1:22; Hebrews 10:10; 13:12

What he called us to be

Christ called the church 'to make her holy' (v 26) and 'holy and blameless' (v 27), making provision for our 'washing' through the word of God.

See also John 15:3; 17:17

Why he called us

Christ called us because he wants a beautiful bride, 'without stain or wrinkle or any other blemish' (v 27).

See also 2 Corinthians 11:2; Revelation 19:7–8; 21:2

Holiness then is the very aim of our calling (or election). That is why it is God's fundamental requirement of us:

It is God's will that you should be sanctified.

(1 Thessalonians 4:3)

Just as he who called you is holy, so be holy in all you do; for it is written: 'Be holy, because I am holy.'

(1 Peter 1:15–16, quoting Leviticus 11:44–45)

See also Romans 12:1; 1 Corinthians 1:2; 6:19–20; 2 Timothy 1:9

The problem starts when we see holiness as 'yet another demand' on our already-busy lives. Seen that way, we will never achieve holiness! God wants holiness to become part of our daily lives, just as it was with Israel under the old covenant, where no aspect of life was unaffected by it. Glancing through Leviticus and Deuteronomy we see that holiness covered not just 'religious matters' such as sacrifices, but hygiene, work, care of livestock, relationships etc. When seen as something positive like this – living life differently with God – holiness becomes much more exciting!

And just look at Jesus. No holier a man ever lived; there was not a trace of sin in him (e.g. John 8:46; 2 Corinthians 5:21; 1 Peter 2:22; 1 John 3:5); and yet he lived life to the full and enjoyed it. Surely this must tell us something about holiness.

The way of holiness

So, holiness is God's heart for us, and Jesus modelled it in his life; but how do we get there? Well, the amazing thing is: so much of it depends on him, not us!

Christ's union with us

Transferred

Just as football players are transferred from one team to another, so a similar thing has happened to us. When we became Christians, we were transferred from one kingdom to another:

For He rescued us from the domain of darkness, and transferred us to the kingdom of His beloved Son.

(Colossians 1:13, NASB)

See also Acts 26:17–18; Ephesians 2:1–5

We have now been 'separated' from what we used to be part of and 'set apart' ('sanctified') for Christ. Our daily growing in holiness ('sanctification') now works out from this basis, as the things of the old kingdom increasingly have less attraction for us.

But you are a chosen people, a royal priesthood, a holy nation, a people belonging to God, that you may declare the praises of him who called you out of darkness into his wonderful light. Once you were not a people, but now you are the people of God; once you had not received mercy, but now you have received mercy.

(1 Peter 2:9–10)

Note that God considers us to be already a holy nation! Holiness is a basis we work from, not something we work for. Our position needs to be: 'In Christ, I am holy; therefore I will seek to live a holy life', not 'I must be holy in order to be in Christ.'

United

Once transferred, we are now 'united' with Christ by the Spirit through faith.

I have been crucified with Christ and I no longer live, but Christ lives in me. The life I live in the body, I live by faith in the Son of God, who loved me and gave himself for me.

(Galatians 2:20)

Having been crucified with him, by faith, an end is put to our lives once dominated by sin (Romans 6:6) and we are raised with him to live a new life (Romans 6:4–5, 8). 'Self' has been removed from the throne of our lives and Christ has taken its place. He gives us a new heart (Ezekiel 36:26–27): one that *wants* to love God, respond to him and become more holy, just like he is. Being holy is not about 'trying hard', but about becoming in reality what we already are in principle, through the Spirit's help. 'Become what you are' is the heart of the call to holiness!

153

Starting to see

The more we then go on as believers, the more we start to see 'how terrible and evil sin really is' (Romans 7:13, CEV). Motives, attitudes and thoughts will often appal us. In fact, at times, we might even feel we are going backwards rather than forwards! But we are not on our own when this happens! Paul, for example, after years as a Christian, still struggled with sin at times and felt, 'What a wretched man I am!' (Romans 7:24). What is happening at such times is that we are becoming less comfortable with what we could once live with. The longer we live, the more we see how very much we need Christ and to 'fix our eyes on Jesus' (Hebrews 12:2).

The Spirit's work in us

The Holy Spirit brings holiness

It is the Holy Spirit who brings about holiness. Human attempts at holiness only produce dead religion, as with the Pharisees (see e.g. Matthew 23:1–39). Their origins lay in a 'renewal movement'; but they became so legalistic in their efforts to be holy, that they couldn't even see holiness when it stood in person before them (e.g. Luke 6:1–11).

Trying to become holy through our own efforts will do the same to us. We are certainly to 'work at' our faith, but only as we remember that it is God who is 'at work' in us.

Work out your salvation with fear and trembling; for it is God who is at work in you, both to will and to work for His good pleasure.

(Philippians 2:12–13, NASB)

May the God of peace, who through the blood of the eternal covenant brought back from the dead our Lord Jesus, that great Shepherd of the sheep, equip you with everything good for doing his will, and may he work in us what is pleasing to him, *through Jesus Christ, to whom be glory for ever and ever. Amen.*

(Hebrews 13:20–21)

See also 1 Corinthians 12:6; 15:10; Colossians 1:29

Tools the Holy Spirit uses

The Holy Spirit uses many different means to bring about holiness in us – the Bible, prayer, worship, fellowship, Holy Communion, manifestations of his presence (see Acts 2:42–43). Through these, we see more of what Jesus is like and receive God's grace to make us more like him, as we allow the Spirit to work. As we open ourselves to these objective means, something subjective happens inside us: motives are exposed, thoughts are re-directed, actions are questioned; and consequently habits are changed – not by us, but by the Spirit as he renews our thinking.

Do not conform any longer to the pattern of this world, but be transformed by the renewing of your mind. Then you will be able to test and approve what God's will is – his good, pleasing and perfect will.

(Romans 12:2)

You were taught, with regard to your former way of life, to put off your old self, which is being corrupted by its deceitful desires; to be made new in the attitude of your minds; and to put on the new self, created to be like God in true righteousness and holiness.

(Ephesians 4:22–24)

Why do we fail?

If you are anything like us, there will be times when you fail! We aim to be like Jesus, to love him and follow him completely – and then we stumble. And the worst thing is: sometimes we even do it deliberately! Why does this happen? It is because sin still lives in us and a 'war' is going on inside us (Romans 7:23; 1 Peter 2:11): a war between the still-surviving desires of our old sinful nature and the growing desires of our new nature (Galatians 5:17). In our heart of hearts, we want to please God; but there is antagonism from 'the world, the flesh and the devil'. So sometimes we don't do the good we really want to do, and the bad thing we don't want to do is what we end up doing! Ever felt like that? Then you're exactly the person Paul describes in Romans 7:14–25. (Do read it!)

So what do we do? Give in? Accept that's how things are? That we will have to 'live with it' until we get to heaven? No! With the help of the Spirit there is always hope of change, as we press on.

Not that I have already obtained all this, or have already been made perfect, but I press on to take hold of that for which Christ Jesus took hold of me. Brothers, I do not consider myself yet to have taken hold of it. But one thing I do: Forgetting what is behind and straining towards what is ahead, I press on towards the goal to win the prize for which God has called me heavenwards in Christ Jesus.

(Philippians 3:12–15)

See also 1 Corinthians 9:24–27; Hebrews 6:1–3

Building in progress

Our lives are rather like a building site: old ways are being demolished, and new ways are starting to replace them as Jesus, through his Spirit, builds according to the plans of our Father architect (Hebrews 11:10). At the moment, our lives may look like a 'disaster area' with so many changes going on; yet one day the construction work will result in something beautiful and complete.

In him [Christ] the whole building is joined together and rises to become a holy temple in the Lord. And in him you too are being built together to become a dwelling in which God lives by his Spirit.

(Ephesians 2:21–22)

You also, like living stones, are being built into a spiritual house to be a holy priesthood, offering spiritual sacrifices acceptable to God through Jesus Christ.

(1 Peter 2:5)

Holiness

Crisis or process?

Is sanctification (our becoming more and more holy) a crisis event or a gradual process? The evidence points to the latter.

And we, who with unveiled faces all reflect the Lord's glory, are being transformed into his likeness with ever-increasing glory, which comes from the Lord, who is the Spirit.

(2 Corinthians 3:18)

See also Romans 6:19; Colossians 3:10–14

This does not take away, however, from the reality of our significant encounters with Christ leading to huge leaps forward at times.

Active or passive?

Is sanctification something we must 'fight for' or 'rest in'? The New Testament says 'Both!' We have to rest in Christ and trust him, for he is our holiness (e.g. John 15:1–10; 1 Corinthians 1:30–31; Galatians 2:20; Hebrews 4:9–10); but we must also be active, 'putting off' our old nature and 'putting on' the new (Ephesians 4:22–23). But while it is we who do this, it is with the Spirit's help (Romans 8:13; 12:1–21; Galatians 5:16–25; Colossians 3:1–17; 1 Timothy 6:12). Forget this, and we are heading for legalism!

Relevance for today

Becoming more like Jesus

I can only become more like Jesus as I get to know him better.

I want to know Christ and the power of his resurrection and the fellowship of sharing in his sufferings, becoming like him . . .

(Philippians 3:10)

Paul's first priority was to know Christ; not to know about him, or to know doctrine, but to know Christ. Everything else, including holiness – becoming like him – flows from this.

Happiness equals holiness

I will only become more happy as I become more holy. Pursuing happiness in the things of the world inevitably 'clouds our vision' and steers us away from becoming more like Jesus.

For without him [God], who can eat or find enjoyment? To the man who pleases him, God gives wisdom, knowledge and happiness, but to the sinner he gives the task of gathering and storing up wealth to hand it over to the one who pleases God.

(Ecclesiastes 2:25–26)

Do not love the world or anything in the world. If anyone loves the world, the love of the Father is not in him. For everything in the world – the cravings of sinful man, the lust of his eyes and the boasting of what he has and does – comes not from the Father but from the world. The world and its desires pass away, but the man who does the will of God lives for ever.

(1 John 2:15–17)

Pursue holiness and you will find happiness! Pursue happiness, and you will find neither holiness nor happiness.

See also Esther 5:9–13; Luke 12:13–21

Holiness should pervade everything

Keeping 'faith' and 'life' in separate compartments will lead to a strange view of holiness. Holiness should run through everything we are and do.

Just as he who called you is holy, so be holy in all you do.

(1 Peter 1:15)

Holiness sometimes means saying 'No'

While we do not want to come across as 'kill-joys', there will be times when we have to stand up and say 'no' to things that others invite us to do. We do not need to take a Pharisaic posture as we do so ('God, I thank you that I am not like other men . . .', Luke 18:11); but nor should we be embarrassed at declining invitations to take part in things that will simply do us no good.

What shall we say, then? Shall we go on sinning, so that grace may increase? By no means! We died to sin; how can we live in it any longer?

(Romans 6:1–2)

Holiness through the Spirit

Holiness comes about through the Spirit, not through 'law' (Ephesians 2:8–9). God's requirements are not a Pharisaic 'code of practice' covering every detail of life and behaviour. Rather, he wants us to live in response to his Spirit.

After all, the Law brings death, but the Spirit brings life.

(2 Corinthians 3:6, CEV)

Becoming more holy

The more we grasp the promises of God, the more these should move us into the holiness of God.

Since we have these promises, dear friends, let us purify ourselves from everything that contaminates body and spirit, perfecting holiness out of reverence for God.

(2 Corinthians 7:1)

'What would Jesus do?'

If, in every situation, we ask ourselves, 'What do I think Jesus would do here?', and then do it, we will not go far wrong.

Holy Spirit, truth divine,
Dawn upon this soul of mine;
Word of God, and inward light,
Wake my spirit, clear my sight.

Holy Spirit, love divine,
Glow within this heart of mine;
Kindle every high desire;
Perish self in Thy pure fire.

Holy Spirit, power divine,
Fill and nerve this will of mine;
By Thee may I strongly live,
Bravely bear, and nobly strive.

Holy Spirit, right divine,
King within my conscience reign;
Be my Lord, and I shall be
Firmly bound, for ever free

Holy Spirit, peace divine,
Still this restless heart of mine;
Speak to calm this tossing sea,
Stayed in Thy tranquillity.

Holy Spirit, joy divine,
Gladden Thou this heart of mine;
In the desert ways I'll sing:
Spring, O Well, for ever spring!

Samuel Longfellow, 1819–92

Conclusion

Holy Christians are not those whose lives are aimed at 'holiness', but whose lives are centred fully on Jesus.

For God did not call us to be impure, but to live a holy life.

(1 Thessalonians 4:7)

CHAPTER FIVE

Growing in Fruitfulness

Fruitfulness is a natural by-product of the life of Christ within us.
As we abide in him, certain things begin to instinctively grow.

*The fruit of the Spirit is love, joy, peace, patience, kindness,
goodness, faithfulness, gentleness and self-control.
Against such things there is no law.* (Galatians 5:22–23)

Mike has a plum tree in his garden. It is of good stock, was planted properly and has been fed and pruned. Yet, after several years, the most it has ever managed to produce is half-a-dozen plums. It is, as fruit trees go, completely useless!

There is nothing more useless than a fruitless fruit tree. And likewise, there is nothing more useless than a 'fruitless' Christian. Thankfully, God has made provision through his Spirit for things to be very different. For through his Spirit, God wants to bring forth in our lives the fruitfulness that he had planned from the beginning.

Fruitfulness and the purposes of God

From the very beginning, God's purpose was that both the world and the human race should be fruitful, thereby expressing something of the abundant heart of God. Let us look at some of the very specific promises concerning fruitfulness that he has given us.

Fruitfulness in creation

God blessed them and said, 'Be fruitful and increase in number and fill the water in the seas, and let the birds increase on the earth.'

(Genesis 1:22)

See also Genesis 8:17, 22

Fruitfulness in the human race

So God created man in his own image, in the image of God he created him; male and female he created them. God blessed them and said to them, 'Be fruitful and increase in number; fill the earth and subdue it.'

(Genesis 1:27–28)

See also Genesis 9:1–3; Psalm 128:1–4

Fruitfulness among God's people

Abram fell face down, and God said to him, 'As for me, this is my covenant with you: You will be the father of many nations. No longer will you be called Abram; your name will be Abraham, for I have made you a father of many nations. I will make you very fruitful; I will make nations of you, and kings will come from you.'

(Genesis 17:3–6)

See also Genesis 28:3–4; 35:11–12; Psalm 105:24; Jeremiah 23:3

Fruitfulness in the promised land

The spies Moses sent to explore Canaan came back with the following report:

We went into the land to which you sent us, and it does flow with milk and honey! Here is its fruit.'

(Numbers 13:27)

See also Exodus 3:8; Leviticus 26:9–10; Deuteronomy 28:11; Jeremiah 2:7; Ezekiel 20:6

Fruitfulness for the righteous

The righteous will flourish like a palm tree, they will grow like a cedar of Lebanon; planted in the house of the LORD, they will flourish in the courts of our God. They will still bear fruit in old age, they will stay fresh and green, proclaiming, 'The LORD is

upright; he is my Rock, and there is no wickedness in him.'

(Psalm 92:12–15)

See also Psalm 1:1–3; 128:1–4; Jeremiah 17:7–8

Fruitfulness in God's new creation

'Fruit trees of all kinds will grow on both banks of the river. Their leaves will not wither, nor will their fruit fail. Every month they will bear, because the water from the sanctuary flows to them. Their fruit will serve for food and their leaves for healing.'

(Ezekiel 47:12)

See also Isaiah 65:17–22; Revelation 22:1–2

Fruitfulness, then, runs through God's purposes for his people from beginning to end. It should therefore not surprise us to discover that the Spirit of this God who abounds in fruitfulness wants us to be fruitful also.

Good trees, good fruit

'Fruit' in our lives is seen in various ways in the Bible. One of the main ones is to do with our words and actions, which are seen as 'fruit' growing from our innermost being. Jesus taught that our true character is seen in our words and actions and that you can recognize people 'by their fruit'.

'By their fruit you will recognise them. Do people pick grapes from thornbushes, or figs from thistles? Likewise every good tree bears good fruit, but a bad tree bears bad fruit. A good tree cannot bear bad fruit, and a bad tree cannot bear good fruit. Every tree that does not bear good fruit is cut down and thrown into the fire. Thus, by their fruit you will recognise them.'

(Matthew 7:16–20)

See also Proverbs 11:30; Isaiah 5:1–7; Matthew 12:33–37; John 15:1–8; James 3:12

'Fruit' in our lives finds expression in a number of ways:
- the life we live
(Isaiah 3:10; Ephesians 5:8–9; Philippians 1:11)
- the words we speak
(Proverbs 12:13–14; Matthew 12:33–37; Hebrews 13:15)
- the service we offer
(Colossians 1:10; Philippians 1:22)
- the prayers we pray
(John 15:7–8)
- the witness we bear
(Proverbs 11:30; Colossians 1:6)
- the gifts we give
(Romans 15:25–28)

Throughout the Bible fruitlessness is seen as a shameful thing among God's people (e.g. Isaiah 5:1–7).

The fruit of the Spirit

Fruitfulness needs the help of the Holy Spirit. Without him, it just becomes a matter of sheer will and self-effort. This was what the Galatians were drifting into and was why Paul asked them:

Did you receive the Spirit by observing the law, or by believing what you heard? Are you so foolish? After beginning with the Spirit, are you now trying to attain your goal by human effort?

(Galatians 3:2–3)

They were forgetting that the Christian life can only be lived in the power of the Spirit. As we live by that Spirit, Paul says, old things have a way of 'dying' (Galatians 5:16–21), and new things begin to grow. It was these 'new things' that he described as 'the fruit of the Spirit' – things that grow naturally when he is in control (Galatians 5:22- 25).

The nine 'fruits' are actually seen as one: Paul speaks of the 'fruit' (not 'fruits') of the Spirit. They are not like sweets in a 'Pick'n'Mix' shop where you take some and leave others; they all belong together for they are all the result of the Spirit's work.

Note that every one of them is a characteristic of God himself. It is nothing less than his own nature that his Spirit is seeking to grow within us!

Love

In some ways this could have said it all! For true love ('agape' – 'commitment love') covers all the other fruit. Love, as the greatest Christian virtue (1 Corinthians 13:13), always comes first, for God himself *is* love (1 John 4:8).

Love is not just a feeling; it is a resolved commitment to do what is right and best for my neighbour, whatever the cost to me (e.g. Luke 10:25–37). It is the first fruit that God looks for in our lives, and always brings a blessing.

He who pursues righteousness and love finds life, prosperity and honour.

(Proverbs 21:21)

'A new command I give you: Love one another. As I have loved you, so you must love one another. By this all men will know that you are my disciples, if you love one another.'

(John 13:34–35)

Let no debt remain outstanding, except the continuing debt to love one another, for he who loves his fellow-man has fulfilled the law.

(Romans 13:8)

See also Leviticus 19:18; Proverbs 3:3–4; Romans 5:5; 12:9; 1 Corinthians 13:1–13; Galatians 5:13–14; 1 John 3:16–18

Joy

Wherever Jesus went, he brought joy (e.g. Luke 19:5–6, 37) – gladness, happiness, to use more ordinary words. He himself knew how to be 'full of joy through the Holy Spirit' (Luke 10:21) and wanted his joy to be ours (John 15:11; 17:13). God's kingdom is all about 'righteousness, peace and joy in the Holy Spirit' (Romans 14:17). In fact, words like 'joy', 'joyful' and 'rejoice' occur well over 400 times in the Bible! Luke in particular delights to emphasize this joy (e.g. Luke 2:10; 10:17, 21; 15:10; 24:52; Acts 5:41; 8:8, 39; 13:52; 16:34).

But joy is not restricted to happy feelings; it is about confidence in God, no matter what may come our way. That is why Paul and Silas could sing while they were locked up in jail (Acts 16:25–28). They knew that God was with them. See also Luke 6:22–23, Romans 5:1–5.)

'This day is sacred to our Lord. Do not grieve, for the joy of the LORD is your strength.'

(Nehemiah 8:10)

For the Jews it was a time of happiness and joy, gladness and honour. In every province and in every city, wherever the edict of the king went, there was joy and gladness among the Jews, with feasting and celebrating. And many people of other nationalities became Jews because fear of the Jews had seized them.

(Esther 8:16–17)

You love righteousness and hate wickedness; therefore God, your God, has set you above your companions by anointing you with the oil of joy.

(Psalm 45:7)

See also 1 Chronicles 12:38–40; Esther 9:20–22; Psalm 30:11–12; Isaiah 61:1–3, 7; John 16:24; Romans 15:13; Philippians 4:4–7; 1 Thessalonians 5:16; 1 Peter 1:8

Peace

Once we know we 'have peace with God through our Lord Jesus Christ' (Romans 5:1; see also Part 2, Chapter 4), we can be peaceful within, not fearful when things go wrong, but confident that 'if God is for us, who can be against us?' (Romans 8:31).

I will lie down and sleep in peace, for you alone, O LORD, make me dwell in safety.

(Psalm 4:8)

The LORD gives strength to his people; the LORD blesses his people with peace.

(Psalm 29:11)

Do not be anxious about anything, but in everything, by prayer and petition, with thanksgiving, present your requests to God. And the peace of God, which transcends all understanding, will guard your hearts and your minds in Christ Jesus.

(Philippians 4:6–7)

See also Numbers 6:24–26; Psalm 119:165; John 14:27; Romans 8:6; 14:17; Ephesians 2:14–17

Patience

'Lord give me patience – now!' Ever felt like that? We have! But patience follows naturally from peace. It is about being able to wait for things because we trust God; about being able to withstand wrong behaviour without 'flying off the handle'; about not getting angry in the face of annoyance, opposition or harm.

Commit your way to the LORD; trust in him and he will do this: He will make your righteousness shine like the dawn, the justice of your cause like the noonday sun. Be still before the LORD and wait patiently for him; do not fret when men succeed in their ways, when they carry out their wicked schemes. Refrain from anger and turn from wrath; do not fret – it leads only to evil. For evil men will be cut off, but those who hope in the LORD will inherit the land.

(Psalm 37:5–9)

I waited patiently for the LORD; he turned to me and heard my cry.

(Psalm 40:1)

Better a patient man than a warrior, a man who controls his temper than one who takes a city.

(Proverbs 16:32)

One of Martin's favourite books is a book of games to do while waiting. In our 'instant' society, waiting does not come easily to us; so the games help grow this fruit in him! All of us need prayerful and practical ways to let the Spirit cultivate this fruit of patience in us. It is as we learn to 'wait patiently' that we receive God's promises (Hebrews 6:15) and become more like our patient Father (Nehemiah 9:30; Romans 2:4; 2 Peter 3:9).

See also Romans 12:12; Ephesians 4:2; Colossians 1:10–12; 3:12; 1 Thessalonians 5:14; Revelation 3:10

Kindness

There is often not a lot of kindness in the world today, for people are far too busy with themselves to stop and think of others. So, when kindness is demonstrated (by a Mother Teresa or the like), it is all the more striking.

God wants us to be kind. Why? Because he himself is kind, even to the ungrateful (Luke 6:35–36)! Paul reminds us that 'God's kindness leads you towards repentance' (Romans 2:4). Jesus was known for his kindness, his thoughtful and gentle way of handling people in their need (e.g. Matthew 19:13–14; Luke 8:40–56), and this should characterize us too.

163

'The LORD bless you for showing this kindness to Saul your master by burying him. May the LORD now show you kindness and faithfulness, and I too will show you the same favour because you have done this.'

(2 Samuel 2:5–6)

He who despises his neighbour sins, but blessed is he who is kind to the needy.

(Proverbs 14:21)

He who is kind to the poor lends to the LORD, and he will reward him for what he has done.

(Proverbs 19:17)

See also Proverbs 12:25; 14:31; Jeremiah 9:23–24; Matthew 25:34–40; Ephesians 4:32; Colossians 3:12; 2 Peter 1:5–8

Goodness

Being a 'do-gooder' is generally despised today (normally by those who feel guilty for not having done good themselves!). But as Cliff Richard once said in a TV interview, 'I'd rather be known as a do-gooder than a do-badder.'

God wants us to be good because he himself is good (Psalm 100:5), all he does is good (Genesis 1:31), and all his promises are good (Joshua 23:14).

You are good, and what you do is good.

(Psalm 119:68)

Goodness always benefits others, even our enemies (Luke 6:27–28, 33–36). Goodness demonstrated in our lives can begin to open up people to an understanding of a good God.

Do what is right and good in the LORD's sight, so that it may go well with you.

(Deuteronomy 6:18)

I am still confident of this: I will see the goodness of the LORD in the land of the living. Wait for the LORD; be strong and take heart and wait for the LORD.

(Psalm 27:13–14)

Let us not become weary in doing good, for at the proper time we will reap a harvest if we do not give up. Therefore, as we have opportunity, let us do good to all people, especially to those who belong to the family of believers.

(Galatians 6:9–10)

See also Proverbs 3:27–28; Luke 6:27–36; Romans 2:9–10; Ephesians 2:10; 1 Timothy 6:18–19; Titus 2:14; Hebrews 13:16; James 4:17; 1 Peter 3:10–14; 3 John 11

Faithfulness

We have already seen (Part 1, Chapter 4) that faithfulness is a hallmark of God's character (Exodus 34:6–7). God wants us, as his people, to be faithful too – faithful to God himself, to his word, to his gospel, to his church, to people. Such a faithfulness will withstand any disappointment, deception or mockery.

The Lord rewards every man for his righteousness and faithfulness.

(1 Samuel 26:23)

Let love and faithfulness never leave you; bind them around your neck, write them on the tablet of your heart. Then you will win favour and a good name in the sight of God and man.

(Proverbs 3:3–4)

'Be faithful, even to the point of death, and I will give you the crown of life.'

(Revelation 2:10)

See also Joshua 24:14–15; Psalm 18:25; 31:23–24; 37:28; Matthew 24:45–47; 25:14–30; 1 Corinthians 4:2; 1 Peter 4:10.

Gentleness

Gentleness (or 'meekness') is not a weakness where everyone 'uses us as a doormat'. (Paul certainly did not stand for that! See Acts 16:35–37; 22:22–29.) It means 'strength that has been controlled' (like a wild horse being tamed and trained). Christ himself demonstrated this characteristic (Matthew 11:29–30; 21:5; 2 Corinthians 10:1).

We need to be gentle in our handling of people (Ephesians 4:2; 1 Peter 3:15–16). Even if we have been wronged or have a just point to make, we must do so with gentleness, not arrogance or anger.

A gentle answer turns away wrath, but a harsh word stirs up anger.

(Proverbs 15:1)

Your beauty should not come from outward adornment . . . Instead, it should be that of your inner self, the unfading beauty of a gentle and quiet spirit, which is of great worth in God's sight.

(1 Peter 3:3–4)

See also Proverbs 25:15; Ephesians 4:2; Philippians 4:5; Colossians 3:12; 1 Thessalonians 2:6–7; 1 Timothy 6:11; 1 Peter 3:15–16

Self-control

Most of us like to be 'in control' – of other things and other people! But the Bible says that the only thing we should be controlling is – ourselves! Self-control is the means by which we keep ourselves, and the acts of the sinful nature, 'in check'. It is more than saying 'No' to excessive eating or wrong desires (though that is part of it! See e.g. Proverbs 23:1–3; Colossians 3:5). It is saying 'Yes' to God. It is 'taking captive every thought to make it obedient to Christ' (2 Corinthians 10:5); it is saying 'Yes' to the way of the cross (Matthew 16:24–27).

Like a city whose walls are broken down is a man who lacks self-control.

(Proverbs 25:28)

The end of all things is near. Therefore be clear minded and self-controlled so that you can pray.

(1 Peter 4:7)

For this very reason, make every effort to add to your faith goodness; and to goodness, knowledge; and to knowledge, self-control; and to self-control, perseverance; and to perseverance, godliness; and to godliness, brotherly kindness; and to brotherly kindness, love. For if you possess these qualities in increasing measure, they will keep you from being ineffective and unproductive in your knowledge of our Lord Jesus Christ.

(2 Peter 1:5–8)

See also 1 Thessalonians 5:6–9; 1 Timothy 6:6–11; 2 Timothy 1:7; Titus 2:6–8, 11–12; Hebrews 13:4–5; 1 Peter 1:13–16

Relevance for today

How can we see this fruit grow so it can be given away to a starving world – a world starved of love, joy, peace, etc.? The context of our passage shows us:

Since we live by the Spirit, let us keep in step with the Spirit.

(Galatians 5:25)

What does 'keeping in step' or 'keeping up with' him involve?
- Seeking daily to be 'filled with the Holy Spirit' (Ephesians 5:18).
- Submitting our hearts and minds to his control (Romans 8:6–9).
- Feeding our spirits with 'Spirit food' (Scripture, prayer, worship, fellowship) (Acts 2:42; 1 Peter 2:2).
- 'Pulling out the weeds of sin' when they grow (Matthew 13:7, 37–39).
- Allowing him to prune our life 'so that it will be even more fruitful' (John 15:2). It is so reassuring to know that we are carefully looked after by our Father-gardener. As we abide in Jesus (John 15:4–7), fruitfulness really is possible (John 15:8)!

Take time to be holy, let Him be thy guide:
And run not before Him whatever betide:
In joy or in sorrow still follow thy Lord,
And, looking to Jesus, still trust in His Word.

Take time to be holy, be calm in thy soul;
Each thought and each temper beneath His
  control.
Thus led by His Spirit and filled with His
  love,
Thou soon shalt be fitted for service above.

William Dunn Longstaff, 1822–94

Conclusion

Showing the fruit of the Spirit means, quite simply, being like Christ. If we abide in him, we will be fruitful.

'I am the vine; you are the branches. If a man remains in me and I in him, he will bear much fruit; apart from me you can do nothing.'

(John 15:5)

Take time to be holy, speak oft with thy
  Lord;
Abide in Him always, and feed on His Word.
Make friends of God's children, help those
  who are weak;
Forgetting in nothing His blessing to seek.

Take time to be holy, the world rushes on;
Spend much time in secret with Jesus alone.
By looking to Jesus like Him thou shalt be;
Thy friends, in thy conduct, His likeness shall
  see.

CHAPTER SIX

Growing in Power

The Holy Spirit wants to give us his power so that our lives can be holy and effective for God.

'You will receive power when the Holy Spirit comes on you; and you will be my witnesses in Jerusalem, and in all Judea and Samaria, and to the ends of the earth.' (Acts 1:8)

A person's final words have special significance – whether those of a politician leaving office, of someone famous ending their career or of a loved one slipping from this world to the next. The words are often special, something to be kept and remembered.

Likewise, the final words of Jesus before returning to heaven would have held great significance for his disciples. And those final words were to do with his sending a *person* who would bring with him *power*. Words worth remembering!

The person and the power

'You will receive power' (Acts 1:8). For the next ten days the disciples must have pondered about what Jesus meant; and then, at Pentecost, it happened. The promise was kept; the person and the power had arrived!

It is very important that we remember the link between the person and the power. God's power is not something that can be manipulated, like some primitive magic (as Simon Magus discovered to his cost; see Acts 8:9–24); God's power comes in the package of a person – the person of the Holy Spirit – and so needs calling upon in the right way. We are not calling for 'it' but for 'him'.

> We sometimes forget that the Holy Spirit is a person, perhaps because of the images that are used to describe him when he comes. For example, he comes in the form of:
> - wind (1 Kings 19:11; Ezekiel 37:9–10; John 3:8; Acts 2:2)
> - fire (Isaiah 4:4; Matthew 3:11; Acts 2:3)
> - water (Isaiah 44:3; Ezekiel 47:1–12; John 7:37–38)
> - oil (1 Samuel 16:13: Isaiah 61:1–3)
> - dove (Matthew 3:16; John 1:32)
>
> These images generally describe what it is that he has come to do; they are not meant to describe what he is.

Supernatural power

When the Holy Spirit comes with power, it is 'dynamite'! In fact the English word 'dynamite' comes from the Greek word for the 'power' that the Spirit brings. And this power is not about 'adding a little extra something' to human abilities; it is something quite supernatural that lifts people beyond what they themselves could do.

Supernatural power in the Old Testament

The Old Testament saints did not hesitate to call on God's power to demonstrate that the Lord alone was God and that 'besides him there is no other' (Deuteronomy 4:35). These demonstrations of power were all the work of the Spirit.

The Spirit of the LORD came upon him [Samson] in power so that he tore the lion apart with his bare hands as he might have torn a young goat.

(Judges 14:6)

'The Spirit of the LORD will come upon you in power, and you will prophesy with them; and you will be changed into a different person. Once these signs are fulfilled, do whatever your hand finds to do, for God is with you.'

(1 Samuel 10:6–7)

He [Elisha] picked up the cloak that had fallen from Elijah and went back and stood on the bank of the Jordan. Then he took the cloak that had fallen from him and struck the water with it. 'Where now is the Lord, the God of Elijah?' he asked. When he struck the water, it divided to the right and to the left, and he crossed over. The company of the prophets from Jericho, who were watching, said, 'The spirit of Elijah is resting on Elisha.'

(2 Kings 2:13–15)

See also Exodus 7:1–7; Deuteronomy 4:32–38; 34:12; 1 Kings 18:11–12; 1 Chronicles 28:12; Ezekiel 3:12–14; Zechariah 4:6

Supernatural power in the Gospels

From the time that Jesus was anointed with the Spirit's power at his baptism (Luke 3:21–22) and then went out 'in the power of the Spirit' (Luke 4:14), he constantly drew on that power to demonstrate the presence of the kingdom and the Father's love. He challenged those who were well-versed in the Scriptures but had no understanding of the power of God (Mark 12:24).

'If I drive out demons by the Spirit of God, then the kingdom of God has come upon you.'

(Matthew 12:28)

A large crowd of his disciples was there and a great number of people from all over Judea, from Jerusalem, and from the coast of Tyre and Sidon, who had come to hear him and to be healed of their diseases. Those troubled by evil spirits were cured, and the people all tried to touch him, because power was coming from him and healing them all.

(Luke 6:17–19)

When Jesus had called the Twelve together, he gave them power and authority to drive out all demons and to cure diseases, and he sent them out to preach the kingdom of God and to heal the sick.

(Luke 9:1–2)

See also Luke 4:18–19, 36; 5:17–26; 12:11–12

Supernatural power in the book of Acts

Power is one of Luke's dominant themes, both in his Gospel and in Acts. In Acts we see the Spirit's power in:

• releasing heartfelt praise (2:11)
• bringing forth bold witnessing (1:8; 4:29, 33)
• inspiring the preaching of the gospel and applying the Scriptures (2:14–41; 4:8–20)
• bringing unity (2:42–47)
• leading believers in prayer (4:31)
• giving 'spiritual gifts' (1 Corinthians 12:1), such as 'speaking in tongues' (2:4; 10:44–46; 19:6; see also 1 Corinthians 12:10, 28; 14:1–28), prophecy (2:17; 11:28; 19:6; 21:9–11; see also 1 Corinthians 12:10, 28; 14:3–5, 29–32; Ephesians 4:11), and miracles and healings (2:19; 3:1–16; 4:16; 6:8; 8:13; 14:3; see also 1 Corinthians 12:9–10, 28)
• releasing servanthood (6:1–7)
• giving guidance to individuals (8:29; 11:12; 16:6–9) and churches (13:2)
• bringing in 'outsiders'. It was the Spirit who brought those who were 'beyond the pale', spiritually speaking, into the church:

Samaritans, who were seen as 'half-Jews', (8:4–7, 14–17), an Ethiopian eunuch, who could never have become a Jew (8:26–40; see Leviticus 21:16–20), and Gentiles, who were definitely not Jews (e.g. 10:1–48; 13:1–4, 42–52). When the church could not grasp just how much the Spirit wanted to do this, he simply took over (see Acts 10:44–48)!

Everything the early church did, it did in the power of the Spirit.

Supernatural power in the New Testament letters

In the letters of the New Testament, the power of God's Spirit is seen as lying behind everything. It was demonstrated supremely in the resurrection of Jesus, and the same power is said to be now at work in us and is a vital part of our inner resources.

And if the Spirit of him who raised Jesus from the dead is living in you, he who raised Christ from the dead will also give life to your mortal bodies through his Spirit, who lives in you.

(Romans 8:11)

I pray that out of his glorious riches he may strengthen you with power through his Spirit in your inner being, so that Christ may dwell in your hearts through faith. And I pray that you, being rooted and established in love, may have power, together with all the saints, to grasp how wide and long and high and deep is the love of Christ, and to know this love that surpasses knowledge – that you may be filled to the measure of all the fulness of God. Now to him who is able to do immeasurably more than all we ask or imagine, according to his power that is at work within us, to him be glory in the church and in Christ Jesus throughout all generations, for ever and ever! Amen.

(Ephesians 3:16–21)

I want to know Christ and the power of his resurrection.

(Philippians 3:10)

See also Romans 1:4; 15:13; 1 Corinthians 6:14; Ephesians 1:18–21

Paul recognized that any effective ministry through him had been entirely 'by the power of signs and miracles, through the power of the Spirit' (Romans 15:19); that the gospel had been preached by him 'not with wise and persuasive words, but with a demonstration of the Spirit's power, so that your faith might not rest on men's wisdom, but on God's power' (1 Corinthians 2:4; see also 1 Thessalonians 1:5); that even his 'thorn in the flesh' helped him experience more of God's power as he learned that, 'My grace is sufficient for you, for my power is made perfect in weakness' (2 Corinthians 12:9). Here was a man who believed in the power of the Spirit! And he warned his churches to have nothing to do with those 'having a form of godliness but denying its power' (2 Timothy 3:5).

Supernatural power and us

We cannot dismiss these demonstrations of supernatural power, or confine them to a narrow band of time or people. The power of the Spirit is always available, for the person of the Spirit is always available. As his presence becomes more fully released under the new covenant, so his power is increasingly released also, just as he promised (e.g. Joel 2:28–32).

Jim Packer writes: 'Supernatural living through supernatural empowering is at the very heart of New Testament Christianity, so that those who, while professing faith, do not experience and show forth this empowering are suspect by New Testament standards' (*Keep in Step with the Spirit*).

What a challenge that is to you and me! But also, what a promise!

Some 'power' promises

'Not by might nor by power, but by my Spirit,' says the LORD Almighty.

(Zechariah 4:6)

I am not ashamed of the gospel, for it is the power of God for salvation to everyone who believes.

(Romans 1:16, NASB)

For the message of the cross is foolishness to those who are perishing, but to us who are being saved it is the power of God.

(1 Corinthians 1:18)

For the kingdom of God is not a matter of talk but of power.

(1 Corinthians 4:20)

The weapons we fight with are not the weapons of the world. On the contrary, they have divine power to demolish strongholds.

(2 Corinthians 10:4)

Finally, my brethren, be strong in the Lord and in the power of His might.

(Ephesians 6:10, NKJV)

For God did not give us a spirit of timidity, but a spirit of power, of love and of self-discipline.

(2 Timothy 1:7)

See also 1 Chronicles 29:11; Isaiah 40:10, 29–31; Daniel 7:14; Luke 24:49; 2 Corinthians 4:7; Philippians 3:10; 2 Peter 1:3

The cry of our hearts?

If we're honest, don't we need this sort of power in our lives? Power to tell others about Jesus; power to live godly lives; power to love and serve others? Often we can know what to do, but can't do it; we lack the power. We may go to conference after conference and learn new methods and programmes, yet still lack the power to put them into practice. What we need are not more conferences, but more power! With Isaiah, we need to cry:

Oh, that you would rend the heavens and come down, that the mountains would tremble before you! As when fire sets twigs ablaze and causes water to boil, come down to make your name known to your enemies and cause the nations to quake before you!

(Isaiah 64:1–2)

So how does this power come to be ours? The following steps may be helpful.

Recognize our need of God

'Be filled with the Spirit' (Ephesians 5:18) is a daily command, not a one-off experience. In responding to it, we are saying, 'I need you God!' If our attitude is, 'I can do it!' we will never be in the place where the Spirit can help us. But those who call out to him will find he answers.

Yet I am poor and needy; come quickly to me, O God. You are my help and my deliverer; O LORD, do not delay.

(Psalm 70:5)

See also Psalm 27:7–8; 86:1–7; 109:22; Jeremiah 29:12–14; 33:3

Seek God

Ask

'Asking' is a key to receiving anything from God, including the Holy Spirit.

'If you then, though you are evil, know how to give good gifts to your children, how much more will your Father in heaven give the Holy Spirit to those who ask him!'

(Luke 11:13)

You do not have, because you do not ask.

(James 4:2)

It sounds so obvious, doesn't it? But often we lack the Spirit's power simply because we do not *ask*.

See also Matthew 7:7–11; Mark 11:24; John 15:16; 16:24; 1 John 5:14–15

Thirst

Another key word is 'thirst' (e.g. Matthew 5:6). Are we hungering and thirsting for *God* and *his righteousness?* Or are we just looking for an exciting experience? Do we want power, or do we want God? Do we want others to say, 'There goes a powerful man/woman of God!' and have them notice *us* and *our* 'gifting', or do we want power for God's glory and the sake of others? How *thirsty* we are for *him* is a good measure of how truly thirsty we are.

Let them give thanks to the LORD for his unfailing love and his wonderful deeds for men, for he satisfies the thirsty and fills the hungry with good things.

(Psalm 107:8–9)

For I will pour water on the thirsty land, and streams on the dry ground.

(Isaiah 44:3)

O God, you are my God, earnestly I seek you; my soul thirsts for you, my body longs for you, in a dry and weary land where there is no water. I have seen you in the sanctuary and beheld your power and your glory.

(Psalm 63:1–2)

Believe

As in anything in the Christian life, 'believing' is foundational to how we live and grow, and to how we experience more of the Spirit.

On the last and greatest day of the Feast, Jesus stood and said in a loud voice, 'If anyone is thirsty, let him come to me and drink. Whoever believes in me, as the Scripture has said, streams of living water will flow from within him.' By this he meant the Spirit, whom those who believed in him were later to receive.

(John 7:37–39)

Did you receive the Spirit by observing the law, or by believing what you heard? Are you so foolish? After beginning with the Spirit, are you now trying to attain your goal by human effort? . . . Does God give you his Spirit and work miracles among you because you observe the law, or because you believe what you heard?

(Galatians 3:2–3, 5)

Put right what is wrong

When God shows us things in our lives that need to change, we need to take action. If we don't, it is like leaving a dam in place when the river is trying to flow. Unconfessed sin, unresolved issues, unforgiveness and holding on to things that need to go, will all hinder the flow of God's Spirit, and therefore of God's power, in our lives. God loves to release his blessing among us as we deal with our sin!

For if you live according to the sinful nature, you will die; but if by the Spirit you put to death the misdeeds of the body, you will live, because those who are led by the Spirit of God are sons of God.

(Romans 8:13–14)

The one who sows to please his sinful nature, from that nature will reap destruction; the one who sows to please the Spirit, from the Spirit will reap eternal life.

(Galatians 6:8)

Be vulnerable!

Ouch! Being vulnerable feels like it could hurt! Well, the truth is, it may – at first! But there is tremendous joy in finding a fellow Christian whom we trust and with whom we can share our inner life – our failures as well as our successes. We have both known such times of sharing together in seeking God honestly have been a tremendous blessing.

As iron sharpens iron, so one man sharpens another.

(Proverbs 27:17)

See also Malachi 3:16; 2 Corinthians 6:11–13; James 5:16

'Give it away'

It is hard to understand Christians who claim to have 'the power' but do nothing with it, especially in a world of desperate need. They remind us of a rocket that is ready for lift-off but which stays on the launch-pad! If there really is power within us, then surely it will show in service and in reaching out to bless others. It is as we give it away that we get refilled.

See e.g. Luke 10:1–9, 17–20

Relevance for today

Power for today
The Spirit's power is for today, not for yesterday. There is absolutely no reason for relegating the power of God's Spirit to bygone times. The promise made *then* is for *now*.

'The promise is for you and your children and for all who are far off – for all whom the Lord our God will call.'

(Acts 2:39)

Power for everyone
The Spirit's power is for everyone, not just 'special people'.

'And afterwards, I will pour out my Spirit on all people. Your sons and daughters will prophesy, your old men will dream dreams, your young men will see visions. Even on my servants, both men and women, I will pour out my Spirit in those days.'

(Joel 2:28–29)

Power greater than ours
The power of the Spirit is not about 'me doing my best'. If we reduce it to this, there is little that distinguishes us from the world around us. God does not want us to resort to worldly resources to do his work, but rather to his power.

'Not by might nor by power, but by my Spirit,' says the LORD Almighty.

(Zechariah 4:6)

Power for a purpose
We have been given power for selfless service (Acts 1:8), not selfish enjoyment (Acts 8:18–23).

'But you will receive power when the Holy Spirit comes on you; and you will be my witnesses . . .'

(Acts 1:8)

Power in a person
The power is still focused in the *person of the Holy Spirit*. Remember: I need more of 'him' not more of 'it'.

Pause for thought
Does my life show I trust in a supernatural God? Does my view of the Holy Spirit really make room for him to demonstrate his power today – in my life and in my church? Or am I afraid of the 'supernatural'?

Spirit of the living God, fall afresh on me
Spirit of the living God, fall afresh on me
Break me, melt me, mould me, fill me;
Spirit of the living God, fall afresh on me.

Conclusion

No matter how it finds expression – in the 'spectacular' or the more ordinary – the Spirit's power is 'dynamite'! If we are living with less than this, we are living with less than Jesus promised.

We have this treasure in jars of clay to show that this all-surpassing power is from God and not from us.

(2 Corinthians 4:7)

CHAPTER SEVEN

Growing in Reality

> The Holy Spirit wants to keep our relationship with Jesus fresh so that we can serve him in the world and prepare the way for God to come in power.
>
> *We, who with unveiled faces all reflect the Lord's glory, are being transformed into his likeness with ever-increasing glory, which comes from the Lord, who is the Spirit.*
> (2 Corinthians 3:18)

'Virtual reality' has become increasingly common. Through powerful computer technology, 'virtual' (we used to call them 'pretend'!) worlds can be created, allowing airline pilots to practise handling emergencies or games enthusiasts to combat some imaginary foe. It is all to do with the illusion of participation in a created world. What you see and do looks and feels real; but in reality it is only a computer simulation.

This is certainly not how the Christian life is meant to be! There is nothing 'virtual' about it; either in terms of our experience of the Spirit or our impact on the world. God wants us to live and grow in reality. And his Spirit is the means to ensure this happens.

In this chapter, we look at some of the commands that help us to live in the Spirit's reality and will therefore help us to be used to bring the world back to reality also.

Do not resist the Holy Spirit

Although the Holy Spirit is the Spirit of the all-powerful God, there is a very real possibility of resisting him. This comes out in Acts 7, where Stephen's speech ends in a very blunt way!

'You stiff-necked people, with uncircumcised hearts and ears! You are just like your fathers: You always resist the Holy Spirit!'

(Acts 7:51)

So, let's look at what resisting the Holy Spirit can involve:

Opposition to his purposes

It is easy to remain blind, deaf and opposed to his purposes. Just because we are God's people is no guarantee that we will hear God, let alone obey him. God often had to call his people back because they had drifted away, challenging their blindness and deafness (e.g. Isaiah 42:19–20) and calling them to 'circumcise their hearts' again (e.g. Jeremiah 4:3–4). Leaders, sadly, can sometimes be the most blind (e.g. Matthew 15:14; 23:16) or most resistant to God because they can feel threatened by 'change' (e.g. John 7:45–49; 8:31–41).

However, it was promised that the Messiah, when he came, would open blind eyes to see God and his purposes.

See, a king will reign in righteousness and rulers will rule with justice. Each man will be like a shelter from the wind and a refuge from the storm, like streams of water in the desert and the shadow of a great rock in a thirsty land. Then the eyes of those who see will no longer be closed, and the ears of those who hear will listen.

(Isaiah 32:1–3)

See also Psalm 119:18; Isaiah 35:5–10; 42:6–7

If we ask God, he will open our spiritual eyes to see what is going on around us, just as Elisha asked it for his servant:

And Elisha prayed, 'O LORD, open his eyes so that he may see.' Then the LORD opened the servant's eyes, and he looked and saw the hills full of horses and chariots of fire all round Elisha.

(2 Kings 6:17)

If we are not to resist the Holy Spirit, we need to ask him to help us keep our 'spiritual' eyes and ears open to God and to help us to be open to what he is doing.

Ascribing his work to the devil

The Pharisees were always quick to challenge Jesus whenever he cut across their understanding or traditions (e.g. Matthew 12:1–14; 15:1–2, 12; Luke 11:37–54). The climax of this was their ascribing to the devil what he did in the power of the Spirit (Matthew 12:22–32), which Jesus described as unforgivable 'blasphemy against the Spirit'.

'And so I tell you, every sin and blasphemy will be forgiven men, but the blasphemy against the Spirit will not be forgiven. Anyone who speaks a word against the Son of Man will be forgiven, but anyone who speaks against the Holy Spirit will not be forgiven, either in this age or in the age to come.

(Matthew 12:31–32)

This is certainly one of the more solemn promises of the Bible! And it is one that needs careful understanding, for church leaders have often had to reassure people that a particular sin they have committed is not the unforgivable sin! In context, Jesus says that the unforgivable sin is the persistent refusal to accept who he is, just as the Pharisees were doing, expressed specifically here in their ascribing his work to the devil (v 24).

We should take care not to do the same, especially where others' experience of the Spirit's work is different to ours, or we may well find ourselves resisting what God is doing. Whenever we are uncertain about something, the advice of Gamaliel is still sound:

'Leave these men alone! Let them go! For if their purpose or activity is of human origin, it will fail. But if it is from God, you will not be able to stop these men; you will only find yourselves fighting against God.'

(Acts 5:38–39)

The key to not resisting the Spirit is to keep a tender heart towards God (e.g. Deuteronomy 10:16; 30:6; Psalm 139:23–24; Isaiah 57:15; Matthew 5:8).

Grieving the Holy Spirit

It is possible for us to make the Holy Spirit sad – to grieve him (Isaiah 63:10; Ephesians 4:30). We can do this by:

Failing to live appropriately

Paul's comment about grieving the Spirit comes in the context of his explaining (or rather, 'insisting', see Ephesians 4:17!) how we should live as Spirit-filled Christians (Ephesians 4:17–5:21). He includes things like, not lying or getting angry (4:25–27), not stealing (4:28), not using inappropriate or bad language (4:29), not engaging in immorality or greed (5:3), avoiding obscenity and coarse jokes (5:4). All of this grieves the Holy Spirit. Why? Because we are his holy temple! Just as God promised (e.g. Ezekiel 11:19; 36:26–27), the Spirit has come to live within us, both individually (1 Corinthians 6:19–20) and corporately (1 Corinthians 3:16–17); and therefore anything 'dirty' offends him and his holiness.

Don't you know that you yourselves are God's temple and that God's Spirit lives in you? If anyone destroys God's temple, God will destroy him; for God's temple is sacred, and you are that temple.

(1 Corinthians 3:16–17)

Do you not know that your body is a temple of the Holy Spirit, who is in you, whom you have received from God? You are not your own; you were bought at a price. Therefore honour God with your body.

(1 Corinthians 6:19–20)

God wants us to keep his Spirit's temple clean, and it grieves him when we don't. But remember: holiness is not about our 'trying harder' (see Chapter 4 of this section); it is about following the Spirit's leading and doing whatever he says.

So I say, live by the Spirit, and you will not gratify the desires of the sinful nature.

(Galatians 5:16)

See also Romans 8:5–14; Galatians 5:24–25

Pretending to be what we are not

Deception is contrary to God's very nature and is therefore something he detests (Proverbs 12:22) and commands us to shun (Leviticus 19:11; Proverbs 24:28; 1 Peter 2:1). We, the children of truth, should be known for our truthfulness (e.g. 2 Corinthians 4:2; Ephesians 4:25). And anyway, God knows everything and everyone (e.g. 1 Chronicles 28:9; Psalm 139:1–6); so how can we hide things from him (e.g. 1 Corinthians 4:5; 14:25)? One day everything will be brought into the light (1 Corinthians 3:13).

Just how seriously the Holy Spirit sees deception was revealed in a stark way when Ananias and Sapphira dropped dead for trying to deceive him and the church (Acts 5:1–11). While this is a sober lesson, it does bring home just how much the Spirit is grieved by deception and pretence.

The positive side of all this is for us to remember that God wants us to 'bring everything into the light'. What we keep in the darkness, the devil keeps power over; but what we bring into the light can be forgiven and dealt with.

If we claim to have fellowship with him yet walk in the darkness, we lie and do not live by the truth. But if we walk in the light, as he is in the light, we have fellowship with one another, and the blood of Jesus, his Son, purifies us from all sin.

(1 John 1:6–7)

See also Psalm 89:15; Isaiah 2:5; Ephesians 5:8–11

Refusing to use his gifts

If God gives us a 'spiritual gift' (Romans 12:3–8; 1 Corinthians 12:7–11, 28–31; Ephesians 4:7–13), we have a responsibility to use it (Romans 12:6). How sad the Spirit must be when we fail to exercise the gifts he has given, whether for building up the body of Christ (1 Corinthians 14:12) or sharing the gospel (Acts 1:8). In fact, when the Jerusalem church would not use its evangelistic gifts, the Holy Spirit arranged for a little bit of persecution to thrust them out of their cosy nest (Acts 8:1, 4). Perhaps he just became too tired of waiting!

Sometimes people are almost paralysed and do not use their gifts, spiritual or natural, for fear of making a mistake or of not pleasing God (see e.g. Matthew 25:24–25). But God would rather we 'had a go', even if we get it wrong, than that we never stepped out. Even Peter was encouraged by Jesus to 'give it a go' when he wanted to walk on the water with him (Matthew 14:28–29); there was time for Jesus to comment on his lack of faith later (Matthew 14:31)!

Do not put out the Spirit's fire

Paul wrote: 'Do not put out the Spirit's fire' (1 Thessalonians 5:19); or, as other versions put it, 'Do not quench the Spirit' (NKJV, NRSV, NASB). More recent versions translate it as: 'Do not hold back the work of the Spirit' (NCV); 'Do not stifle the Spirit' (NLT); 'Don't turn away God's Spirit' (CEV); 'Don't suppress the Spirit' (The Message).

The context of this verse (immediately before) is the issue of idleness, and (immediately after) prophecy. Paul says that sheer idleness can put out the Spirit's fire in us, and hence the Bible has many warnings about it (e.g. Proverbs 10:4; Ecclesiastes 10:18; 11:6; Matthew 25:26–30; 2 Thessalonians 3:6–12; Hebrews 6:12). If we are too lazy to read our Bibles, pray, worship with others and be active in the church, then it should not surprise us if the Spirit's fire burns low within us. But Paul also says that failure to receive prophecy (or any other spiritual gift, no doubt) can also quench the Spirit's fire. Of course, we should test prophecy and spiritual gifts (v 21); but we should never treat them with contempt (v 20).

There are many other things too that can 'hold back' or 'stifle' the work of the Spirit; things like fear, vested interests, half-heartedness, jealousy, bitterness, to name but a few. Remember: there is a solemn warning about becoming lukewarm; but also a promise for those who recognize it and do something about it:

'I know your deeds, that you are neither cold nor hot. I wish you were either one or the other! So, because you are lukewarm – neither hot nor cold – I am about to spit you out of my mouth. You say, "I am rich; I have acquired wealth and do not need a thing." But you do not realise that you are wretched, pitiful, poor, blind and naked. I counsel you to buy from me gold refined in the fire, so that you can become rich; and white clothes to wear, so that you can cover your shameful nakedness; and salve to put on your eyes, so that you can see. Those whom I love I rebuke and discipline. So be earnest, and repent. Here I am! I stand at the door and knock. If anyone hears my voice and opens the door, I will come in and eat with him, and he with me.'

(Revelation 3:15–20)

Keep in step with the Spirit

Let's turn now to some of the positive commands about keeping real with the Spirit.

Since we live by the Spirit, let us keep in step with the Spirit.

(Galatians 5:25)

We are reminded in the preceding verses of the need to 'live by the Spirit' (v 16), to be 'led by the Spirit' (v 18), to avoid what is not of the Spirit (vv 19–21), and to allow the Spirit's fruit to grow in us (vv 22–23). But while it is the Spirit who does the leading, it is we who must do the following (v 25). The Greek word means 'to draw up in line' or 'to keep in line', rather like soldiers marching in a row. Likewise, the Holy Spirit wants us follow him closely, keeping in step with him and everything he does. He wants to 'move us on', both individually, and as churches.

So, what about us? How are we doing? Are we moving or are we 'stuck'? Stuck in a time-warp of three hundred years ago, or thirty years ago, or even three years ago? The Spirit does not want us to keep in step with what he was doing then, but with what he is doing *now*; and not just a little group of us within the church, lost in some higher, more spiritual realm while the rest stay put; but the whole church, as a people bound together by the Spirit (Ephesians 4:3), keeping in step with him and so moving on with God. The Galatians had started out by keeping in step with the Spirit, but then had drifted away from that; so Paul asked them:

Are you so foolish? After beginning with the Spirit, are you now trying to attain your goal by human effort?

Galatians 3:3

Unless we are keeping in step with the Spirit today, the answer from us is 'Yes!'

Be aglow with the Spirit

Romans 12:11 reads, 'Keep your spiritual fervour'; but the RSV translates it as 'Be aglow with the Spirit'; other translations include 'eagerly follow the Holy Spirit' (CEV) and be 'fervent in spirit' – i.e. in your own human spirit (KJV, NASB). Our human spirit can only be kept 'on fire' by God's Holy Spirit.

Paul did not want his readers to be 'lukewarm', half-hearted, or lacking in enthusiasm, but to be set on fire by the Spirit! Note that the context of these verses is the laying down of our lives as 'living sacrifices' (12:1), both towards God (vv 1–3) and one another (vv 4–21). To live this way, we certainly need the Spirit's fire.

So how does this happen? Well, like any fire, the 'fire' of the Spirit needs fuel; things like Bible reading and prayer (not as some dry duty, but expecting the Spirit to speak through them!), worship, sharing our faith, and using our spiritual gifts.

Keep in the fellowship of the Spirit

The 'fellowship of the Holy Spirit' (2 Corinthians 13:14) is not just the final third of 'the grace' spoken at the end of some meetings. It is a reference to our sharing in his work.

The word 'fellowship' means 'participation in something together' and was used of 'business partnerships', for example. What the Holy Spirit is saying is: 'I want us to be business partners! You and me, and all these others I have brought to the Father.' This 'partnership' is his gift to us as much as grace is the gift of Jesus and love is the gift of the Father.

The 'fellowship of the Holy Spirit' is not a warm glow to make as feel good as we leave a meeting; it is the assurance of his presence as we go into the world to make a difference, and the assurance of his uniting us with others in the body of Christ. Fellowship with the Spirit will always be demonstrated in fellowship with one another (e.g. Philippians 2:1–2). If it doesn't, there is something terribly wrong.

As Bruce Milne puts it: 'The Spirit knows nothing of one-man-band Christians and ministries.'

Relevance for today

Revive us, Lord!

Don't we need constantly to know the Spirit breaking into our lives in a fresh way, keeping God's presence real and living? In times of revival – when God comes among his people in a special way – believers have a heightened sense of his presence and of the power of his word, and therefore of their own sinfulness before him. Such times have happened in many nations! Why should they not happen again?

There are many green shoots appearing for those with eyes to see. Things like the Alpha Course have brought a breath of fresh air to churches across the world. Through it, many Christians have found new boldness to share their faith, and countless numbers have found faith in Christ. And this is just one of the things God is doing. Let's keep praying for a genuine Holy Spirit revival to sweep across the world! And let's be ready when he comes to us!

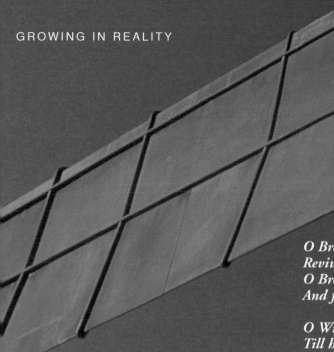

Will you not revive us again, that your people may rejoice in you?

(Psalm 85:6)

LORD, I have heard of your fame; I stand in awe of your deeds, O LORD. Renew them in our day, in our time make them known; in wrath remember mercy.

(Habakkuk 3:2)

This is what the LORD Almighty says: 'Many peoples and the inhabitants of many cities will yet come, and the inhabitants of one city will go to another and say, "Let us go at once to entreat the LORD and seek the LORD Almighty. I myself am going." And many peoples and powerful nations will come to Jerusalem to seek the LORD Almighty and to entreat him.' This is what the LORD Almighty says: 'In those days ten men from all languages and nations will take firm hold of one Jew by the hem of his robe and say, "Let us go with you, because we have heard that God is with you." '

(Zechariah 8:20–23)

See also Psalm 80:16–19; Ezekiel 37:1–14; Hosea 6:1–3; Micah 4:1–5

O Breath of Life, come sweeping through us,
Revive Thy church with life and power,
O Breath of Life, come, cleanse, renew us,
And fit Thy church to meet this hour.

O Wind of God, come, bend us, break us,
Till humbly we confess our need;
Then in Thy tenderness remake us,
Revive, restore; for this we plead.

O Breath of Love, come, breathe within us,
Renewing thought and will and heart:
Come, Love of Christ, afresh to win us,
Revive Thy church in every part.

Revive us, Lord! Is zeal abating
While harvest fields are vast and white?
Revive us, Lord, the world is waiting,
Equip Thy church to spread the light.

Elizabeth Ann Head, 1850–1936

Conclusion

As we seek to keep in step with the Spirit, we truly live in reality and are preparing for him to come in reviving power across the nations of the world.

May the . . . fellowship of the Holy Spirit be with you all.

(2 Corinthians 13:14)

PART FOUR

Belonging to the Church

CHAPTER ONE

The Promise of the Church

One of the deepest human needs is to know that we belong. As Christians we have the privilege of belonging to the family of God, his church.

God placed all things under his feet and appointed him to be head over everything for the church, which is his body, the fulness of him who fills everything in every way.
(Ephesians 1:22–23)

Ask the average person what they first think of when they hear the word 'church', and it will almost certainly be a building – one with funny-shaped windows, and perhaps a tower or spire. Some might think of weddings, brides and confetti; or, less happily, of funerals, coffins and mourners; others might think of the denomination that they grew up in many years ago and its apparent intolerance of 'the others' down the road. All in all, it will be a rather drab and unexciting picture.

To suggest to them that such an answer couldn't possibly be further from the truth would come as something as a shock! But shock it must be; for 'church' is none of these things. Church is nothing less than a family; God's family.

What do we mean by 'church'?

Before we explore what 'church' really means, let's note that the word is used in two main ways in the Bible: what is often called the 'universal church', and the 'local church'.

Universal and local

The 'universal church' is made up of everyone who truly believes in Jesus, whether living or dead. The church in this sense spreads through time and space, cuts across boundaries of colour, race, nationality and class (e.g. Galatians 3:28), and is destined to overcome everything in its path (e.g. Matthew 16:18)! It is used in this way, for example, in Matthew 16:18; Ephesians 1:22; 3:10, 21; 5:23–32.

The 'local church' is made up of a particular group of believers in a particular area. The New Testament letters, except those to individuals, are addressed to specific churches, whether in a city (e.g. 1 Corinthians 1:2; Ephesians 1:1; 1 Thessalonians 1:1) or in a region (e.g. Galatians 1:2; 1 Peter 1:1; Revelation 1:4). Jesus himself foresaw such local gatherings of his followers (Matthew 18:17–20).

Universal or local?

'So, is it possible to be part of one without being part of the other?' people sometimes ask. New Testament Christians would be astonished at such a question! They had absolutely no concept of such a thing; no concept of 'lone rangers' who see themselves as part of the great 'universal church', but who cannot, for some reason or other, settle down into a local expression of it. You can't have one without the other!

So, whether universal or local, what does 'church' actually mean?

The called ones

The word for 'church' in Greek is *ekklesia* (from which we get our word 'ecclesiastical'). It comes from a verb meaning 'to call out', and was used of any group of people who were called to meet together for some purpose – an 'assembly' (e.g. Acts 19:32, 39, 41). But the word also has a Hebrew background; for in the Greek translation of the Old Testament the word *ekklesia* was used to translate the Hebrew word *qahal*, 'the congregation of God's people' or 'the assembly' (e.g. Psalm 1:5; 22:25). Together the two word groups occur more than 700 times in the Bible.

It was this word that the early church used of themselves, for they understood they were a people with a special calling on their lives together.

Called out

As surely as Israel was called out of Egypt (Hosea 11:1), so Christians have been 'called out' – not from a place, but from sin and death; transferred from the kingdom of darkness to the kingdom of light.

But you are a chosen people, a royal priesthood, a holy nation, a people belonging to God, that you may declare the praises of him who called you out of darkness into his wonderful light.

(1 Peter 2:9)

For he has rescued us from the dominion of darkness and brought us into the kingdom of the Son he loves, in whom we have redemption, the forgiveness of sins.

Colossians 1:13–14)

See also Romans 1:6; 1 Corinthians 1:26–30; 2 Peter 1:3–4

Called for

We are not simply 'called out'; we are also called *for* a relationship with God – to know him, love him and serve him. This is the expression of God's covenant (see Part 1, Chapter 3), his drawing us into the 'family business'. We are not a holy club, with a list of do's and don'ts, we are people who have been called to enjoy a living relationship with the living God. Paul underlined this promise in one of his prayers:

I pray also that the eyes of your heart may be enlightened in order that you may know the hope to which he has called you, the riches of his glorious inheritance in the saints, and his incomparably great power for us who believe.

(Ephesians 1:18–19)

See also Romans 8:28–29; 2 Thessalonians 2:13–14

Called together

God calls us as individuals, but as individuals destined to become a new community. Like the spokes of a wheel, the closer we come to the centre (i.e. God), the closer we come to one another. Being a Christian is more than something involving just 'me and Jesus'; it is something we do together – or better, something we are together. Our faith must be personal, but it can never be private.

Just look again at the corporate nature of 1 Peter 2:9 (see above): a chosen people; a royal priesthood; a holy nation; none of these can happen with just one person! That is what makes solitary Christianity so impossible.

As you come to him, the living Stone – rejected by men but chosen by God and precious to him – you also, like living stones, are being built into a spiritual house to be a holy priesthood.

(1 Peter 2:4)

See also Ezekiel 37:1–10; Romans 12:4–5; 1 Corinthians 12:12; Ephesians 4:1–6

Being called together in this way is not just about going to meetings. If that is our understanding, then we are little more than balls in a game of pool that leave their pockets once a week to 'click around' on the table before returning to their own corner. Being 'called together' is about a

depth of relationship between us, and is far more important than the number of activities we're involved in. We can be very 'active' yet never demonstrate the 'togetherness' that Christ has promised for his people.

Called to

As Israel was called out of Egypt and into the promised land of Canaan (Exodus 3:7–10), we too are called to a future inheritance. For Christians the destination at the end of our journey is heaven and, ultimately, God's new creation (Revelation 21:1–4).

But our citizenship is in heaven. And we eagerly await a Saviour from there, the Lord Jesus Christ, who, by the power that enables him to bring everything under his control, will transform our lowly bodies so that they will be like his glorious body.

(Philippians 3:20–21)

See also 1 Corinthians 15:50–57; 2 Corinthians 5:1–5; Philippians 3:12–14; 1 Thessalonians 4:13–18; 2 Peter 3:10–13

But if our only hope is to 'get to heaven one day', then we are missing out now! There are many things that God calls us to along the way; it is a call to an adventure through life with him! Abraham was not told exactly where God would take him when he was called; he was simply told to 'go to the land I will show you' (Genesis 12:1). Have we lost something of a sense of going somewhere, of a sense of adventure with God?

Each of these aspects of being 'called' is part of the whole package of what it means to be a Christian: called out, called for, called together, called to. We cannot pick and choose the bits we like or that seem most comfortable or convenient; we either embrace them all, or we do not embrace them at all. Yet when each aspect is so full of God's promises, how silly it is to leave any of them on the shelf.

187

The church's birth

So, how did this church come into being? Well, like anything else 'living', it was born! It came into being through –

The plan of the Father

While the church was 'born' some two thousand years ago, that is not where its story begins. Before the beginning of human history, God already had the plan for his church in his heart!

For he chose us in him before the creation of the world to be holy and blameless in his sight.

(Ephesians 1:4)

See also Matthew 25:34; Ephesians 1:4–14

The promise and death of Jesus

The church was not the later invention of Jesus' disciples – a sort of club where they could gather to prop one another up or to tell their stories. Jesus himself promised its coming into being.

'*And I tell you that you are Peter, and on this rock I will build my church, and the gates of Hades will not overcome it.*'

(Matthew 16:18)

Our confidence for the success and growth of the church is based on the sure promise of Jesus. Your own church may have struggled to grow, or perhaps has even shrunk, this year; but meanwhile the church in China, for example, has grown by millions. The church of Jesus is growing! So let us not get discouraged. He has promised to build his church, and this is a promise he will keep. Our part in the process is simply to 'seek first his kingdom' (Matthew 6:33); it is his part to build his church.

But Jesus' promise in itself was not sufficient to bring the church to birth; for we first needed cleansing so that we could become God's community of renewed people. It was Christ's death on the cross that alone makes it possible for sinful people to be drawn into God's new family (Ephesians 2:14–22).

. . . the church of God, which he bought with his own blood.

(Acts 20:28)

See also Colossians 1:18–20

The work of the Holy Spirit

The church, planned by the Father, and promised and made possible by the Son, was brought to birth by the Spirit at Pentecost. It was only as he came and baptized the disciples in his very self, just as Jesus promised (Acts 1:5), that the disciples began to boldly proclaim the risen Jesus – and some three thousand were 'added to their number that day' (Acts 2:41).

Then the church throughout Judea, Galilee and Samaria enjoyed a time of peace. It was strengthened; and encouraged by the Holy Spirit, it grew in numbers, living in the fear of the Lord.

(Acts 9:31)

The ministry of apostles and prophets

While the ultimate foundation of the church is Christ alone (1 Corinthians 3:11), the apostles and prophets were seen, in a secondary sense and from a human point of view, as the foundation of the church.

Consequently, you are no longer foreigners and aliens, but fellow-citizens with God's people and members of God's household, built on the foundation of the apostles and prophets, with Christ Jesus himself as the chief cornerstone.

(Ephesians 2:19–20)
See also Matthew 16:17–18; 1 Corinthians 3:10–11

Promises for the church

Not only was the church itself promised, it was given many promises. Here are just some of them:

Headship
Jesus will be the head of the church.

And God placed all things under his feet and appointed him to be head over everything for the church.

(Ephesians 1:22)
See also Ephesians 4:15; 5:23; Colossians 1:18; 2:19

Foundation
Jesus will be the cornerstone of the church.

For in Scripture it says: 'See, I lay a stone in Zion, a chosen and precious cornerstone, and the one who trusts in him will never be put to shame.'

(1 Peter 2:6)
See also Matthew 21:42; Ephesians 2:20–21

Authority
Jesus has given the church authority to go and make disciples.

'All authority in heaven and on earth has been given to me. Therefore go and make disciples of all nations, baptising them in the name of the Father and of the Son and of the Holy Spirit, and teaching them to obey everything I have commanded you. And surely I am with you always, to the very end of the age.'

(Matthew 28:18–20)
See also Mark 16:15–20; Acts 1:8

Gifts
Jesus has given gifts to the church.

But to each one of us grace has been given as Christ apportioned it. This is why it says: 'When he ascended on high, he led captives in his train and gave gifts to men.'

(Ephesians 4:7–8)
See also Romans 12:4–8; 1 Corinthians 12:7–11; Ephesians 4:11–13

Care
Jesus will care for the church.

After all, no-one ever hated his own body, but he feeds and cares for it, just as Christ does the church.

(Ephesians 5:29)

See also Ephesians 5:25; 1 Peter 5:7

Protection

Jesus will protect the church.

'I will build my church, and all the powers of hell will not conquer it.'

(Matthew 16:18, NLT)

See also John 10:11–15, 27–29

Presence

Jesus will always be with the church.

'For where two or three have gathered together in My name, I am there in their midst.'

(Matthew 18:20, NASB)

See also John 14:16; Hebrews 13:5

Wisdom

God's wisdom will be made known through the church.

His intent was that now, through the church, the manifold wisdom of God should be made known to the rulers and authorities in the heavenly realms.

(Ephesians 3:10)

See also 1 Corinthians 2:6–10

Glory

God's glory will be shown through the church.

Now to him who is able to do immeasurably more than all we ask or imagine, according to his power that is at work within us, to him be glory in the church and in Christ Jesus throughout all generations, for ever and ever! Amen.

(Ephesians 3:20–21)

See also Colossians 1:27

Unity

Unity is the birthright of the church.

'Holy Father, protect them by the power of your name – the name you gave me – so that they may be one as we are one'

(John 17:11)

See also John 17:21–22; 1 Corinthians 10:17; 12:12–31; Galatians 3:28; Ephesians 4:3–4

Love

Love will be the hallmark of the church.

'By this all men will know that you are my disciples, if you love one another.'

(John 13:35)

See also 1 John 3:11–16; 4:7–21

Growth

Growth is part of the 'genetic make-up' of the church. Just look in the book of Acts and see how the church kept growing, just as Jesus promised, in a variety of very different situations:

'I will build my church . . .'

(Matthew 16:18)

See also Acts 1:8; 2:47; 4:4; 5:14; 6:7; 8:12; 9:31; 11:21; 12:24; 13:49–52; 14:1–3; 16:13–15; 17:4, 12, 34; 18:7–8; 19:1–20

Future

A glorious future is the sure destiny of the church.

'In my Father's house are many rooms; if it were not so, I would have told you. I am going there to prepare a place for you. And if I go and prepare a place for you, I will come back and take you to be with me that you also may be where I am.'

(John 14:2–3)

See also Ephesians 5:27; Revelation 21:1–5, 9–14

Relevance for today

❏ 'Church' is not a place we go to, but rather a living, dynamic expression of Christ's activity in the world today; a body in which we all have a vital part to play (1 Corinthians 12:12–27).

Now you are the body of Christ, and each one of you is a part of it.

(1 Corinthians 12:27)

❏ If the church is so in God's heart, then we cannot dismiss it as an irrelevance or additional extra for today.

Christ loved the church and gave himself up for her.

(Ephesians 5:25)

If this is so, and if I claim to be his follower, then how can I do any less?

❏ 'Church' is not just a meeting to go to on Sundays; it is the sphere of an exciting adventure with God and all his people.

You have come to Mount Zion, to the heavenly Jerusalem, the city of the living God. You have come to thousands upon thousands of angels in joyful assembly, to the church of the firstborn, whose names are written in heaven. You have come to God, the judge of all men, to the spirits of righteous men made perfect, to Jesus the mediator of a new covenant, and to the sprinkled blood that speaks a better word than the blood of Abel.

(Hebrews 12:22–24)

❏ If I have fallen into the trap of being a 'lone Christian', I need to look whether I am holding on to some past hurt or disappointment that I simply need to release rather than continue to nurse it and remain isolated.

Let us not give up meeting together, as some are in the habit of doing, but let us encourage one another – and all the more as you see the Day approaching.

(Hebrews 10:25)

❏ Jesus will build his church (Matthew 16:18) if we will 'seek first his kingdom and his righteousness' (Matthew 6:33).
.

191

The church's one foundation
Is Jesus Christ her Lord;
She is His new creation
By water and the Word;
From heaven He came and sought her
To be His holy bride;
With His own blood He bought her,
And for her life He died.

Elect from every nation,
Yet one o'er all the earth;
Her charter of salvation –
One Lord, one faith, one birth;
One holy Name she blesses,
Partakes one holy food;
And to one hope she presses,
With every grace endued.

Though with a scornful wonder
Men see her sore oppressed,
By schisms rent asunder,
By heresies distressed,
Yet saints their watch are keeping,
Their cry goes up, 'How long?'
And soon the night of weeping
Shall be the morn of song.

'Mid toil and tribulation,
And tumult of her war,
She waits the consummation
Of peace for evermore;
Till with the vision glorious
Her longing eyes are blest,
And the great church victorious
Shall be the church at rest.

Yet she on earth hath union
With God the Three in One,
And mystic sweet communion
With those whose rest is won.
O happy ones and holy!
Lord, give us grace that we,
Like them, the meek and lowly
On high may dwell with Thee!

Samuel John Stone, 1839–1900

Conclusion

The church of Christ is made up of all those who are saved. It is his church: he is active in it and through it to fulfil his purposes.

'I will build my church, and the gates of Hades [or hell] will not overcome it.'

(Matthew 16:18)

CHAPTER TWO

God's Plan for the Church

Different pictures of 'the church' in the New Testament reveal how exciting God's plan is for it, and for our part in it.

But you are a chosen people, a royal priesthood, a holy nation, a people belonging to God, that you may declare the praises of him who called you out of darkness into his wonderful light. Once you were not a people, but now you are the people of God; once you had not received mercy, but now you have received mercy. (1 Peter 2:9–10)

Trying to change our mindset about things can be difficult. Imagine how people must have felt when they discovered that the earth was not flat, or that people could fly, or that pictures could be transmitted. Such things are hard to get your mind around at first!

That's how it is for many people with 'the church'. For them, as we saw in the previous chapter, the church is a building. But God wants them to realise that the church is not about buildings but about people.

Changing our mindset

God really wants to change our mindset – the way we look at life and approach it (Romans 12:2). There are two key areas in our thinking about 'church' which he wants to change:

Becoming 'a part'

In the New Testament, whenever anyone became a Christian, they were immediately baptized and became part of the local group of Christians, the church (see e.g. Acts 2:37–41; 9:26–28; 18:1–11). Paul links being baptized with the Spirit with becoming part of the church:

For we were all baptised by one Spirit into one body – whether Jews or Greeks, slave or free – and we were all given the one Spirit to drink.
(1 Corinthians 12:13)

They had no concept of 'go-it-alone' Christians, reflected in the fact that the word 'saint' (a synonym for 'Christian') is always in the plural in the New Testament. Even the one apparent singular usage in the Authorized (King James) Version is corporate: 'Salute [greet] every saint in Christ Jesus' (Philippians 4:21). This should tell us something! In the words of Michael Griffiths, 'the concept of a solitary saint is foreign to the New Testament writers'. At conversion, Christians identified themselves with the local church where they 'became a part'.

Thinking 'us' not 'them'

A second area where God wants to change our thinking concerns 'us' and 'them'. Martin was once at a meeting where the speaker asked everyone to write a sentence about 'the church'. Most people began with 'It' or 'They'. But to be fully biblical, the sentence should have begun with 'We' ('We do this . . .', 'We are this . . .'). The church is not 'them', but 'us'!

Zephaniah has a beautiful picture of this corporate togetherness that God promises for his people:

'Then will I purify the lips of the peoples, that all of them may call on the name of the LORD and serve him shoulder to shoulder.'
(Zephaniah 3:9)

'Shoulder to shoulder' is how God wants his people standing together! Us, not them.

God's plan for the church, then, is not that it should be a building (that's just a place where we can gather!), but a community of his people, made up of those who see that, as God's children, we cannot live as isolated believers, but must stand firmly together, shoulder to shoulder.

Getting the picture

God's plan for us is reflected in the various pictures that the New Testament uses of 'church' – although to call them 'pictures' is in some ways misleading. These are not simply illustrations to make a point; they are the reality of how God sees us and wants us to live together.

A Family

Right back with Abraham, God promised to build a big family for himself (Genesis 12:1–3; 17:3–6). It should not surprise us then to see the church described as a 'family' or a 'household'.

Consequently, you are no longer foreigners and aliens, but fellow-citizens with God's people and members of God's household.

(Ephesians 2:19)

For this reason I kneel before the Father, from whom his whole family in heaven and on earth derives its name.

(Ephesians 3:14–15)

See also Galatians 6:10; 1 Timothy 3:15; 1 Peter 4:17

At ease together

'Family' speaks of being together and being at ease. No one should be left out or feel a stranger (e.g. Hebrews 13:1–3; James 2:1–9), but should be integrated as children in the family. 'This is what the congregation ought to mean to us – a place where we feel safe, can be ourselves, and have no need to be boarded up behind a façade, a place where we are cared for and care for one another' (Michael Griffiths). The church should be where we can relax, rather than where we feel we have to 'perform' – whether through the way we dress, behave, take part or whatever.

Church in the home

It's so good that the church has been rediscovering the importance of using homes for some meetings, for this helps build a sense of real family. Using homes was a key feature of early church life; in fact, when Paul was a persecutor of the church, it wasn't to some central building that he went to round them up, but rather 'from house to house' (Acts 8:3). Homes played a key part (see e.g. Acts 2:46; 20:20; Romans 16:5; 1 Corinthians 16:19; Colossians 4:15), not simply because they didn't have church buildings yet, but because they really helped to express 'family'.

A Body

The picture of the church as a body brings home three key facts:

Christ is the head

It is only as we let Christ be the head and draw life from him that the church can grow:

Christ is the head of the church, his body, of which he is the Saviour.

(Ephesians 5:23)

See also Ephesians 1:9–10, 22–23; Colossians 1:18, 24; 2:19;

Speaking the truth in love, we will in all things grow up into him who is the Head, that is, Christ. From him the whole body, joined and held together by every supporting ligament, grows and builds itself up in love, as each part does its work.

(Ephesians 4:15–16)

. . . the Head, from whom the whole body, supported and held together by its ligaments and sinews, grows as God causes it to grow.

(Colossians 2:19)

No matter what our church structures might be, there is only one head of the church (whether local or universal). Jesus alone is the head; he makes the decisions, brings the direction and supplies the life.

Every member is vital

In 1 Corinthians 12 Paul shows just how important every part of the human body is; and so it is with the church, he says. Each of us is a part of Christ's body; together those parts express Christ in the world.

Just as each of us has one body with many members, and these members do not all have the same function, so in Christ we who are many form one body, and each member belongs to all the others.

(Romans 12:4–5)

The body is a unit, though it is made up of many parts; and though all its parts are many, they form one body. So it is with Christ.

(1 Corinthians 12:12)

Now you are the body of Christ, and each one of you is a part of it.

(1 Corinthians 12:27)

See also 1 Corinthians 10:16–17; 12:12–31; Ephesians 3:6

One of Martin's friends once broke her little toe. Not only was it very painful, it made her far less mobile. Even when it is something so small out of joint, the whole body cannot function properly. So it is with the body of Christ. No member of it is unimportant (1 Corinthians 12:14–18) or unnecessary (1 Corinthians 12:21–26). Equally, no members are more important than others; all are needed in different ways, but equally (1 Corinthians 12:27–30). If you ask most Christians what the most important jobs in the church are they will probably reply 'preaching' or 'pastoring'. But the Bible says: the most important tasks are – all of them! Just think of a church service: we might thank the preacher at the end; but what about those who helped him to preach? What about those who put out chairs, welcomed visitors, operated the PA equipment, produced the news sheet, played the instruments, served the tea, swept up our mess at the end? All of them are important; all need each other; all have a vital place in the body; all are valued by Christ, the head, for their service to him.

Leaders equip the body

So, what is the role of leaders then – whether pastors, group leaders or youth leaders? Well, the Bible says they are not there to 'do the work'! Rather, their role is to equip the members to do the work!

It was he [Jesus] who gave some to be apostles, some to be prophets, some to be evangelists, and some to be pastors and teachers, to prepare God's people for works of service, so that the body of Christ may be built up until we all reach unity in the faith and in the knowledge of the Son of God and become mature, attaining to the whole measure of the fulness of Christ.

(Ephesians 4:11–13)

Don't expect your leaders to do everything! That's not what they are there for. God has given them to us to ensure that the body functions. When a church operates like this, Paul says, it is really becoming mature!

A Building

People often talk about 'the house of God' – meaning a building of some sort, whether tiny chapel or grand cathedral; but actually, the house of God is people!

'Living stones'

In the Old Testament King David wanted to build a 'house' for God – a great temple (2 Samuel 7:1–2); but God said to him, 'I'm going to build a house for you instead!' (2 Samuel 7:4–29). Initially a 'royal house' or dynasty, it would become a vast family through David's descendant, Jesus. God has always had it in his heart to have a house of people, not of stones.

For we are . . . God's building

(1 Corinthians 3:9)

You also, like living stones, are being built into a spiritual house to be a holy priesthood, offering spiritual sacrifices acceptable to God through Jesus Christ.

(1 Peter 2:5)

See also Ephesians 2:19–22

Still under construction

And in him [Jesus] you too are being built together to become a dwelling in which God lives by his Spirit.

(Ephesians 2:22)

Note it says we are being built. The 'building' is still under construction! This means, first, that we will have to exercise patience and tolerance with one another at times (ask anyone who has worked on a building site!); and second, that we need to take care how we build.

By the grace God has given me, I laid a foundation as an expert builder, and someone else is building on it. But each one should be careful how he builds. For no-one can lay any foundation other than the one already laid, which is Jesus Christ. If any man builds on this foundation using gold, silver, costly stones, wood, hay or straw, his work will be shown for what it is, because the Day will bring it to light. It will be revealed with fire, and the fire will test the quality of each man's work. If what he has built survives, he will receive his reward. If it is burned up, he will suffer loss; he himself will be saved, but only as one escaping through the flames.

(1 Corinthians 3:10–15)

Christ alone is the cornerstone

No matter how important good leadership might be, we must remember that God's plan for the church focuses on Jesus. No leader, however gifted, can take Jesus' place. Indeed, Paul said, it is stupid to promote one leader over another when all are simply servants of Christ (1 Corinthians 1:10–17). Christ alone is the cornerstone of the church.

Consequently, you are no longer foreigners and aliens, but fellow-citizens with God's people and members of God's household, built on the foundation of the apostles and prophets, with Christ Jesus himself as the chief cornerstone.

(Ephesians 2:19–20)

For in Scripture it says: 'See, I lay a stone in Zion, a chosen and precious cornerstone, and the one who trusts in him will never be put to shame.'

(1 Peter 2:6)

See also Matthew 21:42; Acts 4:11; 1 Peter 2:7

A Bride

Perhaps the most beautiful picture of the church in the New Testament is that of a bride.

'Come, I will show you the bride, the wife of the Lamb.'

(Revelation 21:9)

What a thought: the church is to be 'married' to Christ! Such a picture speaks to us of:

Love and intimacy

Husbands, love your wives, just as Christ loved the church and gave himself up for her to make her holy, cleansing her by the washing with water through the word, and to present her to himself as a radiant church, without stain or wrinkle or any other blemish, but holy and blameless . . . 'For this reason a man will leave his father and mother and be united to his wife, and the two will become one flesh.' This is a profound mystery – but I am talking about Christ and the church.

(Ephesians 5:25–27, 31–32)

While Song of Songs is essentially a song in praise of God-given love, written in the style of Wisdom literature, many Christians over the centuries have also seen in it a beautiful picture of the intimate relationship between Christ and his bride.

Like an apple tree among the trees of the forest is my lover among the young men. I delight to sit in his shade, and his fruit is sweet to my taste. He has taken me to the banquet hall, and his banner over me is love.

(Song of Songs 2:3–4)

Devotion and purity

'The bride belongs to the bridegroom.'

(John 3:29)

I [Paul] am jealous for you with a godly jealousy. I promised you to one husband, to Christ, so that I might present you as a pure virgin to him.

(2 Corinthians 11:2)

Preparation

Just as a human bride prepares herself to look her very best on 'the great day', so the church should be preparing now, in anticipation of its final transformation on the last 'Great Day'.

'Let us rejoice and be glad and give him glory! For the wedding of the Lamb has come, and his bride has made herself ready.'

(Revelation 19:7)

I saw the Holy City, the new Jerusalem, coming down out of heaven from God, prepared as a bride beautifully dressed for her husband.

(Revelation 21:2)

See also Ephesians 5:25–27

Other pictures of the church

As well as the main pictures we have looked at, the New Testament also uses a number of others. These include:

• Army (2 Corinthians 10:3–4; Ephesians 6:10–17)
• Branches of the vine (John 15:1–5)
• City (Hebrews 12:22; Revelation 21:2, 10)
• Field (1 Corinthians 3:9)
• Flock (John 10:16; 1 Peter 5:2)
• God's holy people (Ephesians 5:3; 2 Thessalonians 1:10)
• Israel of God (Galatians 6:16)
• Multitude (Revelation 7:9–17)
• Nation (1 Peter 2:9)
• Priesthood (1 Peter 2:5, 9; Revelation 1:6; 5:10)
• Temple (2 Corinthians 6:16)
• Zion (Romans 9:33; Hebrews 12:22–23)

Note how all these images are corporate or demand corporate response. It is impossible for just one person to be them! God's plan is truly for us to know him and follow him together.

Relevance for today

A unique church
The church is the unique expression of Christ in the world. There is no organization on earth that can do what the church can do; it alone is the expression of Christ's 'fullness' and the carrier of God's wisdom.

God placed all things under his feet and appointed him to be head over everything for the church, which is his body, the fulness of him who fills everything in every way.

(Ephesians 1:22–23)

His intent was that now, through the church, the manifold wisdom of God should be made known to the rulers and authorities in the heavenly realms.

(Ephesians 3:10)

The reality of the church
The church is about 'us' not 'them'. Have I grasped this and am I living it? Do I understand that images of the church in the New Testament are not just 'pictures', but realities, and am I living in the light of that?

The local church
Living faith in Jesus is expressed in a living church of Jesus. Have you 'become part' of a local church? Or have you simply made excuses (see, e.g., the parable in Luke 14:15–24). There is no such thing as a 'lone Christian' in the Bible.

Jesus challenges the church
Jesus, as head, has the right to challenge his church. When we drift from his plan or his ways, or when our hearts grow cold, Jesus has the right to challenge us and to demand change, just as he did with the seven churches in Revelation (see Revelation 2:1–3:22).

Leadership
Leaders are there to equip us. If we look to our church leaders to do all the work, we have a defective view of why Jesus gave them to us; they are there to 'equip' not to 'do'.

Their responsibility is to equip God's people to do his work and build up the church, the body of Christ.

(Ephesians 4:12, NLT)

Discernment
We are called to be family towards one another, soldiers towards the devil. Sadly, the church sometimes mixes those up! Let us love one another, and fight against the devil, not vice-versa. Know when it's time for what!

Church of God, elect and glorious,
holy nation, chosen race;
called as God's own special people,
royal priests and heirs of grace:
know the purpose of your calling,
show to all his mighty deeds;
tell of love which knows no limits
grace which meets all human needs.

God has called you out of darkness
into his most marvellous light;
brought his truth to life within you,
turned your blindness into sight:
let your light so shine around you
that God's name is glorified;
and all find fresh hope and purpose
in Christ Jesus crucified.

Once you were an alien people,
strangers to God's heart of love,
but he brought you home in mercy,
citizens of heaven above:
let his love flow out to others,
let them feel a Father's care;
that they too may know his welcome,
and his countless blessings share.

Church of God, elect and holy,
be the people he intends;
strong in faith and swift to answer
each command your master sends:
royal priests, fulfil your calling
through your sacrifice and prayer;
give your lives in joyful service
sing his praise, his love declare.

James Seddon, 1915–1983

Conclusion

The church is a living fellowship, not a dead building; an organism not an organization; a close family, not a bunch of individuals. God's plan is for us now to become this people, preparing as the bride of Christ for the day when we come to full and perfect beauty for our wedding with the Lamb.

Christ loved the church and gave himself up for her . . . to present her to himself as a radiant church, without stain or wrinkle or any other blemish, but holy and blameless.

(Ephesians 5:25, 27)

CHAPTER THREE

The Marks of a Church

Certain characteristics stand out in the life of one church in the New Testament. If we are courageous enough to work them through ourselves, God will produce similar results in our churches today, for his glory.

It was in Antioch that the disciples were for the first time called Christians. (Acts 11:26, The Message)

Every aspect of life has an example that is quite outstanding and that 'sets the benchmark' for all that follows: Abraham Lincoln in American politics, Elvis Presley in rock music, Henry Ford in car manufacturing, and so on. In terms of church life, it was undoubtedly, not Jerusalem or Rome, but Antioch that 'set the benchmark' for what normal Christian life was all about. While the Jerusalem church got stuck within its narrow confines, Antioch pushed back the boundaries and cast its influence across the known world. Who wouldn't want to be part of a church like that!

Antioch: a model church

Antioch: population 300,000, third largest city in the Roman Empire, situated by the north-eastern corner of the Mediterranean; clearly a place with great potential for the Christian church. And it was potential that was realized. The church grew through people being converted (Acts 11:21, 24), both Jew and Gentile alike (Acts 11:19–20). It refused to be inward-looking; whenever God spoke, they responded positively and pushed back the boundaries (Acts 11:28–30; 13:2–3). In fact, the church was so 'successful' that it was here, for the first time, that 'the disciples were called Christians' (Acts 11:26) – 'Christ-people' (quite possibly a nickname at first). The word used for 'were called' actually means 'to transact business in someone's name'. In other words, everything these disciples did had the hallmark of being done in the name of Jesus! Little wonder they were called after him; little wonder they grew!

So, what were some of the secrets of their 'success'? It all grew out of their vision for what 'church' was all about.

A vision for involving all

Church life at Antioch involved everyone, not just the 'specialists' or the 'experts'. They really did believe in the church as 'the body of Christ' (see Chapter 2 of this section).

Evangelism

When persecution arose in Jerusalem, the main leaders stayed there (Acts 8:1), while the 'ordinary' Christians had been scattered (Acts 11:19–20). What did they do? Clam up? No! They simply got on with sharing the gospel (v 20). And the result?

The Lord's hand was with them, and a great number of people believed and turned to the Lord.

(Acts 11:21)

There were no 'big names'; no well-known speakers or travelling ministries; even Barnabas didn't come till later when they heard what was going on (v 22)! The 'ordinary' believers just shared the gospel naturally by speaking to people and telling them the good news about Jesus (see also Acts 8:4).

What about us? Do we want to 'leave it to the experts'? Do we think it's enough just to live an upright life and never talk to anyone about Jesus? Our lifestyle is indeed often a key in

preparing the ground, and good deeds often water that ground; but ultimately, the seed must be sown; and the seed is 'the word of God' (Luke 8:11).

How can people have faith in the Lord and ask him to save them, if they have never heard about him? And how can they hear, unless someone tells them? And how can anyone tell them without being sent by the Lord? The Scriptures say it is a beautiful sight to see even the feet of someone coming to preach the good news.

(Romans 10:14–15, CEV)

Compassion

A second area where the 'ordinary' church members were actively involved was in the 'ministry of compassion'. Alerted to an impending famine through prophecy, 'the disciples, each according to his ability, decided to provide help for the brothers living in Judea' (Acts 11:29). Compassionate ministry is a hallmark of all true biblical faith, for compassion is a hallmark of God himself (e.g. Exodus 34:6; see Part 1, Chapter 5). God's people should demonstrate that same compassion.

If there is a poor man among your brothers in any of the towns of the land that the LORD your God is giving you, do not be hard-hearted or tight-fisted towards your poor brother. Rather be open-handed and freely lend him whatever he needs . . . Give generously to him and do so without a grudging heart; then because of this the LORD your God will bless you in all your work and in everything you put your hand to.

(Deuteronomy 15:7–8, 10)

All they asked was that we should continue to remember the poor, the very thing I [Paul] was eager to do.

(Galatians 2:10)

See also Job 29:11–16; Proverbs 28:27; Matthew 6:2–4; Acts 2:44–45; 4:32–35; Romans 15:25–27

A vision for worship

In the church at Antioch there were prophets and teachers . . . While they were worshipping the Lord and fasting, the Holy Spirit said, 'Set apart for me Barnabas and Saul for the work to which I have called them.' So after they had fasted and prayed, they placed their hands on them and sent them off.

(Acts 13:1–3)

Even in this short passage, we get some insights into their attitude to worship.

Worship is central

Note that, while this was a meeting of leaders, rather than of the whole church, it was nonetheless a model. This was not just a 'business meeting'; they were eager to touch God's heart in order to find God's direction. (Leaders please note! What leaders do not model, the church will not pick up.) God's people should always be eager to gather together, and worship should always have a central place whenever they do.

I rejoiced with those who said to me, 'Let us go to the house of the LORD.' Our feet are standing in your gates, O Jerusalem. Jerusalem is built like a city that is closely compacted together. That is where the tribes go up, the tribes of the LORD, to praise the name of the LORD.

(Psalm 122:1–4)

See also Exodus 33:7–11; 2 Kings 17:27–28; 2 Chronicles 7:1–3; 20:18–22; Nehemiah 8:5–6; 9:3; Acts 4:23–31

Worship is serious

Note that it included, on this occasion at least, fasting. Fasting – denying ourselves food or drink for a period of time to seek God – shows our seriousness before him. It is helpful for drawing closer to God to seek his direction, and often leads to significant spiritual breakthrough, just as here in Antioch (Acts 13:2). It is a practice commended both in Old and New Testaments.

There, by the Ahava Canal, I proclaimed a fast, so that we might humble ourselves before our God and ask him for a safe journey for us and our children, with all our possessions. I was ashamed to ask the king for soldiers and horsemen to protect us from enemies on the road, because we had told the king, 'The gracious hand of our God is on everyone who looks to him, but his great anger is against all who forsake him.' So we fasted and petitioned our God about this, and he answered our prayer.

(Ezra 8:21–23)

See also 2 Chronicles 20:2–4; Nehemiah 9:1–4; Esther 4:16; Daniel 9:1–3; Joel 2:12–14; Matthew 4:1–2; Mark 2:18–20; Acts 14:23

When we do fast, however, it is important that we do so in the right way and with the right spirit.

'When you fast, do not look sombre as the hypocrites do, for they disfigure their faces to show men they are fasting. I tell you the truth, they have received their reward in full. But when you fast, put oil on your head and wash your face, so that it will not be obvious to men that you are fasting, but only to your Father, who is unseen; and your Father, who sees what is done in secret, will reward you.'

(Matthew 6:16–18)

See also Isaiah 58:3–9

Worship is sensitive

As they worshipped, they were sensitive to God and, no doubt, to each other. They made room for *silence* – so they could listen to God – and *spontaneity* – so they could bring his word (Acts 13:2). Would that we gave God's Spirit more room in our own meetings! While there is still need of preparation, some of our meetings are so one hundred per cent predictable that God couldn't break in if he tried!

Paul encouraged the Corinthians to develop such sensitivity to the Spirit (even though they often got it wrong!) and promised that such responsiveness to the Spirit could have a powerful effect.

If an unbeliever or someone who does not understand comes in while everybody is prophesying, he will be convinced by all that he is a sinner and will be judged by all, and the secrets of his heart will be laid bare. So he will fall down and worship God, exclaiming, 'God is really among you!'

(1 Corinthians 14:24–25)

Worship includes the word

Luke tells us that 'for a whole year Barnabas and Saul met with the church and taught great numbers of people' (Acts 11:26). Their teaching, and their putting it into practice, was so Christ-centred that they were given the name 'Christians'. Right at the heart of the leadership team were 'teachers'.

Without the word of God having a central place, we are open to the danger of drifting from the truth.

We must pay more careful attention, therefore, to what we have heard, so that we do not drift away.

(Hebrews 2:1)

See also 1 Corinthians 15:2; 2 Thessalonians 2:15; 1 Timothy 1:18–20; 2 Timothy 2:17–19

But the word is not just for hearing, but also for doing.

Do not merely listen to the word, and so deceive yourselves. Do what it says. Anyone who listens to the word but does not do what it says is like a man who looks at his face in a mirror and, after looking at himself, goes away and immediately forgets what he looks like. But the man who looks intently into the perfect law that gives freedom, and continues to do this, not forgetting what he has heard, but doing it – he will be blessed in what he does.

(James 1:22–25)

See also Deuteronomy 4:1–2; 1 Kings 6:11–13; Matthew 7:21–27; 1 John 5:2–3

Of course, obeying the word is fairly easy to do when there is no personal cost involved. But the church at Antioch obeyed, even when it was sacrificial! When they were convinced that God had called two of their top men, they were obedient and released them (Acts 13:2–3). That took courage on the part of the leadership and the church; thoughts of 'Our best men can't go – how will we manage without them?' don't seem to have figured much. They acted in obedience to God, whatever the sacrifice meant to them, knowing that God would 'make up the shortfall'.

Worship includes giving

When they heard the prophecy about the coming famine, they dug into their pockets 'each according to his ability' (Acts 11:29) to help the Jerusalem church. Generous giving is a hallmark of true worship.

There are two main aspects of giving in the Bible:

Tithing

Tithing – the giving of one tenth of our income to God – is a risky business (after all, you are giving a tenth of your money away!); but it is something that God has commanded his blessing over.

'Will a man rob God? Yet you rob me. But you ask, "How do we rob you?" In tithes and offerings. You are under a curse – the whole nation of you – because you are robbing me. Bring the whole tithe into the storehouse, that there may be food in my house. Test me in this,' says the LORD *Almighty, 'and see if I will not throw open the floodgates of heaven and pour out so much blessing that you will not have room enough for it.'*

(Malachi 3:8–10)

See also Leviticus 27:30; Numbers 18:25–29; Deuteronomy 14:22–29; 2 Chronicles 31:3–10

Some Christians dismiss tithing on the grounds that it belongs to the Jewish Law; but in fact, it was practised long before the Law came into being, arising instinctively in the hearts of God's faithful servants long before God actually commanded it (e.g. Genesis 14:20; 28:22). Even Jesus did not challenge its practice, simply the perverted way of doing it (Matthew 23:23). The first Christians, converted as they were from Judaism, would almost certainly have continued tithing.

Giving

In addition to tithing, God's word made provision for 'freewill offerings' (see e.g. Exodus 35:29; Deuteronomy 12:5–6; 16:10; Ezra 1:3–4). In other words, the tithe was just the beginning! God wants his people to be as generous-hearted as he himself is. So, by all means do not tithe – as long as your giving far exceeds it!

To catch the spirit of giving in the New Testament church, we need to read the whole of 2 Corinthians 8–9; but here are just a few key verses to whet your appetite!

Our desire is not that others might be relieved while you are hard pressed, but that there might be equality. At the present time your plenty will supply what they need, so that in turn their plenty will supply what you need. Then there will be equality, as it is written: 'He who gathered much did not have too much, and he who gathered little did not have too little.'

(2 Corinthians 8:13–15)

Remember this: Whoever sows sparingly will also reap sparingly, and whoever sows generously will also reap generously. Each man should give what he has decided in his heart to give, not reluctantly or under compulsion, for God loves a cheerful giver. And God is able to make all grace abound to you, so that in all things at all times, having all that you need, you will abound in every good work.

(2 Corinthians 9:6–8)

A vision to develop leaders

Every church needs good leadership (Acts 14:23; Ephesians 4:11–12), and Antioch certainly had that. Barnabas, 'Mr Encouragement', quickly gave himself to nurturing the new believers (Acts 11:23). As a man 'full of the Holy Spirit and faith', his presence also seems also to have spurred on further evangelistic reaping (Acts 11:24). But Barnabas was aware of his own limitations; he knew he couldn't do everything himself, no matter how gifted he was; so he went and found Paul and brought him back to help (Acts 11:25–26). We soon find a *team* of leaders in place (Acts 13:1), releasing yet another team to go and do more work (Acts 13:2–3).

Plural leadership was characteristic of early church life (see e.g. Acts 6:2–6; 15:6; 20:17; Ephesians 4:11–12; Philippians 1:1), and it was all the more effective because of it – though no doubt painful at times! At Antioch there were prophets and teachers (Acts 13:1) – a real combination for tension! Michael Green writes: 'It would be hard to find more uncomfortable

bedfellows than that. The prophet is always tending to move on instinct; you never know what the man is going to do next. And the teacher is painfully predictable. To use contemporary language, the prophet is "charismatic" and the teacher is not. This is one of the hottest issues in a number of churches of all denominations all over the world at the moment. Antioch solved it by having both types represented in the leadership. How wise they were! This meant that the worship combined the warm spirituality of the charismatics and the balanced teaching ministry of the teachers. How rarely is that balance found in a modern church, but what a power it is when the combination comes off.'

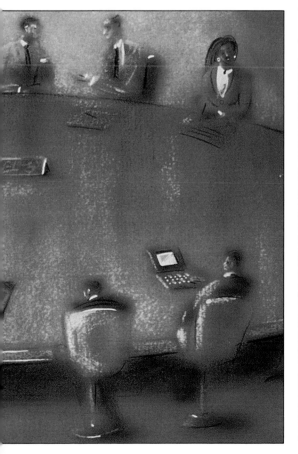

A vision to innovate

Some churches are content to 'hold the fort until Jesus comes'; but not Antioch! For them, it was not an issue of 'status quo' but 'status go'! They had a passion to constantly break new ground. It was one of the first churches to take up the challenge of preaching to, and integrating, both Jews and Gentiles (Acts 11:19–20; 13:4–5, 44–48; 14:26–28; 15:1–4). 'They were not afraid to do something new. They were not always looking over their shoulder and asking: "Is this the way the top brass in Jerusalem do things?" They were prepared to think for themselves from Scripture about such questions as: Does this approach truly glorify Christ? Does this method honestly sow the word? Does it make the gospel clear? If so, let's do it!' (John Benton)

Let's be those who, like Antioch, are constantly ready for God to show us new things!

Relevance for today

God is still looking for 'Antioch' churches. Will your church be one? Does it conform to the model set out by God? What part are you playing in it?

• An 'Antioch' church has every member functioning, not experts running the show.

• An 'Antioch' church is strong in compassion and giving.

• An 'Antioch' church looks beyond itself and its own needs.

• An 'Antioch' church 'gives its best away'.

• An 'Antioch' church has leaders who do not look to 'build their own little empires' but to extend the kingdom of God.

• An 'Antioch' church looks to the Spirit to break fresh ground in worship and its evangelizing this present generation.

• An 'Antioch' church has a heart for the nations?

Facing a task unfinished,
That drives us to our knees,
A need that, undiminished,
Rebukes our slothful ease,
We, who rejoice to know Thee,
Renew before Thy throne
The solemn pledge we owe Thee
To go and make Thee known.

Where other lords beside Thee
Hold their unhindered sway,
Where forces that defied Thee
Defy Thee still today,
With none to heed their crying
For life, and love, and light,
Unnumbered souls are dying,
And pass into the night.

We bear the torch that flaming
Fell from the hands of those
Who gave their lives proclaiming
That Jesus died and rose.
Ours is the same commission,
The same glad message ours,
Fired by the same ambition,
To Thee we yield our powers.

O Father who sustained them,
O Spirit who inspired,
Saviour, whose love constrained them
To toil with zeal untired,
From cowardice defend us,
From lethargy awake!
Forth on Thine errands send us
To labour for Thy sake.

Frank Houghton, 1894–1972

Conclusion

Antioch was a dynamic church, not because it was 'special', but because it took God at his word and allowed the Holy Spirit to lead it. Lord Jesus, make our church more like the church at Antioch!

When he [Barnabas] reached Antioch and saw how God had blessed the people, he was glad. He encouraged all the believers in Antioch always to obey the Lord with all their hearts, and many people became followers of the Lord.

(Acts 11:23–24, NCV)

CHAPTER FOUR

The Meetings of the Church

It is in our meeting together that we can experience the reality of belonging to God and his family and can encourage one another in our walk with him.

Let us not give up meeting together, as some are in the habit of doing, but let us encourage one another – and all the more as you see the Day approaching. (Hebrews 10:25)

For many people, church services are epitomized in an incident portrayed by the British TV character, Mr Bean, a hapless individual who manages to get everything wrong. In one programme he attends a traditional church service and 'does it all wrong'; he stands when everyone sits, and sits when everyone stands; he sings at the wrong time; he gets caught putting a sweet in his mouth; in short, he is constantly the 'odd one out'.

That is exactly how church meetings may seem to people; an alien environment with strange words and even stranger rituals. Yet this is not what God wants for us! When the church meets together, Jesus is there in the midst of us in a special way; and he wants us to be at ease with the Father and to know and enjoy his presence.

Why do we meet?

So, why does God want his people to meet together?

Knowing his presence

'For where two or three are gathered together in my name, there am I in the midst of them.'

(Matthew 18:20, KJV)

This promise of Jesus has proved precious to countless believers through the ages, whether to those hiding from antagonistic authorities, or to the faithful few gathering for prayer. For all of us, however, it is the heart of what our meetings should be about: his presence. Both in Old and New Testament times, it was God's presence that transformed things – and people!

Moses and Aaron then went into the Tent of Meeting. When they came out, they blessed the people; and the glory of the LORD appeared to all the people. Fire came out from the presence of the LORD and consumed the burnt offering and the fat portions on the altar. And when all the people saw it, they shouted for joy and fell face down.

(Leviticus 9:23–24)

After two days he will revive us; on the third day he will restore us, that we may live in his presence. Let us acknowledge the LORD; let us press on to acknowledge him. As surely as the sun rises, he will appear; he will come to us like the winter rains, like the spring rains that water the earth.

(Hosea 6:2–3)

See also Exodus 33:14–15; Deuteronomy 4:37; 1 Samuel 2:21; 1 Kings 19:11–13; 1 Chronicles 29:22; Psalm 16:11; Acts 4:31; 10:33

Sharing his presence

Yet here is the strange thing: when we are spiritually down, sometimes the last thing we want is to meet with God or other Christians! And, of course, the devil heightens such thoughts. 'You're better off by yourself.' 'No one cares about you anyway.' 'You wouldn't be missed.' 'You've got to get through this on your own.' 'You had fewer troubles before you

became a Christian.' Perhaps it was these sort of thoughts that the writer to the discouraged Hebrew Christians had in mind when he reminded them of the importance of gathering together to share in God's presence and to encourage one another.

And let us consider how we may spur one another on towards love and good deeds. Let us not give up meeting together, as some are in the habit of doing, but let us encourage one another – and all the more as you see the Day approaching.

(Hebrews 10:24–25)

See also Deuteronomy 12:4–14; 16:16; Acts 2:42; Hebrews 3:13

Throughout the Bible, God makes provision for his people to know his presence together.

Enjoying his presence

Not only does God want us to know his presence (for that in itself could be a fearful thing!), he also wants us to enjoy his presence. When we know we are right with God, there is nothing to fear, only everything to enjoy!

Moses and Aaron, Nadab and Abihu, and the seventy elders of Israel went up and saw the God of Israel. Under his feet was something like a pavement made of sapphire, clear as the sky itself. But God did not raise his hand against these leaders of the Israelites; they saw God, and they ate and drank.

(Exodus 24:9–11)

See also Exodus 18:9–12; Deuteronomy 12:7; 1 Thessalonians 3:9; Revelation 3:20

God truly wants us to enjoy his presence. This means that our meetings should be enjoyable. We are not being unholy or presumptuous if they are! When we praise and worship God, we are enjoying him.

'Great!' 'Fantastic!' 'Brilliant!' 'Wow!' 'Cool!' are modern words of enjoyment. This is the sort of heart God wants to find in us as we come together in our meetings! This is what it means to be truly 'lost in wonder, love, and praise'.

So, how can we make our meetings times of knowing, sharing and enjoying his presence?

The purpose of meeting

The first time Christians gathered together as a church seems a good place to begin to answer this question as to what should happen when we meet.

They devoted themselves to the apostles' teaching and to the fellowship, to the breaking of bread and to prayer. Everyone was filled with awe, and many wonders and miraculous signs were done by the apostles. All the believers were together and had everything in common. Selling their possessions and goods, they gave to anyone as he had need. Every day they continued to meet together in the temple courts. They broke bread in their homes and ate together with glad and sincere hearts, praising God and enjoying the favour of all the people. And the Lord added to their number daily those who were being saved.

(Acts 2:42–47)

The phrase 'devoted themselves to' could be translated as 'they were passionate about' or even 'they were addicted to'. Clearly these things were important to them!

Teaching

They devoted themselves to the apostles' teaching . . .

Their teaching was not about 'anything they fancied' (see 2 Timothy 4:3), but was 'the apostles' teaching': a clear body of truth about Jesus and what he came to do; a 'pattern' to be followed (2 Timothy 1:13–14). Teaching had a central place in their life together (e.g. Acts 5:42; 11:26; 15:35; 18:11, 24–26; 20:20) and leaders were to stick at it, even if it was 'hard going' at times (2 Timothy 4:2–5). Teaching was not 'an end in itself', but aimed to bring believers to maturity. Our goal is the one that Paul wanted for Philemon:

. . . a full understanding of every good thing we have in Christ.

(Philemon 6)

This teaching aimed to:
- Produce right understanding (Ephesians 3:4–5; Colossians 2:2–4; 2 Timothy 3:14–15)
- Produce right living (Ephesians 4:22–24; 2 Timothy 3:7, 17)
- Proclaim truth and correct error (2 Timothy 2:25–26; 3:16)
- Bring believers to maturity in Christ (Colossians 1:28)
- Cover 'the whole counsel of God' (Acts 20:27, NKJV), not pet theories or emphases.

Whether through sermons, Bible studies or discussions, the word of God still needs a central place whenever we meet together. In the words of Paul:

Let the word of Christ dwell in you richly as you teach and admonish one another with all wisdom . . .

(Colossians 3:16)

Fellowship

They devoted themselves to . . . the fellowship

As we have already seen (Part 3, Chapter 7) 'fellowship' means 'participation or partnership in something together'. But not only does God wants us to be 'in partnership' with him; he also wants us to be in partnership with one another.

'Fellowship' is not just Christians chatting at the end of a meeting over a cup of tea; or a pleasant time together at a Bible Week. Important as these times may be, they need not necessarily be 'fellowship'. True Christian fellowship has to do with a real sharing – first of all 'vertically' (with God), and then 'horizontally' (with one another).

We proclaim to you what we have seen and heard, so that you also may have fellowship with us. And our fellowship is with the Father and with his Son, Jesus Christ.

(1 John 1:3)

Fellowship with one another will mean:
- Meeting together (Acts 20:7; Hebrews 10:24–25)
- Sharing our spiritual gifts for the benefit of one another (1 Corinthians 14:26)
- Sharing our resources (Acts 2:44; 4:32–35)
- Being real friends (Acts 15:25–26; Romans 16:3–16; Colossians 4:14; 1 Thessalonians 2:8)
- Opening our homes to one another (Acts 2:46; 16:15; 18:26; Philemon 2)

Breaking of bread

They devoted themselves to . . . the breaking of bread

In Holy Communion (or the Lord's Supper), we remember Christ's death through the symbols of bread and wine, representing his body and blood given for us (Matthew 26:26–29). But this 'meal' is not just about fellowship with him, but also fellowship with one another.

Is not the cup of thanksgiving for which we give thanks a participation in the blood of Christ? And is not the bread that we break a participation in the body of Christ? Because there is one loaf, we, who are many, are one body, for we all partake of the one loaf.

(1 Corinthians 10:16–17)

See also 1 Corinthians 11:17–29

We are remembering that he died for *us*, not just for *me*. That is why Paul says that in this 'meal' we must give due regard to one another (11:17–21) as well as to Christ (11:27). When we break bread together, we are thanking Jesus for what he has done for us personally and corporately; we are together receiving God's grace, strength and help afresh for our lives; we are together looking forward to his coming again (11:26).

Prayer

They devoted themselves to . . . prayer

(Acts2:42)

Praying with one another and for one another was a key and constant element of early church life. And it was certainly powerful praying!

After they prayed, the place where they were meeting was shaken. And they were all filled with the Holy Spirit and spoke the word of God boldly.

(Acts 4:31)

And pray in the Spirit on all occasions with all kinds of prayers and requests. With this in mind, be alert and always keep on praying for all the saints.

(Ephesians 6:18)

Be joyful always; pray continually; give thanks in all circumstances, for this is God's will for you in Christ Jesus.

(1 Thessalonians 5:16–18)
See also e.g. Acts 6:4; 12:5, 12; 13:3; 14:23; 20:36; Romans 15:30–32; 1 Corinthians 14:15; 2 Corinthians 1:10–11; 1 Timothy 2:1–2, 8

Corporate prayer is the powerhouse of a church. Unspectacular, hard work it may be; but if we neglect it, we should not be surprised if our churches are weak and our evangelism unfruitful.

Praying together, whether in our main meetings or in home groups, can include –

- Praying for opportunities and boldness in witnessing (Acts 4:29–30; Colossians 4:3–4)
- Praying for 'the Lord of the harvest to send out workers into his harvest field' (Matthew 9:38)
- Praying for people to be saved (Romans 10:1)
- Praying for believers in difficult situations (Acts 12:5)
- Praying for wisdom and direction (Acts 1:24–26; James 1:5–8)
- Praying for the sick (James 5:14–16)
- Praying for one another and one another's needs (Ephesians 6:18)
- Praying for our nation and government (1 Timothy 2:1–4)

Other aspects of meeting

Besides these four key aspects in Acts 2:42, there were other things that characterized how the first Christians met:

Baptism

As soon as someone was born again, they were baptized.

Those who accepted his message were baptised, and about three thousand were added to their number that day.

(Acts 2:41)

'Look, here is water. Why shouldn't I be baptised?'

(Acts 8:36)
See also Acts 8:12, 38; 10:47–48; 16:15, 33; 18:8; 19:1–6

Baptism is –
- A symbol of washing (Acts 22:16)
- A symbol of new life (Romans 6:1–11)
- A symbol of becoming part of the church (Acts 2:41; 1 Corinthians 12:13)

Singing

The Bible encourages us to express our praise and thanksgiving to God in song, whatever the circumstances.

Speak to one another with psalms, hymns and spiritual songs. Sing and make music in your heart to the Lord, always giving thanks to God the Father for everything, in the name of our Lord Jesus Christ.

(Ephesians 5:19–20)

Is any one of you in trouble? He should pray. Is anyone happy? Let him sing songs of praise.

(James 5:13)

See also e.g. Ezra 3:10–13; Psalm 33:3; 95:1–2; 98:1–9; 100:1–2; 149:1–5; Acts 16:25; 1 Corinthians 14:15; Colossians 3:16; Revelation 5:9–14

Remember: we don't have to have a good voice – just a good heart! In fact, the Authorized (King James) Version often translates the phrase 'Shout for joy' as 'Make a joyful noise' – something all of us can do!

Encouragement

The ministry of encouragement played a big part in early church life (Acts 11:22–24; 15:32; 16:40; 18:27; 20:1–2; 28:15; Romans 1:12; 12:8; 15:4–6; 1 Corinthians 14:31; Ephesians 6:22; 1 Thessalonians 3:2; 5:11; Titus 2:15). (Just the sheer number of those references should tell us something!) One of their leaders, Joseph, was such an encourager that the apostles renamed him Barnabas, 'Son of Encouragement' (Acts 4:36). Encouragement played a major part in the health and growth of the church.

Then the church throughout Judea, Galilee and Samaria enjoyed a time of peace. It was strengthened; and encouraged by the Holy Spirit, it grew in numbers, living in the fear of the Lord.

(Acts 9:31)

May our Lord Jesus Christ himself and God our Father, who loved us and by his grace gave us eternal encouragement and good hope, encourage your hearts and strengthen you in every good deed and word.

(2 Thessalonians 2:16–17)

But encourage one another daily, as long as it is called Today, so that none of you may be hardened by sin's deceitfulness.

(Hebrews 3:13)

Responding to the Spirit

The New Testament believers sought to respond to the Holy Spirit – as individuals (e.g. Acts 8:26–39), as leaders (e.g. Acts 13:1–3), and as churches (1 Corinthians 12:1–11; 14:26–31). In their meetings, they were open to both Spirit-inspired teaching and Spirit-inspired gifts, the purpose of which was to 'build up the church'.

Since you are eager to have spiritual gifts, try to excel in gifts that build up the church.

(1 Corinthians 14:12)

See also 1 Corinthians 14:1–5

We have already seen in Part 3 how the Spirit energizes and vitalizes God's people. He wants to do the same in our meetings too – if we will make room for him!

Relevance for today

God wants us to know him and enjoy his presence. He wants us to fellowship with fellow believers and live effective lives.

Know his presence

The LORD replied, 'My Presence will go with you, and I will give you rest.'

(Exodus 33:14)

Enjoy his presence

You have made known to me the path of life; you will fill me with joy in your presence.

(Psalm 16:11)

Be 'ready to give'

No man should appear before the LORD empty-handed.

(Deuteronomy 16:16)

When you come together, everyone has a hymn, or a word of instruction, a revelation, a tongue or an interpretation. All of these must be done for the strengthening of the church.

(1 Corinthians 14:26)

Enjoy real fellowship

God wants our fellowship with one another to be as real as our fellowship with him.

We proclaim to you what we have seen and heard, so that you also may have fellowship with us. And our fellowship is with the Father and with his Son, Jesus Christ.

(1 John 1:3)

True fellowship means we can confront one another with the truth, without it breaking the relationship (e.g. Galatians 2:11–14).

Give and receive encouragement

Encouragement is a powerful and necessary gift in the body.

I long to see you so that I may impart to you some spiritual gift to make you strong – that is, that you and I may be mutually encouraged by each other's faith.

(Romans 1:11–12)

Be effective, not busy

God wants us to be effective, rather than busy. Some of us can be so busy, attending this committee or that meeting or that conference, that we never get anything done! God wants fruit on his trees, not just leaves (John 15:2); effectiveness not busyness. This may mean our learning how to steward our time better and learning that 'There is a time for everything, and a season for every activity under heaven' (Ecclesiastes 3:1).

Build a sense of family

God is 'for' family, not 'against' it. This needs to be reflected in our meetings, just as in the life and worship of Israel in the Old Testament (e.g. Exodus 12:21–28; Deuteronomy 6:20–25). Children too have a place when we meet with Jesus and should not be excluded (Mark 10:13–16).

Be committed

Starting to miss meetings is a first sign that something is going wrong!

Some people have got out of the habit of meeting for worship, but we must not do that.

(Hebrews 10:25, CEV)

Jesus, we look to Thee,
Thy promised presence claim;
Thou in the midst of us shalt be,
Assembled in Thy Name.

Thy Name salvation is,
Which here we come to prove;
Thy Name is life, and health, and peace,
And everlasting love.

We meet, the grace to take
Which Thou hast freely given;
We meet on earth for Thy dear sake,
That we may meet in heaven.

Present we know Thou art,
But O Thyself reveal!
Now, Lord, let every bounding heart
The mighty comfort feel.

O may Thy quickening voice
The death of sin remove;
And bid our inmost souls rejoice
In hope of perfect love!

Charles Wesley, 1707–88

Conclusion

God wants us to know him and enjoy him when
we meet together. Whatever does not serve this
end is 'religious clutter', superfluous to the life
of the church.

'For where two or three come together in my
name, there am I with them.'

(Matthew 18:20)

CHAPTER FIVE

The Mission of the Church

A healthy church is one that is concerned not just with its own affairs, but also with making disciples both on its own doorstep and beyond.

'Go and make disciples of all nations . . . ' (Matthew 28:19)

Everything that is healthy in this world relates to something beyond itself; what is concerned only for itself ultimately dies. A doctor can see this in human bodies. For example, when a cell that cares only for itself becomes cancerous, its very attempts to survive kill the whole body. A pastor can see it in human lives, where those who think only of themselves become the most dissatisfied of people. What cares only for itself, dies; what looks beyond itself, lives.

The church is no different. In the first century, the church in Jerusalem found it difficult to look beyond itself, and so was ultimately sidelined in God's bigger plan. Antioch, however, looked beyond itself and so became one of the most significant churches in the early centuries of church history. Which sort of church will we be?

Ever-widening circles

Before Jesus ascended to heaven, he gave his disciples a command:

'All authority in heaven and on earth has been given to me. Therefore go and make disciples of all nations, baptising them in the name of the Father and of the Son and of the Holy Spirit, and teaching them to obey everything I have commanded you. And surely I am with you always, to the very end of the age.'

(Matthew 28:18–20)

219

This was not just a command to those first disciples, but was a command 'to the very end of the age'. That therefore includes us! It is a command that has ever-widening circles in terms of human history.

But it is also a command with ever-widening circles in terms of human geography. Jesus' disciples could think only about God's purpose for Israel, a tiny nation in the world; but Jesus was thinking way beyond that to all the nations of the world.

So when they met together, they asked him, 'Lord, are you at this time going to restore the kingdom to Israel?' He said to them: 'It is not for you to know the times or dates the Father has set by his own authority. But you will receive power when the Holy Spirit comes on you; and you will be my witnesses in Jerusalem, and in all Judea and Samaria, and to the ends of the earth.'

(Acts 1:6–8)

Note the ever-widening geographic circles: Jerusalem, Judea, Samaria, the ends of the earth. As Luke records the rapid expansion of the church in Acts, this is the pattern that he will follow. Jesus indeed intended to keep his promise!

Why should we go?

So, why should we be involved in this mission of ever-widening circles? What are the reasons that compel us to go and become involved?

The heart of God

While God chose Israel as the vehicle for his love, he never intended it to stop there. From the earliest days (Genesis 12:1–4), his heart was not just for one nation, but all nations. God has a passion to see them all saved!

Ask of me, and I will make the nations your inheritance, the ends of the earth your possession.

(Psalm 2:8)

In the last days the mountain of the LORD's temple will be established as chief among the mountains; it will be raised above the hills, and all nations will stream to it. Many peoples will come and say, 'Come, let us go up to the mountain of the LORD, to the house of the God of Jacob. He will teach us his ways, so that we may walk in his paths.'

(Isaiah 2:2–3)

'My house will be called a house of prayer for all nations.'

(Isaiah 56:7)

'I will shake all nations, and the desired of all nations will come, and I will fill this house with glory,' says the LORD Almighty.

(Haggai 2:7)

See also Isaiah 11:10; 42:1–4; 51:4–6; 52:10; Jeremiah 3:17; 16:19–21; Daniel 7:13–14; Malachi 1:11; Revelation 5:9–10; 7:9–10; 21:24–26; 22:1–2

But all this is not a cold, clinical plan on God's part. It is rooted in his love. God loves the whole world; and that is why we should go!

God loved the people of this world so much that he gave his only Son, so that everyone who has faith in him will have eternal life and never really die.

(John 3:16, CEV)

See also John 1:29; 4:42; 2 Corinthians 5:19; 1 John 2:2; 4:14

The command of Jesus

'If you love me, you will obey what I command.'

(John 14:15)

That's a fairly stark saying, isn't it? But it is a sentiment that is repeated again and again (see e.g. John 14:21–24; 15:10; James 1:22–25; 1 John 2:3–6; 5:3). If we are true disciples, Jesus expects us to do what he tells us; and one of the things he told us to do was to 'go', continuing the mission that he had begun (Matthew 28:18–20; Acts 1:8). How can we claim to be his followers unless 'going' is written through our hearts, just as it is through his?

The thrust of the Spirit

From the very beginning (Genesis 1:1–2) the Holy Spirit has always been eager to push out to the next stage of God's plan and purpose. Jesus made it clear to his disciples that there would be an outward-moving thrust to his Spirit's work among them (Acts 1:6–8). If we are 'filled with the Spirit', then a natural consequence should be that we share in the Spirit's outward thrust.

'But you will receive power when the Holy Spirit comes on you; and you will be my witnesses in Jerusalem, and in all Judea and Samaria, and to the ends of the earth.'

(Acts 1:8)

The need of the world

We only have to watch the TV news or read the newspaper to see the mess the world is in – politically, economically, morally and spiritually. Even creation itself is eager to be 'liberated from its bondage to decay' (Romans 8:21) But the world's basic problem is not economics or ecology; but sin (see Part 2, Chapter 2). Because of sin, people are 'perishing', they 'love darkness instead of light' and 'do evil' (John 3:16–20); they are spiritually dead and under God's wrath (Ephesians 2:1–3) – unless God steps in, in mercy and grace, to bring them to faith (Ephesians 2:4–8). But such a response can only be made by those who *hear* the good news – which means someone must go and tell them it.

'Everyone who calls on the name of the Lord will be saved.' How, then, can they call on the one they have not believed in? And how can they believe in the one of whom they have not heard? And how can they hear without someone preaching to them? And how can they preach unless they are sent? As it is written, 'How beautiful are the feet of those who bring good news!'

(Romans 10:13–15)

Where can we go?

Jesus' promise to his disciples in Acts 1:8, as we have already seen, gives us the answer: it was a pattern of ever-widening circles: Jerusalem . . . Judea . . . Samaria . . . the ends of the earth. In other words, we are to start where we are.

This is how Jesus trained his disciples. At first, he simply took them with him; but soon he was sending them out to 'have a go' on their own. He started right on their doorstep however:

These twelve Jesus sent out with the following instructions: 'Do not go among the Gentiles or enter any town of the Samaritans. Go rather to the lost sheep of Israel. As you go, preach this message: "The kingdom of heaven is near." '

(Matthew 10:5–7)

Only later would his followers begin to push back the boundaries further:

Now an angel of the Lord said to Philip, 'Go south to the road – the desert road – that goes down from Jerusalem to Gaza.' So he started out, and on his way he met an Ethiopian eunuch, an important official in charge of all the treasury of Candace, queen of the Ethiopians.

(Acts 8:26–27)

But when the Jews opposed Paul and became abusive, he shook out his clothes in protest and said to them, 'Your blood be on your own heads! I am clear of my responsibility. From now on I will go to the Gentiles.'

(Acts 18:6)

After all this had happened, Paul decided to go to Jerusalem, passing through Macedonia and Achaia. 'After I have been there,' he said, 'I must visit Rome also.'

(Acts 19:21)

After Festus had conferred with his council, he declared: 'You have appealed to Caesar. To Caesar you will go!'

(Acts 25:12)

Ever-increasing circles! For all of us, mission begins right on our doorstep – among our unsaved family, with our neighbours, at school or college, in the office or workplace. It is as we are faithful in doing this that God can prepare us for being stretched. One thing is certain: we will never be bold enough to speak to the nations if we aren't bold enough to speak to the neighbours!

How can we go?

So, how can our mission to the world be expressed? Here are some suggestions.

Prayer

One way that all of us can 'go' is by praying. It is in praying that we start to catch hold of God's heart and share in the compassion for the lost that Jesus had.

When he saw the crowds, he had compassion on them, because they were harassed and helpless, like sheep without a shepherd. Then he said to his disciples, 'The harvest is plentiful but the workers are few. Ask the Lord of the harvest, therefore, to send out workers into his harvest field.'

(Matthew 9:36–38)

Praying – for God to revive his church, to give us compassion for the lost, to give us more boldness to witness, to save our friends – is where mission begins. Even when the early church was threatened and commanded to stop preaching (Acts 4:18), all that did was to drive them to more prayer to be even more effective (Acts 4:29–31)! Praying is where all mission begins.

See also Acts 13:1–3; Romans 10:1; 15:30–33; Ephesians 6:19–20; Colossians 4:2–4; 2 Thessalonians 3:1; Philemon 6

Involvement with people

Praying is not a substitute for doing. The disciples in Acts 4 had a powerful prayer meeting and encounter with the Holy Spirit (v 31), but they then immediately turned that into action. What did they do? They got involved with people (e.g. Acts 5:12–16). They were, to use John Stott's phrase, both holy and worldly: 'The church is a people that is simultaneously holy (distinct from the world because belonging to God) and worldly in the sense of being immersed in the life of the people around it.' (See John 17:11, 14–18.) Mission flows out of the biblical doctrine of 'the church in the world'. If we do not remain God's people, holy and distinct, we will have nothing to say, because we will be compromised; but if we do not remain 'the world's people', in the sense of being involved with its people, then we will have no one to say it to!

Involvement with people in the New Testament included:

- Acts of kindness (e.g. Acts 9:36; 10:38; 1 Timothy 2:10; 1 Peter 2:12)
- Praying for the sick (e.g. Mark 1:40–42; 2:1–12; Acts 3:1–9; 8:5–8)
- Serving well in the workplace (e.g. Ephesians 6:5–9; 1 Thessalonians 4:11–12; Titus 2:9–10; 1 Peter 2:18–22)
- Telling them about Jesus (e.g. Acts 4:33; 8:4–5, 26–40; 14:1–3; 17:16–34)

All of this is an aspect of mission! It is all about demonstrating God's love. When we are genuine with people, are ready to serve them with 'no strings attached', and are not out to see how many converts we can notch up; when we are simply 'ourselves' with people, then we will start to 'build bridges' over which we can walk to people and they can walk to Jesus.

Catch the vision

Where there is no vision, the people perish.
(Proverbs 29:18, KJV)

While this promise is translated variously in English versions, the heart of it is: where people do not get clear direction brought to them, they are prone to 'do their own thing'. This is no less true in the area of mission where, left to ourselves, we would all take the more comfortable option of doing nothing! So, how can we help one another to catch the vision?

- By teaching

Paul constantly taught his churches about the need to think 'beyond themselves' (e.g. 2 Corinthians 8:1–5; Philippians 1:12–14)

- By leading

Leaders have a responsibility for ensuring that mission stays central and not peripheral to the church's life. New Testament leaders set an excellent example in this (e.g. Acts 13:1–3).

- By informing

Up-to-date news about the exciting things that God is doing is important, as the early church recognized (e.g. Acts 14:27). These days, with facilities like e-mail, camcorders, and video links, keeping in touch is relatively easy. 'Live' reports of what God has done from those who have just returned can build our faith; and praying for nations that have been in the news keeps God's big world in our focus.

Go!

But of course, the best way to be involved in mission is simply to go! For it is in going that we 'catch something'. Mike confesses to having been rather uninterested in 'mission' for many years. But that all changed when a colleague invited him, many years ago now, to go on a ministry trip to Uganda. He was 'bitten by the bug' and has been infected ever since! And his ministry and churches have been all the more healthy ever since because of it.

Many years ago, Amos was bitten by the same bug too, as God called him, a southerner, to go for a season to the northern tribes:

I was neither a prophet nor a prophet's son, but I was a shepherd, and I also took care of sycamore-fig trees. But the LORD took me from tending the flock and said to me, 'Go . . .'

(Amos 7:14–15)

Of course, some can find the call and challenge too overwhelming initially, just like Jonah did:

The word of the LORD came to Jonah son of Amittai: 'Go to the great city of Nineveh and preach against it, because its wickedness has come up before me.' But Jonah ran away from the LORD and headed for Tarshish.

(Jonah 1:1–3)

But God worked in Jonah's life until he began to catch something of God's own heart for those who were lost (Jonah 3:1–10). God does not force us into mission, but he does want to woo us!

And for those of us who feel overwhelmed by it all, is there a word of encouragement? Yes!

The word of the LORD came to me, saying, 'Before I formed you in the womb I knew you, before you were born I set you apart; I appointed you as a prophet to the nations.' 'Ah, Sovereign LORD,' I said, 'I do not know how to speak; I am only a child.' But the LORD said to me, 'Do not say, "I am only a child." You must go to everyone I send you to and say whatever I command you. Do not be afraid of them, for I am with you and will rescue you,' declares the LORD.

(Jeremiah 1:4–8)

Who can go?

In these days of easy travel there is no reason why everyone can't go beyond their doorstep to engage in mission, whether in their own nation or in the nations of the world. The days of going for seven years and returning for a 'furlough' (a strange missionary word for an overdue holiday!) are long past. Many churches take their own short-term teams abroad and many mission agencies accept workers for three or six months. You don't have to be a theologian; in fact, you are more likely to get a visa and be of more help if you are a builder or a nurse! Nor does age (at either end) discount you! In Mike's own church, for example, a couple in their eighties have been on prayer tours in Israel; two ladies in their sixties are going to China to visit longer-term missionaries; many of the young people have been on two-week teams to Africa or India. All come back testifying that their life and attitudes have been changed. So, why not you?

Relevance for today

Mission arises from God's heart

God our Saviour, who wants all men to be saved and to come to a knowledge of the truth.

(1 Timothy 2:3–4)

Mission is simply the outworking of God's desire for all to be saved. If we do not share his passion to see the lost saved, there is something of God's heart that we have not yet touched.

Mission is the church's permanent task

'Therefore go and make disciples of all nations . . . to the very end of the age.'

(Matthew 28:19–20)

No 'people group' is unreachable

We have put our hope in the living God, who is the Saviour of all men, and especially of those who believe.

(1 Timothy 4:10)

In the writers' lifetimes, the apparently impregnable wall of communism fell in response to prayer; why should not every other wall do the same?

Ever-increasing circles

Mission should grow through ever-increasing circles.

'Jerusalem . . . Judea . . . Samaria . . . the ends of the earth'

(Acts 1:8)

Ask God to show you your ever-increasing circle.

Mission is for all

Mission is for the whole body, not just the enthusiastic few.

They were all filled with the Holy Spirit and spoke the word of God boldly.

(Acts 4:31)

Everyone can 'go'!

No one is too old and no one too young; even new Christians are not excluded (think of the apostle Paul! see Acts 9:20). Why not ask God to open up an opportunity for you to 'go', perhaps on a short-term team. It will change your life for ever!

225

We have heard the joyful sound:
Jesus saves!
Spread the tidings all around:
Jesus saves!
Bear the news to every land,
Climb the steeps and cross the waves;
Onward! 'tis our Lord's command:
Jesus saves!

Sing above the battle's strife:
Jesus saves!
By His death and endless life,
Jesus saves!
Sing it softly through the gloom,
When the heart for mercy craves;
Sing in triumph o'er the tomb:
Jesus saves!

Give the winds a mighty voice:
Jesus saves!
Let the nations now rejoice:
Jesus saves!
Shout salvation full and free,
Highest hills and deepest caves;
This our song of victory:
Jesus saves!

Priscilla Jane Owens, 1829–1907

Conclusion

'A Christian who is not dedicated to world evangelism is living an unbiblical life, and a church that is not dedicated to missionary vision is an unbiblical church' (Pete Lowman).

'You will be my witnesses in Jerusalem, and in all Judea and Samaria, and to the ends of the earth.'

(Acts 1:8)

The Warfare of the Church

God's church is an army, soldiers called to fight together. We are engaged in a battle that is ongoing, but whose outcome is assured.

Your enemy the devil prowls around like a roaring lion looking for someone to devour. Resist him, standing firm in the faith.
(1 Peter 5:8–9)

'There are two equal and opposite errors into which our race can fall about the devils. One is to disbelieve in their existence. The other is to believe, and to feel an excessive and unhealthy interest in them' (C.S. Lewis, *The Screwtape Letters*). The liberal theologian, or the believer who cannot accept what science cannot explain, has dismissed any thoughts of devils or spiritual warfare as merely the world-view of a primitive people. In contrast, some Christians have found 'demons under every bed' and would minister to others until Mary Magdalene, 'from whom seven demons had come out' (Luke 8:2), looked like a mere beginner in the realm of demonization. But somewhere between these two positions, a real warfare is taking place; a warfare experienced by Jesus and the apostles; a warfare that any believer ignores at their peril.

A real battle

When Jesus came to earth, he entered a battle zone. The devil had no intention of giving up what he had falsely claimed, and so contested Jesus at every point: he tried to slaughter him at birth (Matthew 2:16); to deflect him from obedience towards his Father (Luke 4:3–13); to get a mob to kill him (Luke 4:28–30); he deceived one of the disciples into betraying him (Luke 22:3–6); he finally conspired to bring about his arrest and execution (Mark 14:43–50; 15:1–15). The battle was real; and it was not just against people or institutions. As Paul put it:

For our struggle is not against flesh and blood, but against the rulers, against the authorities, against the powers of this dark world and against the spiritual forces of evil in the heavenly realms.

(Ephesians 6:12)

The battle was not just his. Jesus warned his followers they could expect little better!

'Blessed are you when people insult you, persecute you and falsely say all kinds of evil against you because of me. Rejoice and be glad, because great is your reward in heaven, for in the same way they persecuted the prophets who were before you.'

(Matthew 5:11–12)

'Then you will be handed over to be persecuted and put to death, and you will be hated by all nations because of me . . . but he who stands firm to the end will be saved.'

(Matthew 24:9, 13)

'Remember the words I spoke to you: "No servant is greater than his master." If they persecuted me, they will persecute you also.'

(John 15:20)

Paul taught exactly the same:

'We must go through many hardships to enter the kingdom of God.'

(Acts 14:22)

When we were with you, we kept telling you that we would be persecuted. And it turned out that way, as you well know.

(1 Thessalonians 3:4)

In fact, everyone who wants to live a godly life in Christ Jesus will be persecuted.

(2 Timothy 3:12)

What a cheery list of promises with which to begin a chapter! But all of this brings home to us that, when we become a Christian, we do not so much enter a battle arena (it was always there!), as have our eyes opened to see what was going on around us all the time, like Elisha's servant.

When the servant of the man of God got up and went out early the next morning, an army with horses and chariots had surrounded the city. 'Oh, my lord, what shall we do?' the servant asked. 'Don't be afraid,' the prophet answered. 'Those who are with us are more than those who are with them.' And Elisha prayed, 'O LORD, open his eyes so that he may see.' Then the LORD opened the servant's eyes, and he looked and saw the hills full of horses and chariots of fire all round Elisha.

(2 Kings 6:15–17)

The battle is real, then. And that is why the church is described as an army, with you and I as its soldiers (1 Corinthians 9:7; Philippians 2:25; 2 Timothy 2:3–4; Philemon 2), fighting side by side. But the good news is: we already know who wins!

A real enemy

Our enemy, the devil, is real. His one aim is to oppose God, his works and his children. The whole world system is under his control (1 John 5:19), so much so that he is called its 'prince' or 'ruler' (John 14:30); but nothing rightfully belongs to him, for he is but a 'thief and a robber' (John 10:1, 10).

His origin

Satan was originally one of God's highest angels. Many Christians see a description of him in Ezekiel's prophecy about the king of Tyre (Ezekiel 28:12–17). Pride, and a desire to be like God himself, arose in his heart, and so he was cast out of heaven (Isaiah 14:12–15; Ezekiel 28:17; Revelation 12:7–9).

His names

The devil has many names in the Bible, reflecting different aspects of his wicked work. These include:

- Beelzebub/Beelzebul ['Lord of the flies/Exalted Baal'] (Matthew 10:25–27; 12:24)
- Devil ['Slanderer'] (Matthew 4:1; John 13:2; Acts 13:10; James 4:7)
- Evil One (Matthew 13:19; Ephesians 6:16; 2 Thessalonians 3:3)
- Father of lies (John 8:44)
- God of this age (2 Corinthians 4:4)
- Prince of this world (John 12:31)
- Satan ['Adversary'] (1 Chronicles 21:1; Job 1:6–12; Zechariah 3:1–2; Luke 10:18; Acts 5:3; Romans 16:20)
- Serpent (Genesis 3:1–15; Revelation 12:9; 20:2)
- Tempter (Matthew 4:3; 1 Thessalonians 3:5)

His tactics

The devil's tactics to bring about his destructive work are wide-ranging and include:

- Accusation (Zechariah 3:1; Revelation 12:10)
- Affliction (Job 2:3–8; Luke 13:16)
- Blinding minds (2 Corinthians 4:4)
- Craftiness and cunning (Genesis 3:1; 2 Corinthians 11:3)
- Deception (Acts 13:10; 2 Thessalonians 2:9–10)
- Disguising himself as 'an angel of light' (2 Corinthians 11:14)
- Lies (John 8:44)
- Setting traps (1 Timothy 3:7; 2 Timothy 2:26)
- Temptation (Matthew 4:1; 1 Thessalonians 3:5)

His servants

Jesus spoke of 'the devil and his angels' (Matthew 25:41). For reasons we are not told, the devil seduced some of God's angels, who were expelled from heaven along with him (2 Peter 2:4; Revelation 12:9) and who now do his business. Jesus took their presence and activity seriously, and he distinguished between sickness and their oppressing work (e.g. Matthew 8:16; 10:8). He did not operate as the exorcists of his time (e.g. Acts 19:13), but simply 'drove out the spirits with a word' (Matthew 8:16). Commanding demons to leave was no big deal and required no lengthy counselling!

His limits

While the devil may be powerful, however, he is not all-powerful. Only God is! The devil is a created being (Ezekiel 28:15) and will therefore always be less than God. Some Christians seem to forget that and almost have a view of two equal and opposing powers, struggling against one another. Such is not the case, and the devil's end is assured (Revelation 20:10).

His defeat

On the cross, Christ broke once and for all the hold that the devil had on humanity (Colossians 2:13–15; Hebrews 2:14–15). The devil and his hosts are truly defeated!

God stripped the spiritual rulers and powers of their authority. With the cross, he won the victory and showed the world that they were powerless.

(Colossians 2:15, NCV)

However, the devil does not now stand idly by. He may be defeated, but he is resolved to go down fighting! While he can never regain complete power over us as Christians, he certainly tries to make our lives difficult.

A real strategy

In the light of all this, the church needs a strategy – and God has given us one! While we should be careful of Satan, we needn't be afraid of him. As with most bullies, we simply need to stand up against him in the strength and with the resources that God gives us.

Submit yourselves, then, to God. Resist the devil, and he will flee from you.

(James 4:7)

Be self-controlled and alert. Your enemy the devil prowls around like a roaring lion looking for someone to devour. Resist him, standing firm in the faith, because you know that your brothers throughout the world are undergoing the same kind of sufferings.

(1 Peter 5:8–9)

How, practically, can we do this? Paul's teaching on 'spiritual warfare' in Ephesians 6 gives us some answers.

Our God

The first thing to remember is that 'it is not by sword or spear that the LORD saves; for the battle is the LORD's' (1 Samuel 17:47). (See also 2 Chronicles 20:15–17; Psalm 24:8; Proverbs 21:31; Hosea 1:7.) Our focus must not be on ourselves, but on God; victory comes only from him. He alone is our strength. That's why Paul begins by saying,

Finally, be strong in the Lord and in his mighty power.

(Ephesians 6:10)

See also Psalm 62:11–12; Proverbs 18:10; Isaiah 35:3–4; Jeremiah 9:23–24; Daniel 10:18–19; Haggai 2:4; Zechariah 12:5; 1 Corinthians 1:8; 2 Timothy 2:1; 1 Peter 5:10

Our weapons

In Ephesians 6:10–20 all the instructions are in the plural. Although there will be constant individual skirmishes, it is together that we stand against the devil's schemes; it is together that we are to be strong in the Lord. That is why relationships amongst God's people must always be protected.

Finally, be strong in the Lord and in his mighty power. Put on the full armour of God so that you can take your stand against the devil's schemes. For our struggle is not against flesh and blood, but against the rulers, against the authorities, against the powers of this dark world and against the spiritual forces of evil in the heavenly realms. Therefore put on the full armour of God, so that when the day of evil comes, you may be able to stand your ground, and after you have done everything, to stand. Stand firm then, with the belt of truth buckled round your waist, with the breastplate of righteousness in place, and with your feet fitted with the readiness that comes from the gospel of peace. In addition to all this, take up the shield of faith, with which you can extinguish all the flaming arrows of the evil one. Take the helmet of salvation and the sword of the Spirit, which is the word of God. And pray in the Spirit on all occasions with all kinds of prayers and requests. With this in mind, be alert and always keep on praying for all the saints.

(Ephesians 6:10–18)

Note that Paul tells us to put on 'the full armour of God' (vv 11, 13). The word used ('panoply') is the term for the Roman soldier's full battle gear. All the armour is needed for battle.

Note too that we are to put the armour on *now* 'so that when the day of evil comes', we will be ready. This suggests that 'putting on the armour' is not a prayer to be said before 'spiritual warfare', but is part of a lifestyle we adopt so that we will always be ready.

Let's look at the equipment he mentions.

The belt of truth

Before any strenuous activity, the first thing men would do was to tuck their long garment into their belt so they did not trip over it. Truth is the first thing that needs to be in place, Paul says (v 14). Unless we are people of truth, integrity, honesty, sincerity, we will get tripped up. We will open the door to the devil's accusations and rob our testimony of effectiveness. We also need to be those who base their lives completely and confidently on the Truth, the Bible.

We have renounced secret and shameful ways; we do not use deception, nor do we distort the word of God. On the contrary, by setting forth the truth plainly we commend ourselves to every man's conscience in the sight of God.

(2 Corinthians 4:2)

See also Psalm 26:1–3; 119:29–32; Proverbs 23:23; John 1:14; 7:18; 1 Corinthians 5:8; 2 Corinthians 6:7; 13:8; Ephesians 4:25; 1 Timothy 3:14–15; 3 John 4

The breastplate of righteousness

The breastplate covered the main body area and protected the soldier's vital organs. The Christian soldier's breastplate is righteousness (v 14); first, righteousness is *given to us* by God through Christ (Romans 3:21–26; 4:3–8), and secondly, it is to be *lived by us* through the help of the Holy Spirit (Romans 14:17). With this righteousness on, we cannot live with inconsistencies in our lives, either towards God or others.

For surely, O LORD, you bless the righteous; you surround them with your favour as with a shield.

(Psalm 5:12)

I strive always to keep my conscience clear before God and man.

(Acts 24:16)

See also Genesis 7:1; 15:6; Deuteronomy 6:24–25; 2 Samuel 22:21–25; Psalm 1:6; Proverbs 10:9; Isaiah 61:3; Hosea 2:19; Matthew 5:6; Romans 1:17; 2 Corinthians 6:3–7

The feet of readiness

Paul is referring here to the Roman soldier's 'half-boot', with its studded soles which give a good grip when marching or in battle. Firmness and mobility were essential requirements. We, as Christ's soldiers together, need to 'have our boots on' so we are always ready to share our faith or make our stand at any moment (v 15).

The gospel sets us at peace, so we can always be at peace in our readiness to share it with others.

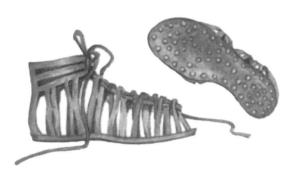

Always be ready to answer everyone who asks you to explain about the hope you have, but answer in a gentle way and with respect.

(1 Peter 3:15–16, NCV)

See also Proverbs 22:17–18; Isaiah 52:7; Jeremiah 1:17–19; Matthew 24:44; Luke 12:35–38; Colossians 4:6

The shield of faith

Roman soldiers had shields; one that was small and round, ideal for hand-to-hand combat, and another that was rather like today's police riot shield, body-length and slightly curved. It is the latter word that Paul uses here. Such shields, when held together, could form a solid wall or roof that stopped every missile. An individual alone was vulnerable; but in a group, with their shields put together, they had a tremendous defence. So it is with us: we need other believers in the spiritual battles we're fighting; we need to stand *together* in faith against 'all the flaming arrows of the evil one' (v 16). It's as we stand in faith together, claiming the promises of God, that the arrows are put out.

This is the victory that has overcome the world, even our faith.

(1 John 5:4)

See also Genesis 15:1; Deuteronomy 32:10–11; 33:12; Psalm 3:3; 18:2; Proverbs 30:5; Isaiah 31:5; 1 Peter 1:5

233

The helmet of salvation

The soldier's head needed special protection, and hence the helmet. We too need to protect our mind (v 17) – the very place where we remember the greatness of our salvation and God's promises to us so that we 'will not grow weary and lose heart' (Hebrews 12:3). Little wonder, therefore, that the devil tries to attack our minds and what goes on there! We need to constantly remind ourselves that we are saved, that nothing can separate us from God's love (Romans 8:31–39), no matter how we fail or what happens; we need to 'fix our eyes on Jesus' (Hebrews 12:2) rather than on any present difficulties or doubts.

Since we belong to the day, let us be self-controlled, putting on faith and love as a breastplate, and the hope of salvation as a helmet.

(1 Thessalonians 5:8)

See also Isaiah 26:1–3; 59:16–17; Romans 8:6; 12:2

The sword of the Spirit

Paul is thinking here of the Roman soldier's short sword, used in one-to-one battle, and this is the only offensive weapon in his list. Our only weapon is the word of God (v 17), the Bible; for it is here that we see God's character and promises. It was the weapon that Jesus himself used when tempted by the devil in the wilderness. The word of God has a powerful effect, whether used to face temptation, claim God's promises or release others from the enemy's grip. But we can only do this effectively if we believe that it really is the word of God (2 Timothy 3:16; 2 Peter 1:20–21) and are feeding on it regularly. Mixed with prayer in the Spirit (v 18), the word is a powerful weapon.

For the word of God is living and active. Sharper than any double-edged sword, it penetrates even to dividing soul and spirit, joints and marrow; it judges the thoughts and attitudes of the heart.

(Hebrews 4:12)

See also Matthew 4:1–11; Colossians 3:16; 1 Thessalonians 2:13; 2 Timothy 2:9

Relevance for today

The battle still continues

The book of Revelation shows that the battle continues until the very end, and therefore we are still in it.

When the dragon saw that he had been hurled to the earth, he pursued the woman [God's people] who had given birth to the male child . . . . the dragon was enraged at the woman and went off to make war against the rest of her offspring.

(Revelation 12:13, 17)

The enemy is still real

Be careful! Watch out for attacks from the Devil, your great enemy. He prowls around like a roaring lion, looking for some victim to devour. Take a firm stand against him, and be strong in your faith.

(1 Peter 5:8–9, NLT)

However, don't look for the devil or demons; look for Jesus!

The victory is still effective

But thanks be to God! He gives us the victory through our Lord Jesus Christ.

(1 Corinthians 15:57)

The weapons still work

The weapons we fight with are not the weapons of the world. On the contrary, they have divine power to demolish strongholds.

(2 Corinthians 10:4)

The army is still needed

His intent was that now, through the church, the manifold wisdom of God should be made known to the rulers and authorities in the heavenly realms.

(Ephesians 3:10)

The outcome is still assured

And the devil, who deceived them, was thrown into the lake of burning sulphur, where the beast and the false prophet had been thrown. They will be tormented day and night for ever and ever.

(Revelation 20:10)

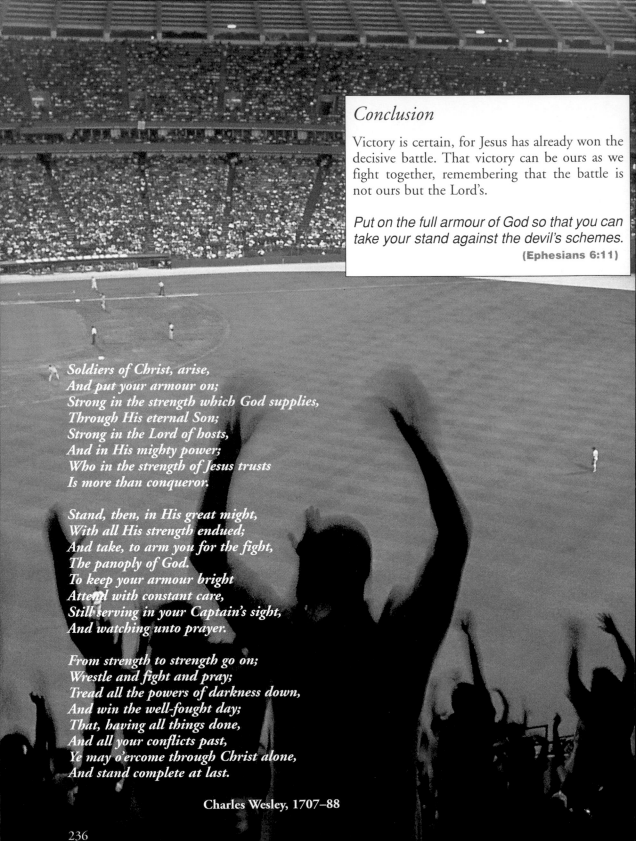

Conclusion

Victory is certain, for Jesus has already won the decisive battle. That victory can be ours as we fight together, remembering that the battle is not ours but the Lord's.

Put on the full armour of God so that you can take your stand against the devil's schemes.

(Ephesians 6:11)

Soldiers of Christ, arise,
And put your armour on;
Strong in the strength which God supplies,
Through His eternal Son;
Strong in the Lord of hosts,
And in His mighty power;
Who in the strength of Jesus trusts
Is more than conqueror.

Stand, then, in His great might,
With all His strength endued;
And take, to arm you for the fight,
The panoply of God.
To keep your armour bright
Attend with constant care,
Still serving in your Captain's sight,
And watching unto prayer.

From strength to strength go on;
Wrestle and fight and pray;
Tread all the powers of darkness down,
And win the well-fought day;
That, having all things done,
And all your conflicts past,
Ye may o'ercome through Christ alone,
And stand complete at last.

Charles Wesley, 1707–88

CHAPTER SEVEN

The Unity of the Church

All true Christians are already 'one'; this unity, based on God's love and truth, now needs to be worked out in and between our churches.

You are all sons of God through faith in Christ Jesus, for all of you who were baptised into Christ have clothed yourselves with Christ. There is neither Jew not Greek, slave nor free, male nor female, for you are all one in Christ Jesus.
(Galatians 3:26–28)

People can have an amazing way of gathering round things. Think of the average football match: thousands of supporters, all cheering for their team to win, all comrades together, but who, beyond the gates, would have little or nothing to do with one another. Yet a common cause has a powerfully uniting effect.

If that can happen for football – or for business, politics, or war – how much more can it happen for the church. For what joins us together is not a cause but a person. That person, Jesus, brings us into his family, his body. It is now to everyone's loss if we do not live as though we really belonged to it.

What is unity?

'Unity' can sound a somewhat uninspiring concept; rather static and lacking in dynamic purpose. But once we begin to see what the Bible means by it, it takes on a different dimension. Certainly the psalmist saw it as an exciting thing!

How good and pleasant it is when brothers live together in unity! It is like precious oil poured on the head, running down on the beard, running down on Aaron's beard, down upon the collar of his robes. It is as if the dew of Hermon were falling on Mount Zion. For there the LORD bestows his blessing, even life for evermore.

(Psalm 133:1–3)

The Bible sees unity as:

The gift of God

Unity is one of the gifts God gives his people, and so should be especially treasured and embraced by us.

The hand of God was on the people to give them unity of mind to carry out what the king and his officials had ordered, following the word of the LORD.

(2 Chronicles 30:12)

May the God who gives endurance and encouragement give you a spirit of unity among yourselves as you follow Christ Jesus, so that with one heart and mouth you may glorify the God and Father of our Lord Jesus Christ.

(Romans 15:5–6)

This gift of unity should not come as a surprise to us; for, after all, unity lies at the very heart of our God's being.

'Holy Father, protect them by the power of your name – the name you gave me – so that they may be one as we are one.'

(John 17:11)

The prayer of Jesus

In John 17, Jesus prays for his followers; not just those gathered with him in that upper room, but also 'for those who will believe in me through their message' (v 20). His longing is for those who believe in him to be truly one, to be truly united.

'My prayer is not for them alone. I pray also for those who will believe in me through their message, that all of them may be one, Father, just as you are in me and I am in you. May they also be in us so that the world may believe that you have sent me. I have given them the glory that you gave me, that they may be one as we are one: I in them and you in me. May they be brought to complete unity to let the world know that you sent me and have loved them even as you have loved me.'

(John 17:20–23)

Such a unity is not about structures or organizations, but is based on truth (v 17) and heart-felt love (John 13:34–35; 1 John 4:7–12), both indispensable foundations to this unity. Little will be achieved by our loving one another if it is not on the basis of Bible truth; but equally, little is achieved if we are strong on Bible truth but cannot love, or cannot love those who hold to the basics of the gospel but express some things in a different way to us. Paul said that we were not to pass judgment on others over 'disputable matters' (Romans 14:1). Various English versions translate this verse as: 'Don't criticize them for having beliefs that are different to yours' (CEV); 'Don't argue with them about what they think is right or wrong' (NLT); 'Do not argue about opinions' (NCV); 'Don't jump all over them every time they do or say something you don't agree with' (The Message). There are some secondary matters on which Christians have different viewpoints, and there must be room to accept these. As someone has said, 'In necessary things, unity; in doubtful things, liberty; in all things, charity.'

The work of the Spirit

One of the first things that happened when the believers were baptized in the Holy Spirit was that a tremendous unity was released among them. They really knew they were in this together! And this Spirit-given unity had a powerful effect.

All the believers were one in heart and mind. No-one claimed that any of his possessions was his own, but they shared everything they had. With great power the apostles continued to testify to the resurrection of the Lord Jesus, and much grace was upon them all.

(Acts 4:32–33)

See also Acts 2:44–47; 4:34–37; 1 Corinthians 12:13

The Spirit is the one who baptizes the body into unity. How sad it is, then, when we allow his work among us today to do the very opposite at times.

The goal of history

God's world, perfect when he first made it and then spoilt by sin, will one day be renewed, and unity in everything will be its hallmark once again.

And he made known to us the mystery of his will according to his good pleasure, which he purposed in Christ, to be put into effect when the times will have reached their fulfilment – to bring all things in heaven and on earth together under one head, even Christ.

(Ephesians 1:9–10)

See also Isaiah 11:6–9; Colossians 1:20

One in Christ Jesus

You are all sons of God through faith in Christ Jesus, for all of you who were baptised into Christ have clothed yourselves with Christ. There is neither Jew nor Greek, slave nor free, male nor female, for you are all one in Christ Jesus.

(Galatians 3:26–28)

Once the Spirit has brought us to new birth and has baptized us into the body of Christ, then we really are one. Barriers, whether racial or religious (Jew and Greek), social (slave and free), or sexual (male and female), are broken through and broken down and are now to be abandoned. In Christ, all are equal; every barrier has been removed.

For he himself is our peace, who has made the two one and has destroyed the barrier, the dividing wall of hostility, by abolishing in his flesh the law with its commandments and regulations. His purpose was to create in himself one new man out of the two, thus making peace, and in this one body to reconcile both of them to God through the cross, by which he put to death their hostility. He came and preached peace to you who were far away and peace to those who were near. For through him we both have access to the Father by one Spirit.

Consequently, you are no longer foreigners and aliens, but fellow-citizens with God's people and members of God's household, built on the foundation of the apostles and prophets, with Christ Jesus himself as the chief cornerstone. In him the whole building is joined together and rises to become a holy temple in the Lord. And in him you too are being built together to become a dwelling in which God lives by his Spirit.

(Ephesians 2:14–22)

But this does not mean that we are all 'the same' – a concept that western egalitarian thinking finds hard to grasp at times. The Bible teaches that, within this unity (1 Corinthians 12:12–13), there is both *diversity* (1 Corinthians 12:14–26) and *order* (1 Corinthians 12:28). These differences must never become grounds for jealousy among us, however. This is simply how Christ himself has chosen, in his sovereignty, to put his body together.

The effects of disunity

Disunity spoils. It spoils our own life, because of the bad attitudes it produces within us (e.g. Genesis 37:3–4; 1 Samuel 18:6–9); it spoils the lives of others, because of the way those attitudes affect them (e.g. 3 John 9–10); it spoils the life and witness of the local church as people hear about it (e.g. 1 Corinthians 1:11–12; 11:18).

Little wonder, then, that Paul was constantly appealing to his churches to make unity a priority.

I appeal to you, brothers, in the name of our Lord Jesus Christ, that all of you agree with one another so that there may be no divisions among you and that you may be perfectly united in mind and thought.

(1 Corinthians 1:10)

As a prisoner for the Lord, then, I urge you to live a life worthy of the calling you have received. Be completely humble and gentle; be patient, bearing with one another in love. Make every effort to keep the unity of the Spirit through the bond of peace. There is one body and one Spirit – just as you were called to one hope when you were called – one Lord, one faith, one baptism; one God and Father of all, who is over all and through all and in all.

(Ephesians 4:1–6)

If you have any encouragement from being united with Christ, if any comfort from his love, if any fellowship with the Spirit, if any tenderness and compassion, then make my joy complete by being like-minded, having the same love, being one in spirit and purpose.

(Philippians 2:1–2)

Therefore, as God's chosen people, holy and dearly loved, clothe yourselves with compassion, kindness, humility, gentleness and patience. Bear with each other and forgive whatever grievances you may have against one another. Forgive as the Lord forgave you. And over all these virtues put on love, which binds them all together in perfect unity.

(Colossians 3:12–14)

The blessings of unity

When we read such exhortations, maybe we feel we still have a long way to go; but seeing that we do can be the start of the process. Unity is something that grows, and that grows as we work at it. That's why Paul says, 'Make every effort . . .' (Ephesians 4:3). But once we see the blessings that it brings, it spurs us on to 'go for it'. Here are just some of those blessings:

• Unity allows God to command his blessing among us (Psalm 133:3)
• Unity releases Jesus to answer our prayers (Matthew 18:19–20)
• Unity allows the Spirit to move (Acts 2:1–4; 4:32–33)
• Unity lets us all use our gifts without vying with one another (1 Corinthians 12:14–27)
• Unity keeps us humble (Romans 14:1–12) It keeps us from 'majoring in minors' and from becoming too full of our own opinions.
• Unity pushes us outwards (Acts 2:1–41; 13:1–3)

Remember: The ultimate purpose of unity isn't to make us inward-looking, constantly taken up with ourselves, but rather that the world may know the God of love who sent Jesus into the world (John 17:21, 23).

241

Relevance for today

The call to unity

Unity remains a call on our lives until the end. It also means making an effort

The mystery of his will . . . to bring all things in heaven and on earth together under one head, even Christ.

(Ephesians 1:9–10)

Let us therefore make every effort to do what leads to peace and to mutual edification.

(Romans 14:19)

Trusting others

Unity develops where there is trust. This is true both within churches and between churches. Trust comes as we let the barriers down and begin to get to know one another, to operate with honesty and openness, rather than with suspicion and hostility.

After David had finished talking with Saul, Jonathan became one in spirit with David, and he loved him as himself . . . And Jonathan made a covenant with David because he loved him as himself.

(1 Samuel 18:1, 3)
See also 2 Corinthians 8:16–24

Accepting our differences

Unity does not mean we have to agree on everything. We simply need to accept and respect some differences in an atmosphere of love. Doing things together can often be the way that we get the important things in perspective.

One man considers one day more sacred than another; another man considers every day alike. Each one should be fully convinced in his own mind.

(Romans 14:5)

A time for silence

Unity means sometimes keeping our views to ourselves! We need to exercise the gift of discernment.

So whatever you believe about these things keep between yourself and God. Blessed is the man who does not condemn himself by what he approves.

(Romans 14:22)

A time for speaking

Unity mean sometimes speaking up whatever the cost. A fundamental truth of the gospel was at risk here, so Paul had no alternative but to speak up. But he wanted to redeem the situation and he was successful in this (Acts 15:1–35).

When Peter came to Antioch, I [Paul] opposed him to his face, because he was clearly in the wrong. Before certain men came from James, he used to eat with the Gentiles. But when they arrived, he began to draw back and separate himself from the Gentiles because he was afraid of those who belonged to the circumcision group. The other Jews joined him in his hypocrisy, so that by their hypocrisy even Barnabas was led astray.

(Galatians 2:11–13)

Thinking well of others

How the Christian scene in our nation would be transformed if we all pledged –
- not to pass on gossip (even if it is true)
- not to be negative about others
- not to speak badly of other churches
- not to dismiss the gifting of other leaders or speakers
- not to leave our wrong attitudes about others unchallenged.

THE UNITY OF THE CHURCH

Lord from whom all blessings flow,
Perfecting the church below,
Steadfast may we cleave to Thee,
Love, the mystic union be;
Join our faithful spirits, join
Each to each, and all to Thine;
Lead us through the paths of peace
On to perfect holiness.

Move and actuate and guide;
Divers gifts to each divide;
Placed according to Thy will,
Let us all our work fulfil;
Never from our office move;
Needful to each other prove;
Use the grace on each bestowed,
Tempered by the art of God

Sweetly may we all agree,
Touched with softest sympathy;
There is neither bond nor free,
Great nor servile, Lord, in Thee:
Love, like death, hath all destroyed,
Rendered all distinctions void;
Names and sects and parties fall,
Thou, O Christ, art All in all.

Charles Wesley, 1707–88

Conclusion

Christians who are united, even though they worship in different churches or in different ways, can present a powerful witness to their community. Are you playing your part in this?

My purpose is that they may be encouraged in heart and united in love, so that they may have the full riches of complete understanding, in order that they may know the mystery of God, namely, Christ, in whom are hidden all the treasures of wisdom and knowledge.

(Colossians 2:2)

243

PART FIVE

Living in the World

CHAPTER ONE

Enjoying God's Word

The Bible is not merely a book for meditation by recluses or for analysis by academics; it is God's word, given to change us and the way we live in thc world.

All Scripture is God-breathed and is useful for teaching, rebuking, correcting and training in righteousness, so that the man of God may be thoroughly equipped for every good work.
(2 Timothy 3:16–17)

Best sold, least read, worst understood. That, sadly, sums up the Bible. It is certainly a world bestseller (though many copies end up as unread gifts for christenings or weddings); but it is probably the least read and worst understood bestseller. After all, is it not (the average person thinks) a dusty old book full of genealogies and 'Thou shalt nots'?

Such thinking couldn't be further from the truth! For this book is nothing less than the word of God – exciting, encouraging, challenging, relevant for today – the very voice of God into our needy souls and world.

It might seem strange to begin this part on 'Living in the world' by considering God's word. And yet, why do we read our Bibles? So that we can become walking encyclopedias of Bible facts? No! It is so that we can know God and his ways, and so be the kind of people that he wants us to be in his world. Paul understood that once we grasp that the Bible is 'God-breathed', we will quickly see how it can make us 'thoroughly equipped for every good work' (2 Timothy 3:17) – in the world, as well as in the church.

The God-breathed word

As we have already seen (Part 3, Chapter 2) the Bible is not just a book like any other book; it is the 'God-breathed' word (2 Timothy 3:16). It is not people's attempts to describe God or recount their experiences of him; it is the very 'breath' of God, breathed into the writers by God's Spirit, so that what they wrote was exactly what God wanted written. This is why this book can be trusted, and why it is still so relevant for today.

How is the Bible seen?

Psalm 119 is a beautifully constructed psalm, each stanza beginning with the next letter of the Hebrew alphabet. But not only is it beautifully written, it is passionately written. The writer was passionate about the Scriptures! This comes out in the wide range of terms he uses to describe God's word.

Law(s) (45 times)

Blessed are they whose ways are blameless, who walk according to the law of the LORD. (v 1)
    Great peace have they who love your law, and nothing can make them stumble. (v 165)

Statutes (23 times)

Blessed are they who keep his statutes and seek him with all their heart. (v 2)
    Your statutes are my delight; they are my counsellors. (v 24)

Precepts (21 times)

I will walk about in freedom, for I have sought out your precepts. (v 45)
    I will never forget your precepts, for by them you have preserved my life. (v 93)

Decrees (22 times)

Teach me, O LORD, to follow your decrees; then I will keep them to the end. (v 33)
    Your decrees are the theme of my song wherever I lodge. (v 54)

Commands (22 times)

I run in the path of your commands, for you have set my heart free. (v 32)
    To all perfection I see a limit; but your commands are boundless. (v 96)

Word(s) (30 times)

I have hidden your word in my heart that I might not sin against you. (v 11)
    Your word is a lamp to my feet and a light for my path. (v 105)

Promise(s) (13 times)

My comfort in my suffering is this: Your promise preserves my life. (v 50)
    Your promises have been thoroughly tested, and your servant loves them. (v 140)

Clearly this psalmist loved God's word! But it was not love of it for its own sake; he saw how transforming it was as he applied it in everyday life.

Other words used

Besides these seven words in Psalm 119, other words are also used to describe the Bible, including:
- **The Book**, usually in conjunction with other words, including 'the Book of the Covenant' (e.g. Exodus 24:7), 'the Book of the Law' (e.g. Joshua 1:8), 'the Book of Truth' (Daniel 10:21)
- **The Law of Moses** (e.g. 1 Kings 2:2–3; Acts 13:39)
- **The Scriptures** (e.g. Matthew 22:29; Luke 24:27; 2 Timothy 3:15)
- **The scroll** (e.g. Psalm 40:7; Isaiah 34:16)
- **The word of truth** (e.g. Ephesians 1:13; 2 Timothy 2:15)

What is the Bible like?

The Bible uses a number of different pictures of itself to bring home to us the breadth of God's purpose in it.

A judge

The Bible is like a judge.

For the word of God is living and active. Sharper than any double-edged sword, it penetrates even to dividing soul and spirit, joints and marrow; it judges the thoughts and attitudes of the heart.

(Hebrews 4:12)

The Bible reaches parts that no other book can reach. It discerns our heart and motives. It sees what goes on deep down inside, beneath the veneer we put on for others, and passes judgment on 'what makes us tick'. We have probably all experienced this uncomfortable uncovering of wrong as we have listened to a sermon or read our Bibles. But such judgment is not designed to leave us in condemnation, but rather to bring us to God who loves to cleanse whatever is confessed (1 John 1:8–9).
　　See also Acts 2:37; 1 Corinthians 14:24–25

We also need to remember that the Bible is there to judge us, not the other way round. This means that we cannot lay aside the bits that we don't like, or rationalize certain parts as relevant only for a bygone age. This book is the eternal word of God (e.g. Psalm 119:89), expressing his eternal truth. Rather than judge it, we should 'humbly accept the word planted in you, which can save you' (James 1:21).

Water

The Bible is like rain or water.

As the rain and the snow come down from heaven, and do not return to it without watering the earth and making it bud and flourish, so that it yields seed for the sower and bread for the eater, so is my word that goes out from my mouth: It will not return to me empty, but will accomplish what I desire and achieve the purpose for which I sent it.

(Isaiah 55:10–11)

As surely as God sends literal rain on the land, feeding and refreshing it, so he brings 'spiritual rain' on his people to feed and refresh them through his word. Don't we all need God to break up our barrenness by the renewing of the Spirit-inspired word of God?

Water is also used for washing, and Jesus wants to clean up his church, 'cleansing her by the washing with water through the word' (Ephesians 5:26). The word of God can sanctify us (John 17:17), cleansing us from the dirt we pick up out there in the world.

See also Deuteronomy 32:2; Psalm 68:9; 147:15–18

Seed

The Bible is like a seed.

The seed is the word of God.

(Luke 8:11)

The promise here is of fruitfulness. The seed itself is living (Mark 4:26–29) and imperishable (1 Peter 1:23). Therefore our part is simply to sow the seed (e.g. Ecclesiastes 11:6; Luke 8:5–8; 2 Corinthians 9:6); the responsibility for its growth lies with God.

I [Paul] planted the seed, Apollos watered it, but God made it grow. So neither he who plants nor he who waters is anything, but only God, who makes things grow.

(1 Corinthians 3:6–7)

'This is what the kingdom of God is like. A man scatters seed on the ground. Night and day, whether he sleeps or gets up, the seed sprouts and grows, though he does not know how. All by itself the soil produces corn – first the stalk, then the ear, then the full grain in the ear. As soon as the grain is ripe, he puts the sickle to it, because the harvest has come.'

(Mark 4:26–29)

This is why it is worth 'sticking at it' when sowing the seed, even if it seems hard going; for the joy of harvest will surely come.

Those who sow in tears will reap with songs of joy. He who goes out weeping, carrying seed to sow, will return with songs of joy, carrying sheaves with him.

(Psalm 126:5–6)

A sword

The Bible is like a sword.

Take . . . the sword of the Spirit, which is the word of God.

(Ephesians 6:17)

For the word of God is living and active. Sharper than any double-edged sword . . .

(Hebrews 4:12)

We have already seen that this is our only weapon against our spiritual enemies (see Part 4, Chapter 6). This sword is 'double-edged' – a contemporary metaphor meaning 'exceedingly sharp'. Jesus used this weapon against both spiritual opponents (Matthew 4:4, 7, 10) and natural opponents (Matthew 22:41–46). But, as for any soldier, this weapon is only as effective in battle as we have made it in training.

See also Isaiah 49:2; Revelation 1:16; 2:12; 19:15

Fire

The Bible is like a fire.

But if I say, 'I will not mention him or speak any more in his name,' his word is in my heart like a fire, a fire shut up in my bones.
(Jeremiah 20:9)

'Is not my word like fire', declares the LORD . . .
(Jeremiah 23:29)

Fire often symbolizes God's presence and holiness (e.g. Exodus 3:1–6; 24:15–17; 2 Chronicles 7:1–3; Isaiah 4:4–6; Hebrews 12:29). The Bible is like fire because it reveals what God is like in all his holiness, but then points me to the one who can burn up all that is unholy in my life, refining me like precious metal (e.g. Zechariah 13:9; Malachi 3:2–3).

Fire also speaks of power and swift movement. The power of fire was seen with the disciples at Pentecost when 'tongues of fire' on their heads became 'words of fire' in bold preaching (Acts 2:3–4).

A hammer

The Bible is like a hammer.

'Is not my word like fire', declares the LORD, 'and like a hammer that breaks a rock in pieces?'

(Jeremiah 23:29)

The human heart can be amazingly hard (e.g. Exodus 7:13; Proverbs 28:14; Daniel 5:20; Zechariah 7:12; Matthew 19:8; Ephesians 4:18; Hebrews 3:15). There are times when God woos those hearts gently; but there are also times when hearts become so hard that only a hammer can crack them open. God's word, Jeremiah says, is such a hammer. It breaks open rock-like hearts so that his life can burst in – whether into an unbeliever responding to the gospel, or into a believer repenting of careless living.

But hammers are also used to smooth and shape objects (e.g. Exodus 25:31; Isaiah 41:7); and the Bible also fashions our lives to God's plan. This is an aspect of 'rebuking, correcting and training in righteousness' (2 Timothy 3:16).

A lamp

The Bible is like a lamp.

Your word is a lamp to my feet and a light for my path.

(Psalm 119:105)

The unfolding of your words gives light.

(Psalm 119:130)

Lift stones in the garden, and insects will scurry for cover as they are exposed to the light. That's what the Bible does: it 'brings things into the light', just like Jesus himself did (e.g. John 3:19–21). We need its light to dispel the darkness – the darkness loved by the fallen world (John 3:19), and that in our own human hearts (2 Corinthians 4:6). The Bible's light shows up the dirt; but God's intention in doing so is only to help us clear up the rubbish. We can't clean up what we don't know is there!

But everything exposed by the light becomes visible, for it is light that makes everything visible.

(Ephesians 5:13–14)

A mirror

The Bible is like a mirror.

Anyone who listens to the word but does not do what it says is like a man who looks at his face in a mirror and, after looking at himself, goes away and immediately forgets what he looks like. But the man who looks intently into the perfect law that gives freedom, and continues to do this, not forgetting what he has heard, but doing it – he will be blessed in what he does.

(James 1:23–25)

A mirror both reveals and reflects. When we stand before a mirror, we see ourselves as we really are – warts and all! Mirrors don't lie (except those at fun-fairs that deliberately distort!); and this mirror, the Bible, is no different. We see God exactly as he is; and we see ourselves exactly as we are. 'The promise of a perfect revelation of God and ourselves is ours when we accept the Bible as the divine mirror' (Herbert Lockyer).

Again, the promise is very practical. We don't look into a mirror and then forget what we see, do we? No, we act on it, adjusting our

hair or clothes, etc. Similarly, the Bible calls us not to be casual passive listeners, but doers of the word (James 1:22, 25). And as we act on what we see, we are gradually changed to become like Jesus (2 Corinthians 3:18).

Food

The Bible is like food. We all need food in order to live; and the same is true spiritually. Without a regular intake of spiritual food, we will never grow up and become 'thoroughly equipped' (2 Timothy 3:17). This food is described in various ways:

Milk

Like newborn babies, crave pure spiritual milk, so that by it you may grow up in your salvation, now that you have tasted that the Lord is good.

(1 Peter 2:2–3)

Milk is generally the food of babies and the young to help them grow up and become strong. Likewise, the Bible helps us grow up spiritually, whether we are young in physical years (2 Timothy 3:15) or in spiritual experience (1 Corinthians 3:1–2). But just as babies are weaned and move on to solids, so we need to go deeper with God in our Christian 'diet'.

See also Isaiah 28:9–10; Hebrews 5:12–13

Solid food ('Strong meat', KJV)

In fact, though by this time you ought to be teachers, you need someone to teach you the elementary truths of God's word all over again. You need milk, not solid food! Anyone who lives on milk, being still an infant, is not acquainted with the teaching about righteousness. But solid food is for the mature, who by constant use have trained themselves to distinguish good from evil.

(Hebrews 5:12–14)

251

Imagine the sadness of parents whose children never grew up! That's how the writer of Hebrews felt when so many in the church were not growing up spiritually. And that's how God feels too. He wants us to 'get our teeth into' his truth, to 'chew it over', to take it in, to make it part of our very selves. That's what will make us grow up and be useful to him in the world.

Don't give up when you get to some of the 'more chewy bits' of the Bible. Even Peter found Paul hard to understand at times (see 2 Peter 3:15–16)! But it is as we 'chew it over' that God's Spirit begins to speak to us through it.

Bread

Jesus answered, 'It is written: "Man does not live on bread alone, but on every word that comes from the mouth of God." '

(Matthew 4:4)

For our physical life, we need daily bread, daily sustenance. How much more is that true of God's word! So, are we nourishing ourselves with slices of God's strengthening 'bread' each day? We may think we can do without it; but when the pressures of the day come along, we'll soon see how very hungry we really are!

See also Deuteronomy 8:3

Honey

Then he said to me, 'Son of man, eat this scroll I am giving you and fill your stomach with it.' So I ate it, and it tasted as sweet as honey in my mouth.

(Ezekiel 3:3)

When Martin feels under the weather, he loves a slice of bread and honey. He enjoys it and it cheers him up. That's just what God's word is like! It is meant to be a sheer delight to us as we take it in.

Relevance for today

The Bible is old, but not dead!

It is very much alive and active.

He [Moses] received living words to pass on to us.

(Acts 7:38)

For you have been born again, not of perishable seed, but of imperishable, through the living and enduring word of God.

(1 Peter 1:23)

The Bible can still 'burn within us'

'Were not our hearts burning within us while he talked with us on the road and opened the Scriptures to us?'

(Luke 24:32)

The Bible is one of God's resources for us to stand against sin

I have hidden your word in my heart that I might not sin against you.

(Psalm 119:11)

The Bible is to be worked out practically in everyday living

How can a young man keep his way pure? By living according to your word.

(Psalm 119:9)

All Scripture is God-breathed and is useful for teaching, rebuking, correcting and training in righteousness, so that the man of God may be thoroughly equipped for every good work.

(2 Timothy 3:16–17)

The Bible is worth giving time to

Do your best to present yourself to God as one approved, a workman who does not need to be ashamed and who correctly handles the word of truth.

(2 Timothy 2:15)

Good workers know their tools; and a daily 'quiet time' gives us an opportunity to get familiar with this most basic of tools for the Christian life.

When you don't understand, get help!

When you find that some parts of the Bible are not easy to understand at first, take encouragement that you are not on your own (e.g. Acts 8:30–35; 18:24–26; 2 Peter 3:15–16)! But don't stay in the dark; speak to your pastor or group leader and ask; get hold of Bible reading notes or a good Study Bible. The answers are there for those who can be bothered to look!

Lord, Thy Word abideth,
And our footsteps guideth;
Who its truth believeth
Light and joy receiveth.

When our foes are near us,
Then Thy Word doth cheer us,
Word of consolation,
Message of salvation.

When the storms are o'er us,
And dark clouds before us,
Then its light directeth,
And our way protecteth.

Who can tell the pleasure,
Who recount the treasure,
By Thy Word imparted,
To the simple-hearted?

Word of mercy, giving
Succour to the living;
Word of life, supplying
Comfort to the dying!

O that we, discerning
Its most holy learning,
Lord, may love and fear Thee,
Evermore be near Thee!

Henry Williams Baker, 1821–77

Conclusion

Time spent in the Bible each day is never wasted; it is God's very own enduring food being put into our lives.

The grass withers and the flowers fall, but the word of our God stands for ever.

(Isaiah 40:8)

254

CHAPTER TWO

Growing in Prayer

Prayer is not meant to be a duty or a ritual, but an exciting adventure in our relationship with God to help us engage with the world.

'Ask and it will be given to you; seek and you will find; knock and the door will be opened to you. For everyone who asks receives; he who seeks finds; and to him who knocks, the door will be opened.' (Matthew 7:7–8)

For the vast majority of us, prayer is something we know we ought to do, but never quite get round to; or at least, we don't get round to as much of it as we know we ought to. We are, in the words of *Newsweek* magazine, following a survey of the spiritual life of theological students, 'artful dodgers of a disciplined prayer life'. Family, work, children, study, tiredness, even church meetings, all provide our excuses. We are addicted to the drug of busyness; and, like Martha long ago (Luke 10:38–42), just don't know how to stop and spend time with Jesus. For this is what prayer is: spending time in friendship with him. In the words of the Early Church Father, Clement of Alexandria, 'Prayer is happy company with God.' Our Father wants our company so he can make us different and send us out to change his world.

What prayer isn't

- **Prayer isn't a ritual** – a duty to be to be fitted into an already busy schedule, but whose heart has been forgotten (e.g. Isaiah 29:13; 58:2–4). Prayer done in this way is a burden that clouds its true significance which inoculates us against the real thing.
- **Prayer isn't a self-congratulatory exercise** – an opportunity for rehearsing how good we have been or for reminding the Almighty how fortunate he is to have us (e.g. Luke 18:11–12). Prayer done in this way will lock us out of the Father's heart.
- **Prayer isn't a competition** – to see who can use the most or the finest words (e.g. Matthew 6:7). Prayer done in this way glorifies us, not God.
- **Prayer isn't an insurance policy** – a tipping of our cap to the Almighty lest a thunderbolt come our way (e.g. Acts 8:24). Prayer done in this way is shallow and self-centred.
- **Prayer isn't magic** – something to be used to get our own way or bolster us up (e.g. Acts 8:15–23). Prayer done in this way wants *things* to change, but not *us*.

What prayer is

Prayer is exploring a friendship with God. It is about who I am before God rather than what I do for God. I am his child; he is my Father. It is therefore the most natural thing in the world to turn to him and talk.

'When you pray, say: "Father . . ."'
(Luke 11:2)

Because you are sons, God sent the Spirit of his Son into our hearts, the Spirit who calls out, 'Abba, Father.'
(Galatians 4:6)

Once we understand that our identity, security and destiny are in the hands of God,

our Father and our friend, then prayer is bound to follow. We will want to talk to him! And because it is about friendship, we will listen as well as speak. (It's a poor friend who talks your head off but never listens!) God's Spirit helps us in all this (see Part 3, Chapter 3).

In the same way, the Spirit helps us in our weakness. We do not know what we ought to pray for, but the Spirit himself intercedes for us with groans that words cannot express.
(Romans 8:26)

- 'Prayer is not wrestling with God's reluctance to bless us; it is laying hold of his willingness to do so' (John Blanchard).
- 'It is because God has promised certain things that we can ask for them with the full assurance of faith' (A. W. Pink).
- 'To pray is nothing more than to lie in the sunshine of his grace' (O. Hallesby).
- 'Prayer allows us a direct relationship with the one person who can save us from the evil that invades our hearts' (James Houston).

Sticking at it

For the most part, our problem is not that we don't know that prayer works, that it changes things, that it changes us, that it changes circumstances. Our problem is actually doing it, and keeping doing it. Jesus understood this, and so he taught his disciples to 'stick at it'.

'Keep on asking, and you will be given what you ask for. Keep on looking, and you will find. Keep on knocking, and the door will be opened. For everyone who asks, receives. Everyone who seeks, finds. And the door is opened to everyone who knocks.'

(Matthew 7:7–8, NLT)

These verses are a great stimulus to prayer, if ever we needed it; for they promise answers: 'you will be given . . . you will find . . . the door will be opened'. And these are promises to 'everyone'! Wow! But note how we have to 'stick at it'. We deliberately chose the New Living Translation of Matthew 7:7–8 because it brings out the meaning of the original Greek: *keep on* asking, *keep on* looking, *keep on* knocking. In other words, don't ask once and then give up because it didn't happen; stick at it!

See also Luke 11:5–13; 18:1–8

Promises in prayer

So, why should we 'stick at it'? Jesus said: because your Father is good and will answer!

'Which of you, if his son asks for bread, will give him a stone? Or if he asks for a fish, will give him a snake? If you, then, though you are evil, know how to give good gifts to your children, how much more will your Father in heaven give good gifts to those who ask him!'

(Matthew 7:9–11)

The Bible is full of such promises, that God answers his children when they call to him. Here are just some, from the New Testament:

'I tell you that if two of you on earth agree about anything you ask for, it will be done for you by my Father in heaven.'

(Matthew 18:19)

'If you remain in me and my words remain in you, ask whatever you wish, and it will be given you.'

(John 15:7)

'If you believe, you will receive whatever you ask for in prayer.'

(Matthew 21:22)

'Whatever you ask for in prayer, believe that you have received it, and it will be yours.'

(Mark 11:24)

'And I will do whatever you ask in my name, so that the Son may bring glory to the Father. You may ask me for anything in my name, and I will do it.'

(John 14:13–14)

'You did not choose me, but I chose you and appointed you to go and bear fruit – fruit that will last. Then the Father will give you whatever you ask in my name.'

(John 15:16)

'In that day you will no longer ask me anything. I tell you the truth, my Father will give you whatever you ask in my name. Until now you have not asked for anything in my name. Ask and you will receive, and your joy will be complete.'

(John 16:23–24)

[We] receive from him anything we ask, because we obey his commands and do what pleases him.

(1 John 3:22)

This is the confidence we have in approaching God: that if we ask anything according to his will, he hears us.

(1 John 5:14)

Note that all of these promises have conditions, however; they are not ours for the automatic taking. We have to play our part: asking in faith, asking 'in Jesus' name' (not as a catchphrase, but in line with his purposes), agreeing with others, bearing fruit, etc. It is as we do these things that God releases his power from heaven.

Hindrances in prayer

But there are things that can hinder our praying and restrict God from releasing the full blessing that he wants to give; things like –

- Sin that remains unconfessed (Psalm 66:18)
- Wrong motives (James 4:3)
- Double-mindedness (James 1:5–8)
- Cherishing unforgiveness in our heart (Mark 11:25–26)
- Wrong relationships (Matthew 5:23–24)
- Vain repetition (Matthew 6:7)
- Pride (Job 35:12–13)
- Lack of faith (Mark 11:22–24)
- Focusing only on 'me' (James 4:3)
- Wrong attitudes in marriage (1 Peter 3:7)
- Not asking! (James 4:2)

The 'mechanics' of prayer

When can we pray?

Anytime! For if we have understood that prayer is part of our relationship, then questions like, 'How often should I talk to my friend?' are meaningless! But equally, just as in marriage, not having times set aside to talk sometimes means it never happens! So in the Bible we find different patterns of prayer: morning (e.g. Psalm 5:3; 88:13; Mark 1:35), morning and evening (e.g. 1 Chronicles 23:30), three times a day (e.g., Psalm 55:17; Daniel 6:10), at mealtimes (e.g. John 6:11; 1 Timothy 4:3–5); during the night (e.g. Luke 6:12; Acts 16:25), 'night and day' [i.e. constantly!] (Nehemiah 1:4–6; Luke 2:36–37). The most important thing is that we do it!

And pray in the Spirit on all occasions ...
(Ephesians 6:18)

Be joyful always; pray continually; give thanks in all circumstances, for this is God's will for you in Christ Jesus.
(1 Thessalonians 5:16–18)

Where can we pray?

Anywhere! We do not need to go to a special place to pray or to be better heard. While we may sometimes find this helpful, reliance on a special location can be superstitious nonsense. While we certainly find people praying in the temple (e.g. 1 Kings 8:22–30), we also find them praying in the open air (e.g. Luke 5:16), in public places (e.g. Acts 21:5), under trees (1 Kings 19:4), in rooms, whether privately (e.g. Daniel 6:10) or corporately (e.g. Acts 1:13–14), on the roof (e.g. Acts 10:9). Pretty wide-ranging, isn't it? With God, what matters is not where we pray, but whether we pray. Clearly there is value in getting alone with God, for this prevents us 'playing to the crowd' and gives us the chance to pour out our heart intimately and honestly, just as Jesus spoke about:

'And when you pray, do not be like the hypocrites, for they love to pray standing in the synagogues and on the street corners to be seen by men. I tell you the truth, they have received their reward in full. But when you pray, go into your room, close the door and pray to your Father, who is unseen. Then your Father, who sees what is done in secret, will reward you.'

(Matthew 6:5–6)

But this does not mean that there is no value in praying as we walk down the street, or travel on the bus, or wait at the school gate, or talk with a friend on the phone. Indeed, praying in such settings often provokes us to pray for things that we would normally never think of.

How can we pray?

Anyhow! There is no right or wrong way to pray. In the Bible we find people standing (e.g. Luke 18:10–13), sitting (e.g. 2 Samuel 7:18), bowing (e.g. Exodus 34:8–9), kneeling (e.g. Acts 9:40), prostrating (e.g. 1 Chronicles 29:20), lifting or spreading hands (e.g. Exodus 9:29), praying in their own language and praying in tongues (e.g. 1 Corinthians 14:15). The key issue does not seem to be the body, but the heart. We should not be afraid of using our bodies in prayer or worship (any such fear is a very Greek, rather than Hebrew, view of ourselves). In fact, our body will often help to express what our prayer is trying to say.

And pray in the Spirit on all occasions with all kinds of prayers and requests. With this in mind, be alert and always keep on praying for all the saints.

(Ephesians 6:18)

What can we pray for?

Anything! The very fact that there are over 20 different words in the Bible for 'prayer' – indicating request, entreaty, intercession, crying out, sighing, praising, rejoicing – reflects the breadth of prayer and the emotions involved. We cannot possibly include here everything that we can pray for; but some of the things we can confidently pray for include:

For the progress of the gospel

Jesus promised that 'this gospel of the kingdom will be preached in the whole world as a testimony to all nations' (Matthew 24:14) and he commissioned his disciples to take it out there (Matthew 28:18–20). So we can confidently pray for this to happen (e.g. Romans 10:1; Ephesians 6:19–20; Colossians 4:3–4; 2 Thessalonians 3:1), including our own witness, our church's outreach, Christian workers in other nations, and the effective preaching of the word (e.g. Isaiah 55:10–11).

For God's blessing on others

Paul's letters reveal how very much he prayed for others, both for individuals and for churches, and how he recognized that he needed their prayers too (e.g. Romans 1:9–10; 2 Corinthians 1:10–11; Ephesians 1:16; Philippians 1:4–5; Colossians 1:9–12; 1 Thessalonians 1:2–3). Clearly our family and our friends form part of such praying.

For our nation and government

We are struck by the fact that in both Jeremiah 29:7 and 1 Timothy 2:1–4, God's people are told to pray for the blessing of governments that were hostile to them – Babylon and Rome. Clearly Jeremiah and Paul would have little sympathy for Christians who will not pray for a government that they did not vote for!

For the workplace

Paul insisted that Christians behave with the highest standards of integrity in the workplace (e.g. Ephesians 6:5–9; Colossians 3:22–4:1) – not only for the sake of 'gospel witness', but because God is a God of righteousness and justice, who hates 'sharp practices' (e.g. Leviticus 19:35–36; Proverbs 11:1). We should be praying for righteousness, and the consequent blessing of God, on the place where we work.

For our own needs

Jesus encouraged us to bring our daily needs before God – though in the Lord's prayer (Matthew 6:9–13; Luke 11:2–4), these do not come until halfway through. Prayer which starts out self-centred will probably remain self-centred, and so will we ourselves.

Relevance for today

Prayer is about remaining dependent

We all know that we constantly need God; but there is a danger that, as we become 'mature' Christians, we don't need his help as much as we used to. Prayer means bringing our weakness, not our strength, to God. Remember: he is unimpressed by any of our achievements!

'We do not know what to do, but our eyes are upon you.'

(2 Chronicles 20:12)

'God opposes the proud but gives grace to the humble.' Humble yourselves, therefore, under God's mighty hand, that he may lift you up in due time. Cast all your anxiety on him because he cares for you.

(1 Peter 5:5-7)

See also 2 Chronicles 7:14; 33:12–13; 34:26–27; Ezra 8:21–23

Prayer is about being honest

Prayer demands honesty – about who we are, what we have done, and about what we are praying for and truly have faith for. There is no point 'pumping ourselves up' about what we do not really believe! God prefers the honest approach!

The LORD is near to all who call on him, to all who call on him in truth.

(Psalm 145:18)

During the days of Jesus' life on earth, he offered up prayers and petitions with loud cries and tears to the one who could save him from death, and he was heard because of his reverent submission.

(Hebrews 5:7)

See also Psalm 15:1–2; 51:6; Proverbs 16:13; Jeremiah 20:7–12

Prayer is effective when rooted in the Bible

Prayer goes hand in hand with discovering the treasures and promises of the Bible. The more I discover, the more I can confidently claim:

Do good to your servant according to your word, O LORD.

(Psalm 119:65)

Pray using the prayers of the Bible

While God does not want us to pray by rote, the prayers of the Bible, and especially the Psalms, can be a great source of inspiration when it comes to praying, particularly when we are finding it hard to pray. If your spirit is dry, make some of the prayers in this chapter your own.

Pray in 'the market place'

Prayer is not just for 'holy huddles'. Much praying in the early church took place out in the world, whether unembarrassingy praying in public places (e.g. Acts 2:1–12, 46; 16:13–15; 21:5) or praying for unbelievers (Acts 3:6–10; 16:16–18; 28:7–9). Let's not keep this powerful weapon hidden or be embarrassed by it!

Prayer's great cop-out

'The phrase "If it be thy will" is more often than not a cop-out . . . It is lazy pseudo-reverence' (John White). Of course Jesus prayed it; but he prayed it because he knew what the Father's will was, not because he didn't (Matthew 26:39, 42).

Prayer's poor substitute

Saying 'I will think about you' is a poor substitute for 'I will pray for you'. 'Thinking about someone' helps no one; praying for them makes a difference!

What a Friend we have in Jesus,
All our sins and griefs to bear!
What a privilege to carry
Everything to God in prayer!
O what peace we often forfeit,
O what needless pain we bear,
All because we do not carry
Everything to God in prayer!

Have we trials and temptations?
Is there trouble anywhere?
We should never be discouraged:
Take it to the Lord in prayer.
Can we find a friend so faithful,
Who will all our sorrows share?
Jesus knows our every weakness:
Take it to the Lord in prayer.

Are we weak and heavy-laden,
Cumbered with a load of care?
Precious Saviour, still our refuge:
Take it to the Lord in prayer.
Do thy friends despise, forsake thee?
Take it to the Lord in prayer;
In His arms He'll take and shield thee,
Thou wilt find a solace there.

Joseph Medlicott Scriven, 1819–86

Conclusion

Prayer isn't a 'twisting of God's arm' to make him fit in with our purposes. It is an exploring and enjoying of our friendship with him, a learning to submit our wills to his, a discovering of his will, so that we can live it out in the world.

The prayer of a righteous man is powerful and effective.

(James 5:16)

CHAPTER THREE

The Promise of Strength

Every day of our lives God's strength is available to equip us for everyday situations.

'Your strength will equal your days.' (Deuteronomy 33:25)

'Lord, give me strength!' the cry often goes up. In many cases, it is simply a cry of exasperation in trying circumstances, rather than a genuine prayer. Yet it is a prayer that God is happy for us to make. For the Bible is full of promises of God's strength for those who come to him, acknowledging that they have no strength of their own.

The secret of strength

'Tell me the secret of your great strength,' Delilah asked Samson (Judges 16:6), sent by the Philistines to ensnare him. The apparent source was the Nazirite vow to which Samson had been dedicated from conception (Judges 13:2–5); but the true source of his strength was not the vow, nor his unshorn hair, but the God to whom he had been dedicated. Still today the God of Samson comes to bring his supernatural strength into the lives of his people for every need and circumstance.

God alone

The secret of our strength is God alone, as so many writers of the Scriptures testified:

'The LORD is my strength and my song; he has become my salvation.'

(Exodus 15:2)

Look to the LORD and his strength; seek his face always.

(1 Chronicles 16:11)

The LORD is my strength and my shield; my heart trusts in him, and I am helped.

(Psalm 28:7)

Surely God is my salvation; I will trust and not be afraid. The LORD, the LORD, is my strength and my song.

(Isaiah 12:2)

He gives strength to the weary and increases the power of the weak. Even youths grow tired and weary, and young men stumble and fall; but those who hope in the LORD will renew their strength. They will soar on wings like eagles; they will run and not grow weary, they will walk and not be faint.

(Isaiah 40:29–31)

The Sovereign LORD is my strength; he makes my feet like the feet of a deer, he enables me to go on the heights.

(Habakkuk 3:19)

He [Christ] will keep you strong to the end, so that you will be blameless on the day of our Lord Jesus Christ.

(1 Corinthians 1:8)

I can do everything through him who gives me strength.

(Philippians 4:13)

Strongest when weak

This strength that we are promised is not a 'pulling ourselves up by the bootstraps' sort of strength. In fact, the weaker we are, the better (which is so encouraging for many of us!); because the more aware we are of our weakness, the more God can show his power.

This is why it is so important not to look at the external or apparent strength of the opposition, but to look to God alone who is bigger than it all. Two well-known incidents from the Old Testament bring this home.

David said to the Philistine, 'You come against me with sword and spear and javelin, but I come against you in the name of the Lord Almighty, the God of the armies of Israel, whom you have defied. This day the LORD will hand you over to me, and I'll strike you down and cut off your head. Today I will give the carcasses of the Philistine army to the birds of the air and the beasts of the earth, and the whole world will know that there is a God in Israel. All those gathered here will know that it is not by sword or spear that the LORD saves; for the battle is the LORD's, and he will give all of you into our hands.'

(1 Samuel 17:45–47)

This is what the LORD says: 'Let not the wise man boast of his wisdom or the strong man boast of his strength or the rich man boast of his riches, but let him who boasts boast about this: that he understands and knows me, that I am the LORD, who exercises kindness, justice and righteousness on earth, for in these I delight,' declares the LORD.

(Jeremiah 9:23–24)

Let the weakling say, 'I am strong!'

(Joel 3:10)

'My grace is sufficient for you, for my power is made perfect in weakness.' Therefore I will boast all the more gladly about my weaknesses, so that Christ's power may rest on me. That is why, for Christ's sake, I delight in weaknesses, in insults, in hardships, in persecutions, in difficulties. For when I am weak, then I am strong.

(2 Corinthians 12:9–10)

'Be strong and courageous. Do not be afraid or discouraged because of the king of Assyria and the vast army with him, for there is a greater power with us than with him. With him is only the arm of flesh, but with us is the LORD our God to help us and to fight our battles.'

(2 Chronicles 32:7–8)

No matter what the situation is that we might be facing, it is important to remember that God's weakness is always stronger than the greatest human strength:

For the foolishness of God is wiser than man's wisdom, and the weakness of God is stronger than man's strength.

(1 Corinthians 1:25)

'As thy days, so shall thy strength be'

The words in this heading are from the King James Version; in the NIV the verse reads, 'Your strength will equal your days' (Deuteronomy 33:25). This is God's wonderful promise to us: that he will provide strength for each day. Over the years we have seen this to be true again and again. We have seen people who thought that they would never be able to face something – perhaps unemployment, or severe illness, or bereavement, or tragedy – suddenly find a miraculous grace from God and strength for each day. We don't have to sit and worry whether we will have enough strength for tomorrow or next year or ten years' time. God promises us sufficient resources – himself – for each present day as it comes. Strength isn't given before we need it, but when we need it.

Strength in times of crisis

Being a Christian does not guarantee us immunity from life's trials, sorrows and sufferings. Mike learned the theory of this at Bible college; but he experienced a quick learning curve when he took up the pastorate of his first church. Even before he had been formally received as the pastor, he had to conduct the funeral service of his church treasurer's teenage son, tragically killed in a freak car accident. Over the years many more funerals would follow: young and old who died of cancer, the middle-aged who died of heart attacks, young people killed in accidents, a young man who took his own life when things got on top of him. And all these were God's dear people! Clearly, we as Christians are not immune from the consequences of living in a sin-ridden world. It is at such times, when something earth-shattering happens, when the bottom falls out of our world, that we need God's strength. We need to know with the psalmist:

Even though I walk through the valley of the shadow of death, I will fear no evil, for you are with me; your rod and staff, they comfort me.'
(Psalm 23:4)

In times of major personal disaster, we may indeed know God's miraculous deliverance (e.g. Psalm 34:4–10); but at other times, the deliverance does not come in the way we would choose it to (e.g. Psalm 22:1–2), and it is time instead for us to know his presence, his companionship, in the midst of difficulty, trial or danger (e.g. 2 Corinthians 12:7–10). Paul experienced both in his life; but whatever the outcome, this was his confident assertion:

What, then, shall we say in response to this? If God is for us, who can be against us? He who did not spare his own Son, but gave him up for us all – how will he not also, along with him, graciously give us all things? . . . Who shall separate us from the love of Christ? Shall trouble or hardship or persecution or famine or nakedness or danger or sword? As it is written: 'For your sake we face death all day long; we are considered as sheep to be slaughtered.' No, in all these things we are more than conquerors through him who loved us. For I am convinced that neither death nor life, neither angels nor demons, neither the present nor the future, nor any powers, neither height nor depth, nor anything else in all creation, will be able to separate us from the love of God that is in Christ Jesus our Lord.

(Romans 8:31–32, 35–39)

Here was indeed a man who had discovered the reality of finding strength in God, no matter what the situation.

Strength in times of temptation

Temptation is something that all of us face, and if we are going to stand against it, we need God's strength and help. We need to remember that, because Jesus himself was tempted, he really can help us.

Because he himself suffered when he was tempted, he is able to help those who are being tempted.

(Hebrews 2:18)

See also Hebrews 4:15–16

With Christ's help we are 'more than conquerors through him who loved us' (Romans 8:37) and there is strength to stand and to escape if we will ask for it.

No temptation has seized you except what is common to man. And God is faithful; he will not let you be tempted beyond what you can bear. But when you are tempted, he will also provide a way out so that you can stand up under it.

(1 Corinthians 10:13)

When we become Christians, we become 'a new creation' (2 Corinthians 5:17) and things are different. Sin is no longer the controlling factor in our lives (Romans 6:1–14). That old relationship with sin is over and done with; our new master – God himself – is the only one who has a legitimate claim on us, and he will provide strength to his children to 'stand against the devil's schemes' (Ephesians 6:11). But even if we do stumble, God does not give up on us!

If you return to the Almighty, you will be restored.

(Job 22:23)

If we confess our sins, he is faithful and just and will forgive us our sins and purify us from all unrighteousness.

(1 John 1:9)

Remember: no matter how big a mess we make of things, God can always redeem it.

Strength in daily life

But it's not just in the crisis times that God wants us to look to him for strength. It's in the ordinary (dare we say it? – monotonous!) days, when things just keep ticking along. Even here, God wants us to derive our strength from him. In fact, the challenge not to do things in our own strength, especially when they are routine and familiar, is all the greater.

Jesus stressed the need to look to God for strength in even the most basic areas of life:

'Give us today our daily bread . . .'

(Matthew 6:11)

There are certainly strong words for those who look to their own strength, rather than to God:

This is what the LORD says: 'Cursed is the one who trusts in man, who depends on flesh for his strength and whose heart turns away from the LORD. He will be like a bush in the wastelands; he will not see prosperity when it comes. He will dwell in the parched places of the desert, in a salt land where no-one lives. But blessed is the man who trusts in the LORD, whose confidence is in him. He will be like a tree planted by the water that sends out its roots by the stream. It does not

fear when heat comes; its leaves are always
green. It has no worries in a year of drought
and never fails to bear fruit.'

(Jeremiah 17:5–8)

See also Psalm 118:8–9; Isaiah 2:22; 30:1–2;
31:1

How do we become strong?

So, how do we become strong, then? How do
we get God's strength into our lives? Well,
just like an athlete, we need to 'get into training'
(e.g. 1 Corinthians 9:24; 2 Timothy 2:5;

Hebrews 12:1). Investing in things now will mean we are ready for whatever comes; learning to be dependent on God on a daily basis will make it easier to be dependent when the crisis time comes. So, what sort of things help to 'build up our spiritual strength'?

- Holding firmly to the gospel, the means by which God's power comes to work in us (Romans 1:16; 1 Corinthians 1:18).
- Submitting ourselves to God each day (James 4:6–7).
- Acknowledging our dependence on God daily (Philippians 4:12–13).
- Coming to God in faith (Hebrews 11:6; 1 John 5:4), not in an attitude of unbelief (Romans 4:20), but of quietness and trust (Psalm 27:14; Isaiah 30:15).
- Growing in God's joy (Nehemiah 8:10; Isaiah 12:2–3).
- Remembering that God's power at work in us is the same as that by which he raised Jesus from the dead (Ephesians 1:19–20).
- Drawing from his word (Colossians 3:16; 2 Timothy 3:16–17) and letting it do its work in us (1 Thessalonians 2:13).
- Strengthening one another. In 1 Samuel 23:16 we read: 'Jonathan went to David . . . and helped him to find strength in God.' Sometimes we can't get by on our own; in fact, God has designed life that way. We need each other's help; others who will encourage us to look to God when we're struggling or down, who will urge us to keep going when it's tough (Hebrews 12:1).

Strength for the weak and fearful

Nobody knows us like God! And he knows that there are times when all of us feel weak or fearful. Even to a leader like Joshua, about to lead God's people into the promised land, God had to speak words of encouragement. Three times in four verses (Joshua 1:6, 7, 9) we find the phrase 'Be strong and courageous'. Clearly Joshua needed to hear these words! And often so do we; that is why the Bible has promises specifically for such times.

'Be strong and courageous . . . The LORD himself goes before you and will be with you; he will never leave you nor forsake you. Do not be afraid; do not be discouraged.'
(Deuteronomy 31:7–8)

'But as for you, be strong and do not give up, for your work will be rewarded.'
(2 Chronicles 15:7)

Be strong, take heart and wait for the LORD.
(Psalm 27:14)

Say to those with fearful hearts, 'Be strong, do not fear; your God will come.'
(Isaiah 35:4)

'Do not be afraid, O man highly esteemed . . . Peace! Be strong now; be strong.'
(Daniel 10:19)

'So will I save you, and you will be a blessing. Do not be afraid, but let your hands be strong.'
(Zechariah 8:13)

Be on your guard; stand firm in the faith; be men of courage; be strong.
(1 Corinthians 16:13)

Finally, be strong in the Lord and in his mighty power.
(Ephesians 6:10)

Relevance for today

We all need encouragement to learn how to become strong in God, through his strength, not ours.

God is strong and loving

One thing God has spoken, two things I have heard: that you, O God, are strong, and that you, O Lord, are loving.

(Psalm 62:11)

Strength through weakness

God brings his strength to us when we acknowledge our weakness.

Whom have I in heaven but you? And earth has nothing I desire besides you. My flesh and my heart may fail, but God is the strength of my heart and my portion for ever.

(Psalm 73:25–26)

See also 1 Corinthians 2:2–5; 2 Corinthians 12:9; 13:4, 9

Strength through dependence

Strength in God is dependent on trust in God.

The LORD is my strength and my shield; my heart trusts in him, and I am helped.

(Psalm 28:7)

See also Psalm 18:1–3; 112:6–8; Isaiah 26:3–4

Strength from God's Spirit

True strength comes from God's Spirit, not our own efforts.

'Not by might nor by power, but by my Spirit,' says the LORD Almighty.

(Zechariah 4:6)

See also 1 Samuel 2:9–10; Ezekiel 37:1–10

God's strength is greatest

No crisis has power that is greater than God's strength. When the Israelites were faced with the impenetrable barrier of the Red Sea ahead of them and the invincible might of Pharaoh's army behind them, listen to what Moses said:

'Do not be afraid. Stand firm and you will see the deliverance the LORD will bring you today . . . . The LORD will fight for you; you need only to be still.'

(Exodus 14:13–14)

See also Deuteronomy 3:21–24; Joshua 10:6–14; 2 Chronicles 20:2–30

Strength through God's grace

God wants us to be strong, above all, in his grace.

You then, my son, be strong in the grace that is in Christ Jesus.

(2 Timothy 2:1)

It is as we are strong in God's grace that all the resources for all of life can be found.

Strength for action

Knowing we have God's strength should prompt us to action.

'The people that do know their God shall be strong, and do exploits.'

(Daniel 11:32, KJV)

Do we not need more strong Christians who will 'do exploits' for God? If your answer is 'Yes!', then our question is: 'Why not let it start with you now?'

'We rest on Thee', our Shield and our
   Defender!
We go not forth alone against the foe;
Strong in Thy strength, safe in Thy keeping
   tender,
'We rest on Thee, and in Thy Name we go.'

Yes, 'in Thy Name', O Captain of salvation!
In Thy dear Name, all other names above;
Jesus our Righteousness, our sure Foundation,
Our Prince of glory and our King of love.

'We go' in faith, our own great weakness
   feeling,
And needing more each day Thy grace to
   know;
Yet from our hearts a song of triumph pealing:
'We rest on Thee, and in Thy Name we go.'

'We rest on Thee', our Shield and our
   Defender!
Thine is the battle; Thine shall be the praise
When passing through the gates of pearly
   splendour,
Victors, we rest with Thee through endless days.

Edith Adeline Gilling Cherry 1872–97

Conclusion

'God's strength reinforces the fragile abilities of man. This enables him to do great exploits for God' (Wayne Detzler).

'*Yours, O L*ORD*, is the greatness and the power . . . In your hands are strength and power to exalt and give strength to all.*'
(1 Chronicles 29:11–12)

274

CHAPTER FOUR

The Promise of Comfort

None of us gets through life without meeting trouble or sorrow at some point; but that is exactly when we can experience the comfort and love of God in our lives.

The God of all comfort, who comforts us in all our troubles.
(2 Corinthians 1:3–4)

What do you think of when you hear the word 'comfort'? Settling down into your favourite armchair? Lying in the bath away from the kids for half an hour? Munching your way through a box of chocolates to cheer yourself up? Upgrading your car to something a little better? None of these pictures come anywhere near what the Bible means by 'comfort'. For true comfort is nothing less than a divine invasion of God's grace, encouragement and strength for the hard times of life; not just to 'give us a bit of relief' or to 'keep us going', but to so fortify us that we will have more than enough left over to pass on to others.

The source of comfort

There is no other book of comfort in the whole world that is comparable to the Bible. That should hardly surprise us, for God himself is described in it as 'the God of all comfort'.

Praise be to the God and Father of our Lord Jesus Christ, the Father of compassion and the God of all comfort, who comforts us in all our troubles, so that we can comfort those in any trouble with the comfort we ourselves have received from God.

(2 Corinthians 1:3–4)

Comfort for ourselves, and comfort to pass on; that sums up so much about the Bible and the God it reveals. Just look at the following testimonies of those who found that God brought them comfort:

Give me a sign of your goodness, that my enemies may see it and be put to shame, for you, O LORD, have helped me and comforted me.

(Psalm 86:17)

My comfort in my suffering is this: Your promise preserves my life.

(Psalm 119:50)

Shout for joy, O heavens; rejoice, O earth; burst into song, O mountains! For the LORD comforts his people and will have compassion on his afflicted ones.

(Isaiah 49:13)

O my Comforter in sorrow . . .

(Jeremiah 8:18)

Promises of comfort

God's promises of comfort are not just for reflecting upon, as though they were some mystical or philosophical thoughts on life, but for living in the world. They are associated with help and encouragement in times of stress, sorrow and difficulty, and show that God is deeply interested in all that goes on in our lives. Here are just some of the areas where God promises his comfort to us.

When afraid

The LORD is my light and my salvation – whom shall I fear? The LORD is the stronghold of my life – of whom shall I be afraid? When evil men advance against me to devour my flesh, when my enemies and my foes attack me, they will stumble and fall. Though an army besiege me, my heart will not fear; though war break out against me, even then will I be confident. One thing I ask of the LORD, this is what I seek: that I may dwell in the house of the LORD all the days of my life, to gaze upon the beauty of the Lord and to seek him in his temple. For in the day of trouble he will keep me safe in his dwelling; he will hide me in the shelter of his tabernacle and set me high upon a rock.

(Psalm 27:1–5)

See also Psalms 34; 46; 56; 91; Proverbs 3:24–26; Isaiah 12:2-3; 41:10–14; Matthew 8:23–27; 10:19–20, 26–31; John 14:27; Acts 18:9–10; Hebrews 13:6

When anxious or worried

'Therefore I tell you, do not worry about your life, what you will eat; or about your body, what you will wear. Life is more than food, and the body more than clothes. Consider the ravens: They do not sow or reap, they have no storeroom or barn; yet God feeds them. And how much more valuable you are than birds! Who of you by worrying can add a single hour to his life? Since you cannot do this very little thing, why do you worry about the rest?'

(Luke 12:22–26)

Cast all your anxiety on him because he cares for you.

(1 Peter 5:7)

See also Psalm 94:18–19; Isaiah 43:1–13; Matthew 6:25–34; Luke 10:40–42; 21:14–15; Philippians 4:6–7

When bereaved or mourning

The Spirit of the Sovereign LORD is on me, because the LORD has anointed me to preach good news to the poor. He has sent me to bind up the broken-hearted, to proclaim freedom for the captives and release from darkness for the prisoners, to proclaim the year of the LORD'S favour and the day of vengeance of our God, to comfort all who mourn, and provide for those who grieve in Zion – to bestow on them a crown of beauty instead of ashes, the oil of gladness instead of mourning, and a garment of praise instead of a spirit of despair.

(Isaiah 61:1–3)

'Blessed are those who mourn, for they will be comforted.'

(Matthew 5:4)

See also Psalm 23:1–6; Isaiah: 25:6–8; Jeremiah 31:13; John 11:21–27; 1 Corinthians 15:51–57; 1 Thessalonians 4:13–18; Revelation 21:1–5

277

When discouraged

The LORD *is close to the broken-hearted and saves those who are crushed in spirit.*

(Psalm 34:18)

Why are you downcast, O my soul? Why so disturbed within me? Put your hope in God, for I will yet praise him, my Saviour and my God.

(Psalm 42:5)

See also Psalm 40:1–3; Lamentations 3:19–24; Romans 8:28–39; 2 Corinthians 4:7–18; 7:6

When facing difficulties

'Fear not, for I have redeemed you; I have summoned you by name; you are mine. When you pass through the waters, I will be with you; and when you pass through the rivers, they will not sweep over you. When you walk through the fire, you will not be burned; the flames will not set you ablaze. For I am the LORD*, your God, the Holy One of Israel, your Saviour.'*

(Isaiah 43:1–3)

See also Psalm 4:1; 25:16–18; 40:1–5; 91:3–15; Jonah 2:1–10; 2 Corinthians 12:7–10

When failure or falling comes

'I have seen his ways, but I will heal him; I will guide him and restore comfort to him.'

(Isaiah 57:18)

'Simon, Simon, Satan has asked to sift you as wheat. But I have prayed for you, Simon, that your faith may not fail. And when you have turned back, strengthen your brothers.'

(Luke 22:31–32)

See also Psalm 51; Isaiah 40:1–2; Luke 15:11–24; 2 Timothy 2:11–13

When feeling far from God

'I have chosen you and have not rejected you. So do not fear, for I am with you; do not be dismayed, for I am your God.'

(Isaiah 41:9–10)

'My Father, who has given them to me, is greater than all; no-one can snatch them out of my Father's hand.'

(John 10:29)

See also Psalm 22:1–19; 71:9–21; 139:1–18; John 6:37; Acts 17:24–27; James 4:8–10

When ill or in pain

When Jesus landed and saw a large crowd, he had compassion on them and healed their sick.

(Matthew 14:14)

'My grace is enough; it's all you need. My strength comes into its own in your weakness.'

(2 Corinthians 12:9, The Message)

See also Psalm 41:3; 103:1–4; Isaiah 53:4–5; Ezekiel 34:1–16; Romans 8:18–25; 2 Corinthians 4:16–18; James 5:14–16

When lonely

'Can a mother forget the baby at her breast and have no compassion on the child she has borne? Though she may forget, I will not forget you! See, I have engraved you on the palms of my hands.'

(Isaiah 49:15–16)

See also Psalm 25:16–20; 68:4–6; 73:23–25; Isaiah 49:14–16; John 14:15–21

When needing peace

You will keep in perfect peace him whose mind is steadfast, because he trusts in you.

(Isaiah 26:3)

Do not be anxious about anything, but in everything, by prayer and petition, with thanksgiving, present your requests to God. And the peace of God, which transcends all understanding, will guard your hearts and your minds in Christ Jesus.

(Philippians 4:6–7)

See also Numbers 6:24–26; Psalm 85:8; Isaiah 40:1–8; John 14:27; 16:33; Romans 5:1–5; Philippians 4:6–7

When in trouble

The LORD is good, a refuge in times of trouble. He cares for those who trust in him.

(Nahum 1:7)

Call upon me in the day of trouble; I will deliver you, and you will honour me.

(Psalm 50:15)

See also Job 5:7–18; Psalm 9:9; 27:4–5; 32:7; 46:1–2; 138:7–8; 2 Corinthians 4:16–18; James 5:13

When weak

For we do not have a high priest who is unable to sympathise with our weaknesses, but we have one who has been tempted in every way, just as we are – yet was without sin. Let us then approach the throne of grace with confidence, so that we may receive mercy and find grace to help us in our time of need.

(Hebrews 4:15–16)

See also Joshua 1:6–9; Psalm 72:12–14; Isaiah 40:29–31; 1 Corinthians 1:27–31; 2 Corinthians 11:24–12:10; Philippians 4:12–13

When weary

'Come to me, all you who are weary and burdened, and I will give you rest. Take my yoke upon you and learn from me, for I am gentle and humble in heart, and you will find rest for your souls. For my yoke is easy and my burden is light.'

(Matthew 11:28–30)

See also Exodus 33:14; Psalm 68:9; 119:28; Isaiah 40:28–31; Jeremiah 31:25; 2 Corinthians 4:16–18; Hebrews 12:1–3

Ever asked 'why?'

None of us gets through life without meeting trouble and sorrow at some time or other (Job 5:7). At such times we may wonder where God is; we may not feel he is near us; we may even be tempted to ask, 'Why?' Certainly there were people in the Bible who did (e.g. Job 3:11–16; 21:7; 24:1; Psalm 10:1; 44:23–24; Jeremiah 12:1; 15:18; Habakkuk 1:13). Ultimately, the answer to why someone suffers or seems to get an 'unfair deal' remains a profound mystery. The problem, at its most basic level, is that we live in a fallen world, one originally made good but spoilt dreadfully by sin, and one in which, as a consequence, things go dreadfully wrong at times. Suffering may be the direct result of our own sin (e.g. Job 4:8); but more often than not, it is simply 'one of those things' in life in a fallen world (e.g. Luke 13:1–5; John 9:1–3), and all of us are affected by it.

The Christian message therefore is one of comfort in the midst of trouble (e.g. Psalm 9:9; 46:1; Hebrews 11:32–38). God does not always rescue us from it (though sometimes he may, e.g. Psalm 50:15; 2 Timothy 3:10–11); but he certainly always provides his grace and strength in the midst of it (e.g. 2 Corinthians 12:8–10). Our confidence is in the God who has already acted in history, identifying himself with us fully (e.g. Hebrews 2:14) and dealing with the root problem of sin through the sacrifice of his Son on the cross (e.g. Isaiah 53:3–12).

Our assurance is that, one day, at the end of human history, everything will be put right again:

Then I saw a new heaven and a new earth, for the first heaven and the first earth had passed away, and there was no longer any sea. I saw the Holy City, the new Jerusalem, coming down out of heaven from God, prepared as a bride beautifully dressed for her husband. And I heard a loud voice from the throne saying, 'Now the dwelling of God is with men, and he will live with them. They will be his people, and God himself will be with them and be their God. He will wipe every tear from their eyes. There will be no more death or mourning or crying or pain, for the old order of things has passed away.'

(Revelation 21:1–4)

In the meantime, hardships can be embraced with Christ's help, and can even be turned to our good (Romans 8:28–39). They may serve as discipline (Hebrews 12:5–13), or lead to a deeper revelation of God (Job 42:1–5), or strengthen our character (Psalm 119:67, 71; Romans 5:3–4). It can certainly all be to God's glory (John 9:1–7).

What we can be sure of is the fact that God can be trusted (e.g. Psalm 20:7; 31:14–16). 'Will not the Judge of all the earth do right?' Abraham asked (Genesis 18:25). 'Yes!' the universe cries out in response! We may not always understand what God is doing; but we can be sure that, even through the hard things, he is doing something that will turn out for our good and not for our harm (Romans 8:28). The more we get to know him and trust him in the

easy times, the easier it will be to keep hold of this in the hard times. Whatever comes our way, however, we can be sure of this:

The eternal God is your refuge, and underneath are the everlasting arms.

(Deuteronomy 33:27)

Pass it on!

The last thing that any of us wants to be is 'glib comforters'; purveyors of trite truths dispensed without thought or feeling. Job had 'friends' like that, and he described them as 'miserable comforters' whose 'long-winded speeches never end' (Job 16:2–3). But this does not mean that there is not a very real way in which we can share with others out of the experiences that we ourselves have been through. Once we have 'come out the other side', we often find that we can help those who are going through the same things. We can share our first-hand experience of God's comfort and help from a position of real understanding; and as long as we do so with sensitivity and a caring heart, it will be appreciated and do its work. This is true fellowship!

All praise to the God and Father of our Lord Jesus Christ. He is the source of every mercy and the God who comforts us. He comforts us in all our troubles so that we can comfort others. When others are troubled, we will be able to give them the same comfort God has given us. You can be sure that the more we suffer for Christ, the more God will shower us with his comfort through Christ. So when we are weighed down with troubles, it is for your benefit and salvation! For when God comforts us, it is so that we, in turn, can be an encouragement to you. Then you can patiently endure the same things we suffer. We are confident that as you share in suffering, you will also share God's comfort.

(2 Corinthians 1:3–7, NLT)

THE PROMISE OF COMFORT

Relevance for today

God comforts us in person

'I, even I, am he who comforts you.'

(Isaiah 51:12)

'And I will pray the Father, and he shall give you another Comforter, that he may abide with you for ever; even the Spirit of truth.'

(John 14:16–17, KJV)

See also Isaiah 49:15–16; Jeremiah 8:18; 2 Corinthians 1:3–4

God comforts us tenderly

Comfort, comfort my people, says your God. Speak tenderly to Jerusalem . . .

(Isaiah 40:1–2)

'As a mother comforts her child, so will I comfort you; and you will be comforted over Jerusalem.'

(Isaiah 66:13)

See also Hosea 2:14–23; Luke 1:78

God comforts us through others

But God, who comforts the downcast, comforted us by the coming of Titus, and not only by his coming but also by the comfort you had given him.

(2 Corinthians 7:6–7)

See also 1 Samuel 23:16; Colossians 4:11

God comforts us in every circumstance

No matter what our situation, God has a comfort appropriate to it.

I have learned to be content whatever the circumstances . . . I can do everything through him who gives me strength.

(Philippians 4:11, 13)

Bringing God's comfort to others

God wants us to pass our comfort on.

He [God] comes alongside us when we go through hard times, and before you know it, he brings us alongside someone else who is going through hard times so that we can be there for that person just as God was there for us.

(2 Corinthians 1:4, The Message)

God's comfort for the future

Any discomforts in this life will, for believers, be more than made up for in the life to come.

'But Abraham replied, "Son, remember that in your lifetime you received your good things, while Lazarus received bad things, but now he is comforted here and you are in agony." '

(Luke 16:25)

See also Matthew 25:31–46; Luke 6:21; Revelation 20:11–21:5; 22:1–5

How firm a foundation, ye saints of the
  Lord,
Is laid for your faith in His excellent Word!
What more can He say than to you He has
  said –
You, who unto Jesus for refuge have fled?

In every condition- in sickness, in health,
In poverty's vale, or abounding in wealth;
At home or abroad, on the land, on the sea,
As days may demand, shall thy strength ever
  be.

Fear not, I am with thee, O be not dismayed!
I, I am thy God, and will still give thee aid:
I'll strengthen thee, help thee, and cause thee
  to stand,
Upheld by My righteous, omnipotent hand.

When through the deep waters I cause thee to
  go,
The rivers of woe shall not thee overflow;
For I will be with thee, thy troubles to bless,
And sanctify to thee thy deepest distress.

When through fiery trials thy pathway shall
  lie,
My grace all-sufficient shall be thy supply;
The flame shall not hurt thee: I only design
Thy dross to consume, and thy gold to refine.

The soul that on Jesus has leaned for repose
I will not, I will not desert to its foes;
That soul, though all hell should endeavour
  to shake,
I'll never, no never, no never forsake!

'K' in Rippon's Selection, 1787

Conclusion

God is the sure foundation of our Christian lives. He never stops looking after us, even when circumstances are hard or when we don't feel he is near. Absolutely nothing can cut us off from him and his love.

I am convinced that neither death nor life, neither angels nor demons, neither the present nor the future, nor any powers, neither height nor depth, nor anything else in all creation, will be able to separate us from the love of God that is in Christ Jesus our Lord.

(Romans 8:38–39)

CHAPTER FIVE

The Promise of Guidance

Because God is our Father, we can be confident that his promises to guide us will be fulfilled.

Trust in the LORD with all your heart and lean not on your own understanding; in all your ways acknowledge him, and he will make your paths straight. (Proverbs 3:5–6)

So many people look for guidance each day. Sadly, most of them look in the wrong place. For millions it is to the horoscopes in the nation's newspapers that they turn. It is amazing how people so governed by 'science' in the rest of life can believe that the planets' positions affect what might happen to them that day. For Christians, such things are not only forbidden, they are completely unnecessary; for God himself – our Father! – has promised to guide us.

God has plans for us!

How amazing to think that the sovereign, eternal God of the universe (and beyond!) has, not just plans, but plans for you and me. This is what the Bible tells us again and again:

Many, O LORD my God, are the wonders you have done. The things you planned for us no-one can recount to you; were I to speak and tell of them, they would be too many to declare.

(Psalm 40:5)

'For I know the plans I have for you,' declares the LORD, 'plans to prosper you and not to harm you, plans to give you hope and a future.'

(Jeremiah 29:11)

See also 2 Kings 19:25; Job 23:13–14; 42:1–3; Psalm 33:10–11; Proverbs 19:21; Isaiah 14:24–27; 25:1; Ephesians 1:11; Hebrews 11:40

But God's plans for our life are not cold and deterministic; and here lies a major difference between 'the God and Father of our Lord Jesus Christ' (Ephesians 1:3) and the Muslim god 'Allah'. In Islam, whatever Allah wills, happens; man's lot is simply to accept it. But with Father God, while his will is always carried out, we can, amazingly, be 'God's fellow-workers' in it (1 Corinthians 3:9; 2 Corinthians 6:1). We can resist that will (e.g. Acts 7:51; 11:17) or respond to it (e.g. Acts 16:14); but if God doesn't get to us through the front door, he has a way of coming in through the back! This is a far more exciting and dynamic view of God and his plans for our lives. Such is how a Father deals with his children.

The God of guidance

There are many times in life when we have to make decisions. Some are ordinary and run-of-the-mill; but some are more significant, even life-changing. It is easy to feel paralysed at such times, overwhelmed by the possibilities. So it is good to know two things:

God wants to guide us

The constant testimony of Scripture is that God guides his people.

'In your unfailing love you will lead the people you have redeemed. In your strength you will guide them to your holy dwelling.'

(Exodus 15:13)

'My Presence will go with you, and I will give you rest.'

(Exodus 33:14)

For this God is our God for ever and ever; he will be our guide even to the end.

(Psalm 48:14)

The lot is cast into the lap, but its every decision is from the LORD.

(Proverbs 16:33)

Whether you turn to the right or to the left, your ears will hear a voice behind you, saying, 'This is the way; walk in it.'

(Isaiah 30:21)

See also Exodus 13:21; Nehemiah 9:19–20; Psalm 23:3; 25:9; 31:3; 73:23–24; 139:9–10; Isaiah 42:16; 58:11; John 16:13

God knows all the 'what ifs' of life

Sometimes we can be paralysed by thinking, 'But what if this . . .' or 'What if that . . .?'. That's when it's good to remember that God, who is outside of time, knows all the 'what ifs' of life. He already knows all the possibilities and conceivable options – and has a plan 'up his sleeve' for every one of them! We may not be able to see around the corner, but he can! That is why we can be sure he will guide and reassure us.

The guidance of God

Let's be honest: guidance is a problem. How do I know which job to take? Where to live? What to study? Who to marry? And besides these bigger questions, there are the more 'routine' issues of everyday life. For all of these, we need God's guidance.

The guidance of God becomes clearer as we get to know the God of guidance better. The more we learn about him, the more we learn about his ways, and the more we know what is right to do. Knowing what to do only assumes enormous proportions if we are uncertain about God himself. He is infinitely more than a celestial careers adviser, there to help when we ring up; he is our Father who is constantly 'there' for us and watches over us. We do not have to persuade him to guide; he is there guiding always.

I lift up my eyes to the hills – where does my help come from? My help comes from the LORD, the Maker of heaven and earth. He will not let your foot slip – he who watches over you will not slumber; indeed, he who watches over Israel will neither slumber nor sleep. The LORD watches over you – the LORD is your shade at your right hand; the sun will not harm you by day, nor the moon by night. The LORD will keep you from all harm – he will watch over your life; the LORD will watch over your coming and going both now and for evermore.

(Psalm 121)

Ways of guidance

Guidance is like a rope made up of strands; when all the strands are woven together our conviction will be clear and we will have a strong 'rope' that is not easily broken when tested. But if only one strand is present, it is probably wiser to wait for others to come into place. So, what are some of those 'strands' that God brings to us?

God's voice

While hearing the audible voice of God may not be the norm for most of us, it is impossible to read the Bible without seeing that this was a common means of God speaking to his people.

'The LORD our God has shown us his glory and his majesty, and we have heard his voice from the fire. Today we have seen that a man can live even if God speaks with him.'

(Deuteronomy 5:24)

See also Exodus 19:18–19; Numbers 7:89; Deuteronomy 4:11–12; Psalm 29:3–9; Isaiah 6:8; Ezekiel 10:5; Matthew 3:16–17; Acts 8:26, 29; 9:3–7

Even if we do not hear God's voice audibly, there may be times when we hear his voice 'within' – often characterized by great clarity or by a thought unusual to our language or way of thinking. Sometimes God's direction may come to us through visions or dreams (e.g. Genesis 15:1; Acts 10:9–15), or even angelic visitations (e.g. Acts 8:26; 10:3–6).

God's word

A more ordinary way of guidance comes as we regularly read God's word. The Bible contains many testimonies concerning the blessing, guidance and light that it brings.

Your word is a lamp to my feet and a light for my path.

(Psalm 119:105)

The unfolding of your words gives light.

(Psalm 119:130)

See also Joshua 1:7–8; 2 Timothy 3:14–17

But how do we use the Bible in guidance? Not just by opening it at random and picking out the first verse that looks suitable (or that supports what we want to do!). Rather, as we 'let the word of Christ dwell in [us] richly' (Colossians 3:16), we begin to get to know God's mind on the issues that face us. As we regularly receive God's input into our lives through his word (whether through reading it, hearing sermons or discussing it with others), so our minds begin to get renewed (Romans 12:2) and we increasingly come to have 'God's mind' on matters. How he thinks about things begins to affect how we think and instils in us fundamental attitudes, values, and understandings.

Our own testimony is that, as we have read God's word over the years, not only has it built God's principles into our life, but many times the right passage just 'happens' to have been in our reading programme on just the right day to bring God's more specific guidance to us. A verse has leapt from the page! Of course, such verses need to fit in with the broad tenor of the Bible's teaching (it's amazing how we can stretch a point if we want to!) and need to be checked out with other strands of guidance too.

God's prophets

While it may not be common in some of our churches, there is no doubt that prophecy played a key part in bringing God's guidance in Bible times. The guidance could vary from the fairly mundane, such as where your lost donkeys were (1 Samuel 9:3–20), to the crucial, such as the destiny of the nation (e.g. 2 Kings 19:5–7) or the future of the church (e.g. Acts 11:27–30; 13:1–3; 21:10 14). Clearly, God is a God who loves to speak to his people!

'Call to me and I will answer you and tell you great and unsearchable things you do not know.'

(Jeremiah 33:3)

Surely the Sovereign LORD does nothing without revealing his plan to his servants the prophets.

(Amos 3:7)

See also Numbers 11:29; Deuteronomy 18:17–22; Isaiah 38:1–8; Acts 2:17; 15:32; 21:9; 1 Corinthians 14:1–3

All prophecy must be carefully weighed (1 Corinthians 14:29). This means we should not base a decision on a prophetic word alone. Prophecy will generally confirm what we have already been hearing or thinking, or will itself be confirmed by other events.

God's hand

God is not remote and distant, but is involved in his world and his people's lives. That is why it is common in the Bible to see God's hand involved in bringing guidance through *circumstances*. By circumstances we include things that happen around us, opportunities that come our way, doors that open or close, existing commitments or obligations, and so on. For example:

- Joseph was released from jail and introduced to Pharaoh only when God stirred the cupbearer's memory to think back to him (Genesis 41:9–14).
- Ruth went out to glean in the fields and 'as it turned out, she found herself working in a field belonging to Boaz' (Ruth 2:3), their kinsman-redeemer.
- Paul, eager to spread the gospel, 'tried to enter Bithynia, but the Spirit of Jesus would not allow them to' (Acts 16:6–7).

God is bigger than any of our circumstances and can use all of them. Equally, he can override them when they get in his way.

When God took the Israelites 'the long way round' from Egypt to Canaan (Exodus 13:17–18), it would have been easy for them to complain (and many of them did!). But it avoided a head-on confrontation with the Philistines on the coastal plain. God blocked what would have been the obvious way for them to go (just a ten-day journey). If they had resisted it, they would have been in big trouble. We need to learn not to fight when God seems to resist our plans at times!

God's people

We saw earlier in this book that while God calls us personally, he does not call us privately. He calls us into his family. This 'togetherness' operates in the area of guidance too.

A wise man listens to advice.

(Proverbs 12:15)

Plans fail for lack of counsel, but with many advisers they succeed.

(Proverbs 15:22)

For waging war you need guidance, and for victory many advisers.

(Proverbs 24:6)

See also Exodus 18:13–26; Proverbs 13:10; 19:20; Acts 15:5–31

Counsel from friends

If we are too proud to take counsel from others, we will end up in trouble. Remember: 'The heart is deceitful above all things' (Jeremiah 17:9) and has an amazing way of convincing us why we should do certain things. If we simply tell our Christian friends what we intend to do, rather than being open to their perspectives, if we ask for their advice only when we know they'll agree with us, then we are not serious about receiving their input. Often, others are better judges of our own characters, gifts, and shortcomings than we are ourselves. Real friends will always be honest with us (Proverbs 27:6), and we should let them be. Remember: it's not unspiritual or immature to ask for others' help, advice and prayers. Even the apostle Paul asked others to pray for him (e.g. Romans 15:31–32; Ephesians 6:19).

Counsel from leaders

Church leaders are God's gift to us, given to help us grow into maturity and fruitful service

(Ephesians 4:11–13). The advice of the elders was always taken seriously in the Bible, and leaders were held in high esteem (e.g. Hebrews 13:17). If we are wise, therefore, we will involve our leaders in major decisions in our life as one of the strands of our hearing from God. This does not mean getting them to decide for us! But it does mean listening seriously to their observations. Rehoboam brought disaster upon the nation because of his failure to take seriously the advice from the elders (1 Kings 12:1–19).

God's whispers

The LORD said, 'Go out and stand on the mountain in the presence of the LORD, for the LORD is about to pass by.' Then a great and powerful wind tore the mountains apart and shattered the rocks before the LORD, but the LORD was not in the wind. After the wind there was an earthquake, but the LORD was not in the earthquake. After the earthquake came a fire, but the LORD was not in the fire. And after the fire came a gentle whisper.

(1 Kings 19:11–12)

After the exciting demonstrations of God's power in the contest with the prophets of Baal on Mount Carmel (1 Kings 18), Elijah was exhausted. What he needed now was not power, but the gentle whisper of God's voice, reassuring him that God was still with him and bringing guidance for the way ahead (1 Kings 19:13–18).

God still wants to bring his whispers and his 'nudges' to us today. This comes as we take time to stop and put God at the centre of everything again.

Be still before the LORD and wait patiently for him.

(Psalm 37:7)

'Be still, and know that I am God.'

(Psalm 46:10)

But I have stilled and quietened my soul; like a weaned child with its mother, like a weaned child is my soul within me.

(Psalm 131:2)

Paul wrote: 'Let the peace of Christ rule in your hearts' (Colossians 3:15). The phrase means: let Christ's peace act as an umpire, an arbiter, in the decisions that you have to make. In other words, we should have a sense of peace when we come to a right decision. If the peace isn't there, the decision probably isn't right.

Prohibited ways of guidance

While God is eager for us to receive guidance, there are some means of guidance that the Bible clearly forbids, because of their link to occult powers. These include:

- **Astrology** (e.g. Deuteronomy 4:19; 17:2–5; Jeremiah 8:1–2)
- **Consulting mediums or spiritists** (e.g. Leviticus 19:31; 20:6; Deuteronomy 18:10–12; 1 Samuel 28:7–20; 2 Kings 21:6; 1 Chronicles 10:13–14; Isaiah 8:19–20)
- **Divination of any sort** (e.g. Leviticus 19:26; Deuteronomy 18:10–12; 1 Samuel 15:23; 2 Kings 21:6)
- **Magic** (e.g. Ezekiel 13:18–20; Acts 8:9–13; 19:18–20; Revelation 21:8; 22:15)

Sometimes you have to jump!

At the end of the day we have to make decisions. Wherever possible, we need to wait until our 'strands' of guidance have come together and we are sure before God that a particular course of action is right. In these days of instant everything, that's not always easy for us, and we often want 'instant guidance' from God. But when we have sought God to the best of our ability and it is time to decide, even though all the strands may not be in place, then we need to make the decision and trust God that it is the right one. Sometimes you just have to jump! We can trust him to take us on to the next stage, not anxious about the decision we've made, not 'worrying it', and not going back on it. If it's wrong, our Father loves us enough to turn the circumstances round again.

In all your ways acknowledge him, and he will make your paths straight.

(Proverbs 3:6)

Relevance for today

God has a plan for each of us

In him we were also chosen, having been predestined according to the plan of him who works out everything in conformity with the purpose of his will, in order that we, who were the first to hope in Christ, might be for the praise of his glory.

(Ephesians 1:11–12)

God's plans are certain and sure

But the plans of the LORD stand firm for ever, the purposes of his heart through all generations.

(Psalm 33:11)

God's plans always prevail

There is no wisdom, no insight, no plan that can succeed against the LORD.

(Proverbs 21:30)

Devise your strategy, but it will be thwarted; propose your plan, but it will not stand, for God is with us.

(Isaiah 8:10)

God wants to guide us

I will instruct you and teach you in the way you should go; I will counsel you and watch over you. Do not be like the horse or the mule, which have no understanding but must be controlled by bit and bridle or they will not come to you.

(Psalm 32:8–9)

God's promises come true

What God has promised will surely happen – so wait for it!

For the revelation awaits an appointed time; it speaks of the end and will not prove false. Though it linger, wait for it; it will certainly come and will not delay.

(Habakkuk 2:3)

Look for confirmation

God's guidance is surest when the 'strands' are strongest. We should seek to bring together as many 'strands' of guidance as we can; but in the end, we have to jump!

Be prepared to repent

Wrong guidance can be remedied by repentance. If you have sought guidance through horoscopes, tarot cards, mediums, etc, you need to put that right by clearly repenting of it. As with anything else, God will be quick to forgive us and release us from any bondage.

Be still, my soul: the Lord is on thy side;
Bear patiently the cross of grief or pain;
Leave to thy God to order and provide;
In every change He faithful will remain.
Be still, my soul: thy best, thy heavenly
  Friend
Through thorny ways leads to a joyful end.

Be still, my soul; thy God doth undertake
To guide the future as He has the past.
Thy hope, thy confidence, let nothing shake;
All now mysterious shall be bright at last.
Be still, my soul: the waves and winds still
  know
His voice who ruled them while He dwelt
  below.

Be still, my soul: the hour is hastening on
When we shall be for ever with the Lord,
When disappointment, grief and fear are
  gone,
Sorrow forgot, love's purest joys restored.
Be still, my soul: when change and tears are
  past,
All safe and blessed we shall meet at last.

Katharina von Schlegel, born 1697
tr. by Jane Laurie Borthwick, 1813–97

Conclusion

God is not reluctant to show us what he wants
for our lives. He has already given us so much in
Christ, so we should not doubt that he will
continue to guide us.

I will instruct you and teach you in the way
you should go; I will counsel you and watch
over you.

(Psalm 32:8)

CHAPTER SIX

Promises for the Market Place

God's promises are not for enjoyment in holy huddles, but are to be taken out into 'the market place' of life to do our world good.

So he [Paul] reasoned in the synagogue with the Jews and the God-fearing Greeks, as well as in the market-place day by day with those who happened to be there. (Acts 17:17)

Have you ever thought that throughout Jesus' ministry, his focus was not the church, but the kingdom (e.g. Mark 1:15)? It was 'this gospel of the kingdom' (Matthew 24:14) that he sent his followers out to preach. Sadly, we have often focused on 'the church' rather than 'the kingdom', the 'meeting place' rather than the 'market place'. Yet 'the market place' – for us, the world of work, or school, or neighbours – is where we spend most of our lives. Might it not be, therefore, that God has a plan for us there; that his promises are as much for 'out there' as for 'in here'? The Bible's answer would seem to be 'Yes!'

293

What is work?

Ask most people what we mean by 'work' and they will think of their job – in the office, on the shopfloor, at the hospital, etc. This is one aspect of 'work'; but work also includes keeping the home, looking after the children, doing the garden, studying and voluntary work. In other words we are all workers in some way or other, just how God designed us to be.

Work is the gift of God

'I like work; it fascinates me. I could sit and look at it for hours.' So ran the words of an office poster. Perhaps a sentiment shared by many!

But work is not a nuisance to be avoided; it is the gift of God.

From the beginning, God designed us to work:

• 'Be fruitful and increase in number' (Genesis 1:28) – the work involved in family life.
• 'Fill the earth and subdue it' (Genesis 1:28) – the work involved in ruling nature (vv 28–30).
• 'The LORD God took the man and put him in the Garden of Eden to work it and take care of it' (Genesis 2:15) – the work involved in taking responsibility.

This should hardly surprise us, for God himself is a God who works (e.g. Genesis 2:3;

John 5:17; Philippians 2:13). Since we are made in his image (Genesis 1:26–27), we too are designed to be workers.

After the fall, however, things changed. Sin got into the very fabric of life and things began to deteriorate. But it was not *work* that was cursed as a result of sin, but rather the *ground*.

To Adam he [God] said, 'Because you listened to your wife and ate from the tree about which I commanded you, "You must not eat of it," Cursed is the ground because of you; through painful toil you will eat of it all the days of your life.'

(Genesis 3:17)

In other words, work would now be hard at times; but work itself is not under the curse of God. That is why we can ask him to bless it, and why he promises to do so.

Work has the blessing of God

Then the LORD your God will make you most prosperous in all the work of your hands and in the fruit of your womb, the young of your livestock and the crops of your land. The LORD will again delight in you and make you prosperous, just as he delighted in your fathers, if you obey the LORD your God and keep his commands and decrees that are written in this Book of the Law and turn to the LORD your God with all your heart and with all your soul.

(Deuteronomy 30:9–10)

Moreover, when God gives any man wealth and possessions, and enables him to enjoy them, to accept his lot and be happy in his work – this is a gift of God.

(Ecclesiastes 5:19)

See also e.g. Deuteronomy 5:33; 28:11; 2 Chronicles 14:7; Job 1:1–3; Psalm 128:1–6; Proverbs 31:10–31; Jeremiah 29:4–7; Acts 20:35; Romans 16:12

Work is the calling of God

There are, of course, times when some of us cannot work; a period of enforced unemployment, prolonged sickness, unusual family circumstances, etc. But the Bible's general call to us is to work hard, not being wrongly dependent on others, for hard work has God's blessing on it and is a good witness.

Make it your ambition to lead a quiet life, to mind your own business and to work with your hands, just as we told you, so that your daily life may win the respect of outsiders and so that you will not be dependent on anybody.

(1 Thessalonians 4:11–12)

In the name of the Lord Jesus Christ, we command you, brothers, to keep away from every brother who is idle and does not live according to the teaching you received from us. For you yourselves know how you ought to follow our example. We were not idle when we were with you, nor did we eat anyone's food without paying for it. On the contrary, we worked night and day, labouring and toiling so that we would not be a burden to any of you. We did this, not because we do not have the right to such help, but in order to make ourselves a model for you to follow. For even when we were with you, we gave you this rule: 'If a man will not work, he shall not eat.' We hear that some among you are idle. They are not busy; they are busybodies. Such people we command and urge in the Lord Jesus Christ to settle down and earn the bread they eat.

(2 Thessalonians 3:6–12)

See also Ephesians 4:28

At work in the workplace

How, then, should we conduct ourselves in the workplace so as to make an impact for God?

Work as if working for God

Whatever you do, work at it with all your heart, as working for the Lord, not for men, since you know that you will receive an inheritance from the Lord as a reward. It is the Lord Christ you are serving.

(Colossians 3:23–24)

This means giving our work our very best, not seeing it as a nuisance compared to 'the real work' at church.

Work hard!

God expects us to work hard as a matter of integrity. Jesus set us an example, spending far more years in the family carpentry business than he did in 'full-time ministry'.

All hard work brings a profit, but mere talk leads only to poverty.

(Proverbs 14:23)

In everything I [Paul] did, I showed you that by this kind of hard work we must help the weak, remembering the words the Lord Jesus himself said: 'It is more blessed to give than to receive.'

(Acts 20:35)

See also Luke 5:5; Romans 16:6, 12; 1 Corinthians 4:12; 2 Corinthians 6:5

Work with integrity

Integrity and honesty make a tremendous impact – whether it be by refusing to join in 'the little fiddles' (stretching our expense claims, 'borrowing' things from the office, taking longer breaks than we should) or telling the shop assistant when we've been undercharged. Even if no one else notices, God does; and God promises to bless honesty and integrity.

I know, my God, that you test the heart and are pleased with integrity.

(1 Chronicles 29:17)

The man of integrity walks securely, but he who takes crooked paths will be found out.

(Proverbs 10:9)

See also Exodus 20:15; Leviticus 19:11, 35–36; Deuteronomy 25:13–16; 2 Kings 12:15; Psalm 25:21; 97:11; Proverbs 11:6, 11; 30:7–9; Matthew 24:45–51; Romans 13:9–10

Work with sincerity

In the Bible, the key issue is not so much what work you do, as how you do it. Hence, Paul didn't challenge slavery head on (though he had views on it, see Philemon 8–21), but rather challenged the attitudes of both slaves and masters.

Slaves, obey your earthly masters with respect and fear, and with sincerity of heart, just as you would obey Christ. Obey them not only to win their favour when their eye is on you, but like slaves of Christ, doing the will of God from your heart. Serve wholeheartedly, as if you were serving the Lord, not men, because you know that the Lord will reward everyone for whatever good he does, whether he is slave or free. And masters, treat your slaves in the same way. Do not threaten them, since you know that he who is both their Master and yours is in heaven, and there is no favouritism with him.

(Ephesians 6:5–9)

See also Colossians 3:22–4:1; 1 Timothy 6:1–2

How industry, business and commerce would change if people took to heart the call to do their best always, not just when someone was watching them!

Work with a servant attitude

Servanthood lies at the heart of the kingdom, for it was established by him who came among us as 'one who serves' (Luke 22:27). He did not insist on his position, but selflessly gave himself for others and now calls us to do the same:

Your attitude should be the same as that of Christ Jesus: Who, being in very nature God, did not consider equality with God something to be grasped, but made himself nothing, taking the very nature of a servant, being made in human likeness. And being found in appearance as a man, he humbled himself and became obedient to death – even death on a cross!

(Philippians 2:5–8)

When an argument broke out among the disciples about 'position', Jesus said this:

'You know that the rulers of the Gentiles lord it over them, and their high officials exercise authority over them. Not so with you. Instead, whoever wants to become great among you must be your servant, and whoever wants to be first must be your slave – just as the Son of Man did not come to be served, but to serve, and to give his life as a ransom for many.'

(Matthew 20:25–28)

We can adopt this sort of servant attitude whether we are the Chief Executive who sits in the office or the cleaner who comes in later to tidy it up. None of us ever gets beyond being a servant, and servanthood in the workplace and society can make a powerful impact.

See also Mark 9:35; Luke 17:7–10; John 12:24–26; 1 Corinthians 3:5; 2 Corinthians 6:3–10; Ephesians 6:7; Colossians 3:23–24

Exercise faith

Successful businesses are those whose leaders take bold steps – 'faith', to put it another way. God wants us, too, to exercise faith in the world and in the workplace. Faith is not just for Sundays, but for Mondays to Fridays too! Remember:

Without faith it is impossible to please God . . . he rewards those who earnestly seek him.

(Hebrews 11:6)

God wants us to pray about our work, its pressures, difficulties, opportunities and challenges, and to exercise faith in it, asking him for wisdom in this matter (James 1:5) as much as in anything else.

At work in society

Church is not meant to be the sum total of my life and work; it is the base from which I do my work. 'My destiny is not the church; the church is there to ensure that I fulfil my destiny wherever God has called me' (Dave Oliver).

God wants his people in significant places of influence in society where they can use their position for the good of God's people and the nation. Consider the following:

- Joseph – who used his promotion to high office in Egypt (Genesis 41:39–43) to bless the nation of Egypt (Genesis 41:46–57) and to save God's people (Genesis 45:25–46:27).
- Daniel – who used his position in the Babylonian civil service to bring God's wisdom and revelation to the king (e.g. Daniel 2:25–28), opening up more opportunities as he did so (Daniel 2:46–49). (But note that there were some things that he made his stand on! See Daniel 1:8–16.)
- Esther – whose position in the royal harem would not have been of her choosing, but who trusted God enough to let him use it to bring her to the throne and thereby to save her people (Esther 4:12–16; 8:1–17).

For all those who hold positions of influence, the words of Mordecai to Esther are still a challenge and encouragement:

'Who knows but that you have come to royal position for such a time as this?'

(Esther 4:14)

Sometimes this may involve releasing people from 'church' commitments for the wider impact they can make on society. Let's face it, church leaders find this hard! Yet it can bring great fruitfulness for the kingdom.

Martin was part of his church leadership team and also a governor of a local school. He found it difficult to do both satisfactorily but

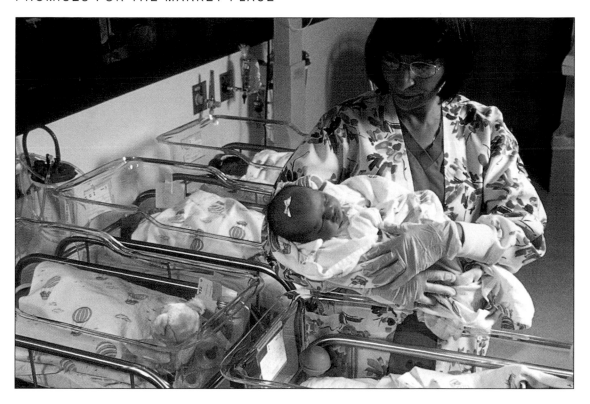

nevertheless continued in both roles. After his initial four years as governor elapsed, his links with the school became fewer, although he remained in touch and continued to support and pray for the school community. A couple of years later, the school approached him, after a school inspection, asking him to become a governor again – the very day after he had passed the school and had been praying for them! After prayer and discussion, he came off the church leadership team and is now active as a school governor, seeking to bring a Christian influence to bear in the school.

Mike's church is increasingly seeking to release their members to influence the workplace. One, a pharmacist, has helped shape the policy of the World Health Organization; another, an economist, has shaped the policies of companies and government organizations (one proposal even went to the Prime Minister's office!); another advises multinationals and governments on their energy policies. All have a place in the church; but their ministry is as much 'out there' as 'in here', and they need supporting in it.

Not all of us hold such obviously influential jobs; but no matter what our work involves, we can be salt and light there.

'You are the salt of the earth. But if the salt loses its saltiness, how can it be made salty again? It is no longer good for anything, except to be thrown out and trampled by men. You are the light of the world. A city on a hill cannot be hidden. Neither do people light a lamp and put it under a bowl. Instead they put it on its stand, and it gives light to everyone in the house. In the same way, let your light shine before men, that they may see your good deeds and praise your Father in heaven.'

(Matthew 5:13–16)

Watch out – the devil's about!

Having pleaded for greater involvement in society and the world of work, we now need to issue a caution. The devil would love us to get so engrossed in all of this that church becomes secondary, even optional, to our lives. We may not always be able to be present at every meeting; but we need to be careful, for we desperately need church as a community of fellowship, strength and accountability for all that we do elsewhere.

And let us consider how we may spur one another on towards love and good deeds. Let us not give up meeting together, as some are in the habit of doing, but let us encourage one another – and all the more as you see the Day approaching.

(Hebrews 10:24–25)

Watch out for signs that we are drifting spiritually, including things like:

- Our own walk with God becoming dry
- Growing dislike of spending time with Christians
- Making excuses to avoid meetings
- Being dismissive of what the church is doing
- Becoming totally 'success' orientated
- Becoming increasingly materialistic.

One of the best ways to ensure that we do not drift is to make ourselves closely accountable to another believer and to let them ask us the awkward questions!

'Full-time' Christian work

The allure of 'full-time' Christian work can become a real 'golden calf' to some. But the thing about 'golden calves' – substitute gods (see Exodus 32:1–4) – is that while they can look so spiritual (e.g. 1 Kings 12:28) they actually take us away from what God intended (e.g. 1 Kings 12:30). To be called to serve God as a minister or missionary is indeed a high calling; but the calling to serve him in the work-place can be just as significant. Consider the following key characters in the Bible. Few were 'full-time'.

- Abraham – successful nomadic farmer (Genesis 13:5–6)
- Joseph – household management (Genesis 39:1–6; 41:41–43)
- Nehemiah – royal household official (Nehemiah 1:11)
- Daniel – civil servant (Daniel 1:3–6)
- Amos – shepherd and grower of sycamore figs (Amos 7:14)
- Lydia – up-market clothing dealer (Acts 16:14)
- Priscilla and Aquila – tent manufacturers (Acts 18:2–3)
- Paul – returned to tent-making when he needed to (Acts 18:1–3; 20:34; 1 Corinthians 4:12)

How our effectiveness would change if we began to see that the workplace and the market place were not diversions from 'real ministry' but were real ministry! Being called to serve God as a pastor or evangelist is indeed a privilege; but we are all called to 'full-time work'; for some of us, that is based in the church; for most, it is based in the world.

William Tyndale summed it up like this: 'There is no work better than another to please God; to pour water, to wash dishes, to be a cobbler, or an apostle, all is one; to wash dishes or to preach is all one as touching the deed, to please God.'

Relevance for today

Enjoying your work

Yes, it's OK to enjoy our work!

So I saw that there is nothing better for a man than to enjoy his work, because that is his lot.

(Ecclesiastes 3:22)

See also Ecclesiastes 2:24; 5:19; 8:15

Seeing God as boss

Your 'boss' is not your boss, God is.

Serve wholeheartedly, as if you were serving the Lord, not men.

(Ephesians 6:7)

Not letting work 'get out of hand'

We shouldn't let work take over our lives or we will end up wearied.

What does a man get for all the toil and anxious striving with which he labours under the sun? All his days his work is pain and grief; even at night his mind does not rest. This too is meaningless.

(Ecclesiastes 2:22–23)

We need to make sure that constant working late or at weekends does not adversely affect other areas of our lives.

Learning when to stop

It's not unspiritual to take time off! We all need to take time to rest and be refreshed.

'Come with me by yourselves to a quiet place and get some rest.'

(Mark 6:31)

See also Exodus 20:8-11; Matthew 11:28-30; Luke 10:38-42; John 4:6

Guarding relationships at work

We must take care not to lower our standards in relationships with the opposite sex at work.

'How then could I do such a wicked thing and sin against God?'

(Genesis 39:9)

Understanding God's bigger purpose

Equipping is for the workplace and not just for the church.

Leaders are called to equip God's people 'for the work of ministry' (Ephesians 4:12, NKJV), which is far wider than what they do in the church.

Sprinkling the salt

Salt can't do its work in the salt-shaker.

'You are the salt of the earth.' **(Matthew 5:13)**

We need to see more and more of the salt unlocked and sprinkled into our rotting world. Christians must be active in the workplace for this to happen.

Conclusion

God loves the world, not just the church; we should love it too, and take every opportunity to influence it for good in his name.

God so loved the world . . .

(John 3:16)

Forth in Thy name, O Lord, I go,
My daily labour to pursue,
Thee, only Thee, resolved to know
In all I think, or speak, or do.

The task Thy wisdom has assigned
O let me cheerfully fulfil;
In all my works Thy presence find,
And prove Thy good and perfect will.

Thee may I set at my right hand,
Whose eyes my inmost substance see;
And labour on at Thy command,
And offer all my works to Thee.

Give me to bear Thine easy yoke,
And every moment watch and pray,
And still to things eternal look,
And hasten to Thy glorious day.

For Thee delightfully employ
Whate'er Thy bounteous grace hath given,
And run my course with even joy,
And closely walk with Thee to heaven.

Charles Wesley, 1707–88

CHAPTER SEVEN

Through all the Changing Scenes of Life

Though our situations in life often change, we can know that the unchanging God is always with us, providing for all our needs.

Godliness with contentment is great gain. For we brought nothing into the world, and we can take nothing out of it. But if we have food and clothing, we will be content with that.
(1 Timothy 6:6–8)

Ever tried clearing out a cupboard? Or a shed? Or a garage? It's amazing what you find there, isn't it? Priceless treasures too good to throw away; documents about important past business; bits and pieces that 'may come in handy one day' – or, to put it another way, a whole load of rubbish! On one occasion Martin cleared just one cupboard and threw out four dustbins-full of rubbish; Mike clears his garage each spring and fills the whole car with rubbish for the refuse dump. What an amazing tendency we all have to clutter our lives – which might just be one of the reasons why we find it so hard to be content.

Our needs

In the animated film *Jungle Book*, Baloo the bear sings a delightful song entitled 'The Bare Necessities' – or should that be 'The Bear Necessities'? He's a lazy sort of character who, as long as there is a paw-paw or two to eat, is remarkably content and can't see why people get in such a fuss about things. A lot of Christians could do with being a bit more like him!

The first Christians were a remarkably content people, summed up in Paul's statement to Timothy:

Godliness with contentment is great gain. For we brought nothing into the world, and we can take nothing out of it. But if we have food and clothing, we will be content with that.

(1 Timothy 6:6–8)

So, let's take a look at some of the 'bare necessities' of life and what God says about these basic human needs.

Food

God's gift

The Bible sees food as God's gift to us. We may earn the money to buy it; but who upholds creation from where our food comes? Who orders the seasons and sends the rain? Our faithful Father God.

Then God said, 'I give you every seed-bearing plant on the face of the whole earth and every tree that has fruit with seed in it. They will be yours for food.'

(Genesis 1:29)

Everything that lives and moves will be food for you. Just as I gave you the green plants, I now give you everything.

(Genesis 9:3)

He makes grass grow for the cattle, and plants for man to cultivate – bringing forth food from the earth: wine that gladdens the heart of man, oil to make his face shine, and bread that sustains his heart.

(Psalm 104:14–15)

See also Psalm 104:27; 111:5; 145:15–16; Matthew 6:11

In the light of this, Jesus reassures us that we need not worry about God providing such basics for us.

'Therefore I tell you, do not worry about your life, what you will eat or drink; or about your

body, what you will wear. Is not life more important than food, and the body more important than clothes? Look at the birds of the air; they do not sow or reap or store away in barns, and yet your heavenly Father feeds them. Are you not much more valuable than they? Who of you by worrying can add a single hour to his life?'

(Matthew 6:25–27)

Our gratitude

The natural response to such provision should, surely, be gratitude. When Mike first visited Uganda, he was just about to drink a cup of tea when his host interjected, 'Shall we give thanks?' Slightly embarrassed, Mike put down his cup and saucer until a heartfelt prayer of gratitude for the provision of God was completed. You see, these people had been through civil war; they genuinely knew what it meant to be grateful for a cup of tea, and they didn't want to forget.

What about us? Are we grateful for our food? Do we despise saying 'grace'? Or has saying 'grace' become a mere ritual? Either way, the Bible encourages us to be thankful for God's provision of food.

Jesus then took the loaves, gave thanks, and distributed to those who were seated as much as they wanted.

(John 6:11)

After he said this, he [Paul] took some bread and gave thanks to God in front of them all. Then he broke it and began to eat.

(Acts 27:35)

See also Romans 14:6; 1 Corinthians 10:30–31; 1 Timothy 4:3–4

Gratitude will also demonstrate itself in our sharing what we have with others, whether through hospitality (e.g. Romans 16:23; Titus 1:8; 1 Peter 4:9; 3 John 8) or relief of those in need (e.g. Acts 11:28–30; Galatians 2:10).

Share with God's people who are in need. Practise hospitality.

(Romans 12:13)

Clothes

Our clothes too ultimately come from God, so once again our anxieties can be allayed.

'And why do you worry about clothes? See how the lilies of the field grow. They do not labour or spin. Yet I tell you that not even Solomon in all his splendour was dressed like one of these. If that is how God clothes the grass of the field, which is here today and tomorrow is thrown into the fire, will he not much more clothe you, O you of little faith? So do not worry, saying, "What shall we eat?" or "What shall we drink?" or "What shall we wear?" For the pagans run after all these things, and your heavenly Father knows that you need them. But seek first his kingdom and his righteousness, and all these things will be given to you as well.'

(Matthew 6:28–33)

A trip to the Third World has a way of putting clothes and 'fashion' into perspective. In the West we spend millions of pounds on 'designer label' clothes – most of them produced in Third World or developing nations for a mere pittance by people who have perhaps just one set of clothes to their name. Perhaps we need to ask ourselves from time to time just how much we spend on such things, especially if it is for the sake of a mere label. It is so easy to make 'idols' out of clothes when, at the end of the day, our health and holiness are far more important. As Jesus said, 'Life is more than food, and the body more than clothes' (Luke 12:23).
See also 1 Timothy 2:9–10; 1 Peter 3:3–4; James 2:2–4; 5:1–5

An appropriate Christian act is to provide clothes for those who have none or few (Matthew 25:34–46; James 2:15–17).

Sleep

Sleep is a precious gift, as any of us know who have found it eluding us! We need sleep. It is essential for our physical wellbeing; and when we cannot sleep, we soon get weary and irritable with others. When we are finding sleep hard we need to claim God's promises:

I will lie down and sleep in peace, for you alone, O LORD, make me dwell in safety.

(Psalm 4:8)

He gives to his beloved sleep.

(Psalm 127:2, RSV)

See also Job 11:19; Psalm 3:5; Proverbs 3:24

Work

As we have seen in the previous chapter, work is a gift of God (Genesis 2:15), and in that sense is a basic 'human right'. We should not be content with any political values that accept it is inevitable for some people not to work, for this robs them of their dignity. It is God's intention that we should enjoy our work (Ecclesiastes 5:18–19) and it is right to expect to receive reasonable pay for the work we do.

The worker deserves his wages.

(Luke 10:7)

See also Matthew 20:9–15; Luke 3:14;
1 Timothy 5:18

Money and possessions

Let's face it, many of us spend lots of time thinking about money: how we can stretch it, or how we can get more of it. But we need to be careful; for this is a sign that money, not God, is becoming our god, and Jesus said we can't serve both.

'No-one can serve two masters. Either he will hate the one and love the other, or he will be devoted to the one and despise the other. You cannot serve both God and Money.'

(Matthew 6:24)

God has promised to give us what we need (Psalm 34:9–10; 37:25; Philippians 4:19) and the Bible warns us about getting so caught up with money and possessions that they become a consuming passion which dangerously spreads.

'Watch out! Be on your guard against all kinds of greed; a man's life does not consist in the abundance of his possessions.'

(Luke 12:15)

For the love of money is a root of all kinds of evil.

(1 Timothy 6:10)

See also Job 31:24–28; Psalm 39:6; 62:10;
Luke 12:16–21, 32–34

The Bible gives us practical guidelines on handling money and possessions, which help ensure they keep their proper perspective. These include –

Get your money honestly

As we saw in the previous chapter, we are to get our money honestly (e.g. 1 Thessalonians 4:11–12). This means there can be no place among us for such things as:

- theft (e.g. Exodus 20:15; Ephesians 4:28)
- fraud (e.g. Leviticus 19:13; Mark 10:19)
- bribes (e.g. Exodus 23:8; Proverbs 15:27)
- sharp business practices (e.g. Deuteronomy 15:9–15; Amos 8:4–7)
- money-lending at interest (e.g. Exodus 22:25; Deuteronomy 15:7–11)

Use your money wisely

In days when we are constantly urged to have 'credit' (for which a more appropriate word is 'debt'!), we need to hear the Bible's teaching here. Wise use of our money means giving priority to things like:

- Providing for our families (e.g. 1 Timothy 5:8)
- Paying our dues, such as taxes (e.g. Matthew 22:21; Romans 13:6–7)
- Providing for our future as best we can (e.g. Proverbs 6:6-8; Luke 16:9)

Handle your money faithfully

The Bible teaches us to see our money and possessions not as our own, but as held in stewardship from God (e.g. Deuteronomy 8:10–18; Matthew 25:14–30; Luke 12:42–46; 16:10–12). It is all his, not ours (which means

that if there is any worrying to be done, let God do it!). Our task is simply to be the best stewards that we can be on his behalf. This means ensuring that our finances are planned, checked, controlled, and that we do not cling onto our possessions at any cost.

Share your money generously

A spirit of generosity was built into the Old Testament law, through regulations governing sabbatical years (Exodus 23:10–11), jubilee years (Leviticus 25:8–17), additional 'third year' tithes (Deuteronomy 14:27–29), gleaning (Leviticus 19:9–10), and so on. The same spirit of generosity pervades the New Testament (e.g. 2 Corinthians 8 & 9), where we are told that our giving should be both generous and happy. (The word 'cheerful' in 2 Corinthians 9:7 – 'God loves a cheerful giver' – is *hilarios,* from which we get our word 'hilarious'!)

Stretch your money amazingly

Want to know the secret of making your money go further? The Bible says: give a tenth of it away! Tithing was a basic value among God's people (e.g. Genesis 14:20; 28:22; Leviticus 27:30–32; 2 Chronicles 31:3–10; Malachi 3:10; Luke 11:42; Hebrews 7:1–2). (See also Part 3, Chapter 3.) Sounds scary? Then remember this: with God, nine-tenths goes further than ten-tenths!

These principles all help produce the contentment that the Bible speaks of (Philippians 4:12–13; 1 Timothy 6:6–8) and are an expression of Jesus' fundamental teaching in this whole area of money and possessions:

'Seek first his kingdom and his righteousness, and all these things will be given to you as well.'

(Matthew 6:33)

Birth and growing up

None of us is 'an accident'. God planned us even before we were conceived (Psalm 139:16) and watched over us in the womb (Psalm 139:15). That is why the Bible says that children are a gift from God (Psalm 127:3). God watches over our growing years (e.g. Exodus 2:1–10; 1 Samuel 2:26; Psalm 121:5–8), just as he did with Jesus (Luke 2:40, 52).

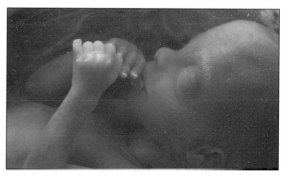

God's word to children

Children, obey your parents in the Lord, for this is right. 'Honour your father and mother' – which is the first commandment with a promise – 'that it may go well with you and that you may enjoy long life on the earth.'

(Ephesians 6:1–3)

See also Exodus 20:12; Proverbs 6:20–23; Colossians 3:20

God's word to parents

Train a child in the way he should go, and when he is old he will not turn from it.

(Proverbs 22:6)

Fathers, do not exasperate your children; instead, bring them up in the training and instruction of the Lord.

(Ephesians 6:4)

See also Deuteronomy 6:6–7; Matthew 19:13–15; Colossians 3:21

Our days

I praise you because I am fearfully and wonderfully made; your works are wonderful, I know that full well. My frame was not hidden from you when I was made in the secret place. When I was woven together in the depths of the earth, your eyes saw my unformed body. All the days ordained for me were written in your book before one of them came to be.

(Psalm 139:14–16)

It is not only our needs, but also our days that God, the God who neither slumbers nor sleeps (Psalm 121:4), watches over, from the moment we are conceived to the moment we come into his presence.

Loving discipline is also a part of this training (Proverbs 3:11–12; 6:23; 13:24; 19:18; 22:15; 23:13; 29:17; Hebrews 12:7–11), and we neglect it to our cost.

Marriage and family life

Marriage

Marriage is given by God (Genesis 2:18–25) and men and women joined in marriage are united by God (Matthew 19:4–6). Marriage is a covenant relationship between one man and one woman for life.

'At the beginning of creation God "made them male and female". "For this reason a man will leave his father and mother and be united to his wife, and the two will become one flesh." So they are no longer two, but one. Therefore what God has joined together, let man not separate.'

(Mark 10:6–9)

The Bible is clear that a Christian may only marry another Christian (1 Corinthians 7:39; 2 Corinthians 6:14–18), though someone who becomes a Christian should not leave their unbelieving partner (1 Corinthians 7:12–16), such is God's high view of marriage. 'Heirs together of the grace of life' (1 Peter 3:7, NKJV) is how Peter describes a Christian husband and wife. The husband's responsibility is to love his wife as Christ loved the church (Ephesians 5:25–33; Colossians 3:19), and the wife's is to submit to her husband as the church submits to Christ (Ephesians 5:22–24, 33; Colossians 3:18).

Singleness

The Bible nowhere suggests that it is 'more holy' to stay single, though it teaches that for some, singleness is God's calling (e.g. Jeremiah 16:1–2; Matthew 19:10–12; 1 Corinthians 7:7), and that singleness can allow us greater freedom to serve him (e.g. 1 Corinthians 7:32–25). Jesus blessed singleness by remaining single himself. Singleness is to be characterized by the rejection of 'sexual immorality' ('fornication', KJV) (e.g. 1 Corinthians 6:13, 18; Ephesians 5:3; Galatians 5:19; 1 Thessalonians 4:3–8), therefore we need to be sure that this is God's call on our lives so that we can draw upon his grace. For both married and single, sexual purity is God's requirement of our lives (e.g. Acts 15:28–29; 1 Corinthians 6:18–20; 1 Timothy 5:2).

Home

The Christian home is to be a place of genuine love and security, but not a fortress that keeps others out. Hospitality should be one of its hallmarks (e.g. Romans 12:13; 16:23; 1 Peter 4:9; 3 John 8).

The increasing years

The day Mike hit fifty he woke up and shouted, 'Yes!' He meant there was lots more life in him yet! While we often think of the young men and women that God used in the Bible (David, Esther, Timothy), there are significant middle-aged and older people in the list too. For example:

• Caleb – sent to explore Canaan at the age of 40 (Joshua 14:7), and still serving the Lord with vigour at 85! (Joshua 14:10–12)

• Moses – 40 years old when he fled from Egypt to Midian (Acts 7:23) and 80 when he returned to Egypt to lead God's people to freedom (Acts 7:30–36) – that's 120 years of walking with God; 40 of them learning how great he was, 40 learning how insignificant he was, and 40 learning how a great God uses insignificant people.

• Anna – still serving God in her 80s (Luke 2:36–38)

The Bible calls us to honour and respect those who are older in years (e.g. Leviticus 19:32; Job 32:6; 1 Timothy 5:5; 1 Peter 5:5) – something largely lacking in western society today where old age is seen as something bad and older people are 'has-beens', to be ignored or forgotten. But the Bible says that old age can still be a time of great fruitfulness (Psalm 92:12–15).

Whether our days are many or few, we have the assurance that 'our strength will equal our days' (Deuteronomy 33:25). God himself will strengthen us and provide for us, through all the changing scenes of life, and that will be sufficient for the needs and trials each day may bring. So let's not worry about tomorrow: tomorrow can take care of itself (Matthew 6:34); let's live one day at a time in the light of our faithful God.

Relevance for today

Be content

I know how to live on almost nothing or with everything. I have learned the secret of living in every situation, whether it is with a full stomach or empty, with plenty or·little. For I can do everything with the help of Christ who gives me the strength I need.

(Philippians 4:12–13, NLT)

Be trusting

So do not worry, saying, 'What shall we eat?' or 'What shall we drink?' or 'What shall we wear?' For the pagans run after all these things, and your heavenly Father knows that you need them. But seek first his kingdom and his righteousness, and all these things will be given to you as well.

(Matthew 6:31–33)

Be grateful

So whether you eat or drink or whatever you do, do it all for the glory of God.

(1 Corinthians 10:31)

Be generous

Remember this: Whoever sows sparingly will also reap sparingly, and whoever sows generously will also reap generously. Each man should give what he has decided in his heart to give, not reluctantly or under compulsion, for God loves a cheerful giver. And God is able to make all grace abound to you, so that in all things at all times, having all that you need, you will abound in every good work.

(2 Corinthians 9:6–8)

Be happy

Moreover, when God gives any man wealth and possessions, and enables him to enjoy them, to accept his lot and be happy in his work – this is a gift of God.

(Ecclesiastes 5:19)

O make but trial of His love,
Experience will decide
How blessed are they, and only they,
Who in His truth confide.

Through all the changing scenes of life,
In trouble and in joy,
The praises of my God shall still
My heart and tongue employ.

Fear Him, ye saints, and you will then
Have nothing else to fear;
Make you His service your delight,
Your wants shall be His care.

Of His deliverance I will boast,
Till all that are distressed
From my example comfort take,
And charm their griefs to rest.

Naham Tate, 1652–1715
and Nicholas Brady, 1659–1726

O magnify the Lord with me,
With me exalt His Name;
When in distress to Him I called,
He to my rescue came.

Conclusion

As we put God and his ways first, so Jesus promises that everything necessary for our well-being will be given to us throughout our lives.

The hosts of God encamp around
The dwellings of the just;
Deliverance He affords to all
Who on His succour trust.

Seek first his kingdom and his righteousness, and all these things will be given to you as well.

(Matthew 6:33)

313

PART SIX

Getting ready for the future

CHAPTER ONE

Facing Death

Male or female; black or white; rich or poor; good or bad – death is the one certainty that faces us all.

Man is destined to die once, and after that to face judgment.
(Hebrews 9:27)

'Death is the ultimate statistic; one out of one die.' So wrote George Bernard Shaw. And it's absolutely true! We may have different backgrounds, jobs, experiences of life; but we all have one thing in common: we all must die one day. No matter what advances might be made in medical science; no matter how long we might feel we can put off 'the fateful day', we will all come to the end of our days on this earth. For death is not simply a biological fact; it is a theological certainty.

Death is an appointment

Sometimes there are appointments in life that we just can't keep; business executives who couldn't make a meeting; parents who couldn't get their children to the dentist; the elderly who were too unwell to turn out to something. But there is one appointment that all of us will have to keep, come what may. And that is our appointment with death.

I know you will bring me down to death, to the place appointed for all the living.

(Job 30:23)

It is appointed for men to die once.

(Hebrews 9:27, NKJV)

So, how did this appointment come to be in our diaries?

The dawn of death

We said in our introduction that death is not simply a biological fact; it is a theological certainty. By that we mean that we don't just die because our bodies wear out or get diseased or damaged beyond repair. We die because that is how God has determined that life in this world must now be.

God had said to Adam,

'You are free to eat from any tree in the garden; but you must not eat from the tree of the knowledge of good and evil, for when you eat of it you will surely die.'

(Genesis 2:16–17)

God is a God who keeps his promises; and so, when Adam disobeyed this command, God released the promised consequence:

'By the sweat of your brow you will eat your food until you return to the ground, since from it you were taken; for dust you are and to dust you will return.'

(Genesis 3:19)

From that moment on, death became a 'normal' feature of human life (e.g. Psalm 39:4–7; 104:29; Ecclesiastes 3:18–21; 12:6–7).

The certainty of death

Not only is death now 'normal' in this life; it is a certainty of this life, a universal and inevitable experience for all Adam's descendants; and will remain so until Jesus returns (1 Corinthians 15:54–55).

Like water spilled on the ground, which cannot be recovered, so we must die.

(2 Samuel 14:14)

When Adam sinned, sin entered the entire human race. Adam's sin brought death, so death spread to everyone, for everyone sinned.

(Romans 5:12, NLT)

The wages of sin is death.

(Romans 6:23)

See also Genesis 6:3; Joshua 23:14; 1 Kings 2:2; Job 4:18–21; 21:22–26; 30:23; 2 Peter 1:13–14

Because we are still part of this world Christians, too, face death (e.g. Romans 14:8); it is not something that we can avoid. Only those who are alive on the day Jesus returns will have the amazing experience of avoiding death and being instantly caught up into his presence (1 Corinthians 15:50–52; 1 Thessalonians 4:15–17).

The timing of death

For each one of us God has fixed the moment when our death will surely come:

Man's days are determined; you have decreed the number of his months and have set limits he cannot exceed.

(Job 14:5)

There is a time for everything, and a season for every activity under heaven: a time to be born and a time to die.

(Ecclesiastes 3:1–2)

No man has power over the wind to contain it; so no-one has power over the day of his death.

(Ecclesiastes 8:8)

See also Deuteronomy 32:39; 1 Samuel 2:6; Psalm 31:14–15; 90:1–4; 104:29; Isaiah 38:5; Luke 12:16–21; Acts 17:26; Revelation 1:18

This does not mean that we can be careless about how we live, nor that we should be fearful of when we die. But it does mean that we can trust God, and that we do not need to cling on to life at any price (e.g. Luke 12:4–7) or be fearful of dying when our day comes (e.g. 2 Timothy 4:6–8). God has a good, acceptable and perfect will for each one of us, and the timing of our death, or the death of a loved one, is part of that. Hard though this is at times, we may rest assured both in God's timing and in God's love.

The sanctity of death

Because it is God who fixes the time of our death, we should leave this matter in his hands alone. That is why Christians oppose anything that removes the determination of life and death from God's hands and seeks to put it into human hands, whether the termination of life at its beginning through abortion, the termination of life at its end through euthanasia (so-called 'mercy-killing') or the termination of life when things get too hard through suicide. No matter what situation may confront us, our Father has grace and help sufficient to the need.

But I trust in you, O LORD; I say, 'You are my God.' My times are in your hands.

(Psalm 31:14–15)

See also Deuteronomy 33:25.

The finality of death

The Bible is clear that we live once and that we die once:

Man is destined to die once . . .

(Hebrews 9:27)

This is the only life that we have in which to find God and to find salvation. The Bible finds no room for such ideas as:

• *Purgatory* – the belief that there is a place that you go to after death where you can 'pay off' your sins, or even have others pay them off for you. Such a belief arose only when people began to fail to understand how, when Christ died on the cross, all our sins were completely forgiven and how, through believing in him, we can be completely 'justified' before the Father (see Part 2, Chapter 3).

• *Reincarnation* – the belief that life is a series of 'lives' in which you return to a better one if you have been good, or a lesser one if you have not, as part of the process of being purified from sin. Once again, such a view fails to understand what Christ did for us through his death on the cross. It was because of his offering of his own perfect life (e.g. 1 Peter 3:18) that such imperfect people as us can come to God as soon as we die.

Jesus taught that, for those who put their trust in him, death would be followed by immediate entry into the presence of God. To the thief on the cross Jesus said:

'I tell you the truth, today you will be with me in paradise.'

(Luke 23:43)

Death is a departure

'When you're dead, you're dead' is a common viewpoint today. 'Wrong!' the Bible says. When you die, you go somewhere, as surely as when you go into the departure lounge at an airport it is because you are going somewhere. In fact, the Bible uses the word 'departure' about death.

Two men, Moses and Elijah, appeared in glorious splendour, talking with Jesus. They spoke about his departure, which he was about to bring to fulfilment at Jerusalem.

(Luke 9:30–31)

I desire to depart and be with Christ, which is better by far.

(Philippians 1:23)

For I am already being poured out like a drink offering, and the time has come for my departure. I have fought the good fight, I have finished the race, I have kept the faith. Now there is in store for me the crown of righteousness, which the Lord, the righteous Judge, will award to me on that day – and not only to me, but also to all who have longed for his appearing.

(2 Timothy 4:6–8)

I think it is right to refresh your memory as long as I live in the tent of this body, because I know that I will soon put it aside, as our Lord Jesus Christ has made clear to me. And I will make every effort to see that after my departure you will always be able to remember these things.

(2 Peter 1:13–15)

Jesus, Paul, and Peter were all looking forward to their 'departure', their leaving this life and going to a better place. But where are we going to, and exactly what happens next?

Goodbye body!

Anyone who has stood alongside someone who has died cannot fail to have seen that at the moment of death, 'something' has 'gone'. It is not simply that the loved one stops moving or breathing, or that the brain is no longer sending its signals; 'life' has gone out of them. In fact, they often don't even look quite the same. What has happened is that the 'soul' (that which makes you 'you') and the 'spirit' (that which relates to God) have separated from the body, and from that moment on, the body, for which we no longer have a need, begins to decay.

'For dust you are and to dust you will return.'
(Genesis 3:19)

You turn men back to dust, saying, 'Return to dust, O sons of men.'
(Psalm 90:3)

Remember him – before the silver cord is severed, or the golden bowl is broken; before the pitcher is shattered at the spring, or the wheel broken at the well, and the dust returns to the ground it came from, and the spirit returns to God who gave it.
(Ecclesiastes 12:6–7)
See also Job 7:21; 21:23–26; 34:14–15; Psalm 103:13–16; 104:29; Ecclesiastes 3:20; Acts 13:36; 1 Corinthians 15:35–57

Hello heaven!

For those who trust in Christ, however, that's not the end of the story! For as we slip away from our body and this life, we immediately pass into the glory of heaven and into God's presence.

Now we know that if the earthly tent we live in is destroyed, we have a building from God, an eternal house in heaven, not built by human hands. Meanwhile we groan, longing to be clothed with our heavenly dwelling, because when we are clothed, we will not be found naked. For while we are in this tent, we groan and are burdened, because we do not wish to be unclothed but to be clothed with our heavenly dwelling, so that what is mortal may be swallowed up by life. Now it is God who has made us for this very purpose and has given us the Spirit as a deposit, guaranteeing what is to come. Therefore we are always confident and know that as long as we are at home in the body we are away from the Lord.
(2 Corinthians 5:1–8)
See also Luke 23:42–43; John 12:26; 14:1–3; Philippians 1:21–23; 1 Thessalonians 5:10; Revelation 7:9–17

Heaven is indeed a wonderful place! There, believers experience –

- seeing God (Psalm 17:15; 1 Corinthians 13:12; Revelation 22:4)
- serving God (Revelation 5:10; 7:15; 22:3)
- God's reward (2 Corinthians 5:10; 2 Timothy 4:7–8)
- being with Christ (Philippians 1:21–23)
- being 'at home' (John 14:3; 2 Corinthians 5:8)
- full joy (Psalm 16:9–11; Matthew 25:19–23; Jude 24)
- rest (Revelation 14:13)
- fellowship with others (Hebrews 12:22–23; Revelation 7:9)
- everything focused on 'him who sits on the throne and . . . the Lamb' (Revelation 5:13)

Little wonder that the psalmist could write:

Precious in the sight of the LORD is the death of his saints.

(Psalm 116:15)

Some people have felt that the Bible teaches that our soul 'sleeps' at death and remains in that state until the return of Christ. The Bible indeed uses the picture of 'sleep' (e.g. Psalm 13:3; 1 Corinthians 15:51); but this was simply a metaphor in Bible times for 'death'. The overwhelming weight of evidence in the Bible is that as soon as believers die they immediately enter the presence of the Lord (e.g. Luke 23:43; Philippians 1:23).

Relevance for today

Facing up to death

All of us have to face up to the reality of death.

What man can live and not see death, or save himself from the power of the grave?

(Psalm 89:48)

The question we must all ask ourselves is: Am I ready to die? Have I 'made my peace' with God? God urges us, in an insistent yet tender way, to turn to him now, for it will certainly be too late then.

'In the time of my favour I heard you, and in the day of salvation I helped you.' I tell you, now is the time of God's favour, now is the day of salvation.

(2 Corinthians 6:2)

Being free from the fear of death

While no one looks forward to the physical experience of dying, we do not need to fear death, for Christ has broken its power and fear once and for all.

Since the children have flesh and blood, he too shared in their humanity so that by his death he might destroy him who holds the power of death – that is, the devil– and free those who all their lives were held in slavery by their fear of death.

(Hebrews 2:14–15)

Confidence about our inheritance

Christ's resurrection means that he cannot die again; death no longer has mastery over him for he died to sin once for all (Romans 6:9–10). But not only is he alive for ever and ever (Revelation 1:18), through our faith in him he has raised us with him to share in that new spiritual life that can never end (Ephesians 2:4–10).

Praise be to the God and Father of our Lord Jesus Christ! In his great mercy he has given us new birth into a living hope through the resurrection of Jesus Christ from the dead, and into an inheritance that can never perish, spoil or fade – kept in heaven for you, who through faith are shielded by God's power until the coming of the salvation that is ready to be revealed in the last time.

(1 Peter 1:3–5)

Coping with bereavement

The shortest verse in the Bible sums up God's heart towards us in times of bereavement:

Jesus wept.

(John 11:35)

This is Jesus' 'permission slip' to us to have a good cry when a loved one dies! Tears are not a sign of lack of faith; they are a sign that we have truly loved (e.g. Genesis 49:33–50:1; 2 Samuel 1:11–12; 3:31–32; Mark 16:10; John 11:33; 20:10–11).

But while our tears are real, there can be an undergirding confidence that our loved one, if a believer, is now with Christ and has 'gained' not 'lost', and so our grieving is not without hope.

For me, to live is Christ and to die is gain.

(Philippians 1:21)

Brothers, we do not want you to be ignorant about those who fall asleep, or to grieve like the rest of men, who have no hope. We believe that Jesus died and rose again and so we believe that God will bring with Jesus those who have fallen asleep in him.

(1 Thessalonians 4:13–14)

See also Psalm 23; 49:15; John 14:1–6; Romans 8:35–39; 1 Thessalonians 5:10; 2 Timothy 4:6–8

Responsibility towards the bereaved

Christians have a particular responsibility to help and encourage those who have been bereaved.

Religion that God our Father accepts as pure and faultless is this: to look after orphans and widows in their distress . . .

(James 1:27)

See also Exodus 22:22; Deuteronomy 24:17–22; Psalm 68:5–6; Isaiah 1:17; 1 Timothy 5:3–16

And in the meantime . . .

We are not to sit around twiddling our thumbs, waiting for Jesus to come! We are to live our lives 'packed up and ready to go', yet equally are to be 'wholly committed to Christ's service each day. Don't touch sin with a barge-pole. Keep short accounts with God. Think of each hour as God's gift to you, to make the most and best of. Plan your life, budgeting for seventy years (Psalm 90:10), and understanding that if your time proves shorter that will not be unfair deprivation but rapid promotion' (Jim Packer, *God's Words*).

Lord, it belongs not to my care
Whether I die or live;
To love and serve thee is my share!
And this thy grace must give.

If life be long, I will be glad
That I may long obey;
If short – yet why should I be sad
To soar to endless day?

Christ leads me through no darker rooms
Than he went through before;
He that into God's kingdom comes
Must enter by this door.

Then shall I end my sad complaints
And weary sinful days,
And join with the triumphant saints
That sing Jehovah's praise.

My knowledge of that life is small,
The eye of faith is dim;
But it's enough that Christ knows all,
And I shall be with him.

Richard Baxter, 1615–91

Conclusion

Life is short and uncertain; God wants us therefore to be ready to live, but also to be ready to die.

Teach us to number our days aright, that we may gain a heart of wisdom.

(Psalm 90:12)

CHAPTER TWO

Christ's Second Coming

The personal return of Christ at the end of the age is not a doctrine for speculation but rather for provocation to live the Christian life right now.

But do not forget this one thing, dear friends: With the Lord a day is like a thousand years, and a thousand years are like a day. The Lord is not slow in keeping his promise, as some understand slowness. He is patient with you, not wanting anyone to perish, but everyone to come to repentance. But the day of the Lord will come . . . (2 Peter 3:8–10)

Knowing God . . . Trusting Jesus . .. Growing in the Spirit . . . Belonging to the church . . . Living in the world. Where does all this lead? What is it all for? Where are we all going? Does the Bible say anything about the future, about our future? Yes! The answer is a resounding, glorious yes! The climax of the future – of our future – is the second coming of Jesus Christ.

'I will return!'

The words 'I will return' are often found on the lips of thwarted villains in films or novels, eager to 'have another go'. Sometimes they return, sometimes they don't. But the promise of Jesus to return is no idle promise; it is one he will indeed keep, and one he made often. In fact, there are over 250 references to Christ's 'second coming' in the New Testament. Here are just some of them:

'For the Son of Man is going to come in his Father's glory with his angels, and then he will reward each person according to what he has done.'

(Matthew 16:27)

'And if I go and prepare a place for you, I will come back and take you to be with me that you also may be where I am.'

(John 14:3)

The Lord himself will come down from heaven, with a loud command, with the voice of the archangel and with the trumpet call of God.

(1 Thessalonians 4:16)

Christ was sacrificed once to take away the sins of many people; and he will appear a second time, not to bear sin, but to bring salvation to those who are waiting for him.

(Hebrews 9:28)

He who testifies to these things says, 'Yes, I am coming soon.'

(Revelation 22:20)

See also Matthew 24–25; Mark 13; Luke 21

What will Christ's return be like?

'Impossible to describe!' might be an appropriate answer. For it will be the climactic event of life as we now know it, transcending all experiences that we have ever known and therefore that words can describe. In the light of this, we cannot possibly hope to work out all the details. And even if we could, the Lord would no doubt have surprises up his sleeve!

Because there is no systematic teaching in the Bible about Christ's return, we have to draw our facts from different places. This has inevitably led people to construct different scenarios of what exactly will happen, or in what order it will happen. But nevertheless, some things stand out very clearly.

Christ's return will be physical

Jesus is not going to return in some vague spiritual way, as though it were simply a metaphor for his coming to us when we are born again or when we die, or for the world 'somehow getting better' through him. Jesus promised to come back in person, in a physical way, with eyes actually seeing him, just as he left this earth. In fact, this was the last thing that was underlined to the disciples at his ascension.

'This same Jesus, who has been taken from you into heaven, will come back in the same way you have seen him go into heaven.'

(Acts 1:11)

Christ's return will be public

Christ's first coming was quiet and obscure; but not so his second coming. It will be an utterly public affair.

For as lightning that comes from the east is visible even in the west, so will be the coming of the Son of Man.

(Matthew 24:27)

'At that time men will see the Son of Man coming in clouds with great power and glory.'

(Mark 13:26)

'Look, he is coming with the clouds, and every eye will see him.'

(Revelation 1:7)

Two of the Greek words used in the New Testament bring home the very public nature of Christ's coming again:

- *Parousia* – 'coming' (e.g. Matthew 24:27; 1 Thessalonians 3:13): used of the visits of kings and emperors when all citizens would turn out to welcome them.
- *Apokalypsis* – 'unveiling' or 'revealing' (e.g. Revelation 1:1; 2 Thessalonians 1:7): used of a theatre curtain being lifted for everyone to see the stage.

Christ's return will be sudden

No matter how we might try to work out the date of Christ's return, the simple truth is that Jesus said no one knows when it will be.

'You also must be ready, because the Son of Man will come at an hour when you do not expect him.'

(Luke 12:40)

See also Acts 1:6–7; 1 Timothy 6:14–15

In fact, his return will be a very sudden event, taking everyone by surprise; and this is why we must be constantly ready.

'No-one knows about that day or hour, not even the angels in heaven, nor the Son, but only the Father. As it was in the days of Noah, so it will be at the coming of the Son of Man. For in the days before the flood, people were eating and drinking, marrying and giving in marriage, up to the day Noah entered the ark; and they knew nothing about what would happen until the flood came and took them

all away. That is how it will be at the coming of the Son of Man. Two men will be in the field; one will be taken and the other left. Two women will be grinding with a hand mill; one will be taken and the other left. Therefore keep watch, because you do not know on what day your Lord will come.'

(Matthew 24:36–42)

Now, brothers, about times and dates we do not need to write to you, for you know very well that the day of the Lord will come like a thief in the night. While people are saying, 'Peace and safety', destruction will come on them suddenly, as labour pains on a pregnant woman, and they will not escape.

(1 Thessalonians 5:1–3)

See also Matthew 24:43–44; 25:1–13; Luke 12:35–40; 2 Peter 3:8–10; Revelation 16:15

Christ's return will be glorious

Some amazing spectacles were organized to mark the turn of the millennium. But all of those are nothing in comparison to Christ's return, which will be the most spectacular event ever seen on earth. The glory of God will be seen for what it is!

'They will see the Son of Man coming on the clouds of the sky, with power and great glory.'

(Matthew 24:30)

We wait for the blessed hope – the glorious appearing of our great God and Saviour, Jesus Christ

(Titus 2:13)

See also Matthew 16:27; 25:31; Luke 21:27; Acts 2:20

When will Christ's return happen?

Many Christians have tried to work out an exact timetable for the events surrounding Christ's return. But as we have already seen, it just can't be done. Not even Jesus himself knew the day (Matthew 24:36)! But we are given certain indicators of what life will become like before he returns.

The characteristics of life

Many of the things that the Bible says will characterize life before Jesus returns have been characteristic of every age, ebbing and flowing over the centuries; but it appears that their intensity will increase as the end draws closer. Clear hallmarks include:

Apostasy and false religion

'At that time many will turn away from the faith and will betray and hate each other, and many false prophets will appear and deceive many people. Because of the increase of wickedness, the love of most will grow cold, but he who stands firm to the end will be saved.'

(Matthew 24:10–13)

See also Matthew 24:4–5, 24–25; Mark 13:21–23; 2 Thessalonians 2:9–12; 1 Timothy 4:1–3; 2 Timothy 4:3–4; Revelation 19:20

Increasing godlessness

But mark this: There will be terrible times in the last days. People will be lovers of themselves, lovers of money, boastful, proud, abusive, disobedient to their parents, ungrateful, unholy, without love, unforgiving, slanderous, without self-control, brutal, not lovers of the good, treacherous, rash, conceited, lovers of pleasure rather than lovers of God – having a form of godliness but denying its power. Have nothing to do with them.

(2 Timothy 3:1–5)

See also 2 Peter 3:3–7

Increasing catastrophes and strife

'You will hear of wars and rumours of wars, but see to it that you are not alarmed. Such things must happen, but the end is still to come. Nation will rise against nation, and kingdom against kingdom. There will be famines and earthquakes in various places. All these are the beginning of birth-pains.'

(Matthew 24:6–8)

See also Mark 13:8; Luke 21:9–11; Revelation 6:1–8

Persecution of believers

'Then you will be handed over to be persecuted and put to death, and you will be hated by all nations because of me.'

(Matthew 24:9)

'You will be betrayed even by parents, brothers, relatives and friends, and they will put some of you to death. All men will hate you because of me. But not a hair of your head will perish. By standing firm you will gain life.'

(Luke 21:16–19)

See also Mark 13:9–13; Luke 21:12–15; 2 Timothy 3:12; Revelation 7:13–14; 13:5–10

The appearance of antichrist

Dear children, this is the last hour; and as you have heard that the antichrist is coming, even now many antichrists have come. This is how we know it is the last hour . . . Who is the liar? It is the man who denies that Jesus is the Christ. Such a man is the antichrist.

(1 John 2:18, 22)

See also 1 John 4:3; 2 John 7

Clearly John was expecting not just one antichrist, but 'many antichrists'. Anyone who opposes Christ, or sets himself up instead of Christ, is an anti-Christ. But it seems there may be one particular figure before Christ's return who will be the summation of all that

opposes him. Paul describes this figure as 'the man of lawlessness' (see 2 Thessalonians 2:1–12). 'The Beast' in Revelation 13 may be this same character, or he may simply be a personification of evil secular power, just as Rome was in John's day.

The spreading of the gospel

So far, it's all been bad news. But there's good news too! Jesus promised that, despite all opposition and persecution, the gospel would spread significantly and the kingdom would be extended.

'And this gospel of the kingdom will be preached in the whole world as a testimony to all nations, and then the end will come.'
(Matthew 24:14)
See also Mark 13:10; Revelation 14:6

The idea of a faithful few believers 'holding the fort until Jesus comes' does not tie in with New Testament teaching. Things will get worse; but things will also get better! Wickedness will increase; but the kingdom will increase also. And the kingdom is going to triumph!

This comes out particularly in Jesus' parables in Matthew 13 that show how the kingdom will triumph despite all opposition; the wheat will surely come to harvest despite the weeds (vv 24–30, 36–43); the mustard seed will surely become the biggest tree (vv 31–32); the yeast will surely permeate the whole batch of dough (v 33); the net will surely bring in its catch (vv 47–50).

Are we ready?

Whenever Christians have tried to work out a timetable for Christ's return, they have always got it wrong. (Shouldn't that tell us something?) All we get are general indicators – and even some of those will probably happen in a way that will surprise us all! But the Bible's emphasis in this whole area is not theoretical or speculative, but practical. It asks us the question: are we ready?

'Therefore keep watch, because you do not know on what day your Lord will come. But understand this: If the owner of the house had known at what time of night the thief was coming, he would have kept watch and would not have let his house be broken into. So you also must be ready, because the Son of Man will come at an hour when you do not expect him.'
(Matthew 24:42–44)

But the day of the Lord will come like a thief. The heavens will disappear with a roar; the elements will be destroyed by fire, and the earth and everything in it will be laid bare. Since everything will be destroyed in this way, what kind of people ought you to be? You ought to live holy and godly lives as you look forward to the day of God and speed its coming.
(2 Peter 3:10–12)
See also Matthew 25:1–30; Luke 12:35–46; 1 Thessalonians 5:4–11

Why will Christ come again?

So, what are the purposes of this glorious event for which we must all be ready? We can summarize them as being:

To destroy all evil

Ask most people what their one wish for the world would be and it would be for evil and suffering to be removed. Well, it's going to happen!

The lawless one will be revealed, whom the Lord Jesus will overthrow with the breath of his mouth and destroy by the splendour of his coming.
(2 Thessalonians 2:8)

The present heavens and earth are reserved for fire, being kept for the day of judgment and destruction of ungodly men.

(2 Peter 3:7)

See also 1 Corinthians 15:24–28;
2 Thessalonians 1:7–10; Revelation 20:10, 14;
21:8

To bring about the resurrection

Death is not the end. At Christ's return, all who have ever lived – both Christian and non-Christian – will be restored to life to receive either judgment or salvation.

'Do not be amazed at this, for a time is coming when all who are in their graves will hear his voice and come out – those who have done good will rise to live, and those who havo done evil will rise to be condemned.'

(John 5:28–29)

See also 1 Corinthians 15:50–57;
1 Thessalonians 4:16–17; Chapter 3 of this part

To judge all people

At God's final judgment there will be a division between those who are acquitted and those who are condemned, on the basis of their faith in Christ.

'When the Son of Man comes in his glory, and all the angels with him, he will sit on his throne in heavenly glory. All the nations will be gathered before him, and he will separate the people one from another as a shepherd separates the sheep from the goats. He will put the sheep on his right and the goats on his left. Then the King will say to those on his right, "Come, you who are blessed by my Father; take your inheritance, the kingdom prepared for you since the creation of the world . . .« Then he will say to those on his left, "Depart from me, you who are cursed, into the eternal fire prepared for the devil and his angels." '

(Matthew 25:31–34, 41)

See also Matthew 13:37–43; 16:27; John
5:21–23, 28–29; Acts 17:31; 2 Corinthians 5:10;
Hebrews 9:27; Jude 14–15; Chapter 3 of this part

To complete the work of salvation

As Christians, we need not fear God's judgment. For through Christ, we have already been justified – that is, received God's 'Not guilty' verdict (Romans 5:1–2); but there is so much more to come!

For the Lord himself will come down from heaven, with a loud command, with the voice of the archangel and with the trumpet call of God, and the dead in Christ will rise first. After that, we who are still alive and are left will be caught up together with them in the clouds to meet the Lord in the air. And so we will be with the Lord for ever.

(1 Thessalonians 4:16–17)

See also Philippians 3:20–21; Colossians 3:4;
1 Thessalonians 5:23–24; 2 Thessalonians 2:1;
2 Timothy 4:8; 1 John 3:2

To establish the new creation

Heaven is not our ultimate home. It is but a glorious 'waiting room' (though nothing like those at railway stations!) until God prepares his new creation for us to enjoy with him for ever.

That day will bring about the destruction of the heavens by fire, and the elements will melt in the heat. But in keeping with his promise we are looking forward to a new heaven and a new earth, the home of righteousness.

(2 Peter 3:12–13)

See also Revelation 21:1–22:21

What a message all this is to a world that has lost its direction! God is saying: the world is going somewhere, and it's going somewhere purposeful. History will come to a close; the problem of evil will be resolved. And, as the final curtain falls at the end of time, the Author of the drama of life will walk on to the world's stage and everyone will see him. Christ will indeed come!

Relevance for today

Christ's coming may seem slow, but it isn't late. We should not give up believing in Christ's return simply because our Father is more patient than we are!

But do not forget this one thing, dear friends: With the Lord a day is like a thousand years, and a thousand years are like a day. The Lord is not slow in keeping his promise, as some understand slowness. He is patient with you, not wanting anyone to perish, but everyone to come to repentance.

(2 Peter 3:8–9)

See also Hebrews 10:37

Christ's coming is always near

We do not walk *towards* the end, but *along* it, as if walking by a cliff edge. It is constantly close and at any point God could give the nudge that 'pushes us over'.

The hour has come for you to wake up from your slumber, because our salvation is nearer now than when we first believed.

(Romans 13:11)

The time is near.

(Revelation 1:3)

See also James 5:8; 1 Peter 4:7

The date of Christ's coming is unknown

Some have ignored Christ's teaching that we cannot work out when he will return, and so have looked foolish or, even worse, have led others into tragic death. Only God knows the date. Let us leave it with him; it is safer that way!

'No-one knows about that day or hour, not even the angels in heaven, nor the Son, but only the Father.'

(Matthew 24:36)

Christ's coming provokes us to 'get on with the job'

Having written of Christ's resurrection and return, Paul concluded with the following words:

Therefore, my dear brothers, stand firm. Let nothing move you. Always give yourselves fully to the work of the Lord, because you know that your labour in the Lord is not in vain.

(1 Corinthians 15:58)

See also 1 Thessalonians 5:6–11; 2 Peter 3:11–12

Lo! He comes with clouds descending,
Once for favoured sinners slain;
Thousand thousand saints attending
Swell the triumph of His train:
Hallelujah!
God appears on earth to reign.

Every eye shall now behold Him
Robed in dreadful majesty;
Those who set at nought and sold Him,
Pierced and nailed Him to the tree,
Deeply wailing,
Shall the true Messiah see.

Every island, sea, and mountain,
Heaven and earth, shall flee away;
All who hate Him must, confounded,
Hear the trump proclaim the day;
Come to judgment!
Come to judgment! come away!

Now redemption, long expected,
See in solemn pomp appear!
All His saints, by man rejected,
Now shall meet Him in the air:
Hallelujah!
See the day of God appear!

Yea, Amen! let all adore Thee,
High on Thine eternal throne!
Saviour, take the power and glory;
Claim the kingdom for Thine own:
O come quickly!
Hallelujah! come, Lord, come!

John Cennick, 1718–55
and Charles Wesley, 1707–88

Resurrection and Judgment

The time is coming when everyone who has ever lived will be judged by God. But we can be ready for it!

'Do not be amazed at this, for a time is coming when all who are in their graves will hear his voice and come out – those who have done good will rise to live, and those who have done evil will rise to be condemned.' (John 5:28–29)

High above the buildings of the Old Bailey in London stands the statue of 'Justice' – a blindfolded lady with scales in her hand, epitomizing the justice promised in the courts below. Sadly, our human courts are not always just, for a variety of reasons. But there is one courtroom in which all of us will stand where justice will be absolutely impartial. It is the courtroom of God at the end of this age. Need we be afraid of it? Not at all!

The glorious resurrection

As we saw briefly in the previous chapter, the resurrection of the dead is an important accompaniment to Christ's return, and was foreseen in the Old Testament.

Prophecies in the Old Testament

The view of the 'afterlife' in Old Testament times was somewhat limited. People believed that at death everyone, good and bad alike, went to Sheol ('Hades' in Greek). This was a gloomy half-life; a place of darkness (Job 10:21) and dust (Job 17:16), of silence (Psalm 94:17) and lack of knowledge of God (Psalm 88:10–12). In later Judaism, Sheol was divided into separate areas for the righteous and the wicked. Jesus picked up this popular belief in his parable of the rich man and Lazarus (Luke 16:19–31).

But against this gloomy background, there were glimpses of God having something far better for his people.

I know that my Redeemer lives, and that in the end he will stand upon the earth. And after my skin has been destroyed, yet in my flesh I will see God; I myself will see him with my own eyes – I, and not another.

(Job 19:25–27)

Multitudes who sleep in the dust of the earth will awake: some to everlasting life, others to shame and everlasting contempt. Those who are wise will shine like the brightness of the heavens, and those who lead many to righteousness, like the stars for ever and ever.

(Daniel 12:2–3)

See also Psalm 49:14–15; 73:23–26; Isaiah 26:19; Ezekiel 37:12–13

Teaching in the New Testament

By New Testament times, two views about the resurrection prevailed. The Pharisees firmly believed in it, while the Sadducees didn't. (Paul, a Pharisee by upbringing, would appeal to this distinction on one occasion – see Acts 23:6–8.) Jesus confidently taught about the resurrection (and demonstrated it in his own life!) and his disciples confidently did the same.

'And this is the will of him who sent me, that I shall lose none of all that he has given me, but raise them up at the last day. For my Father's will is that everyone who looks to the Son and believes in him shall have eternal life, and I will raise him up at the last day.'

(John 6:39–40)

'I am the resurrection and the life. He who believes in me will live, even though he dies; and whoever lives and believes in me will never die. Do you believe this?'

(John 11:25–26)

See also Matthew 22:29–32; John 5:25–29; 1 Corinthians 15:12–57; Philippians 3:20–21; 1 John 3:2

Transformed bodies

The end-time resurrection marks the completion of God's plan of redemption, as our bodies become redeemed and transformed just as our spirits have been.

We know that the whole creation has been groaning as in the pains of childbirth right up to the present time. Not only so, but we ourselves, who have the firstfruits of the Spirit, groan inwardly as we wait eagerly for our adoption as sons, the redemption of our bodies.

(Romans 8:22–23)

At the resurrection God will give us a different sort of body (1 Corinthians 15:35–49), just as he gave one to Jesus at his resurrection – one that could be touched (e.g. John 20:27) and that could eat (e.g. Luke 24:30), but that was so gloriously transformed that he wasn't recognized immediately (e.g. Luke 24:15–16) and that seemed to appear in places at will (e.g. John 20:19). Yet it was still the same Jesus. This sounds really exciting!

So, why the need for the transformation? For the simple reason that a new environment demands a new type of body.

The body that is sown is perishable, it is raised imperishable; it is sown in dishonour, it is raised in glory; it is sown in weakness, it is raised in power; it is sown a natural body, it is raised a spiritual body.

If there is a natural body, there is also a spiritual body. So it is written: 'The first man Adam became a living being'; the last Adam, a life-giving spirit. The spiritual did not come first, but the natural, and after that the spiritual. The first man was of the dust of the earth, the second man from heaven. As was the earthly man, so are those who are of the earth; and as is the man from heaven, so also are those who are of heaven. And just as we have borne the likeness of the earthly man, so shall we bear the likeness of the man from heaven.

I declare to you, brothers, that flesh and blood cannot inherit the kingdom of God, nor does the perishable inherit the imperishable. Listen, I tell you a mystery: We will not all sleep, but we will all be changed – in a flash, in the twinkling of an eye, at the last trumpet. For the trumpet will sound, the dead will be raised imperishable, and we will be changed. For the perishable must clothe itself with the imperishable, and the mortal with immortality. When the perishable has been clothed with the imperishable, and the mortal with immortality, then the saying that is written will come true: 'Death has been swallowed up in victory.'

(1 Corinthians 15:42–54)

Note that it is only at this point that death loses its powers over believers. 'The last enemy to be destroyed is death' (1 Corinthians 15:26). But as surely as Christ has delivered our souls from the power of death (John 5:24; 1 John 3:14), so he will deliver our bodies (John 5:25–29).

God's righteous judgment

Let's face it; none of us likes to think about being judged – whether it be school exams, appraisals at work – or God's final judgment! But the Bible tells us that everyone who has ever lived will be judged by God. Nothing will be hidden; there will be an incomparable 'action replay' of our lives. What we really are, what we have thought, what we have done and not done, will all be brought to light.

Nothing in all creation is hidden from God's sight. Everything is uncovered and laid bare before the eyes of him to whom we must give account.

(Hebrews 4:13)

The judge and justice

Throughout the Old Testament, there was a profound conviction that God was a righteous judge who always judged fairly. It was on this basis that Abraham could even challenge God!

'Far be it from you to do such a thing – to kill the righteous with the wicked, treating the righteous and the wicked alike. Far be it from you! Will not the Judge of all the earth do right?'

(Genesis 18:25)

The prophets foresaw the day when this righteous judge would bring his judgment upon sinners on 'the day of the Lord'.

'The day of the LORD is near for all nations. As you have done, it will be done to you; your deeds will return upon your own head.'

(Obadiah 15)

See also e.g. Isaiah 3:13; 13:6–13; 41:1; 66:15–16; Ezekiel 7:1–3; Joel 2:11; 3:1–2; Amos 5:18–20; Zephaniah 1:14–18; Malachi 4:5–6

Israel had always felt that the day of the Lord would be a time of punishment for the Gentiles; much to their surprise, however, they were told that the punishment would start with them! Peter summed this up like this:

For it is time for judgment to begin with the family of God; and if it begins with us, what will the outcome be for those who do not obey the gospel of God? And, 'If it is hard for the righteous to be saved, what will become of the ungodly and the sinner?'

(1 Peter 4:17–18)

Judgment in the New Testament

Some people think that Jesus is too kind to judge anyone. 'Surely we'll all be saved at the end, won't we?' they ask. But Jesus spoke often about the reality and seriousness of God's judgment, and his disciples taught the same.

'Moreover, the Father judges no-one, but has entrusted all judgment to the Son . . . And he has given him authority to judge because he is the Son of Man . . . By myself

I [Jesus] can do nothing; I judge only as I hear, and my judgment is just, for I seek not to please myself but him who sent me.'

(John 5:22, 27, 30)

'He [Jesus] commanded us to preach to the people and to testify that he is the one whom God appointed as judge of the living and the dead.'

(Acts 10:42)

'In the past God overlooked such ignorance, but now he commands all people everywhere to repent. For he has set a day when he will judge the world with justice by the man he has appointed. He has given proof of this to all men by raising him from the dead.'

(Acts 17:30–31)

See also Matthew 7:1–2; 13:37–43; 25:31–46; John 5:21–30; Romans 2:16; 2 Corinthians 5:10; 2 Timothy 4:1; Hebrews 9:27; 12:23; James 4:12; 1 Peter 4:5; Jude 14–15

The basis of our judgment

The basis of this judgment is how we have responded to Christ. Those who have rejected him will have this, their own choice, underlined; those who have trusted him will be saved from condemnation.

'For God did not send his Son into the world to condemn the world, but to save the world through him. Whoever believes in him is not condemned, but whoever does not believe stands condemned already because he has not believed in the name of God's one and only Son.'

(John 3:17–18)

See also Mark 16:16; John 3:16; 2 Thessalonians 1:6–9

337

Judgment and Christians

Christians have nothing to fear in this judgment however. Indeed, at the very moment they trust in Christ, they receive God's end-time 'Not guilty!' – right then! This doctrine of 'justification of faith', lost under centuries of church traditions but rediscovered at the Reformation, assures us that God justifies, not the godly but the ungodly; and that he does so, not at the end of time, but right now. This is utterly amazing!

Therefore, since we have been justified through faith, we have peace with God through our Lord Jesus Christ, through whom we have gained access by faith into this grace in which we now stand.

(Romans 5:1–2)

Therefore, there is now no condemnation for those who are in Christ Jesus.

(Romans 8:1)

The only aspect of judgment that now remains for Christians to face, therefore, is the judgment of their works.

For we must all appear before the judgment seat of Christ, that each one may receive what is due to him for the things done while in the body, whether good or bad.

(2 Corinthians 5:10)

See also Matthew 10:40–42; 19:27–30

The New Testament teaches that there will be different 'degrees' of reward for Christians, appropriate to our service. In Jesus' parable of the ten minas (Luke 19:11–27), the servant who put his mina (about three months' wages) to work and added ten more to it was given ten cities to rule; the one who turned his mina into five more was given five cities to rule; the one who did nothing with it, out of sheer fear (v 21), ended up with no reward at all, though he certainly was not treated like 'those enemies of mine' (v 27). His salvation was assured, but his reward was lost. Maybe something in us reacts to this; but the Bible says that this is not favouritism (Colossians 3:25), but justice!

'Behold, I am coming soon! My reward is with me, and I will give to everyone according to what he has done.'

(Revelation 22:12)

See also 1 Corinthians 3:10–15

What about those who have never heard?

Often this question is simply a diversion from those who don't want to face the challenge of the gospel themselves. But nevertheless, it is a question which the Bible answers. It tells us that different degrees of knowledge of God's will, and so differing abilities to fulfil it, will be taken into account by the righteous judge who knows all things (Matthew 11:21–24; Romans 2:12–16) – though Paul doubts people's abilities even to live up to their own standards and consciences, let alone God's standards (e.g. Romans 1:18–32). God's judgment will be utterly righteous. There will be no facts missed, no extenuating circumstances not considered, no injustices not put right. 'Will not the Judge of all the earth do right?' (Genesis 18:25). Most certainly, yes!

The awfulness of hell

But judgment is not the final word in this matter; for judgment has consequences. And this is where we need to talk about hell.

Any talk of hell tends to be discredited by the fanatical, with their upholding of gruesome medieval imagery, or disbelieved by the respectable, who think that God is too 'kind' for there to be such a place – well, at least for them! For others, hell is 'hell on earth' – the pain or hardships that some have to live through. But the truth is that Jesus spoke solemnly about the reality of hell as the destination of those who reject him.

Hell is described in the Bible as:

• *a place of punishment* (some would say, destruction) for those who reject Christ (e.g. Matthew 5:29; 10:28; 13:40–42; 25:41; Mark 9:42–48; Romans 2:7–8; 2 Peter 3:7; Jude 7; Revelation 20:10–15; 21:6–9)

• *a place of exclusion from God's presence* (e.g. Matthew 7:21–23; 2 Thessalonians 1:6–10)

• *a place from which there is no escape* (Luke 16:19–31)

A variety of imagery is used to describe hell (including a place of wrath, torment, destruction, unquenchable fire, weeping, darkness and death), so perhaps we should not hold to any one image in too literal a way. The simple fact is: the Bible says that hell is not a pleasant experience and that no one in their right mind would want to go there! Indeed, no one needs to, for God has made full provision for our escaping it through the death of Christ his Son.

A new heaven and a new earth

Once evil is dealt with, including the judgment of Satan himself (Revelation 20:10), then the way is cleared for God to renew all things and to bring about his new creation.

'Behold, I will create new heavens and a new earth. The former things will not be remembered, nor will they come to mind. But be glad and rejoice for ever in what I will create.'

(Isaiah 65:17–18)

See also Isaiah 66:22; 2 Peter 3:12–13; Revel-ation 21:1–22:21

Revelation 21 and 22 show how God's presence will be among us (21:3) and his throne at the centre of everything (22:3), and therefore there will be no place for tears or death or mourning (21:4), no place for anything impure or unclean (21:8; 22:15), no place for sickness or curse (22:1–3). Truly this will be the city of God! (Do read through Revelation 21 and 22 slowly and take it all in!)

Relevance for today

This teaching about the future is not designed to feed our curiosity, but to stir us up to be different people. It challenges and encourages us to:

Be hopeful

Too many Christians are pessimists! We are meant to be a hopeful people: we know where we are going, where the church is going, where the world is going. God is Lord of his world and he will not – he cannot – lose his grip on his unfolding plan for it.

May our Lord Jesus Christ himself and God our Father, who loved us and by his grace gave us eternal encouragement and good hope, encourage your hearts and strengthen you in every good deed and word.

(2 Thessalonians 2:16–17)

Therefore, prepare your minds for action; be self-controlled; set your hope fully on the grace to be given you when Jesus Christ is revealed.

(1 Peter 1:13)

See also Titus 3:7; Hebrews 3:6

Be comforted

Because of Christ's resurrection and the assurance of his coming again, we can be comforted in times of bereavement.

Brothers, we do not want you to be ignorant about those who fall asleep, or to grieve like the rest of men, who have no hope. We believe that Jesus died and rose again and so we believe that God will bring with Jesus those who have fallen asleep in him . . . Therefore encourage each other with these words.

(1 Thessalonians 4:13–14, 18)

See also John 14:1–6; 1 Thessalonians 5:10–11

Be holy

Because our ultimate destination will be free of sin, now is a good time to start practising to live like that!

Since everything will be destroyed in this way, what kind of people ought you to be? You ought to live holy and godly lives as you look forward to the day of God and speed its coming.

(2 Peter 3:11–12)

See also 1 Thessalonians 5:23–24; 1 John 3:2–3

• *spreading the gospel*. It is only after the gospel has been preached in the whole world, that 'then the end will come' (Matthew 24:14).

• *preparing the church*. When Christ returns, the church will be presented to him as a bride to her husband (Revelation 21:2). Our task is to help make the church ready.

• *being involved in society*. In God's new creation, justice, love, and peace will reign supreme. This is the sort of society that God wants us to start bringing about even now.

I pray that you may be active in sharing your faith.

(Philemon 6)

Be watchful

'Therefore keep watch because you do not know when the owner of the house will come back – whether in the evening, or at midnight, or when the cock crows, or at dawn. If he comes suddenly, do not let him find you sleeping. What I say to you, I say to everyone: "Watch!" '

(Mark 13:35–37)

God does not want us to be so wrapped up in the affairs of this world that we neglect spiritual matters (Matthew 24:36–44). We can enjoy this life, but it can never be our main focus.

Be prayerful

'Your kingdom come.'

(Matthew 6:10)

Come, O Lord!

(1 Corinthians 16:22)

Be active

Teaching about Christ's return is always turned into practical action in the Bible. We are not to be idle, sitting around waiting for Jesus to come (e.g. 1 Thessalonians 5:14; 2 Thessalonians 3:6–10). Rather, we are to work faithfully, as good stewards (Luke 19:11–27), and patiently (James 5:7–8), giving ourselves fully to God's work (1 Corinthians 15:58). God wants us to be active in –

341

Thou Judge of quick and dead,
Before whose bar severe,
With holy joy, or guilty dread,
We all shall soon appear;
Our cautioned souls prepare
For that tremendous day,
And fill us now with watchful care,
And stir us up to pray.

To pray, and wait the hour,
That aweful hour unknown,
When, robed in majesty and power,
Thou shalt from heaven come down,
The immortal Son of Man,
To judge the human race,
With all Thy Father's dazzling train,
With all Thy glorious grace.

O may we thus be found
Obedient to His Word,
Attentive to the trumpet's sound,
And looking for our Lord!
O may we thus ensure
A lot among the blest;
And watch a moment to secure
An everlasting rest!

Charles Wesley, 1707–88

Conclusion

Our home for eternity depends upon our decisions now; but our hope for eternity should provoke us into being different people right now.

Since everything will be destroyed in this way, what kind of people ought you to be? You ought to live holy and godly lives as you look forward to the day of God and speed its coming.

(2 Peter 3:11–12)

CHAPTER FOUR

The Future Starts Now!

Just 'waiting to get to heaven' is to miss out on so much that God has for us right now.

'The kingdom of God is within you.' (Luke 17:21)

Having a hope for the future is all well and good. But does it have any relevance for right now? Yes! For in contrast to his contemporaries, who saw God's kingdom as something wholly in the future, Jesus said that the kingdom was in fact already here. The future isn't just something to prepare for; with Jesus, the future starts now!

A king and a kingdom

Every kingdom has a king, and the Old Testament was clear that there is no king but God alone.

Lift up your heads, O you gates; be lifted up, you ancient doors, that the King of glory may come in. Who is this King of glory? The LORD strong and mighty, the LORD mighty in battle. Lift up your heads, O you gates; lift them up, you ancient doors, that the King of glory may come in. Who is he, this King of glory? The LORD Almighty – he is the King of glory.

(Psalm 24:7-10)
See also e.g. Psalm 29:10–11; 47; 84:3; 95:1–7

The dominating vision of life was of God's throne at the centre of everything (e.g. Isaiah 6:1; Ezekiel 1:26; Daniel 7:9–14; Revelation 4:1–2; 22:1) and of everything therefore belonging to him (e.g. Psalm 24:1–2) and under his control (e.g. Psalm 96:10). Wherever his rule or 'government' increases, peace increases (Isaiah 9:6–7). All of this, it was believed, would find fulfilment at the end of the age.

'Your kingdom come'

So, when Jesus prayed 'Your kingdom come' (Matthew 6:10) he was praying what every good Jew believed. The prophets had foreseen the day when this kingdom would come and when David's descendant would destroy evil and establish his righteous reign on the earth.

For to us a child is born, to us a son is given, and the government will be on his shoulders. And he will be called Wonderful Counsellor, Mighty God, Everlasting Father, Prince of Peace. Of the increase of his government and peace there will be no end. He will reign on David's throne and over his kingdom, establishing and upholding it with justice and righteousness from that time on and for ever. The zeal of the LORD Almighty will accomplish this.

(Isaiah 9:6-7)

'The days are coming,' declares the LORD, 'when I will raise up to David a righteous Branch, a King who will reign wisely and do what is just and right in the land. In his days Judah will be saved and Israel will live in safety. This is the name by which he will be called: The LORD Our Righteousness.'

(Jeremiah 23:5-6)

'. . . kingship will come to the Daughter of Jerusalem'.

(Micah 4:8)

See also e.g. Psalm 2:1–9; Isaiah 2:2–5; 11:1–9; 32:1; Jeremiah 3:17–18; Daniel 2:31–45; 7:13–27; Micah 4:1–7; Zechariah 14:1–9

By the time of Jesus, the Roman empire was seen as the great enemy that would be overthrown. But opinion was divided: on the one hand, there were those (like the Sadducees) who didn't want to disturb the status quo for fear of losing their political influence; on the other hand, there were the 'freedom fighters' (like Simon 'the Zealot') who wanted to fight. And in between were thousands of ordinary people who felt their life wouldn't change greatly whoever came out on top.

It was into this setting that Jesus came, proclaiming God's kingdom. Yet, rather than looking for its coming, Jesus said it had already arrived.

It's a breakthrough!

If you look at rock faces, the different strata are sometimes clearly visible, and you can even see where one layer has pushed hard against another and has slid over the top of it. That's how it is with God's kingdom. With the coming of Jesus, the future age pushed hard into the present age and 'overlapped it'.

A breakthrough of the future

As believers, we live in a world of 'overlap' or 'breakthrough'. Our life is rooted in the present; and yet the future has overlapped our present and broken through into it so that we can begin to experience the life of 'the age to come' (Matthew 12:32) right now. We don't have to wait for heaven to start experiencing it! The kingdom is here because Jesus is here. Jesus used various images to describe its closeness:

From that time on Jesus began to preach, 'Repent, for the kingdom of heaven is near'.

(Matthew 4:17)

'But if I drive out demons by the Spirit of God, then the kingdom of God has come upon you.'

(Matthew 12:28)

When Jesus saw that he [a teacher of the law] had answered wisely, he said to him, 'You are not far from the kingdom of God.'

(Mark 12:34)

'Do not be afraid, little flock, for your Father has been pleased to give you the kingdom.'

(Luke 12:32)

Once, having been asked by the Pharisees when the kingdom of God would come, Jesus replied, 'The kingdom of God does not come with your careful observation, nor will people say, "Here it is," or "There it is," because the kingdom of God is within you.'

(Luke 17:20–21)

Near – upon – not far – given – within; all this is the language of immediacy and closeness, not of waiting for something yet to come.

A breakthrough of 'eternity'

This idea of the presence of the future comes out in the Greek word for 'eternal' in the New Testament, which literally means 'of the age (to come)'; that is, of God's 'age' or 'dimension', in contrast to that of the human race. So, when Jesus promised 'eternal life', he wasn't so much thinking of never-ending life (though it included that); he was promising life that is characteristic of God's dimension being available to us right now; yet life so powerful that it bursts through the doors of death and continues in the life to come in even fuller expression.

'I tell you the truth, whoever hears my word and believes him who sent me has eternal life and will not be condemned; he has crossed over from death to life.'

(John 5:24)

See also John 3:16; 17:3

Other things that are seen as 'eternal' in the New Testament include:
- gospel (Revelation 14:6)
- salvation (Hebrews 5:9)
- purpose (Ephesians 3:11)
- power (Romans 1:20)
- glory (2 Corinthians 4:17)
- covenant (Hebrews 13:20)
- redemption (Hebrews 9:12)
- kingdom (2 Peter 1:11)
- inheritance (Hebrews 9:15)
- dwellings (Luke 16:9)
- sin (Mark 3:29)
- judgment (Hebrews 6:2)
- fire (Matthew 18:8)
- punishment (Matthew 25:46)

A breakthrough yet to come

While the kingdom was undeniably present, Jesus also taught that there was an aspect of it still to come. We don't have everything yet! The 'overlapping' kingdom was certainly here, but was limited by its co-existence with this present world. But at his return, Jesus said, this world would be wrapped up and all that would remain would be the kingdom (e.g. Revelation 11:15).

As well as teaching about events prior to this future coming of the kingdom (e.g. Matthew 24:1–44), a number of Jesus' parables also underline its future aspect. For example,
- the weeds (Matthew 13:24–30, 36–43)
- the net (Matthew 13:47–50)
- the workers in the vineyard (Matthew 20:1–16)
- the wedding banquet (Matthew 22:1–14)
- the ten virgins (Matthew 25:1–13)
- the talents (Matthew 25:14–30)
- the sheep and the goats (Matthew 25:31–46)

Understanding the kingdom

For Jesus, our getting ready for the future life of the kingdom meant starting to understand it and live it out right now.

An all-embracing kingdom

There is absolutely nothing that God's kingdom cannot reach! It reaches out to:

All nations

No nation is beyond God's reach, no matter what its political or religious persuasions, or what barriers it might put up.

'In the time of those kings, the God of heaven will set up a kingdom that will never be destroyed, nor will it be left to another people. It will crush all those kingdoms and bring them to an end, but it will itself endure for ever'.

(Daniel 2:44)

See also e.g. Psalm 99:1–2; Daniel 2:31–35; 7:13–14; Matthew 28:18–20

All people

God's kingdom doesn't simply reach nations, but also every people group within them. All will be represented around his throne on the last day, so all should be represented among us right now. There is no racism (even by default!) in the kingdom.

And they sang a new song: 'You are worthy to take the scroll and to open its seals, because you were slain, and with your blood you purchased men for God from every tribe and language and people and nation. You have made them to be a kingdom and priests to serve our God, and they will reign on the earth.'

(Revelation 5:9–10)

See also e.g. Galatians 3:26–28; Colossians 3:11; Revelation 7:9–10; 14:6

All of life

There is no aspect of life that God's kingdom doesn't touch. If God is our king, then that impacts everything that we are and do. There were no areas of life that Jesus allowed his followers to retain as 'private'. Discipleship in

the ways of the kingdom (see Part 2, Chapter 7) included training in such areas as character (e.g. Matthew 5:3–10), attitudes (e.g. Matthew 20:20–28), self-control (e.g. Matthew 5:21–22), finances (e.g. Matthew 19:16–30), faithfulness (e.g. Luke 16:10–12), sexual desires (e.g. Matthew 5:27–30), marriage (e.g. Matthew 19:1–9) – not just in how to pray or worship! When people wanted to keep part of their lives to themselves, Jesus sadly let them go (e.g. Matthew 19:21–22). In the kingdom, everything belongs to God; so now is the time to start getting ready for the future.

An all-growing kingdom

The kingdom of God has such power within it that it simply keeps growing.

'This is what the kingdom of God is like. A man scatters seed on the ground. Night and day, whether he sleeps or gets up, the seed sprouts and grows, though he does not know how. All by itself the soil produces corn – first the stalk, then the ear, then the full grain in the ear. As soon as the grain is ripe, he puts the sickle to it, because the harvest has come.'

(Mark 4:26–29)

The parables of the kingdom in Matthew 13 have an overriding message that the kingdom will grow and that nothing can stop it!

The parable of the sower (vv 3–9, 18–23). The sower is generous and the seed is good, so there will be a fruitful harvest.
The weeds (vv 24–30). Despite all opposition from the enemy, the kingdom will prevail.
The mustard seed (vv 31–32). The kingdom may have tiny and insignificant beginnings, but it is destined to take over everything.
The yeast (v 33). The kingdom is like yeast; once it gets to work nothing can stop it until the job is done!

What confidence this should give us!

An all-pervading kingdom

Like sand at the seaside, the kingdom gets absolutely everywhere. There is nothing powerful enough to keep it out. Like yeast, it pervades everything it touches (Matthew 13:33):

'The kingdom of heaven is like yeast that a woman took and mixed into a large amount of flour until it worked all through the dough.'

(Matthew 13:33)

The kingdom is rather like a multi-national company. Such companies are restricted by no governments or borders. In fact, with influence far wider, and often budgets far bigger, they can affect (if not determine) what governments do. That's what God's kingdom is like: limited to no one place or nation, yet having an all-pervading influence in and beyond them all. There is nothing that the kingdom cannot invade and influence – your family, your school, your workplace, your church, your nation. We, as citizens of that kingdom, can be like salt that stops the rot (Matthew 5:13) and light that exposes the darkness (Matthew 5:14–16).

An all-victorious kingdom

Human kingdoms rise and fall, but God's kingdom cannot fail to be victorious.

'You looked, O king [Nebuchadnezzar], and there before you stood a large statue – an enormous, dazzling statue, awesome in appearance. The head of the statue was made of pure gold, its chest and arms of silver, its belly and thighs of bronze, its legs of iron, its feet partly of iron and partly of baked clay. While you were watching, a rock was cut out, but not by human hands. It struck the statue on its feet of iron and clay and smashed them. Then the iron, the clay,

the bronze, the silver and the gold were broken to pieces at the same time and became like chaff on a threshing-floor in the summer. The wind swept them away without leaving a trace. But the rock that struck the statue became a huge mountain and filled the whole earth.'

(Daniel 2:31–35)

Jesus is firmly established on his throne, having broken the power of Satan (e.g. Colossians 2:15; Revelation 5:1–10). What more is there to be conquered therefore?

Jesus and the kingdom

As the focus of Jesus' ministry, God's kingdom was a key feature of all that he did.

Parables – explaining the kingdom

Jesus used parables to explain what the kingdom was like and how it operated. These parables revealed the truth to those with faith, but concealed it from those who thought they already knew all the answers.

The disciples came to him and asked, 'Why do you speak to the people in parables?' He replied, 'The knowledge of the secrets of the kingdom of heaven has been given to you, but not to them. Whoever has will be given more, and he will have an abundance. Whoever does not have, even what he has will be taken from him. This is why I speak to them in parables: Though seeing, they do not see; though hearing, they do not hear or understand. In them is fulfilled the prophecy of Isaiah: "You will be ever hearing but never understanding; you will be ever seeing but never perceiving. For this people's heart has become calloused; they hardly hear with their ears, and they have closed their eyes. Otherwise they might see with their eyes,

hear with their ears, understand with their hearts and turn, and I would heal them." But blessed are your eyes because they see, and your ears because they hear. For I tell you the truth, many prophets and righteous men longed to see what you see but did not see it, and to hear what you hear but did not hear it.'

(Matthew 13:10–17)

Miracles – demonstrating the kingdom

Jesus' miracles were performed, not for their own sake, but to show what the kingdom was like.

Jesus went throughout Galilee, teaching in their synagogues, preaching the good news of the kingdom, and healing every disease and sickness among the people. News about him spread all over Syria, and people brought to him all who were ill with various diseases, those suffering severe pain, the demon-possessed, those having seizures, and the paralysed, and he healed them.

(Matthew 4:23–24)

Miracles of provision (e.g. Matthew 14:15–21; 17:24–27; John 2:1–11) demonstrated that there is no shortage of anything in the kingdom.
Miracles of healing (e.g. Matthew 4:23–24; 8:14–17; Mark 2:1–12) demonstrated that there is no sickness in the kingdom.
Miracles of deliverance (e.g. Matthew 9:32–34; Mark 1:21–28, 34; Luke 9:37–43) demonstrated that there is no place for Satan's destructive work in the kingdom.
Miracles of resurrection (e.g. Matthew 9:18–26; Luke 7:11–17; John 11:1–44) demonstrated that there is no place for death in the kingdom.
All of these point to the presence of the future, assuring us what life will be like when the fullness of the kingdom comes. But we can start preparing for the future right now as we follow Jesus' example in these areas.

Relevance for today

The future starts now!

We don't have to settle for a faith that waits till we get to heaven for everything. The kingdom is already here; the future starts now!

'The kingdom of God is within you.'

(Luke 17:21)

God's kingdom operates differently

When Jesus did not meet Pilate's expectations of what a king should be (John 18:33), Jesus told him:

'My kingdom is not of this world.'

(John 18:36)

God's kingdom operates by principles that are different from every other kingdom. It is built on servanthood, sacrifice and relationship. The presence of the future means that these principles are to be worked out in our lives right here and now.

God's kingdom is still all-embracing

There is no person, nation or issue that God's kingdom doesn't want to embrace.

This gospel of the kingdom will be preached in the whole world as a testimony to all nations, and then the end will come.

(Matthew 24:14)

Here there is no Greek or Jew, circumcised or uncircumcised, barbarian, Scythian, slave or free, but Christ is all, and is in all.

(Colossians 3:11)

God's kingdom is still all-growing

Preparing for the future demands we drop ideas of a struggling and dwindling church. The kingdom is growing and nothing can stop it!

'Night and day, whether he sleeps or gets up, the seed sprouts and grows, though he does not know how. All by itself the soil produces corn.'

(Mark 4:27–28)

God's kingdom is still all-pervading

Don't settle for 'No-man's land', for example, by being told that you should keep your faith and your work separate. The kingdom pervades everything – and always changes it for the better.

'What else is the Kingdom of God like? It is like yeast used by a woman making bread. Even though she used a large amount of flour, the yeast permeated every part of the dough.'

(Luke 13:21, NLT)

God's kingdom is still all-victorious

One day we will hear the cry:

'The kingdom of the world has become the kingdom of our Lord and of his Christ, and he will reign for ever and ever.'

(Revelation 11:15)

In the meantime, don't settle for a Christian life that is resigned to ongoing defeats and is just waiting for heaven to see things conquered. If you fall, get up and fight again!

Greater is He who is in you than he who is in the world.

(1 John 4:4, NASB)

Conclusion

The best way to prepare for the future is to invest our lives fully in the kingdom of God right now.

'But seek first his kingdom and his righteousness . . .'

(Matthew 6:33)

Jesus shall reign where'er the sun
Does his successive journeys run;
His kingdom stretch from shore to shore,
Till moons shall wax and wane no more.

For Him shall endless prayer be made,
And praises throng to crown His head;
His name, like sweet perfume, shall rise
With every morning sacrifice.

People and realms of every tongue
Dwell on His love with sweetest song;
And infant voices shall proclaim
Their early blessings on His name.

Blessings abound where'er He reigns;
The prisoner leaps to lose his chains,
The weary find eternal rest,
And all the sons of want are blest.

Where He displays His healing power,
Death and the curse are known no more;
In Him the tribes of Adam boast
More blessings than their father lost.

Let every creature rise and bring
Peculiar honours to our king;
Angels descend with songs again,
And earth repeat the loud 'Amen.'

Isaac Watts, 1674–1748

CHAPTER FIVE

Jesus: The Focus of the Future

Jesus is the focus of all the promises of the Bible and therefore the focus of the future itself.

The promise of life that is in Christ Jesus. (2 Timothy 1:1)

'A man apt to promise is apt to forget' (Thomas Fuller); 'Promises and pie-crust are made to be broken' (Jonathan Swift); 'He that promises too much means nothing' (traditional proverb). We're all too familiar with broken promises and the people who break them. With God, however, things are utterly different. His promises are not mere 'wishful thinking'; they are firm declarations of intent that he is bound to fulfil, for Jesus is both the grounds and the goal of them all. Jesus is the focus of the promises, the focus of the future.

It all points to Jesus

When Mike was a school teacher, if ever there was trouble in a particular class, he would always know where to look. There were always one or two key individuals who, no matter what the issue, would be involved in it, even if not the instigators of it. All the experience and all the evidence always pointed to them! That's exactly how it is with Jesus and the promises of God; everything points to him. Jesus is their origin, their fulfilment, their goal. It is he himself who is 'the promise of life' (2 Timothy 1:1).

God's Yes and Amen

The apostle Paul summed it up like this:

No matter how many promises God has made, they are 'Yes' in Christ. And so through him the 'Amen' is spoken by us to the glory of God.

(2 Corinthians 1:20)

Two things are being said here:

First, Christ is God's 'Yes' to all the promises in the Scriptures. That is, they all point to him and are fulfilled in him. If our understanding of the promises leads us to anything or anyone other than Christ, then our interpretation is, quite simply, wrong. As Herbert Lockyer puts it, 'All these promises are "of God, in him", that is the Saviour.'

354

But as surely as God is faithful, our message to you is not 'Yes' and 'No'. For the Son of God, Jesus Christ, who was preached among you by me and Silas and Timothy, was not 'Yes' and 'No', but in him it has always been 'Yes'. For no matter how many promises God has made, they are 'Yes' in Christ.

(2 Corinthians 1:18–20)

The promises were spoken to Abraham and to his seed. The Scripture does not say 'and to seeds', meaning many people, but 'and to your seed', meaning one person, who is Christ.

(Galatians 3:16)

Through the gospel the Gentiles are heirs together with Israel, members together of one body, and sharers together in the promise in Christ Jesus.

(Ephesians 3:6)

Second, Christ is God's 'Amen' to all the promises in the Scriptures. As we claim these promises for ourselves, we are simply adding our 'Amen' to the 'Amen' that is Jesus himself. We are not trying to wrestle anything out of his hands; we are simply agreeing with what he has said he wants to do!

The shadow and the substance

Look at a shadow cast on the floor. Is there any reality to it? No, of course not; it is simply the absence of light. But while there is no substance to the shadow, what does a shadow tell you? It tells you that there is a reality somewhere. It points beyond itself to what is real. That is exactly how the Old Testament operates. While it tells of things that really happened, the spiritual realities were not to be found in the events themselves, but in what they were pointing to and preparing the way for. They were just like shadows.

Therefore do not let anyone judge you by what you eat or drink, or with regard to a religious festival, a New Moon celebration or a Sabbath day. These are a shadow of the things that were to come; the reality, however, is found in Christ.

(Colossians 2:16–17)

They [the priests] serve at a sanctuary that is a copy and shadow of what is in heaven. This is why Moses was warned when he was about to build the tabernacle: 'See to it that you make everything according to the pattern shown you on the mountain.'

(Hebrews 8:5)

The law is only a shadow of the good things that are coming – not the realities themselves. For this reason it can never, by the same sacrifices repeated endlessly year after year, make perfect those who draw near to worship.

(Hebrews 10:1)

In other words, as we saw in Part 2, Chapter 1, the Old Testament – whether its stories, rituals or prophecies – comes alive when we put on our 'Jesus spectacles' and look at everything through him. All the promises were made to be confirmed and to come alive through him!

For I tell you that Christ has become a servant of the Jews on behalf of God's truth, to confirm the promises made to the patriarchs so that the Gentiles may glorify God for his mercy.

(Romans 15:8–9)

Looking at the promises through Jesus

Let's see this principle worked out in some examples.

Forgiveness

Did God promise to forgive our sins in the Old Testament? Most certainly! After all, did he not reveal himself as:

'The LORD, the LORD, the compassionate and gracious God, slow to anger, abounding in love and faithfulness, maintaining love to thousands, and forgiving wickedness, rebellion and sin.'

(Exodus 34:6–7)

As such a God, did he not make provision for sinful people in the Old Testament? Indeed he did. The book of Leviticus, for example, is full of instructions on how to offer burnt offerings, grain offerings, fellowship offerings, sin offerings, guilt offerings, and so on (Leviticus 1–7). And to cover any sins that anyone had omitted to confess, the annual Day of Atonement made provision for them (Leviticus 16).

But what did all of these achieve? The writer of Hebrews tells us: they achieved absolutely nothing!

The law is only a shadow of the good things that are coming – not the realities themselves. For this reason it can never, by the same sacrifices repeated endlessly year after year, make perfect those who draw near to worship. If it could, would they not have stopped being offered? For the worshippers would have been cleansed once for all, and would no longer have felt guilty for their sins. But those sacrifices are an annual reminder of sins, because it is impossible for the blood of bulls and goats to take away sins.

(Hebrews 10:1–4)

His argument is stunningly simple: if just one of those sacrifices had really worked, people would have stopped offering them. The fact that they kept going back again and again shows that they knew they weren't forgiven. (It's rather like stopping taking tablets once you get better. But as long as you keep taking them, it proves you are still sick!)

However, as we come to the New Testament, who is it that God provides for our sins to be forgiven? None other than Jesus. And does it work now? Why, of course it does!

In him [Jesus] we have redemption through his blood, the forgiveness of sins, in accordance with the riches of God's grace.

(Ephesians 1:7)

Unlike the other high priests, he [Jesus] does not need to offer sacrifices day after day, first for his own sins, and then for the sins of the people. He sacrificed for their sins once for all when he offered himself.

(Hebrews 7:27)

He [Jesus] did not enter by means of the blood of goats and calves; but he entered the Most Holy Place once for all by his own blood, having obtained eternal redemption. The blood of goats and bulls and the ashes of a heifer sprinkled on those who are ceremonially unclean sanctify them so that they are outwardly clean. How much more, then, will the blood of Christ, who through the eternal Spirit offered himself unblemished to God, cleanse our consciences from acts that lead to death, so that we may serve the living God!

(Hebrews 9:12–14)

See also Part 2, Chapter 2

Jesus is the one that all those Old Testament sacrifices had been pointing to, had been preparing the way for, had been serving as shadows for. When we read about them, therefore, we constantly need to do so with our 'Jesus spectacles' on.

Other promises

Having looked at the previous example in some depth, let's now look at one or two others more quickly to see the same principle at work.

Did God promise to put a new heart within us? Most certainly (e.g. Jeremiah 24:7; Ezekiel 36:26–27). But in Jesus, there is no longer promise but fulfilment (e.g. Acts 2:37–38; Romans 2:28–29; Hebrews 10:19–22; see also Part 2, Chapter 3).

Did God promise the Holy Spirit to us? Most certainly (e.g. Numbers 11:17; Ezekiel 11:19–20; 36:26–27). But in Jesus, the promised Spirit becomes a reality, not just for the few, but for all who believe (e.g. John 7:37–39; Acts 2:33; Romans 8:9–16; 2 Corinthians 1:21–22; Galatians 3:14; see also Part 3, Chapter 1).

Did God promise to never leave us or forsake us? Most certainly (e.g. Deuteronomy 31:6–8; Joshua 1:1–8; Psalm 94:14). But all of this was, at best, for one person or for just one period of time. But in Jesus, Immanuel – 'God with us' (Isaiah 7:14) – has come to us in person (Matthew 1:23). He will now always be there (see also Part 2, Chapter 6).

Did God promise to guide us and provide for us? Most certainly (e.g. Exodus 13:21; Isaiah 42:16; 49:8–10; 58:11). But in the New Testament, the guidance is not by a cloud, or by the events of history, or by something impersonal; it is guidance by the Spirit of Jesus himself (e.g. John 14:16–18, 25–27; 16:12–15; see also Part 3, Chapter 3).

'Jesus spectacles'

In all these examples, putting on our 'Jesus spectacles' brings everything into focus and lifts things to a higher level. Too many Christians read the Old Testament as if the New Testament had never happened! The secret is to put on your 'Jesus spectacles'

every time. Look what has happened, or what is fulfilled, or what doesn't need to happen any more, since Jesus came. (But don't look for 'hidden mysteries' in obscure points!) For example, a theology of the future that sees God once again accepting people on the basis of Old Testament

So the law was put in charge to lead us to Christ that we might be justified by faith.

(Galatians 3:24)

God has no alternative plan of salvation!

The fulfilment of the Law

Another reason we need to approach the Old Testament's rituals and promises through Jesus is that the Bible tells us that he came to 'fulfil' the Old Testament.

'Do not think that I have come to abolish the Law or the Prophets; I have not come to abolish them but to fulfil them. I tell you the truth, until heaven and earth disappear, not the smallest letter, not the least stroke of a pen, will by any means disappear from the Law until everything is accomplished.'

(Matthew 5:17–18)

Jesus could not abolish the Old Testament laws because they were the word of God and therefore eternal (Psalm 119:89) and enduring (1 Peter 1:23). So what Jesus did instead was to fulfil them all – not for himself, for he was perfect and had no need to, but for us. He did this by:

• *Fulfilling its legal requirements*

Christ is the end of the law so that there may be righteousness for everyone who believes.

(Romans 10:4)

See also 1 Peter 2:22.

sacrifices just fails to understand the significance of what Jesus did. With such a view, he might just as well not have come and died! But put on your 'Jesus spectacles' and things inevitably take a different shape. Remember: the role of the Old Testament was simply to bring us to Jesus:

• *Fulfilling its types and shadows*

These are a shadow of the things that were to come; the reality, however, is found in Christ.

(Colossians 2:17)

- *Fulfilling its prophecies*

When evening came, many who were demon-possessed were brought to him, and he drove out the spirits with a word and healed all the sick. This was to fulfil what was spoken through the prophet Isaiah: 'He took up our infirmities and carried our diseases.'

(Matthew 8:16–17)

- *Bringing out its full meaning*

The word used in Matthew 5:17 for 'fulfil' can also mean 'to give them their full meaning' (CEV).

- *Redeeming us from its curse*

By this the New Testament does not mean that the Law itself was a curse; rather, that a curse came upon us because of our failure to keep it.

All who rely on observing the law are under a curse, for it is written: 'Cursed is everyone who does not continue to do everything written in the Book of the Law.' Clearly no-one is justified before God by the law, because, 'The righteous will live by faith.' The law is not based on faith; on the contrary, 'The man who does these things will live by them.' Christ redeemed us from the curse of the law by becoming a curse for us, for it is written: 'Cursed is everyone who is hung on a tree.' He redeemed us in order that the blessing given to Abraham might come to the Gentiles through Christ Jesus, so that by faith we might receive the promise of the Spirit.

(Galatians 3:10–14)

Where is all this leading to?

So, where do all these promises, focused in Jesus, lead us to? Peter sums it up like this:

His divine power has given us everything we need for life and godliness through our knowledge of him who called us by his own glory and goodness. Through these he has given us his very great and precious promises, so that through them you may participate in the divine nature and escape the corruption in the world caused by evil desires.

(2 Peter 1:3–4)

God's promises are designed to do two things: first, to bring us into nothing less than God's nature (and if that doesn't strike you as mind-blowing, you've not understood what you have just read!); second, to help us flee from this world's corruption. The promises, then, are an incentive and encouragement to a life of holiness in preparation for all that is to come.

Since we have these promises, dear friends, let us purify ourselves from everything that contaminates body and spirit, perfecting holiness out of reverence for God.

(2 Corinthians 7:1)

If we find ourselves simply grabbing at the promises that 'bless us', or claiming the promises that are 'nice', but always avoiding the promises that challenge our attitudes or lifestyle, then we are missing the point. The promises are there to help us prepare for the future, a future spent with God. To this end, our focus needs to be much more on the Jesus of the promises rather than just on the promises of Jesus.

'At all times, our eyes must be fixed, not on a promise merely, but on Him, the only foundation of our hopes, and in and through whom alone all the promises are made good to us' (Herbert Lockyer).

Relevance for today

All the promises are focused in Jesus

No matter how many promises God has made, they are 'Yes' in Christ.

(2 Corinthians 1:20)

The Old Testament is focused on Jesus

The Old Testament does not make sense without our 'Jesus spectacles' on, for it was designed for the very purpose of bringing us to Jesus.

Before this faith came, we were held prisoners by the law, locked up until faith should be revealed. So the law was put in charge to lead us to Christ that we might be justified by faith. Now that faith has come, we are no longer under the supervision of the law.

(Galatians 3:23–25)

Expect to experience glory!

While the revelation of the Old Testament is wonderful, it is as nothing in comparison to the revelation that Jesus now brings and that awaits us in the future.

Now if the ministry that brought death, which was engraved in letters on stone, came with glory, so that the Israelites could not look steadily at the face of Moses because of its glory, fading though it was, will not the ministry of the Spirit be even more glorious? If the ministry that condemns men is glorious, how much more glorious is the ministry that brings righteousness! For what was glorious has no glory now in comparison with the surpassing glory. And if what was fading away came with glory, how much greater is the glory of that which lasts!

Therefore, since we have such a hope, we are very bold.

(2 Corinthians 3:7–12)

The God who gave Jesus will keep his promises

Can we honestly think that the God who did not think twice about giving his own Son Jesus on the cross would think twice about fulfilling any promises made through him? Of course not! If he has done the greater thing, he will surely do the lesser.

He who did not spare his own Son, but gave him up for us all – how will he not also, along with him, graciously give us all things?

(Romans 8:32)

Everything finds its meaning in Jesus

Everything in creation and history was made by and for Jesus. It is only in him that everything makes sense; and so it makes sense to keep him as the focus of everything.

He is the image of the invisible God, the firstborn over all creation. For by him all things were created: things in heaven and on earth, visible and invisible, whether thrones or powers or rulers or authorities; all things were created by him and for him. He is before all things, and in him all things hold together.

(Colossians 1:15–17)

Jesus, I am resting, resting
In the joy of what Thou art;
I am finding out the greatness
Of Thy loving heart.
Thou hast bid me gaze upon Thee,
And Thy beauty fills my soul,
For by Thy transforming power
Thou hast made me whole.

CHORUS
Jesus, I am resting, resting
In the joy of what Thou art;
I am finding out the greatness
Of Thy loving heart.

O how great Thy lovingkindness,
Vaster, broader than the sea!
O how marvellous Thy goodness,
Lavished all on me!
Yes, I rest in Thee, Beloved,
Know what wealth of grace is Thine,
Know Thy certainty of promise,
And have made it mine.

Simply trusting Thee Lord Jesus,
I behold Thee as Thou art,
And Thy love, so pure, so changeless,
Satisfies my heart;
Satisfies its deepest longings,
Meets, supplies its every need,
Compasseth me round with blessings,
Thine is love indeed!

Ever lift Thy face upon me,
As I work and wait for Thee;
Resting 'neath Thy smile, Lord Jesus,
Earth's dark shadows flee.
Brightness of my Father's glory,
Sunshine of my Father's face,
Keep me ever trusting, resting;
Fill me with Thy grace.

Jean Sophia Pigott, 1845–82

Conclusion

As we consider God's promises that all focus on Jesus, and as we trust in Jesus, we come to know God more, lead lives that honour him and have a firm hope for the future.

No matter how many promises God has made, they are 'Yes' in Christ.

(2 Corinthians 1:20)

CHAPTER SIX

Waiting Patiently for the Promises

Two New Testament believers are wonderful examples of what it means to patiently live in the light of God's promises.

We do not want you to become lazy, but to imitate those who through faith and patience inherit what has been promised.
(Hebrews 6:12)

What characterizes a good book for you? Or a good film? Perhaps it's a good storyline, or an interesting hero, or a gripping ending. Whatever it is, there will be certain things that mark that book or film out as 'different'. That's how it is with those who are serious about God's promises. They are 'different'. There are certain things that characterize their life and the way they approach the promises which ensures that, ultimately, they are never disappointed.

So, what characterizes the life of a believer who is living in the light of the promises of God? Let's look at two of the people involved in the events after the birth of Christ and see what we can learn from them: Simeon and Anna. Both were looking for the coming of God's kingdom (Luke 2:25, 38); but they found it in a surprising way. It came in the person of a six-week old baby (the ritual of purification happened forty days after the birth of a baby boy, see Leviticus 12:1–8). It was during Joseph and Mary's visit to the temple for this ritual (Luke 2:22–24) that these life-changing encounters happened.

Simeon: Luke 2:25–35

While Simeon was looking for the coming of God's kingdom, he had not sat around idly waiting for it. He had given himself to the things that he could do, while waiting patiently for the things he couldn't do a thing about. Let's look at what sort of man he was:

A man of righteousness

Now there was a man in Jerusalem called Simeon, who was righteous and devout.

(v 25)

The word 'righteous' means that he had been obedient to God's commands, conforming his life to God's requirements. The word 'devout' means that he had been careful in all his religious duties and the outworking of his faith. Whether it was towards God or his fellow human beings, Simeon had sought to live in a godly way. This sort of righteous living pleases God and prepares the way for God to act. It does not save us (only Christ can do that); but it does show we are saved.

God wants all his people to live righteous lives, and in this way to enjoy the present and to prepare for the future.

Since everything will be destroyed in this way, what kind of people ought you to be? You ought to live holy and godly lives as you look forward to the day of God and speed its coming.

(2 Peter 3:11–12)

A man of patience

He was waiting for the consolation of Israel . . .

(v 25)

Promises by their very nature demand patience. They are the assurance that something *will* happen, not *is* happening; and that means – waiting! We don't know how long Simeon had been patient; we aren't told whether he was old or young, though the reference to his seeing the Messiah before he died (v 26) might suggest he was old now; but he had been giving himself to prayerfully watching and waiting. At times that's all you can do with promises!

And so after waiting patiently, Abraham received what was promised.

(Hebrews 6:15)

So do not throw away your confidence; it will be richly rewarded. You need to persevere so that when you have done the will of God, you will receive what he has promised. For in just a very little while, 'He who is coming will come and will not delay. But my righteous one will live by faith. And if he shrinks back, I will not be pleased with him.' But we are not of those who shrink back and are destroyed, but of those who believe and are saved.

(Hebrews 10:35–39)

What was it that Simeon was waiting for? 'The consolation of Israel'. The word 'consolation' means 'comfort' (like the comfort that God promised his people in Isaiah 40:1) or 'encouragement' (like the encouragement the Holy Spirit brought to the church in Acts 9:31).

Simeon was looking for that 'comfort' that God had promised that the Messiah would bring.

Others were looking forward to this too (v 38). They were aware of the dark times they lived in, politically, socially and spiritually. But they took prophecy seriously: they were expectant for God to act; they were patiently waiting for the Messiah's coming. And they weren't prepared to give up on the promise! What about us? Do we ignore the prophecies and promises of God; or do we patiently keep hold of them?

See also Part 3, Chapter 5: 'Patience'

A man of the Spirit

If we are going to embrace God's promises in the way that he wants us to, then we will need to be men and women of the Spirit. For it is the Spirit who directs us to the promises and the Spirit who helps us keep hold of the promises in the time of waiting. The fact that Simeon was a man of the Spirit comes out several times in these verses.

. . . and the Holy Spirit was upon him.

(v 25)

It had been revealed to him by the Holy Spirit that he would not die before he had seen the Lord's Christ.

(v 26)

Moved by the Spirit, he went into the temple courts.

(v 27)

Here was a man who was seeking to live his daily life 'filled with the Spirit' (Ephesians 5:18) so that he could be sensitive to what the Spirit wanted at any moment. It was because he was sensitive to the Spirit in the ordinary affairs of life that he could be moved by the Spirit to go to the temple and so just 'happen to be there' when Jesus' family arrived.

If we are going to be serious about taking hold of the promises of God, we need to be those who are constantly looking to be filled with the Holy Spirit (see Part 3, Chapters 6 and 7).

A man of faith

When the parents brought in the child Jesus to do for him what the custom of the Law required, Simeon took him in his arms and praised God, saying:

'Sovereign Lord, as you have promised, you now dismiss your servant in peace. For my eyes have seen your salvation, which you have prepared in the sight of all people, a light for revelation to the Gentiles and for glory to your people Israel.'

(Luke 2:27–32)

Simeon's song of praise to God has been used by many churches down the ages and is often known as the 'Nunc Dimittis', from its first two words in the Latin Bible.

When you think about it, this expression of praise took some faith! After all, before him was a six-week old baby, nothing more. Yet in faith he spoke out what the Spirit had put in his heart, seeing beyond what his natural eyes could see. He had only seen a baby, but he had seen enough. He gave thanks for what the child meant to him personally and to the whole world – both Gentiles (for whom salvation is light) and Jews (for whom salvation is glory); and now he was happy to die in peace (v 29).

Faith is always a key to seeing the promises of God unlocked to us.

Against all hope, Abraham in hope believed and so became the father of many nations, just as it had been said to him, 'So shall your offspring be.' Without weakening in his faith, he faced the fact that his body was as good as dead – since he was about a hundred years old – and that Sarah's womb was also dead. Yet he did not waver through unbelief

regarding the promise of God, but was strengthened in his faith and gave glory to God, being fully persuaded that God had power to do what he had promised.

(Romans 4:18–21)

A man of prophetic insight

Having offered his prayer of thanksgiving, Simeon then blessed Jesus' parents, adding some amazing words to Mary. (Note that he didn't address Joseph, which may have been a prophetic insight into the fact that Joseph would no longer be alive by the time of the crucifixion and that Mary would have to bear this pain alone.)

Then Simeon blessed them and said to Mary, his mother: 'This child is destined to cause the falling and rising of many in Israel, and to be a sign that will be spoken against, so that the thoughts of many hearts will be revealed. And a sword will pierce your own soul too.'

(vv 34–35)

Simeon made a number of prophecies about the future here:

A stone

Jesus would be like a stone that, to some, would cause them to 'rise up' to God, but to others would cause them to stumble as they took offence at his message. Their reaction to him would show their real spiritual condition.

We preach Christ crucified: a stumbling-block to Jews and foolishness to Gentiles, but to those whom God has called, both Jews and Greeks, Christ the power of God and the wisdom of God.

(1 Corinthians 1:23–24)

As you come to him, the living Stone – rejected by men but chosen by God and precious to him – you also, like living stones, are being built into a spiritual house to be a holy priesthood, offering spiritual sacrifices acceptable to God through Jesus Christ. For in Scripture it says: 'See, I lay a stone in Zion, a chosen and precious cornerstone, and the one who trusts in him will never be put to shame.' Now to you who believe, this stone is precious. But to those who do not believe, 'The stone the builders rejected has become the capstone,' and, 'A stone that causes men to stumble and a rock that makes them fall.' They stumble because they disobey the message – which is also what they were destined for.

(1 Peter 2:4–8)

See also Matthew 21:42–44; Romans 9:33

A sign

Jesus would be like a sign. He saw his miraculous works as 'signs' (e.g. John 2:11; 6:26), designed to point people to the Father. But he himself would be the greatest sign of all (e.g. Isaiah 7:14), confirmed through his resurrection (e.g. Acts 17:31). Despite this amazing sign, people would still speak against him.

A sword

Jesus would be like a sword. Here is the first hint of the destiny of this six-week-old baby as Simeon prophesies Jesus' death that would be like a sword in Mary's heart (v 35).

Anna: Luke 2:36–38

Like Simeon, Anna had given her life to preparing for the coming of Messiah and the kingdom he would bring. Let's look at what we are told about her.

Anna's ministry

Anna is described as a prophetess (v 36), someone who brought to others the revelations God gave her. Her faithfulness in this ministry over the years had prepared her for this 'one last big prophecy'. Faithfulness in our ministry, even in the small things, is important to God (e.g. Luke 16:10–12).

Other prophetesses noted in the Bible include Miriam (Exodus 15:20), Deborah (Judges 4:4), Huldah (2 Kings 22:14), Isaiah's wife (Isaiah 8:3), and the four daughters of Philip (Acts 21:9).

Anna's background

Anna, whose name means 'grace', was from the family of Phanuel (v 36), named after 'Peniel' ('face of God'), where Jacob had seen God face to face, and yet had lived (Genesis 32:30). They were of the tribe of Asher, descended from Jacob's eighth son, way back in Israel's history, which had certainly 'seen life' and had had its share of ups and downs.

Anna's age

She is described as 'very old' (v 36). Anna appears to have been at least 84 years old (v 37), although an alternative rendering suggests that she had been a widow for 84 years, and so would have been even older.

It's good to know that there is no retirement in God's kingdom! As we saw earlier in the book, some of the key people that God used were well advanced in years (e.g. Caleb, see Joshua 14:10–12). There is no reason why that should not include us too.

Anna's devotion

It seems that Anna had deliberately chosen not to marry again, despite what would have been her youthfulness at the time (she would have been about 21!), so that she could give herself wholly to God. It is said of her that:

She never left the temple but worshipped night and day, fasting and praying.

(Luke 2:37)

Anna reminds us of some faithful older believers who joyfully attend the church services on a Sunday and all the meetings through the week, no matter what the weather or what they feel like. They just love being with God's people, worshipping and listening to God's word.

Note too that her devotion found expression not just in worship, but also in fasting and praying (v 37). Fasting shows a seriousness of purpose before God when we are seeking him about something. (See Part 4, Chapter 3.)

Jesus did not oppose fasting, simply the way it was abused by the religious practitioners of his day.

'When you fast, do not look sombre as the hypocrites do, for they disfigure their faces to show men they are fasting. I tell you the truth, they have received their reward in full. But when you fast, put oil on your head and wash your face, so that it will not be obvious to men that you are fasting, but only to your Father, who is unseen; and your Father, who sees what is done in secret, will reward you.'

(Matthew 6:16–18)

How much a part of our life is the practice of fasting?

See also 2 Samuel 1:11–12; 2 Chronicles 20:2–4; Nehemiah 9:1–4; Esther 4:16; Isaiah 58:3-12; Daniel 9:1–3; Joel 2:12–14; Matthew 4:1–2; Mark 2:18–20; Acts 13:2-3; 14:23

Anna's prophecy

[Anna] coming up to them at that very moment, gave thanks to God and spoke about the child to all those who were looking forward to the redemption of Jerusalem.

(Luke 2:38)

'At that very moment' suggests she did so by revelation from God. What she actually said, we will never know; but she had clearly heard God, gave thanks to God confidently for what she had heard, and prophesied to all the others there.

What an example Anna is to young and old alike: a life of worship, fasting, prayer, thankfulness, telling others about the Christ! How do we match up to her devotion, faithfulness, and zeal?

And after the prophecies . . .

What an amazing day that must have been for Mary and Joseph. They certainly got more than they had bargained for! All they had done was to go to the temple to perform the ceremony that the Law required of them; and God had surprised them! (But that is often how it is with prophecy!)

Once the excitement of the prophetic words was over, Mary and Joseph then had to go and 'get on with life' (v 39) – as Jesus himself did (v 40). In fact, it would be thirty years before the prophecies came into play.

It is important that, as we prepare for the future, we do not sit back just because we have had a prophecy or a promise. They are firm declarations of God's intention to do something; but often that 'something' needs a response from us. It may be prayer, or action, or a changed life.

Relevance for today

Don't let the passing years discourage you
Despite the passing years, Simeon and Anna held on to the convictions that God had put in their hearts. Let's be people who, when things don't happen overnight, do the same!

And so after waiting patiently, Abraham received what was promised.

(Hebrews 6:15)

Don't let age disqualify you
Don't accept that increasing years mean that God can't use you or that you are now too old to enjoy God's promises in your lifetime.

So here I [Caleb] am today, eighty-five years old! I am still as strong today as the day Moses sent me out; I'm just as vigorous to go out to battle now as I was then. Now give me this hill country that the LORD promised me that day.

(Joshua 14:10–12)

Don't let impatience frustrate you
Imitate those who through faith and patience inherit what has been promised.

(Hebrews 6:12)

Don't let sin rob you
Simeon and Anna weren't 'waxwork' believers, but flesh and blood like us. Simeon knew he himself needed the salvation he was waiting for (v 30); but he wasn't going to let that rob him. Neither should we.

Since we have these promises, dear friends, let us purify ourselves from everything that contaminates body and spirit, perfecting holiness out of reverence for God.

(2 Corinthians 7:1)

The Lord is King; lift up thy voice,
O earth, and all ye heavens rejoice!
From world to world the joy shall ring:
'The Lord Omnipotent is King!'

The Lord is King! who then shall dare
Resist His will, distrust His care,
Or murmur at His wise decrees,
Or doubt His royal promises?

The Lord is King! child of the dust,
The Judge of all the earth is just:
Holy and true are all His ways;
Let every creature speak His praise.

He reigns! ye saints, exalt your strains:
Your God is King, your Father reigns;
And He is at the Father's side,
The Man of love, the Crucified.

Come, make your wants, your burdens
* known:*
He will present them at the throne;
And angel bands are waiting there,
His messages of love to bear.

One Lord, one empire, all secures:
He reigns – and life and death are yours;
Through earth and heaven one song shall
* ring,*
'The Lord Omnipotent is King!'

Josiah Conder, 1789–1855

Conclusion

Simeon and Anna's patience was rewarded. So will ours be as we follow in their footsteps, and we will truly see God's salvation.

My eyes have seen your salvation, which you have prepared in the sight of all people, a light for revelation to the Gentiles and for glory to your people Israel.

(Luke 2:30–32)

CHAPTER SEVEN

Future Promises, Present Hope

Promises, by their very nature, are for the future. But God wants us to take hold of the future and learn how to bring it into the present.

He [Abraham] did not waver through unbelief regarding the promise of God, but was strengthened in his faith and gave glory to God, being fully persuaded that God had power to do what he had promised. (Romans 4:20–21)

We wrote in the Introduction about the 'Promise Box' of Mike's grandmother. We said there that the promises of God are not for 'pulling out at random', like those little scrolls in the Promise Box were, but rather are to help us get to know the God of the promises. But just to learn about him is as pointless as just pulling out a scroll from the Promise Box; the time comes when the promise must be taken hold of and put into action in life. The future promise has to become a present hope.

Making the promises our own

Charles Spurgeon, the great Baptist preacher of the nineteenth century, wrote, 'I believe all the promises of God, but many of them I have personally tried and proved. I have seen that they are true, for they have been fulfilled to me.'

'They have been fulfilled to me.' That's what we want to explore in this closing chapter: how we can take hold of God's promises and see them fulfilled.

Promises are to be found with eagerness

God loves enthusiasts! He loves people who search for him eagerly, worship him eagerly, serve him eagerly. The Bible promises a blessing for 'the eager', for 'the enthusiasts'. Just look at some of the varied expressions of eagerness in the Bible:

They sought God eagerly, and he was found by them.

(2 Chronicles 15:15)

Now the Bereans were of more noble character than the Thessalonians, for they received the message with great eagerness and examined the Scriptures every day to see if what Paul said was true.

(Acts 17:11)

Therefore you do not lack any spiritual gift as you eagerly wait for our Lord Jesus Christ to be revealed.

(1 Corinthians 1:7)

Therefore, my brothers, be eager to prophesy, and do not forbid speaking in tongues.

(1 Corinthians 14:39)

But by faith we eagerly await through the Spirit the righteousness for which we hope.

(Galatians 5:5)

Jesus Christ, who gave himself for us to redeem us from all wickedness and to purify for himself a people that are his very own, eager to do what is good.

(Titus 2:13–14)

Therefore, my brothers, be all the more eager to make your calling and election sure. For if you do these things, you will never fall, and you will receive a rich welcome into the eternal kingdom of our Lord and Saviour Jesus Christ.

(2 Peter 1:10–11)

Eagerness should characterize every aspect of our life. And this is how we should look for God's promises too. There is a wonderful passage in Job which describes a miner at work deep underground (Job 28:1–11), and which says that this is how we should search for God's wisdom, God's word, God's promises. Just like mining, it may be hard and lonely work at times; but it is always worth it, for it 'brings hidden things to light' (v 11). It goes on to say that wisdom, 'hidden from the eyes of every living thing' (v 21), can be discovered only by those who come 'digging' into God, for 'God understands the way to it and he alone knows where it dwells' (v 23). This is the sort of eager, searching and expectant heart that God wants in us as we come looking for his word and his promises. For it is through God's promises that we find true wisdom:

'Blessed is the man who listens to me [wisdom], watching daily at my doors, waiting at my doorway. For whoever finds me finds life and receives favour from the LORD. But whoever fails to find me harms himself.'

(Proverbs 8:34–36)

Faith

Promises are to be received by faith. Walking with God involves a life of patient faith in God and his promises. That's how it has been ever since Abraham, the founder of the family of faith and the man who is such a model in believing what God has promised.

He [Abraham] did not waver through unbelief regarding the promise of God, but was strengthened in his faith and gave glory to God, being fully persuaded that God had power to do what he had promised.

(Romans 4:20–21)

When God made his promise to Abraham, since there was no-one greater for him to swear by, he swore by himself, saying, 'I will surely bless you and give you many descendants.' And so after waiting patiently, Abraham received what was promised.

(Hebrews 6:13–15)

And the scripture was fulfilled that says, 'Abraham believed God, and it was credited to him as righteousness,' and he was called God's friend.

(James 2:23)

But this life of patient faith, leading to intimate friendship with God, is not just what God wanted for Abraham; it is what he wants for all his people:

Consider Abraham: 'He believed God, and it was credited to him as righteousness.' Understand, then, that those who believe are children of Abraham. The Scripture foresaw that God would justify the Gentiles by faith, and announced the gospel in advance to Abraham: 'All nations will be blessed through you.' So those who have faith are blessed along with Abraham, the man of faith.

(Galatians 3:6–9)

The Scripture declares that the whole world is a prisoner of sin, so that what was promised, being given through faith in Jesus Christ, might be given to those who believe.

(Galatians 3:22)

We do not want you to become lazy, but to imitate those who through faith and patience inherit what has been promised.

(Hebrews 6:12)

And what more shall I say? I do not have time to tell about Gideon, Barak, Samson, Jephthah, David, Samuel and the prophets, who through faith conquered kingdoms, administered justice, and gained what was promised.

(Hebrews 11:32–33)

Some of God's promises may stagger us. They may appear too good to be true – especially if we have just failed God or messed up badly. But

God means all that he says. The problem does not lie with whether God wants to release the promise; it lies with us whether we will receive it; whether we will take the promise and make it a present hope. And faith is what does this.

Our difficulty is that we feel we can't match God's big promises with big faith; so we give up before we start, or get weary halfway through. But Jesus said that it isn't the amount of faith that is the issue. Twice, when the disciples were challenged by their own lack of faith, Jesus said all that they needed was faith the size of a mustard seed (which is very small indeed!).

Then the disciples came to Jesus in private and asked, 'Why couldn't we drive it out?' He replied, 'Because you have so little faith. I tell you the truth, if you have faith as small as a mustard seed, you can say to this mountain, "Move from here to there" and it will move. Nothing will be impossible for you.'

(Matthew 17:19–20)

'If your brother sins, rebuke him, and if he repents, forgive him. If he sins against you seven times in a day, and seven times comes back to you and says, "I repent," forgive him.' The apostles said to the Lord, 'Increase our faith!' He replied, 'If you have faith as small as a mustard seed, you can say to this mulberry tree, "Be uprooted and planted in the sea," and it will obey you.'

(Luke 17:3–6)

The issue is not the amount of faith, but the object of faith; not how much faith you have got, but where your faith is focused. To put it a different way: there is no power in 'faith'; there is only power in Jesus. Faith needs to be faith in him, not faith in 'faith'. Faith is not what makes the promise happen; faith is what keeps us focused on the God who can make it happen.

What does this mean in practice? It means, just as it did for Abraham, facing reality (Romans 4:19), while keeping hold of the promise God has given (Romans 4:20), constantly bringing it back confidently to him (Romans 4:20–21), reminding him of what he has said (Genesis 15:1–3), and telling him we aren't going away until he has done what he has promised, no matter how long we have to wait.

See also 2 Chronicles 20:20; Isaiah 26:1–4; Matthew 8:5–13; 9:27–30; 15:21–28; Mark 2:1–5; Luke 22:31–32; Romans 4:1–25; 2 Corinthians 5:7; Galatians 3:6–14; Hebrews 11

Promises are to be worked out in obedience

Herbert Lockyer said that 'faith and obedience are the two legs a Christian walks with'. If we want to see the future promise become a present hope then we will not only exercise faith in God, but we will obey him too. This is not God saying to his children, 'If you are good, I'll give you a bike for Christmas' (though some Christians live as though they think that's how God operates!). This is God saying: 'If you have grasped who it is that has made the promise, then you will want to live rightly before me and so end up getting the reward that inevitably comes to those who do so.' Obedience is not a duty, but a privilege and a delight!

The Bible clearly links obedience to God with coming into the enjoyment of the promises of God.

All these blessings will come upon you and accompany you if you obey the LORD your God.

(Deuteronomy 28:2)

'Those who honour me I will honour.'

(1 Samuel 2:30)

'Does the LORD delight in burnt offerings and sacrifices as much as in obeying the voice of the LORD? To obey is better than sacrifice, and to heed is better than the fat of rams.'

(1 Samuel 15:22)

'If you are willing and obedient, you will eat the best from the land.'

(Isaiah 1:19)

'Obey me, and I will be your God and you will be my people. Walk in all the ways I command you, that it may go well with you.'

(Jeremiah 7:23)

'Not everyone who says to me, "Lord, Lord," will enter the kingdom of heaven, but only he who does the will of my Father who is in heaven.'

(Matthew 7:21)

'Now that you know these things, you will be blessed if you do them.'

(John 13:17)

You need to persevere so that when you have done the will of God, you will receive what he has promised.

(Hebrews 10:36)

Dear friends, if our hearts do not condemn us, we have confidence before God and receive from him anything we ask, because we obey his commands and do what pleases him.

(1 John 3:21–22)

See also Genesis 22:17–18; Exodus 19:5–6; Leviticus 18:5; Deuteronomy 11:13–15; Joshua 1:7; 1 Kings 3:14; Nehemiah 1:5–9; Isaiah 48:18; Zechariah 6:15; Matthew 28:19–20; John 14:15–16; Hebrews 5:8–10; James 1:22

Obedience and disobedience are what contrast the saved and the unsaved. Christians are 'obedient children' (1 Peter 1:14); those dead in their sins are 'disobedient' (Ephesians 2:2). Let's be what we were designed to be! If there are areas of life where we are holding out against God, if God is telling us to do something or not to do something and we are ignoring him, then we shouldn't be surprised if the promise isn't happening yet. We can't expect to be disobedient and still receive the promise (though in the amazing grace of God probably all of us have known times when God has blessed us despite our disobedience!). And if there are any conditions attached to the promises, as often there are (e.g. 2 Chronicles 7:14; Matthew 11:28–29), we need to face up to them and take them on board. Obedient children are happy children!

Promises are to be presented in prayer

Having discovered the promise, and having received it by faith, seeking to be obedient or to fulfil any conditions, can we sit back and wait? No! We are now to keep bringing God's promise back to him in prayer.

Consider David. When God promised him an unending dynasty, he immediately started to bring the promise back to God.

'O LORD Almighty, God of Israel, you have revealed this to your servant, saying, "I will build a house for you." So your servant has found courage to offer you this prayer. O Sovereign LORD, you are God! Your words are trustworthy, and you have promised these good things to your servant. Now be pleased to bless the house of your servant, that it may continue for ever in your sight; for you, O Sovereign LORD, have spoken, and with your blessing the house of your servant will be blessed for ever.'

(2 Samuel 7:27–29)

In Psalm 119 the author repeatedly uses the phrases 'according to your word' (vv 25, 28, 107, 169) and 'according to your promise' (vv 41, 58, 76, 116, 154, 170) as the basis for his cry to God. He brings back to God what God has already brought to him.

Daniel was another who prayed on the basis of God's promise and word.

In the first year of Darius son of Xerxes (a Mede by descent), who was made ruler over the Babylonian kingdom . . . I, Daniel, understood from the Scriptures, according to the word of the LORD given to Jeremiah the prophet, that the desolation of Jerusalem would last seventy years. So I turned to the LORD God and pleaded with him in prayer and petition, in fasting, and in sackcloth and ashes.

(Daniel 9:1–3)

It was because Daniel was confident about the promise that he prayed. He didn't say, 'God has promised it, so it will happen, whether I do anything or not.' Rather he said, 'God has promised it; therefore I will pray for it to happen.' God's promise was the reason for prayer, not the excuse for inactivity; the reason for activism, not the excuse for fatalism. Within a few months Darius was gone, and Cyrus sent the Jews back home. God had promised it; Daniel prayed for it; and it happened! 'Whatever other lessons we learn from this chapter, we must be sure to grasp this one. The cause of God's acting in history is not simply His promise, but also the prayer of His people' (Stuart Olyott). Such a truth is mind-blowing and is a great provocation, surely, to pray.

Discovering God's promises is part of what it means to pray 'according to his will'. This is not a 'let-out' for unanswered prayers; it is about finding out from the Scriptures what God has promised and then confidently praying for that, knowing that our prayers are right on target.

This is the confidence we have in approaching God: that if we ask anything according to his will, he hears us. And if we know that he hears us – whatever we ask – we know that we have what we asked of him.

(1 John 5:14–15)

God's unfailing promises are given to stimulate our prayers, to be the basis for our prayers. We can confidently ask for whatever is in them and, like the persistent widow in Jesus' parable (Luke 18:1–8), stick at prayer until the answer is released.

Relevance for today

Our final 'Relevance for today' comes from experience 'yesterday'. In *Faith's Checkbook* (cheque-book), a book of Bible promises for daily use, Spurgeon wrote:

'A promise from God may very instructively be compared to a check payable to order. It is given to the believer with the view of bestowing upon him some good thing. It is not meant that he should read it over comfortably, and then have done with it. No, he is to treat the promise as a reality, as a man treats a check.

'He is to take the promise, and endorse it with his own name by personally receiving it as true. He is by faith to accept it as his own. He sets to his seal that God is true, and true as to this particular word of promise. He goes further, and believes that he has the blessing in having the sure promise of it, and therefore he puts his name to it to testify to the receipt of the blessing.

'This done, he must believingly present the promise to the Lord, as a man presents a check at the counter of the bank. He must plead it by prayer, expecting to have it fulfilled. If he has come to Heaven's bank at the right date, he will receive the promised amount at once. If the date should happen to be further on, he must patiently wait till its arrival; but meanwhile he may count the promise as money, for the bank is sure to pay when the due time arrives.

'Some fail to place the endorsement of faith upon the check, and so they get nothing; and others are slack in presenting it, and these also receive nothing. This is not the fault of the promise, but of those who do not act with it in a common-sense, business-like manner. God has given no pledge which He will not redeem, and encouraged no hope which He will not fulfil.'

That really sums up so beautifully how the promises of God operate. They aren't magic formulae, or tomorrow's horoscope, or merely pleasant thoughts for the day. They are part of God's word to us. That's why it's so important to get to know the overall message of the Bible, and not to pick out promises at random, like from the 'Promise Box'. As we do this, we will get to know, not just the promises of God, but the God of the promises. Our prayer is that this book has helped just a little way towards that.

I'm not ashamed to own my Lord,
Or to defend His cause;
Maintain the honour of His Word,
The glory of His cross.

Jesus, my God! I know His Name,
His Name is all my trust;
Nor will He put my soul to shame,
Nor let my hope be lost.

Firm as His throne His promise stands,
And He can well secure
What I've committed to His hands
Till the decisive hour.

Then will He own my worthless name
Before His Father's face;
And, in the new Jerusalem,
Appoint my soul a place.

Isaac Watts, 1674 1748

Conclusion

We can turn future promises into present hope by finding, receiving, obeying, and praying into reality what God has said, and in this way get ready for the future, whatever it may hold.

He who testifies to these things says, 'Yes, I am coming soon.' Amen. Come, Lord Jesus.
(Revelation 22:20)

Index

THE BIBLE CHRONICLE
Derek Williams
• 0 86347 183 8 • 416pp • cased •

READ ALL ABOUT IT!! The stories and people of the Bible presented chronologically alongside contemporary world events in a popular journalistic style in the form of magazine articles. Derek Williams, a former journalist and now an Anglican minister, has taken the events of the Bible, starting with Creation and finishing at about 100AD, and laid them out alongside known events around the world. We read therefore that at the time Joseph was sold into slavery in Egypt, Stonehenge was coming to completion; Nehemiah was rebuilding Jerusalem at the same time that Socrates was expounding his philosophy and Daniel was thrown into the lions' den when Aesop was telling his fables.

Lavishly illustrated throughout, *The Bible Chronicle* contains over 1,000 articles, 600 photographs in colour, 36 maps, many charts and diagrams and background information on beliefs and religions. It is an excellent resource for all the family as well as students and pastors who will appreciate the breadth of its scholarship.

THE BIBLE APPLICATION HANDBOOK

Derek Williams and J I Packer
• 0 86347 300 8 • 416pp • cased •

The only A-Z book-by-book guide to the Bible that provides insights for daily living. *The Bible Application Handbook* aims to open up the meaning of the Bible text so that readers will be able to:

• Understand the Bible's message
• To begin to see its practical relevance to everyday life
• Find their way around the Bible easily
• Obtain a quick overview of each book from the 'at a glance' box

The Bible Application Handbook is a cross between a commentary and Bible dictionary with the emphasis on opening up the meaning of the text and its significance on our life today. Each book in the Bible is presented in a separate chapter, each containing a summary and purpose of that book, its authorship, its place in the canon and its relevance to modern living. *The Bible Application Handbook* is lavishly illustrated throughout with colour pictures, maps and diagrams. Derek Williams has collaborated with respected theologian and writer Dr Jim Packer to produce a scholarly resource that will prove an invaluable aid in discerning and acting upon the truths of the Bible in our postmodern society.